T0305276

THE ECONOMICS OF

BUSINESS VALUATION

THE ECONOMICS OF

BUSINESS VALUATION

Towards a Value Functional Approach

PATRICK L. ANDERSON

STANFORD ECONOMICS AND FINANCE

An Imprint of Stanford University Press

Stanford, California

Stanford University Press
Stanford, California

Special discounts for bulk quantities of Stanford Economics and Finance are available to corporations, professional associations, and other organizations. For details and discount information, contact the special sales department of Stanford University Press. Tel: (650) 736-1782, Fax: (650) 736-1784

Printed in the United States of America on acid-free, archival-quality paper

Library of Congress Cataloging-in-Publication Data

Anderson, Patrick L., author.
  The economics of business valuation : towards a value functional approach / Patrick L. Anderson.
    pages cm
  Includes bibliographical references and index.
  ISBN 978-0-8047-5830-7 (cloth : alk. paper)
  1. Business enterprises—Valuation.   I. Title.
  HG4028.V3A56 2012
  338.5—dc23

                              2012009548

Typeset by Newgen in 10/13.5 Minion

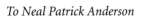

To Neal Patrick Anderson

CONTENTS

PREFACE

PURPOSE OF THIS BOOK

The Poorly Understood Concept of a Business

Despite the enormous literature on corporate finance, accounting, economics, management, and mathematics, two fundamental principles of business remain poorly understood: the definition of the firm and the determination of its value.

Without grasping the purpose of the firm—or naively assuming that it exists to "maximize profits" in some ill-defined way—one cannot understand how a business has market value, or how managers operate it in the face of uncertainty. Furthermore—especially given the daunting statistics on the failure rate of newly formed companies—we cannot hope to understand why an entrepreneur would start one!

Filling the Gap: The Definition of the Firm

This book attempts to fill the yawning gap between the extant theories of business and business value and the reality faced by business managers, investors, and entrepreneurs. To do so, it starts from a fundamental question: What is a firm?

Unfortunately, we have little in the way of an answer! As will be demonstrated, various working definitions must be abandoned once they are confronted with facts.

To fill this gap, I propose a new definition of the firm that allows for a rigorous distinction between a business and the many other entities that have businesslike attributes. This same definition also distinguishes a business from a portfolio of securities. A portfolio is an essential concept in mathematical finance but not a plausible substitute for a firm. Only after properly defining the firm does the book move forward to methods of estimating the value of a firm.

Filling the Gap: The Value of a Firm

Many readers will be familiar with the three traditional business valuation methods, commonly known as the market, asset, and income methods. Each of these has an obvious valuation principle underlying it. However tempting (and commonplace) it is to describe these as the only valuation methods, my research found at least *nine* different well-defined valuation principles that have been articulated in the fields of economics, finance, and accounting, plus an assortment of less well-defined principles that have originated in taxation and management.

A handful of these are fixtures in theoretical work in economics and mathematical finance, and almost completely absent in practical work. Others are ubiquitous in practical work. However, these methods nearly always require significant subjective adjustments, with the adjustments often more important than the theory. In effect, the valuation approaches used in practical work are often a platform from which to make professional judgments. Professional judgment has an important place, but we should have a theory that matches the reality of business, investors, and entrepreneurs.

To these nine extant valuation approaches, I propose a novel principle that grew out of control theory. I argue in the book that this value functional principle avoids many of the shortcomings of its competitors and more correctly matches the actual motivations and information set held by entrepreneurs. However, I also acknowledge its practical limitations.

Colliding with Widely Accepted Notions

The results of the research described in this book collide directly with a small handful of widely accepted notions in the corporate finance, valuation, and management literature. In the book, I argue that this handful is, unfortunately, just plain wrong. I will note three such collisions here:

1. First, I reject the notion that the objective of firms is to maximize profits. This notion, born of neoclassical economics and enshrined in popular culture as well as many fields of study, is contrary to the plain facts of life for almost any entrepreneur.

2. Second, I reject the notion that the value of a business is the estimated net present value of its future earnings. That assertion, and the neoclassical investment rule based on it, has been repeated thousands of times in books and journal articles, especially since its inclusion in the Modigliani-Miller propositions in the 1950s. It has become a pillar of corporate finance.

3. Third, I reject the notion that a portfolio of stocks and bonds issued by a firm is equivalent to the firm itself. That notion may seem odd when written starkly. However, the idea that the value of a firm is the same as the value of a portfolio of its securities—and that this equivalence remains when one buys or sells fractions of the outstanding equity and bonds—underlies much of the work in mathematical finance.

Matching Business Theories to Actual Business Conditions

A valid theory of business and business value should be able to prove itself with a wide range of actual businesses. In this book, I provide some basic empirical data on businesses in the United States and certain other countries—including their number, revenue, size of employment, and forms of organization, as well as the survival rates for the first several years after organization.

A clear finding is that *most* businesses, in the United States and the European Union (EU), are "small." The *vast majority* are privately held. Furthermore, small and medium-sized businesses—overwhelmingly privately held—appear to be responsible for most, if not all, of the net job creation in the United States and the EU. *These* are the firms that should be the main focus of a theory of business and business value.

Unfortunately, much of our corporate finance and mathematical finance theory deals with only a narrow subset of firms: publicly traded, very large corporations. These are the exception, not the rule! Therefore, I seek in this book theories of business and business value that apply to both large corporations *and* companies that do not issue publicly traded stocks and bonds, cannot borrow without constraints, and often rely on entrepreneurs to both finance and manage their operations.

Other Unique Aspects of This Book

This book has certain other unique aspects that bear noting:

1. *It grounds thinking in multiple disciplines and introduces new methodologies.* This book draws on mathematics, finance, economics, accounting, and some elements of statistics and control theory. With this background, it describes existing methodologies in business valuation. It also introduces some new and unusual concepts, such as value functional equations, state and control vectors, real options, Markov decision problems, and dynamic programming.

2. *It recognizes historical development of ideas from around the world.* Much of the literature in contemporary finance and economics effectively dismisses the pioneers in favor of authors that have written in the past half century. This leaves the reader with a poverty of understanding.

In this book, I recognize the tremendous progress that originated in the United States in the last few decades, including the development of modern portfolio theory, the Black-Scholes-Merton option formula, and nearly the entire school of neoclassical finance. It also notes the twentieth-century American and European economists who laid the groundwork, including the deservedly famous such as Irving Fisher, Milton Friedman, and Joseph Schumpeter, and the improperly neglected such as Joan Robinson, John Muth, and Friedrich von Hayek.

However, one shouldn't stop there. I include the century-old contributions of the European and American scholars such as Robert Brown, Norbert Weiner, and Albert Einstein; multiple-century-old works by Adam Smith, David Ricardo, William Blackstone, Bernoulli, Fibonacci, Pacioli, and Renaissance-era Italian traders; and the vital contributions of Islamic scholars such as Al-Khowarizmi and ancient Hindu scholars such as Kautilya. Attentive readers will also learn who first sold the Brooklyn Bridge, who actually invented the Gordon growth formula, what astronomer outlined the net present value algorithm well before corporate finance was recognized as a discipline, after what ancient scholar the term *algorithm* was named, and who described a form of accounting in India a thousand years before Luca Pacioli codified it in Italy.

Limitations

Given its ambitious agenda, this book will invariably suffer from a few limitations:

- First, using ideas from different fields will require introducing nomenclature and mathematical techniques that are not common in other fields. For example, accountants and business school graduates may find the mathematics of dynamic programming challenging. Economists may be daunted by the discussion of accounting concepts. Finance specialists may be confronted with challenges to models that go beyond the derivations offered in most finance texts.

- Second, any pioneer inevitably treads over ground that is considered sacred by others. This will probably be the case here. I have attempted to properly present each theory before critically addressing any of its shortcomings. Inevitably, there will be some qualifications and corrections that, in a perfect world, would have been anticipated. Furthermore, there are differences in how certain recognized techniques are supposed to be used and how they are actually used. This will produce some ambiguities over whether the theory or the practitioner is faulty.

- Third, the arguments for a new definition of a firm, and the explanation of a new valuation method, will be novel. Such novelty necessarily brings with it a difficulty in explaining that, hopefully, I have largely overcome for most readers. I doubt it has been overcome for all readers. Novelty also increases the possibility of errors; those remain the fault of the author.

MY MOTIVATION

I have an unusual background for an author of a book like this, and that background explains my motivation for spending the better part of a decade working on this book. Like most authors, I trained in the standard academic disciplines of economics and finance. However, I spent more of my career actually lending to and investing in businesses and attending the school of hard knocks as an entrepreneur. Those latter two experiences heavily color the scholarly analysis in this book.

My academic training in economics presented a wonderfully clean view of business investment decisions. It also presented a naive view, as I soon learned. The accounting classes I attended at least provided some practical guidance on business management, though the curriculum didn't really pretend to describe why and how investors made decisions.

Early in my career, I was trained in the standard corporate finance valuation methodologies in two separate financial institutions. As a bank economist, I endured the entire loan officer training course and participated in policy decisions on borrowing and lending. Later, I sat on the investment committee for an insurance company, reviewing carefully prepared investment proposals involving real estate, construction, retail, energy, housing, and other industries, including stocks, bonds, private placements, and derivatives.

These gave me an extended education in the standard corporate finance methods, as well as their use in practice. It was in that practice that I observed their serious inadequacies. In particular, despite the seemingly rigorous use of discounted cash flow schedules and cost-of-capital models, the actual decisions were rarely made on the basis of the supposed criteria of exceeding a hurdle rate of return. Good investment managers and business executives—and I worked with some very good ones—looked for something else in the investment. If it wasn't there, we didn't do the deal—regardless of what the cash flow schedule said. If it was there, we would try to make it fit.

These experiences taught me that the existing theories of economics and corporate finance were inadequate to the task of explaining how businesses had value, and why investors supported some and abandoned others. The investors I admired most had a skill for making good investment decisions—but that skill was much different from the theory they supposedly learned in graduate school.

Later in my career I found that the most spectacular and recurring failures of the standard theories arise from their lack of understanding of entrepreneurs. I learned this the hard way—by becoming an entrepreneur myself. If I had allowed the orthodox theory to control my thinking during the early years of my business, I would have abandoned the entire enterprise several times.

Since then, I have studied other entrepreneurs and their businesses. I questioned them personally on their experiences. I visited their business premises. They are an interesting, compelling bunch—and rarely do they describe their critical business decisions using the jargon of corporate finance or the nomenclature of economics!

We entrepreneurs—I'll count myself among the research subjects this time—do not fit into the standard models of corporate finance, or neoclassical economics, or modern portfolio theory, or mathematical finance. We know that most fledgling firms disappear within about five years, but we start businesses anyway. We flout the standard probability-weighted net present value rule, usually risking our own money and reputation along the way.

Why do we do that? I think that question deserves a better answer.

SUGGESTED READING PLANS

I suggest the following reading plans oriented to readers of different interests.

General Reader

In general, I recommend reading in the following order:

- First, the entire Part I, including Chapter 1, "Modern Value Quandaries," and the following chapters in which differing theories of value are presented and the failure of the neoclassical investment rule is demonstrated. These chapters cover essential material not included in standard finance, economics, and valuation texts.

- Part II, "The Nature of the Firm," which rigorously defines a firm and distinguishes it from other organizations. It also provides useful (and often overlooked) data on businesses in the United States and certain other countries. These data are the basis for several arguments presented elsewhere in the book and would be relevant to nearly all readers.

- Any of the chapters on the economics, finance, or traditional methods of valuation. Most readers will be familiar with one or more of these methods. However, these chapters discuss the historical development and the theoretical basis of each method, which is sadly neglected in most practical texts.

- If the reader wishes to understand the value functional method, Chapters 9, 15, and 16.

- Any of the appendixes, such as Appendix A, "Key Formula and Notation Summary," that are relevant.

Scholar in Finance, Mathematics, or Economics

I assume that scholars would already have developed basic mathematical skills, have familiarity with the standard microeconomic model, have some accounting knowledge, and may have also become familiar with the standard corporate finance valuation models. For these readers, I recommend the following:

- All the chapters in Parts I and II, for the reasons discussed earlier.

- Selected chapters in Parts III and IV. In addition, finance scholars may wish to concentrate on Part IV, and economists on Part III, although each could learn from looking at the other part.

- As academic curricula tends to understate the importance of the practical methods described in Part V, my advice to scholars is to recognize that traditional methods, with all their inadequacies, should be accorded respect because they are actually used. The degree to which the practical methods recurrently require adjustments is an interesting focus.

- The novel value functional method presented in Part V, which probably requires also reading the earlier chapter on the modern recursive method.

Advanced Valuation Practitioner

A valuation practitioner is likely to have knowledge of the discounted cash flow methodology and prevailing standards in the fields of valuation; may have completed a degree in accounting, business, finance, or economics; and may have additional professional designations. For such individuals who are interested in studying advanced techniques and identifying the weaknesses of traditional techniques, I recommend concentrating on the following material:

- All the chapters in Part I, which describe nine different valuation methods and introduce a tenth. Valuation practitioners should expect orthodoxies to be challenged here, including the idea that there are only three generally accepted methods of valuation. I ask readers who want to argue with my observations in Part I about the inadequacies of traditional methods to allow that argument to be developed fully in Part V.

- The sections in Part III (on economics theories) and Part IV (on finance theories) that are of particular interest. Chapter 12, "Real Options and Expanded Net Present Value," should not be overlooked if the practitioner performs work on firms that have significant growth options, intellectual property investments, or natural resources interests.

- Any of the topics covered in Part V on traditional methods. Most practitioners will be familiar with these methods but may or may not be aware of their serious limitations. Practitioners can compare their own experience with mine on the frequent use of adjustments in traditional methods.

- The novel value functional method presented in Chapters 15 and 16. Some practitioners will want to only understand the theory; some will want to try out the method and review examples as well.

- If the practitioner wishes to see how the methods described in the book actually work, he or she should also review the three sample firms in Appendix C, "Description of Subject Companies." These are *actual* firms. Using these firms provides a vivid test of whether valuation methods actually work on real companies.

SOLUTIONS MANUAL AND ADDITIONAL RESOURCES

To accompany this book, I have prepared a *Solutions Manual.* An electronic copy of this is available for download free of charge to book purchasers. This volume includes a guide to the mathematics used in the book; additional business data; valuation standards; hints to problems; intermediate results; and notes on software used in the examples presented in this book. See Appendix B, "Guide to the Solutions Manual," for information on obtaining this *Solutions Manual* and an outline of its contents. The *Solutions Manual* can be found at http://www.andersoneconomicgroup.com/books.

ACKNOWLEDGMENTS

I must acknowledge the assistance of the following individuals:

- Erin Agemy Grover prepared a number of the examples listed in these chapters, including the three sample firms used to test individual methods. She also helped me edit the entire book. Mike Hollis and Ilhan Geckil also prepared a number of example valuations used throughout the book.

- Marie-Josée Cros and her colleagues at the Institut National de la Recherche Agronomique in Paris provided their MDP toolbox, which I adapted for use in a number of the example value functional problems.

- I received research assistance from Luke Olson, Justin Eli, and Ralph Dribek during their work at Anderson Economic Group. For their help in editing and correcting the manuscript, I wish to thank Abby Totoraitis, Katie Hayes, and Kimberly Kvorka. I also thank Megan Henriksen, who left Anderson Economic Group around the time the project started and later returned to help me get it completed.

- I also wish to acknowledge the suggestions offered on earlier manuscripts by Patrick Fitzgerald in Texas; Ilhan Geckil in Illinois, Darci Keyes, Bill King, and Ted Bolema in Michigan; and Mike Hanrahan in Alaska. In addition, I want to thank readers Fernando Torres in the United States and Nabil Mikati in Scandinavia.

- I also want to thank a handful of helpful experts who came from other parts of the world, including Paolo Giusto, the Italian engineer-turned-technologist who gave me excellent advice, most of it in California; and the Indian-born statistician Jagdish Rustagi, who patiently pointed me in the direction of several ancient scholars as well as retold several personal anecdotes about his friendships with eminent scholars of the current era.

Finally, I want to thank my wife and children, who patiently allowed me to spend time on this project during many, many weeks across seven years and many family trips.

I   THEORIES OF VALUE

1 MODERN VALUE QUANDARIES

THE FIRM IN ECONOMICS AND FINANCE

For at least two millennia, private businesses have been undertaken by farmers, traders, and artisans across the globe. Such businesses—including small farms, fishing and herding enterprises, textile and clothing producers, and larger ventures—have been the world's primary employers and wealth producers for centuries. Furthermore, for at least the past two centuries society has benefited from the formal study of economics, accounting, and the precursors of finance. What we call a business, enterprise, undertaking, or "firm" figures prominently in all of these fields. Yet with all of this scholarship, we really know very little about the definition and value of the firm. Addressing this poverty is the prime motivation of this book.

For graduates and holders of professional credentials in the fields of accounting, finance, economics, and business, this bold assertion of our lack of knowledge may seem overwrought. However, in this chapter, we pose several quandaries that illustrate this poverty. If we really had a complete, coherent, and valid theory of the firm and its value, these quandaries would not exist. The fact that they *do* exist, and that similar serious self-contradictions exist in related fields of study, motivates this book.

TWO MILLENNIA OF BUSINESS: A BRIEF RECAP

Business from 500 BC to AD 1500

Two millennia ago, accounts of business activity and rules for business behavior appeared in ancient texts such as the books of the Old Testament of the Bible (including the books of the Torah), the books of the New Testament, the Vedas of Hindu literature, and ancient legal codes such as those of the Roman Empire and the Babylonian empire of Hammurabi.[1]

During these twenty centuries, agriculture, hunting, fishing, and herding of game animals were the primary occupations. These farmers, hunters, fishermen, and herders were all engaged in business, and the prospect of hunger and famine made their business very important indeed.

For roughly the last thousand years, the emerging civilizations of the world benefited from mathematics, customs of trade, and other knowledge recorded in Greek and Roman literature, as well as lesser-known literature from other lands. Critical scientific advances that occurred in Egypt, China, India, and the Near East—including the creation of the number system we use today, as well as basic algebra—were transmitted to the West, sometimes with the actual origins forgotten. Much of this knowledge was directly used in business and trade, including weights and measures, arithmetic and numbering, geometry, timekeeping, navigation, water distribution, and cultivation.

Of course, such knowledge was not nicely recorded and widely distributed. Human and civil rights, such as the right to property and the fruits of one's own labor, were denied to many. Life expectancy, literacy, and the need for subsistence were such that relatively few people received a formal education as we now understand it. However, businesses were organized, grew, and failed; trade flourished, was interrupted, and then resumed; people received wages for their work and paid for their purchases; wars and pestilence came and went; and somehow civilization survived—and with it, the institution of business survived and grew.

Business Since AD 1500

In the last five hundred years, business practices were further developed, as were a number of related fields of study, particularly the following:

1500s

- Traders and other businesspeople developed a formal system of accounting to record transactions within a firm. Such practices allowed commerce to grow and are still the bases for trade, contracts, and business investment.

1700s & 1800s

- Economists began writing about the economies of modern societies. Classical economists such as Adam Smith and David Ricardo proposed an explicit labor theory of value.

1900s

- Neoclassical economics emerged as a dominant influence in the whole of social science. It introduced the concepts of marginal cost, consumer utility, and profit maximization, which are now used in economics, law, government, sociology, and commerce. The pervasive idea that prices are set when supply meets demand in an open market took hold.

1940s

- A school of modern finance emerged as a separate discipline. Building on both neoclassical microeconomics and mathematics, modern finance developed notions of arbitrage, martingale pricing, portfolio choice, and mean-variance analysis.

1950s

- Formal credentials were developed for professionals engaged in selling securities of firms, providing advice for individuals investing in firms, accounting or auditing the accounts of firms, and appraising business property. The Modigliani-Miller proposition emerged as a pillar of modern finance. The basis for modern portfolio theory was established.

1970s–2010

- A specialized professional literature in the valuation of business developed. Alongside it grew a smaller literature for forensic economists, who estimate the change in value of firms for the purpose of estimating damages to businesses caused by breaches of contract and natural disasters. A formula for the valuation of certain financial options became widely available. Financial engineering and discounted cash flow analysis became ubiquitous.

We must acknowledge this tremendous progress in the fields of economics, finance, and accounting, and the ongoing efforts of scholars and professional societies dealing with businesses and business value. Indeed, we will devote several chapters to doing exactly that!

THE QUANDARIES

With all this knowledge, we should have a very well-developed theory of the firm and a very well-developed theory of the value of a firm. These theories should be amply tested by reality, comprehensive, and internally consistent.

Unfortunately, few theories provide a sound basis for determining the market value of a privately held firm. Moreover, we still have large gaps in our knowledge about the *rationale* of firms in the modern economy, and no workable universal definition of the firm. Notions of the firm used in microeconomics, accounting, corporate finance, and option pricing all differ. Finally, professionals who seek practical guidance on the definition and value of a firm routinely find it—at least in the United States—from an unlikely source for intellectual enlightenment: the federal taxation authorities.

This unsatisfactory state of affairs can be illustrated by the seven quandaries posed next. Each illustrates a significant gap in the orthodox theories of business drawn from economics, finance, and accounting.

Quandary 1: Mainstream Economics Ignores the Firm

The Neglect of the Firm in Economics

This quandary dates back to the creation of the mathematical models that form the basis of general equilibrium economics. Consider this statement by Léon Walras, the pioneer of welfare economics, writing in the nineteenth century:

Once the equilibrium has been established in principle, exchange can take place immediately. Production, however, requires a certain lapse of time. We shall resolve the second difficulty purely and simply by ignoring the time element at this point. (Walras, 1874, p. 242)

Walras developed the early model of exchange equilibrium, meaning that the buyers and sellers in a market reach agreements at market-clearing prices. However, in order to do this he had to ignore the fact that *production* took some time. It is the firm (or set of firms) that directly internalizes the time, cost, and uncertainty of production. Walras dealt with important issues in economics, and his thought is the basis for much of what we call microeconomics today. But he explicitly ignored the inner workings of the firm. In essence, the firm vanishes from the theoretical model of production, exchange, and consumption.

Next we quote an influential modern-era microeconomist:

> The firm fits into general equilibrium theory as a balloon fits into an envelope: flattened out! Try with a blown-up balloon: the envelope may tear, or fly away: at best, it will be hard to seal and impossible to mail. . . . Instead, burst the balloon flat, and everything becomes easy. Similarly with the firm and general equilibrium—though the analogy requires a word of explanation.

> Jacques H. Drèze, "Uncertainty and the Firm in General Equilibrium Theory," *Economic Journal*, 1985, p. 1.[2]

These observations about the state of economic science are telling.[3] In more than a hundred years, economics had moved quite far—but still typically viewed the firm as a "flattened balloon" abstraction. A few decades later, the standard presentation of the firm in both microeconomics and macroeconomics remains quite primitive.

In the standard microeconomics model, firms are typically assumed to sell homogenous goods using a simple production function. Workers adjust their consumption according to their wages and interest rates. To the extent that firms' production plans are even considered, they are often presented as solutions to single-period profit maximization problems, or as the intersections of average cost curves, assuming static production technology and market structure. Entrepreneurial interests, uncertainty, institutional factors, and numerous financial, managerial, and practical considerations in the organization and operation of the firm are largely assumed away.[4]

To be sure, even this primitive specification of the firm leaves plenty of room for issues such as monetary policy, fiscal policy, trade policy, labor policy, regulation of markets with oligopoly structures, causes of business cycles, and so on. However, it also leaves a rather large void.

The Fulsome Importance of the Firm in the Real Economy

Consider the dimensions in which the firm has an essential, if not dominant, role in society:

- Most firms in the United States are "small" and privately held. Furthermore, these firms appear to employ most of the private-sector workers in the country.

- Equity interests in firms appear to be a very large portion of household wealth.[5]

- One cannot endure an election cycle—at least in the United States—without some businesses, or entire industries being pilloried in campaign rhetoric.[6]

- Much of popular media, entertainment, and sporting events are financed by advertising by firms.[7]
- Successful entrepreneurs have often used their riches to create or endow important charitable, cultural, and educational institutions.[8]
- Finally, a significant portion of the tax revenue of most state and national governments consists of taxes imposed on, or collected by, firms.[9]

The firm is relegated to such inferior status in economics, but not because it is an inferior part of the economy.

Quandary 2: Mainstream Economics Ignores the Entrepreneur

The Much-Loved, but Ignored, Entrepreneur

To understand business value, we must recognize the motivations of those who create businesses and run them. However, neoclassical economics—the dominant school within economics for the past century—largely ignores such people. We discussed earlier how neoclassical economics ignores the inner workings of firms; the entrepreneur can be seen as the inner-inner working of all firms. The relegation of entrepreneurs to an abstraction within neoclassical economics means that these inner workings—so critical to the understanding of business creation, destruction, and value—are also abstracted away. Outside microeconomics, the entrepreneur enjoys a much better public reputation.

Although the notion of the "greedy business executive" is a staple of movies and television shows, the entrepreneur is usually shown in a more favorable light. A good part of popular culture appears to accept the notion that entrepreneurs typically focus on much more than money during their (often long and sometimes unsuccessful) efforts.

Perhaps the most influential modern philosopher of entrepreneurship is George Gilder, whose 1981 book *Wealth and Poverty* became a best-seller and something of a touchstone of the presidency of Ronald Reagan.[10] Gilder writes of the entrepreneur's desire to create, to give, even to love.[11]

This idea of the entrepreneur actually goes back centuries. The Irish economist Richard Cantillon described the entrepreneur as a risk-bearer in the eighteenth century, before Adam Smith wrote his *Wealth of Nations*.[12] Among classic economists, John Stuart Mill and others recognized the vital role of the entrepreneur.

The great twentieth-century economist Joseph Schumpeter coined a phrase that should resonate with anyone who ever worked to build a business, or rebuild it, or expand it. The term is *creative destruction*:

> The opening up of new markets, foreign or domestic, and the organizational development from the craft shop and factory to such concerns as U.S. Steel illustrate the same process of industrial mutation—if I may use that biological term—that incessantly revolutionizes the economic structure *from within*, incessantly destroying the old one, incessantly creating a new one. This process of Creative Destruction is the essential fact about capitalism.
>
> Every piece of business strategy acquires its true significance only against the background of that process and within the situation created by it. It must be seen in its role in the perennial gale of creative destruction; it cannot be understood irrespective of it or, in

fact, on the hypothesis that there is a perennial lull. (Schumpeter, 1975, pp. 83–84; emphasis in original)[13]

Modern Brush-Asides

However prescient Gilder, Cantillon, and Schumpeter's ideas about entrepreneurship may have been, they were not adopted by the mainstream of the economics profession. The importance of entrepreneurship in the dominant economics paradigm diminished greatly in the twentieth century and is still largely missing from general equilibrium economic theory. Some reasons for this disappearance are as follows:

- The neoclassical model relies on equilibrium in a nearly perfect market.[14] This leaves little room for the risk-taking and judgment (not to mention animal spirits) that are the lifeblood of the true entrepreneur.[15]

- The reliance on (some would say infatuation with) mathematical models in modern economics requires much abstraction. Such abstraction cuts against the inclusion of complicated—and mathematically messy—factors such as transaction costs, barriers to entry, uncertainty, and limited ability to finance, all of which are ubiquitous concerns of the entrepreneur.

- A cultural bias exists against "boot strappers" among the well-credentialed academics who write most economics and finance textbooks. This is probably due to a predictable sympathy toward the traditions, mores, and work habits common where one lives and works, and the large differences between the typical life experiences of professors and entrepreneurs.[16]

- There are readily available data on very large, publicly traded firms—providing a convenient basis for academic research and publication opportunities—but relatively little data on privately held firms.[17]

Quandary 3: Entrepreneurs Do Not Maximize Profits

The Profit Maximization Principle

The behavior of entrepreneurs—what they seek, how they think, what they do—should be a core concept in microeconomics. After all, it is entrepreneurs who start businesses. Without them, there are no businesses. What do entrepreneurs try to do?

This question has an easy answer within the world of economics and finance: they maximize profits. Indeed, the idea of businesspeople as mindless profit-maximizers is invoked by politicians, the news media, and popular books and movies.[18] In addition to its elevated position in popular culture, this notion is deeply embedded in the dominant tradition of economics, the neoclassical school.[19] Indeed, we will find that both the traditional neoclassical model and a modern revision of that model assume that the objective of the firm is to "maximize profits."

Entrepreneurs Versus the Economics Books

Of course, the real world is messier than any model. However, I argue the neoclassical model of entrepreneurial behavior is not just incomplete; *it is wrong.*

In particular, entrepreneurs *do not maximize profits*. They *like* profits; they work to *increase* profits at some point; but they do not, as a rule, try to *maximize* them in any one period.

How can this heresy be stated so confidently? It is not heresy to an entrepreneur; it is commonplace. An entrepreneur who attempts to profit-maximize in any one period (say, the first year of business, or the second) will probably find that the optimal "profit-maximizing" production is zero. In other words, shutting down the fledgling firm is what the economics book says he or she ought to do.

Fortunately for all of us, entrepreneurs often refuse to follow the book.

In Chapter 15, "The Value Functional: Theory," we will outline a different objective function of the firm: to maximize *value*. This is *not* the same as maximizing profits in any one period, or every period, or even maximizing the net present value of future expected profits. Instead, it matches what we know about how entrepreneurs actually think and what we can observe about how they act.

Quandary 4: Net Present Value Is Not Value

Much of finance is based on the principle that the value of a firm, and the value of investments in a firm, is defined by the net present value (NPV) of the firm's expected future earnings. The "NPV equals value" principle is embedded deeply in finance. Later in this book, we will date its adoption to the publication and widespread acceptance of the Modigliani-Miller (M-M) propositions approximately a half century ago.[20] However, as a general rule, the net present value of expected future cash flows is *not* the market value of an investment and is rarely the market value of a business.

In Chapter 3, "The Failure of the Neoclassical Investment Rule," we describe several reasons why this is so, including the lack of information from which to estimate net present value (or expected net present value); the ignorance of options, such as the option to wait; and the lack of attention to policy and strategy. Although an entire generation of finance scholars has toyed with the assumptions and implications of the M-M theorem, few have questioned its premise. It is time to do so.

Quandary 5: Managers Do Not Follow the Neoclassical Investment Rule

An important corollary to the "NPV equals value" principle is the *neoclassical investment rule*: a firm should invest in a project when the expected discounted earnings from the investment, less the cost of making the investment, are positive. This is, again, a pillar of modern finance. It is stated and restated in textbooks, magazine articles, journal articles; it is embedded in spreadsheets and models.

However, because NPV is *not* value, the pillar is unstable. In many cases, the neoclassical investment rule leads to the *wrong* decision for the firm, even when the firm's managers have excellent information. By *wrong*, I do not mean merely suboptimal; I mean following the rule causes decisions that *lose money* in amounts that exceed the cost of using a better decision rule. This is, after all, the acid test of a rule.[21]

Of course, the ubiquitous discounted cash flow tables that are taught in standard finance classes are also used in the real business world. Does this mean real managers *follow the rule* when they invest in real life?

In fact, the answer is "only sometimes." Real managers frequently use their judgment to select or reject investments regardless of whether the calculated net present value meets the supposed criteria. Their judgment—not any net present value calculation—is typically the actual determinant.

We will survey extensive empirical evidence on this point in Chapter 3, "The Failure of the Neoclassical Investment Rule." However, we also have the testimony of an unassailable authority on this very question: Stewart Myers. Among other accomplishments, Myers is the co-author (with Richard Brealey) of a widely sold text on corporate finance, which has now been used in various editions by an entire generation of business school students.[22] His decades of experience with actual investment led him and his co-author to coin a "law" of investor behavior:

> According to Brealey and Myers's Second Law, "The proportion of proposed projects having positive NPV is independent of top management's estimate of the opportunity cost of capital."[23]

Real decisions are usually *informed by DCF*, but not *made by DCF*. This means that those who really matter have decided, though perhaps not admitted, that it is not a very good decision rule.

Quandary 6: There Is No Single Coherent Theory of Business Value

The contemporary reader can choose among shelves full of books on valuation methods, odes to the virtues of shareholder value, and strategies to enhance value, however defined. He or she can spend a short career studying mathematical finance models, or learning accounting and finance formulas, or buying and selling investment securities.

That same reader would find no single, valid, coherent theory of business valuation. Yes, we have the intricate mathematics of risk-neutral valuation; we have accounting pronouncements and standards; we have neat formulations for the growth of cash flow and other "value drivers"; and we have the venerable neoclassical investment rule. *None* of these offers a coherent theory of business value.

The most prominent candidate for a coherent theory of business value is Franco Modigliani and Merton Miller's assumption that "the value of a business equals the expected net present value of its profits." This is a cornerstone of capital budgeting theory. Unfortunately, it is incorrect—and, as noted previously, savvy managers often do not follow it anyway.

Quandary 7: Distant and Separate Literatures Cover Business Value Theory

Finance and Economics Literatures Post-1965

There is another consequence—and partially a cause—of this lack of a coherent business value theory. It is the existence of at least two literatures on valuation, almost completely distinct, and often distant from each other:[24]

1. *Finance, accounting, and business management literature.* The concepts of market value and accounting (book) value play a prominent role here, as do management decisions to enhance market value. These books and articles are often heavy on cash flow statements,

finance formulas, and business school jargon. The concept of income alone, for example, is subjected to multiple gradations derived from accounting conventions (gross profit, net profit, operating profit, net operating profit less adjusted taxes [NOPLAT], earnings before interest and taxes [EBIT], earnings before interest, taxes, depreciation, and amortization [EBITDA], "cash flow to the firm," "cash flow to equity," etc.). The value premise is nearly always the net present value rule, with some recent exceptions involving options. Very little attention is paid to underlying economic causes of growth, and any mathematics underlying the valuation premise is often summarized, omitted, or left to appendices.[25]

The capital asset pricing model (CAPM) usually makes an appearance, along with other portfolio-based asset pricing models. However, these are used to describe how investors generally choose assets in a stock market and to estimate discount rates.[26]

2. *The economics and mathematical finance literature.* Entire books within this genre are published without the inclusion of a single accounting statement.[27] Concepts such as "income" and "cash flow" are commonly stated tersely and encapsulated into only one or two variables.

Extensive mathematics (including, in recent decades, set and measure theory, stochastic calculus, and differential calculus) are employed to derive theoretical models. The valuation premise is commonly a pricing-by-arbitrage algorithm or a mathematically sophisticated net present value rule. (In the case of risk-neutral valuation in perfect markets, these are two sides of the same coin.) In recent years, this literature has begun to recognize options, although the pricing techniques discussed are typically variations on the Black-Scholes formula and assume complete markets.

Spending some time in both camps, one is struck by the fact that they are almost entirely separate. Of course, there are exceptions, but contemporary authors in one camp rarely cite those in the other camp and often appear to be unaware of the issues that confront the others.[28] The one stream of literature—and it is a very narrow one—where there is extensive cross-pollination is the valuation and damages texts written by forensic or business economists, which must live in both worlds.[29]

Weakness Within the Stronghold

One may be tempted to dismiss the preceding observations as merely the recognition of the frontiers of research and remain confident that the last half century of modern finance has produced a satisfactory state of affairs. Perhaps it has done so in the classroom but not in the marketplace for business equity.

Even within a fairly narrow subset of finance—the proper portfolio selection for investors with significant investable funds—there is a serious weakness in theory and practice. In particular, the mean-variance framework and its progeny (including the CAPM, arbitrage pricing theory [APT], and their many variations) do not suffice even for portfolio investors.[30] There is no doubting the contributions of the pioneers of the 1950s and 1960s, but there is also no concealing the work that is not yet done.

I was struck by a remark made quite recently by William Sharpe, one of those pioneers in the 1960s. He described the current situation as "not an entirely happy state of affairs."[31]

Although Sharpe was confining his remarks to investment advice largely involving publicly traded securities, his dissatisfaction in this area—the most thoroughly drilled in all finance—indicates an underlying weakness in our knowledge.

A Related Quandary: Intellectuals Seek Advice . . . from the Internal Revenue Service

There is one point on which academics, workers, and ordinary citizens would all agree: politicians who create tax laws are neither oracles of knowledge nor arbiters of fairness.

As a rule, experts in accounting, economics, and finance do not consider "taxable income" as defined by government taxation authorities a reliable indication of the actual earnings of the firm. Publicly traded companies in the United States and many other countries are required to disclose certain financial metrics to the investing public—but those disclosures are typically done according to generally accepted accounting principles, not tax-reporting rules.

Yet when defining a "business" and listing the considerations necessary to estimate its value, experts in these fields often rely on standards promulgated by the taxing authorities. In the United States, the Internal Revenue Service (IRS), or the Internal Revenue Code, is often the most respected authority on such elemental topics such as the standard of value (the definition of *fair market value* in the Internal Revenue Code), the information that must be used to estimate the value of a firm (IRS Revenue Ruling 59-60), types of businesses (Internal Revenue Code definitions of *partnership*, *corporation*, and *sole proprietorship*), and financial data (IRS Statistics of Income data).

When the taxing authorities are also the *intellectual* authorities, the intellectuals should be asking themselves some pointed questions.

ELEMENTS OF A NEW MODEL OF THE FIRM AND ITS VALUE

Modigliani and Miller, who established the concept of business value that has dominated for fifty years, did not proclaim it anything other than a first approximation.[32] This first approximation has lasted for half a century, and it is time to get a second one.

A new valuation approach would ideally incorporate multiple factors that are missing, improperly ignored, or assumed away in the current models. Thus, we would ideally develop a model that would do all of the following:

1. *Establish a definition of the "firm."* Such a definition must distinguish a firm from a worker who pays business taxes (as do many contractors) as well as distinguish a firm from a portfolio of stocks and bonds.

2. *Be informed by empirical data on most firms.* Empirical data on securities issued by publicly traded corporations form the basis for the most empirical work in finance. However, as demonstrated later in this book, more than 99 percent of the firms in the United States are privately held firms that do not issue such securities.

3. *Incorporate risk of the type faced by actual business owners.* Most businesses face very high risks in the first several years of their existence—risks that result in approximately half of

those firms disappearing. Even firms that survive their early years often face a handful of large risks. Such risks are not properly represented by the normal distribution that is often used as the basis for theoretical work in finance.

4. *Assume incomplete markets in equity and debt shares.* Incomplete markets are the rule—not the exception—for private firms.[33] Because complete markets are essential for the "no arbitrage" assumption to be valid, accepting the fact of incomplete markets means accepting the fact that many complete-market pricing methods will not work.

5. *Explicitly identify an objective function for the firm or the entrepreneur.* Identifying an objective function involves replacing the reflexive profit-maximization assumption and changing the implicit time horizon for entrepreneurs. Since most business owners face limitations in trading their equity shares, the one-period neoclassical economics model is untenable as the basis for an objective function for the firm. Similarly untenable is the two-period model underlying modern portfolio theory (MPT).

6. *Take into account factors that are missing in the standard discounted cash flow model.* These would include strategy, policy, and reputation; ideally, the existence of asymmetric information and agency would also be recognized.

7. *Incorporate the benefits of both operating income and real options into the valuation framework.* Actual managers and investors consider both factors.

Each of these objectives is discussed explicitly in one or more of the chapters in this book.[34] We propose a valuation framework that accomplishes most of these objectives, within an integrated model, in Chapter 15, "The Value Functional: Theory."

2 THEORIES OF VALUE

Why Discuss "Business" and "Value"?

In this chapter, we first discuss the idea of *value*. Some readers will wonder why we pause to discuss this concept, rather than plunge headlong into a review of different methods.

This book was written to rigorously define the firm and critically evaluate all known theories of the value of a firm. Such an approach requires rigorously defining *firm* and *value*. Without this foundation, it would be impossible to separate a valid method of business valuation from an invalid one.

We deal with the concept of value in this chapter and again in the next. The definition of a firm is explored in Chapter 4, "The Nature of the Firm."

ECONOMIC VALUE

Common Notions of "Value"

To rigorously discuss the value of businesses, we must start by talking about value. The definition of value is often weak and varies considerably according to the field of literature in which it appears. Here are four important contexts in which the term appears:

1. *Value in common discussion.* In common literature, value is often defined by saying it is the amount something is worth. Such a statement becomes a tautology when *worth* is defined by *value*.[1]

2. *Value in microeconomics.* In neoclassical microeconomics, value is often defined as the product of prices and quantities of commodities that are exchanged.[2] For example, a commodity bundle that included two items that sold for $50 each had a value of $100. This reduces *value* to a mathematical exercise in a useful way for commodities that are sold but not in a useful way for nearly everything else.

3. *Value in accounting.* A fundamental accounting principle is the use of historical cost. The term *book value* for the accounting net worth of a firm (excess of assets over liabilities) is something of a misnomer; accounting authorities explicitly disclaim the accounting balance sheet as an estimate of the market value of a firm [3]

4. *Value in taxation.* Interestingly, tax authorities are the most specific on this topic, probably because they have a material interest in a practical definition that can be the basis for calculating taxes.

In the United States, the Internal Revenue Service and the Code of Federal Regulations have a specific definition of *fair market value*, which has now become the standard legal, accounting, and forensic economics definition of that concept.[4]

5. *Value in life.* Memorable aphorisms and great literature have been written about values; countries have been founded on values in life, and lives have been formed, and sometimes changed, to accord with them. This book deals with something less important: the value of a business. However, we record a selection of thoughts about value made throughout history in Exhibit 2.1.

These treatments are less than satisfying for our purposes. In particular, we need a rigorous concept of *economic value* that cannot be confused with qualitatively different notions of personal life objectives; has meaning to individuals who buy, sell, found, manage, and invest in businesses; and cannot be confused with the variants (and abuses) of the term used in accounting, taxation, microeconomics, law, and other fields.

The Definition of Economic Value

In this book, we use the concept of *economic value* derived from economic theory and available for practical use in business, taxation, and accounting. We define value as a *measurable attribute* that is attached to a *commodity*.

• A *commodity* is any good or service that can be bought and sold. This includes tangible objects (such as wheat, corn, coal, automobiles, and music players); services (including both formal and informal services, legal and illegal services, entertainment, insurance, financial intermediation, and professional services); and real and personal property (including land and buildings as well as leases, easements, and access rights to the use of such properties). The title to the receipt of future commodities is also a commodity; therefore, stocks and bonds, as well as options and other securities, are all considered commodities for this purpose. What we now call *intellectual property* is also a commodity.

• An *attribute* is a condition or characteristic of something else. By defining value as an attribute, we are specifying that value is attached to a commodity but is not intrinsic to the commodity itself.[5]

EXHIBIT 2.1

Thoughts on Value, Worth, and Life

"For what shall it profit a man, if he shall gain the whole world, and lose his own soul?" [Mark 8:36]

"The mind of the superior man is conversant with righteousness; the mind of the mean man is conversant with gain." [Confucius, ancient Chinese philosopher]

"Although gold dust is precious, when it gets in your eyes it obstructs your vision." [Hsi-Tang Chih Tsang, ancient Zen master]

"Not life, but good life, is to be chiefly valued." [Socrates, ancient Greek philosopher]

"What we obtain too cheap, we esteem too lightly; it is dearness only that gives everything its value." [Thomas Paine, American patriot and author]

"There is no value in life except what you choose to place upon it and no happiness in any place except what you bring to it yourself." [Henry David Thoreau, American poet and philosopher]

"Try not to become a man of success but rather try to become a man of value." [Albert Einstein, German-American physicist]

"A business that makes nothing but money is a poor kind of business." [Henry Ford, American industrialist]

"The chief value of money lies in the fact that one lives in a world in which it is overestimated." [H. L. Mencken, American critic]

"Friendship is unnecessary, like philosophy, like art. It has no survival value; rather it is one of those things that give value to survival." [C. S. Lewis, Anglo-Irish author and Christian apologist]

Source: Value Quotes, http://www.valuequotes.com.

People assign value based on the desirability of the commodity to them. This may be manifested in exchanges, transactions, consumption, expressions of interest from others, or the pure enjoyment of the owner. Relative scarcity, usefulness, technology, tastes, and other factors may affect value.[6]

• By *measurable*, we mean there are one or more tractable ways to assign a real number to the attribute, compare it to other such numbers, and use familiar kinds of arithmetic operations on those numbers.[7]

Money and Business Equity as Valuable Commodities

Money or another medium of exchange that can be exchanged for tangible commodities is also a commodity. It has the useful purpose of being a *numeraire*, or basis for numbering a price. Defining money this way also ensures that it is viewed analytically the same way people view it practically: as a commodity that can lose value (such as through inflation); be physically lost, stolen, or confiscated; and have a *convenience yield* or *cost of carry*.[8]

Equity interests in businesses are valuable commodities for at least two reasons:

1. Equity owners are entitled to receive the benefits of future earnings of the firm.

2. Equity owners receive the benefits of exerting control over the enterprise.

We will also explore theories of value that consider one, or both, of these categories of benefits. We also consider carefully later in this text what we mean by the *business* having value; in general we will mean the title to the *equity* in the business has value.

Economic Value Requires Institutions Necessary for Private Enterprise

A valuable commodity must be something that can be defined, legally owned, and transferred for consideration (such as money payment) to another person. This may be summarized by saying a commodity must be the property of an owner.

For property to have economic value, certain institutions in society are required. These include private property rights and enforcement of contract. Without them the business may not be able to rely on contracts to purchase supplies, sell its products, or pay its employees; the manager may not be able to control the enterprise; and the owner of the business may not be able to retain any profits he or she could make. We discuss these specifically in Chapter 4, under the section titled "Institutional Requirements for a Firm."

Market Value in Economics

Market value is the standard on which we base most of the analysis in this book and is a deeply established principle in economics. In general, the market value of any asset is the price for which it is exchanged among willing parties in a *market*, which consists of multiple potential buyers and sellers. The legal definition of *fair market value* is essentially identical: the value *in a market* with *willing buyers and willing sellers*, each with *sufficient information*,[9] and neither under any compulsion.[10]

This fair market value concept from economics is one of the most powerful and useful to emerge from the field. Indeed, it is now codified in countless laws, standards, court cases, individual contracts, and scholarly treatises in the United States and other countries.

TEN PRINCIPLES OF VALUATION

Origin of Valuation Principles

In this book, we identify ten valuation principles articulated in the literature accumulated over the past four centuries; these originated in the fields of economics, accounting, taxation, mathematics, finance, and control theory. Three of these principles have been adapted for use in the professional practice of valuation and have their roots in these fields of study. Others have been largely confined to academic or theoretical use because of novelty, difficulty, or inherent deficiencies. A handful have become available for practical use only recently.

We consider each of these principles distinct from each other, in the sense that each fundamentally derives value from a different source. For example, the labor theory originates value in the amount of labor necessary to produce an asset; the neoclassical economics model originates value in the intersection of supply and demand in a market; and the complete-market models of mathematical finance originate value in the equivalence of pay-offs from a replicating portfolio.

That is not to say that concepts central to one principle are not existent in the others. For example, the supply in the neoclassical economics model is surely connected to the amount of labor necessary to produce the relevant asset. The no-arbitrage assumption central to mathematical finance is often present, at least in a limited sense, in the other theories as well. However, each of the ten fundamental principles is different.

Three of the ten principles presented here are derived from economics; three are traditional methods of valuation; three are derived from mathematical finance; and one novel principle emerges from both economics and control theory.

Valuation in Economics

Three theories of value arise from economics:

1. *The classical labor theory of value.* The classical labor theory of value dates at least as far back as Adam Smith. Within this theory, value arises in principle from the amount of labor required to produce a commodity.

2. *The neoclassical equilibrium theory of value.* The neoclassical equilibrium theory is familiar to anyone who has taken an economics class over the past century. In principle, the value of any commodity is set at the intersection of supply and demand in a one-period competitive market.

3. *The modern recursive equilibrium theory of value.* The modern recursive formulation of a market equilibrium has been largely confined to advanced economics. The valuation principle within this theory is that value to a consumer arises from his or her desire to consume today, rather than to save or invest to secure investment tomorrow.

These approaches are taught in economics classes, with the first two being hallmarks (or low points) of many college educations. It is tempting to say they are often left buried when graduates go on to the "real world," but this would be a mistake. Every time someone quotes a price on the basis of professional time—a common practice in occupations such as lawyer, mechanic, doctor, and consultant—he or she is implicitly using the labor theory of value. Similarly, the neoclassical equilibrium theory arises time and time again in business, even though no one would attempt to value a business using it. The last of these three—the recursive equilibrium theory—arose only recently and provides a basis for new methods of valuation.

We describe these theories in Part 3, "Economic Theories of Value."

Traditional Valuation Methods

Three traditional methods of valuation are commonly used in taxation, accounting, and professional valuation practice:

4. *The market approach.* The market approach relies on the axiom that the market value of any traded asset is defined by actual market transactions. It further relies on the principle that market transactions involving a set of comparable firms can establish another firm's market value.

5. *The income approach.* The income approach relies on the principle, ubiquitous in finance, that the value of a financial asset is the expected net present value of the future earnings from that asset.

6. *The asset approach.* The asset approach is based on the accounting identity: the assets of a firm equal the sum of its liabilities and equity. This implies the principle that the value of a firm is the value of its assets less the value of its liabilities. The common use of the term *book value* is an example of the use of this approach.

Traditional methods are used in most accounting, taxation, and professional valuation work, even though more sophisticated methods are available. For example, the accounting identity is clearly invalid as a universal valuation principle. However, it is handy when an accountant needs to produce the balance sheet of a firm, which is often the first document a prospective buyer wants to review. Similarly, the income method (often described loosely as the *discounted cash flow model*) is a workhorse of corporate finance.

We describe these theories in Part 5, "Traditional Valuation Methods."

Valuation in Mathematical Finance

Three valuation principles have emerged from the field of finance:

7. *Option valuation theory.* Option valuation theory relies on the insight of financial option-pricing models (particularly the seminal Black-Scholes-Merton model), which break the market value of a traded financial option contract into two parts: the intrinsic value and the option premium. The underlying principle is that the equity in a firm is like a call option on the assets of the firm.

8. *Modern portfolio theory.* Modern portfolio theory relies on the notion that the value of a portfolio of investments is set by trade-offs of risk and reward for the portfolio as a whole. The mean-variance approach and its progeny, including the CAPM and other investment models, fall into this category. In principle, the market value of a firm under this theory is determined by the level and variation of its returns compared with those also available for inclusion in an investment portfolio.

9. *Complete-market (no-arbitrage) pricing models.* Complete-market pricing models rely on the findings of mathematical finance that apply to "complete" markets, in which alternative assets can replicate exactly the payoff of any security. Under this theory, the value of any asset is equal in principle to that of a replicating portfolio.

Scholars in the relatively new field of mathematical finance have developed these models of investment behavior largely in the past half century, and they are hard to avoid in the investment field. However, they are almost completely absent from practical work involving business assets that are not widely traded securities.

We describe these theories in some depth in Part 4, "Finance Theories of Value."

The Value Functional Approach from Control Theory

The last principle emerges from economics and control theory and requires a specific definition of the firm:

TABLE 2.1

Ten principles of business valuation

Name of theory	*Fundamental valuation principle; chapter reference*	*Originators (era)*	*Summary comments: theoretical validity; practical usefulness*
ECONOMICS			
Classical	Labor theory of value: value is the sum of labor inputs. See Chapter 7, "Value in Classical Economics."	Smith, Ricardo (18th century); Marx, Sraffa	Invalid as a theory of business valuation (because it is incorrect). Not useful in practice.
Neoclassical	Value theory in "marginalist" school; value is price times quantity of commodities; no theory of producer value. See Chapter 8, "Value in Neoclassical Economics."	Walras (19th century); Marshall, Drèze, Debreu (20th century)	Invalid as a theory of business valuation (because "firm" is an abstraction in this theory). Not useful in practice.
Modern	Recursive general equilibrium model; consumers choose savings (invest) to secure consumption in future periods. See Chapter 9, "Modern Recursive Equilibrium and the Basic Pricing Equation."	Bewley, Lucas, Sargent, Aiyagari (late 20th century)	Valid as a general theory of investment and labor behavior. Does not extend to the value of individual firms. Not useful in practice.
TRADITIONAL APPROACHES			
Asset approach	Value of firm is value of assets less value of liabilities; an adaptation of accounting identity: Assets = Liabilities + Equity. See Chapter 6, "Accounting for the Firm," and Chapter 13, under the section titled "The Asset Method."	Accounting method: Italian trading houses in Renaissance era; first codified by Luca Pacioli (16th century) Practical use in modern era: U.S. Internal Revenue Service (early 20th century)	Accounting identity is invalid as a theory of business valuation. Accounting information is vital for business management and for communication with investors. Asset approach can be useful in practice when "firm" is essentially a collection of assets, for which market values are available.
Market approach	Value of a firm is the market value of similar firms. See Chapter 13, "The Market Approach: Theory."	Traditional	Invalid as a theory of business valuation (because it is a tautology). Very useful in practice, when comparables are available.
Income approach	Value of firm is expected net present value of future earnings; this leads to NPV rule of capital budgeting, also known as the "neoclassical investment rule." See Chapter 13, "The Income Method."	Rational investor income principle: Fisher, Williams (early 20th century); Modigliani and Miller; Dean (mid-20th century) Practical development: Pratt, Damadoran, Brealey, Myers, Reilly (late 20th century)	Partially valid as a theory. Workhorse practical method for private and publicly held firms. Usually requires extensive subjective adjustments to overcome theoretical deficiencies.

	Description	Theoretical development	Validity as theory of business valuation
MATHEMATICAL FINANCE			
Modern portfolio theory	Value of a portfolio and selection of investments within a portfolio is set by trade-off between "risk" and "reward" of portfolio as a whole. See Chapter 11, "Portfolio Pricing Methods."	Mean-variance approach: Markowitz; CAPM: Sharpe and colleagues, Roll Intertemporal model: Merton (mid-20th century)	Invalid as a theory of business valuation. (Valid as a theory about portfolio investments in a single period.) Useful only for publicly traded firms and portfolio investments. Not useful for private firms or nonportfolio investments.
Complete markets ("no arbitrage") methods	In complete markets, no-arbitrage assumption provides unique price for all traded assets ("fundamental theorem of finance"). See Chapter 10, "Arbitrage-Free Pricing in Complete Markets."	State pricing of securities: Arrow, Pratt, Black, Scholes & Merton Enforcement of pricing in stock markets: Modigliani & Miller (mid-20th century) Complete-markets pricing models: Ross, Dybig, Harrison, Kreps (late 20th century)	Valid as a theory for a very narrow class of assets, which includes securities of some firms. Not applicable to noncomplete markets or securities of most firms. Not useful for privately held firms.
Option value	Equity of firm is equivalent to call option on firm's assets. Value of firm is sum of value from continuing operations and real options (including "growth options"). Management flexibility has value. See Chapter 12, "Real Options and Expanded Net Present Value."	Financial option value: Bachelier (early 20th century); Black, Scholes & Merton; Cox, Ross, Rubinstein (late 20th century). Real options: Myers; McDonald & Siegel; Dixit & Pindyck (late 20th century)	Valid as a theory of business valuation, but incomplete as it does not provide a basis for the value of operating companies. Very useful for businesses with IP, natural resources, and similar assets. Useful for most other firms. Often difficult to use practically.
VALUE FUNCTIONAL			
Value functional	Intrinsic value of firm is solution to entrepreneur's value functional equation, given market (state) conditions and ability to control (make policy decisions) in future. See Chapter 15, "The Value Functional Theory."	Optimality principle: Bellman (mid-20th century) Theoretical development: Blackwell, Stokey, Lucas, Sargent (late 20th century) Firm valuation: Anderson (early 21st century)	Valid as a theory of business valuation for both privately held and publicly traded firms. Very useful for most firms, though difficult to implement.

10. *The value functional approach.* The novel value functional approach relies on the concept of the firm as a controlled entity. The underlying valuation principle is that the owner controls the activities of the firm in a manner that maximizes the sum of current income and discounted expected future value, given the control exerted by the owner.

The value functional approach arises from a subfield of mathematics known as control theory, which was first developed about a half century ago.

We describe this approach in Part 6, "The Value Functional Approach."

Summary of the Ten Valuation Principles

Table 2.1 lists each of the ten valuation principles, its key originators, and a chapter reference within this book. The table also provides a brief summary statement about each principle's validity as a theory of business valuation and a comment about the ability of practitioners to actually use the method.

This table can be seen as an appetizer for the material in the rest of the book; as a challenge for readers who are particularly fond of one approach and find it described here as "incomplete" or even "invalid"; or as a summary of much of the material in the later chapters.

Notes on the Classification

NPV Rule Not a Valuation Theory

The neoclassical investment rule, or the *NPV rule*, holds that the firm should undertake investments if the net present value of the income expected from the investment, discounted at the firm's cost of capital, is positive. This rule underlies many finance and capital budgeting theories such as the Modigliani-Miller propositions, and matches the principle of the income method. However, the rule itself is not a valuation method.

Mathematical Finance Not Identical to Option Pricing

The segregation of complete-market models from option valuation models may not be obvious to those steeped in what is sometimes called neoclassical finance, because many option valuation models (including the Black-Scholes-Merton model) are complete-market models.

However, the concept of a firm's equity as a call option on its assets is powerful and separate from any financial option pricing model. Furthermore, real options techniques can often be used without a complete-market assumption. We consider these topics in Chapter 12, "Real Options and Expanded Net Present Value."

New Approaches in Valuation Worth Considering

Both the recursive equilibrium and value functional approaches are so new that most readers are likely to be unfamiliar with them. Furthermore, they are not in common use in practical valuation and do not even have widely accepted names. However, I identify them as separate valuation principles because they are fundamentally different from their predecessors and are at least as logically complete as the others. Indeed, I argue that they are superior in many respects to traditional valuation methods.

3 THE FAILURE OF THE NEOCLASSICAL INVESTMENT RULE

The question of how a company should distribute its profits, as well as how to calculate and record transactions for such a firm, inspired the work of some of the greatest mathematicians in the history of the world. Among their innovations was the net present value algorithm introduced eight hundred years ago by Leonardo of Pisa, the same person who introduced to the Western world the number system we now use.

The related capital-budgeting question—when should a business make an investment?—inspired the inquiry of some of the brightest minds in economics at the beginning and middle of the twentieth century. Their conclusions use the same net present value algorithm introduced by Leonardo of Pisa in 1202: A firm should invest when the net present value of the expected returns of the investment is positive, because that increases the value of the firm. This neoclassical investment rule (or "NPV rule") is a pillar of modern finance.

Failings of the Net Present Value Rule

However, we present telling evidence in this chapter that the value of a firm is *not* the net present value of its expected profits. This is a provocative statement. We support it by presenting six major failings of the NPV rule:

1. Decision makers lack $E(NPV)$ information.
2. The rule ignores option value.
3. The rule ignores policy, strategy, and reputation.
4. Decision makers fail to follow the rule.
5. Liquidity constraints impinge on both firms and investors.
6. "Entrepreneurs are entrepreneurs."

Other Elements of This Chapter

In this chapter, we also:

- Observe the wonderful history of the introduction of Indo-Arabic numerals and the development of algebra and net present value from the work of ancient and medieval scholars in India, Arabia, and Italy.

- Review the seminal Modigliani-Miller propositions, including their implicit definition of the firm and their explicit formula for the value of the firm's securities. We also note the antecedents of the M-M propositions in the work of Irving Fisher and John Burr Williams, as well as the role of Joel Dean in establishing the related neoclassical investment rule.

- Note Modigliani-Miller's definition of the value of the firm as the expected net present value of its future earnings. Observe how this definition leads to the *neoclassical investment rule*: a firm should invest only in projects in which the expected return exceeds their cost of capital.

- Observe the ubiquity of this rule and the related valuation principle in the literature of finance, economics, accounting, and valuation.

- Argue that the value of a bona fide firm often, if not always, deviates from any objective measurement of the expected discounted value of its future profits. Observe that this conclusion relies critically on the definition of the firm and note the difference between applying the neoclassical investment rule to *portfolios* and to *firms*.

We conclude that this rule is not only limited in its application but fails as a principle of valuation—a statement that may appear heretical given the vast literature based on it.

THE APPEARANCE AND REAPPEARANCE OF NET PRESENT VALUE

Fibonacci, "Indian" Numerals, and Net Present Value

In 1202, the great Italian mathematician Leonardo of Pisa, commonly known as Fibonacci, wrote the *Liber Abaci* ("Book of Calculation"). This book introduced to the Western world a revolutionary system of numbers developed in India, the *Modus Indorum*. Fibonacci wrote:

> These are the nine figures of the Indians: 9, 8, 7, 6, 5, 4, 3, 2, 1. With the nine figures, and with this sign 0 which in Arabic is called *sephirium*, any number can be written, as will be demonstrated. (Rubinstein, 2006, p. 3)[1]

These figures were demonstrably superior for purposes of calculation to the Roman numerals (such as I, II, III) that had been used for centuries in Europe and other parts of the world. Quite recently, scholars have rediscovered Fibonacci's contribution to commerce and finance. William Goetzmann (2003) describes how, using the Indian number system, Fibonacci developed the first known solution to the question of the present value of a future stream of earnings.

Goetzmann notes that Fibonacci explicitly described how profits from a business enterprise should be split among investors. Fibonacci then described how to perform a present value analysis using both annual and quarterly compounded interest. Fibonacci's analysis used a novel fraction method, but it calculated the net present value of future cash flows much as we do today. Fibonacci's innovation was clearly the basis for other treatises on mathematics published in the fifteenth century and later.

The Expected Net Present Value Formula

The formal definition of the expected net present value of a discrete series of future cash flows is presented in Appendix A, "Key Formula and Notation Summary." Here we note three critical aspects of the $E(NPV)$ formula:

1. Most cash flows in business are random variables, so the proper measure of these is almost always an *expected* net present value.

2. The expectation is taken based on information available at a specific time, such as $t = 0$. Later-arriving information, therefore, may change this expectation.

3. We assume the discount rate and the statistical distribution of the random variables. Often, an additional assumption is made that those remain constant.

The difficulty of actually using the expected net present value of future earnings should be clear from examining these three assumptions. We discuss this issue further later in this chapter under the section titled "Six Failings of the NPV Rule."

THE POTENT LEGACY OF THE MODIGLIANI-MILLER PROPOSITIONS

The Foundation of Modern Corporate Finance

Few principles are more firmly embedded in corporate finance than that of a firm's value equaling the expected net present value of its future earnings. This principle was not always accepted as a near-universal truth and is seriously questioned here. However, it is well worth reviewing how this principle is intertwined with a foundation of modern corporate finance: the Modigliani-Miller propositions.

Miller later explained what became known as the "M-M" propositions as follows:

> With well-functioning markets (and neutral taxes) and rational investors, who can "undo" the corporate financial structure by holding positive or negative amounts of debt, the market value of the firm—debt plus equity—depends *only* on the income stream generated by its assets. It follows, in particular, that the value of the firm should not be affected by the share of debt in its financial structure or by what will be done with the returns–paid out as dividends or reinvested (profitably). (Modigliani, 1980, p. xiii)

For their contributions, both Modigliani and Miller were honored with the Nobel Prize.[2] Today, the M-M propositions are so well established they are often assumed without much comment, aside from discussion of market imperfections such as taxes, bankruptcy risk, and asymmetric information.[3]

Motivating the M-M Propositions

Before the Modigliani-Miller propositions, opinion on financial markets was largely organized around two schools of thought. The first is that financial markets are little more than fancy casinos, and speculative gains are the fundamental goal of investors.[4] The second—which arose only in the twentieth century—is that investors rationally consider the earning potential of firms and seek the likelihood of earning dividends, interest, and other remunerations from their investments.[5] One indication of the prevalence and intellectual legitimacy of the "casino" school of thought was that John Maynard Keynes, in his 1936 *General Theory*, clearly favored it over the latter.[6]

We discuss in the chapter appendix, "Antecedents of the NPV Rule," how early in the twentieth century Irving Fisher and John Burr Williams laid the groundwork for an income-based theory of investment valuation. Both outlined the key concepts of the market rate of interest; investors choosing among alternative uses of their capital; and the discipline of choosing to use that capital for investment in a firm only when the investor expects a higher rate of return than the cost of that capital. Williams even outlined an explicit discounted cash flow method, under the premise that the value of a firm was the expected net present value of future earnings distributed to shareholders and bondholders.

However, Modigliani and Miller formalized the problem with a number of explicit innovations:

1. Firms could use earnings to repurchase stock, or to reinvest in new projects, as well as distribute earnings to investors.

2. Investors could sell stock instead of waiting for a dividend and borrow and lend to achieve a desired investment portfolio of stocks and bonds.

3. Investors considered a large group of potential investments in the same risk class and seized the opportunity to invest in companies that promise a higher total return, even if it required buying and selling different securities in a manner that eliminated any arbitrage profits.

They also formalized the problem within a near-perfect theoretical world that incorporated these innovations. This synthesis allowed for a much deeper understanding of the capital budgeting problem for the firm and the valuation problem for the investor.

The "Drastic" Assumptions Underlying M-M

Modigliani and Miller acknowledged that their propositions required a number of "drastic" assumptions, including perfect and frictionless markets, lack of default risk for bonds, lack of income taxes, and the availability of the same interest rate to both individual and company borrowers.[7] Although all of these are clearly incorrect, the assumption about income taxes produced the most critical attention and even later disagreement between Modigliani and Miller. In the conclusion to their 1958 article, Modigliani and Miller observe that the "drastic" simplifications were necessary to achieve "at least the foundations of a theory of the valuation of firms and shares under uncertainty."[8]

They certainly achieved that goal.

THE M-M PROPOSITIONS

Proposition I: The Value of the Firm

The first of the M-M propositions is presented in the algebraic formulation shown in Equation 3.1.[9] The proposition contains the following elements:

- A definition of the market value of the firm as the sum of the market values of its (stock and bond) securities: V is defined as $S + D$.

- The assertion that the market value of these securities must be the net present value of the expected returns on the assets of the company: $V = X/\rho$. Modigliani and Miller explicitly describe the future returns as random variables subject to a specific statistical distribution, for which the expected value of the future stream is well defined.

- Based on the assumption of near-perfect capital markets, the assertion that "in any given class the price of every share must be proportional to its expected return," and that factor of proportionality is $1/\rho$, which "can be regarded as the market rate of capitalization for the expected value" of the future profits of firms in that "risk class."[10]

Equation 3.1 M-M Proposition I

V_j = value of firm j

$$V_j \equiv S_j + D_j = \overline{X_j} \Big/ \rho_k$$

where:

S_j = market value of equity shares

D_j = market value of debt

$\overline{X_j}$ = expected return on assets of company j

ρ_k = capitalization rate for companies of risk class k

Once this definition and equation are stated, we can observe that only the capitalization rate for companies of this risk class appears in the equation. From this, Modigliani and Miller state that "our Proposition I asserts that we must have in equilibrium" the following:

That is, the *market value of any firm is independent of its capital structure and is given by capitalizing its expected return at the rate ρ_k appropriate to its class.* (Modigliani and Miller, 1958, p. 268; emphasis in original)

In the corporate finance literature, Proposition I is often described as proving that, at least in a world without income taxes, the value of a levered firm equals that of an unlevered firm with the same assets. However, inspection of Equation 3.1 reveals no such proof.[11] Indeed, the proposition *defines* the market value of the firm as the sum of the market value of its securities, and then equates the sum of those values to the ratio of two unknowns: the expected returns on the firm's assets and the capitalization rate for firms of that risk class. A definition is not a provable theorem. [12]

Proposition II: Irrelevance

The second of the M-M propositions takes an enormous step toward showing, although not quite proving, the famous irrelevance principle. In that proposition, Modigliani and Miller demonstrate how the required returns (the capitalization rates for companies of each risk class) could adjust linearly with the leverage of the firm. If this adjustment exactly matches the change in leverage and the other assumptions also hold, then the capital structure of the firm would indeed be irrelevant to the market value of the firm's securities as defined by Proposition I. Proposition II is shown in Equation 3.2.

Equation 3.2 M-M Proposition II

$$i_j = \rho_k + (\rho_k - r)\frac{D_j}{S_j}$$

where:

i_j = expected rate of return or yield on the stock of company j belonging to the kth risk class

S_j = market value of equity shares in company j

D_j = market value of debt in company j

ρ_k = capitalization rate for companies of risk class k

r = the uniform rate of interest paid on individual and company debt

Here is where Modigliani and Miller actually prove, using their definition of value and their assumptions about perfect markets and a uniform rate of interest, the irrelevance of leverage: they show how investors can trade among securities (arbitrage) to achieve equivalent rates of return on securities within the same risk class. Given this, they conclude:

> That is, *the average cost of capital to any firm is completely independent of its capital structure and is equal to the capitalization rate of a pure equity stream of its class.* (Modigliani and Miller, 1958, p. 269; emphasis in original) [13]

M-M and Arbitrage

The enforcement of the irrelevance result in the M-M model relies on a no-arbitrage assumption about capital markets. This point was reinforced repeatedly in the debate following the original paper. [14] Modigliani and Miller acknowledge in this debate that this enforcement mechanism relies on specific assumptions about the completeness of the market, the uniform interest rate, and absence of transaction costs.

Here, they counter a skepticism of Durand (1959) about the enforcement of prices through arbitrage:

For, whatever the nomenclature, Durand does not seem to disagree that in perfect markets [note 1] enough mechanisms are available to investors and speculators to prevent value discrepancies in a class from being more than ephemeral. And, on our part, we entirely agree with him that real world markets are never perfect and hence that conclusions based on the assumptions of perfect markets *need not* have empirical validity.

[note 1] The term perfect market is to be taken in its usual sense of implying perfect information and absence of transaction costs. In addition to these standard attributes, we also require for a perfect capital market that the rate of interest (or, more generally, the rate of interest function) to the same for all borrowers and lenders. See [p. 268]. (Modigliani and Miller, 1959)

Such a perfect-world borrowing and lending assumption is consistent with the complete-market pricing models we discuss in Chapter 10, "Arbitrage-Free Pricing in Complete Markets."

Proposition III: the Neoclassical Investment Rule

Modigliani and Miller proceed to their version of the neoclassical investment rule:

On the basis of our propositions with respect to cost of capital and financial structure (and for the moment neglecting taxes), we can derive the following simple rule for optimal investment policy by the firm:

Proposition III. If a firm in class k is acting in the best interest of the stockholders at the time of the decision, it will exploit an investment opportunity if and only if the rate of return on the investment, say ρ^*, is as large as or larger than ρ_k. That is, *the cut-off point for investment in the firm will in all cases be ρ_k and will be completely unaffected by the type of security used to finance the investment.* Equivalently, we may say that regardless of the financing used, the marginal cost of capital to a firm is equal to the average cost of capital, which is in turn equal to the capitalization rate for an unlevered stream in the class to which the firm belongs. (Modigliani and Miller, 1959, p. 288; emphasis in original)

The Risk Class, Uniform-Interest-Rate, and Predictable-Profit Assumptions

Contemporary discussions of the M-M model often focus on the effect of taxes, bankruptcy risk, or asymmetric information, each of which violates one or more of the assumptions of the model. Even when maintaining the other definitions and assumptions embedded in the M-M model, relaxing these three assumptions can result in the loss of the irrelevance-of-leverage result.

However, we return to the goal that Modigliani and Miller set for themselves in 1958: to establish the foundation for a theory of value of firms and their securities in a world of uncertainty. What does the relaxation of certain key assumptions mean for the *theory of value* embedded in Proposition I?

Let us consider three assumptions: the adoption of a risk class for both investors and companies, the assumption of infinite streams of profit for each firm, and the assumption of uniform interest rate.

1. *Risk class.* As is explicit in the equations underlying the first two propositions, the arbitrage enforcement occurs among investors in securities of firms *within a certain risk class.* Furthermore, the hurdle rate for investment returns, ρ_k, is defined for each class; see again Equation 3.1.

Now consider any change in investment policy, dividend policy, economic conditions, or management that moves the firm outside its previous risk class. Although Modigliani and Miller assumed no bankruptcy risk and a uniform borrowing rate, they did not assume away uncertainty. Should an uncertain event move the firm outside its previous risk class, it is not clear how arbitrage would enforce the equivalence among returns on securities within the (now uncertain) class to which the firm now belonged.[15] This would render Equation 3.1 untenable for any individual firm.

2. *Uniform interest rate.* One can observe (as Modigliani and Miller did) that interest rates vary among lenders and instruments. Because this is true, one cannot assume that investors can costlessly assemble and reassemble portfolios that achieve the desired balance of debt and equity.[16]

Furthermore, once investors and companies cannot borrow at a uniform rate, dividend policy is no "detail." Hence, the value of the firm can no longer be described by the ratio of expected earnings to a uniform capitalization rate shown in Equation 3.1.

3. *Infinite and predictable streams of profit.* Beginning with Proposition I, the M-M model relies on the assumption of a stream of profit "extending indefinitely into the future," with a mean value that is finite and subject to a specific probability distribution. It combines these assumptions with the risk class and no-bankruptcy assumptions.

What if the profits of the firm are subject to some real-world risks that are not traded in the marketplace and could ultimately result in bankruptcy? Much of the literature asks this question about leverage and dividend policy; we ask it about value. The answer to this question is that nothing in the model describes how arbitrage trading enforces the securities of the firm to trade at values that are equivalent to those of others in the risk class, if the boundaries of such a class are uncertain. Furthermore, given incomplete markets, the arbitrage assumption itself is untenable.[17]

Thus, relaxing any of these key assumptions—even while attempting to maintain the others—makes the valuation equation in Proposition I deeply suspect, if not invalid. Furthermore, this comes not from some market imperfections (such as differing individual and company tax rates, transaction costs, asymmetrical information, or deductibility of interest costs), but from the lack of the arbitrage enforcement that is the source of the discipline in the M-M model. Without such a discipline, the value of a firm, or even the value of its securities, is not necessarily equal to the expected net present value of its earnings.

Conclusion: The Brilliant, but Limited, Modigliani-Miller Propositions

This conclusion does not mean that Modigliani and Miller failed at their goal of establishing "at least the foundations of a theory of the valuation of firms and shares in a world of uncertainty." Indeed, they succeeded brilliantly and did so acknowledging without hesitation the "drastic" assumptions that were necessary for their model.

THE UBIQUITOUS NEOCLASSICAL INVESTMENT RULE

Origin of the Rule

The valuation principle embedded in the M-M propositions has antecedents at least as far back as Irving Fisher, as we demonstrate in the chapter appendix, "Antecedents of the NPV Rule." However, in the middle of the twentieth century this principle became codified by a generation of finance authors into the *neoclassical investment rule*: invest when the net present value of the future earnings exceeds the cost of the investment.

It appears that widespread use of this NPV rule in corporate finance began in the 1950s, with the appearance of Joel Dean's *Capital Budgeting* (1951).[18] The widespread adoption of the Modigliani-Miller propositions after their 1958 article solidified it in economics and the fledgling field of finance. We survey the economics, finance, and professional valuation literatures next and find that the rule is indeed ubiquitous.

The Rule in Economics Literature

The term *neoclassical investment rule* comes from the economics literature, where the following extension from the neoclassical microeconomics model can be made:

> The neoclassical theory of investment starts from a firm's optimization behavior. The objective of the firm is to maximize the present discounted value of net cash flows subject to the technological constraints summarized by the production function. (Hayashi, 1982, p. 213)

This neoclassical extension is usually attributed, in slightly different forms, to Dale Jorgensen (1963) or James Tobin (1969).[19] Stephen LeRoy's (1991) essay on present value in *The New Palgrave* summarizes the contemporary economics curriculum on this topic:

> In introductory finance courses, the present value relation makes an early appearance . . . where it is taught a corporation should accept any investment project that promises a positive net present value (net of costs) and only those. This wealth maximization decision rule— Fisher's separation theorem—is the correct one independent of agents' preferences.

Consistent with this summary, the "rule" appears in numerous economics texts, such as the following statement from a textbook in macroeconomics:

> Under the assumption made, the *fundamental principle of valuation* says that the yield per dollar invested must be the same for all financial assets. . . . The yield on one dollar invested in shares of firm *i* consists of dividend plus capital gains on the price of a share in that firm. . . . Solving . . . by repeated substitutions . . . we find the following expression for [the value of firm *i*] V_t after T substitutions:[20]

$$V_t = \sum \left(\frac{1}{1+r} \right)^{i-t} \cdot \pi_i + \text{terminal value}$$

These authors state the "objective function of the firm" as "the present value of present and future cash flow streams" and again cite the Modigliani-Miller Theorem.

Similar statements appear in historical reviews of economic thought regarding the firm. Douglas Vickers (1987, chap. 2) states the conventional view as follows:

> Consider the profit variable . . . π describing the firm's periodic net income accruing to the owners. The economic value of such an income stream over time, or, that is, the economic value of the ownership, V, will be the present discounted value. . . . We may assume at this stage that the capitalization rate ρ is determined by money capital market conditions. . . . We write $\rho = (risk)$ to indicate the dependence of the required rate of return on the risk being born. . . . We can therefore write:
>
> $$V = \sum_{t=1}^{\infty} \frac{\pi_t}{1+\rho}$$
>
> *or*
>
> $$V = \int_0^{\infty} \pi_t e^{-\rho t} dt$$
>
> *where:*
>
> π_t = periodic net income accruing to the owners
>
> $\rho = \rho(risk)$ = capitalization rate

The Rule in Corporate Finance Literature

The NPV rule has been a foundation of the corporate finance literature, and from there the professional valuation curricula, for at least a generation. So important is this foundation to the subfield of corporate finance that the first edition of the long-running textbook by Richard Brealey and Stewart Myers, *Principles of Corporate Finance* (1981), placed it as the first among the "five most important ideas in finance," saying the "net present value rule" is "obvious when you think about it."[21]

Similar statements appear throughout the professional valuation literature, which is somewhat distinct from the corporate finance literature. For example, the following "theory of valuation" statement appears in both a standard investment analysis and a standard professional valuation text:

> The value of an asset is the present value of the expected returns. (F. Reilly, 1994, pp. 380–381; quoted in Pratt, Reilly, and Schweihs, 1996, p. 151)[22]

Shannon Pratt, Robert Reilly, and Robert Schweihs, collectively authors of several professional valuation texts appearing in multiple editions, state the principle as follows:

> Value today always equals future cash flow discounted at the opportunity cost of capital. (Brealey and Myers, 1991, p. 64; quoted in Pratt, Reilly, and Schweihs, 1996, p. 151)[23]

That ubiquity in the United States is also displayed in a survey of research on investment behavior, primarily in Europe:

Economic theory commonly assumes that an investment project takes place only if the discounted flow of the expected future revenues that it generates exceeds its costs; this is the so-called positive net present value rule. (Butzen and Fuss, 2002, p. 2)

In addition to these cited references, the NPV rule appears in a vast array of other finance, accounting, valuation, law, and economics management references.[24]

Does Ubiquity Mean Validity?

It is hard to overstate the dominance of the neoclassical investment rule, as it is known in the economics literature, or the NPV rule, as it is known in the corporate finance literature. Does that ubiquity confirm validity?

Clearly, it *implies* validity. Is the neoclassical rule *actually* the correct one for investors or managers interested in maximizing shareholder value or another well-accepted objective? We consider that question in the next section.

SIX FAILINGS OF THE NPV RULE

Failure 1: Decision Makers Lack $E(NPV)$ Information

At least three elements are necessary to calculate the expected net present value of a future stream of income: a discount rate, a set of possible outcomes over time, and a probability distribution for the states that could produce the various outcomes.[25] One or more of these is usually *unknown* to a potential investor in a private firm.[26] We consider each next.

1. *The discount rate is not known in advance.* We discuss in this book multiple theories for the establishment of investor discount rates.[27] In general, these theories assume the existence of an available investment alternative or *twin security* with the same maturity, payoff, and risk characteristics as the underlying investment. These characteristics vary with the theory and the type of investment.[28]

Although generations of finance scholars have accepted this device, it suffers from a serious epistemological flaw:

a. Investments by private businesses involve risks that are *not* evident in the markets of widely traded securities; therefore,

b. We often do not know the risk characteristics of the investment and therefore cannot find a twin security for it.

If the neoclassical investment rule works, then those investors must have discounted the expected gain using some type of twin security. Clearly, no such security is traded today for the vast majority of private firms. Thus, the rule cannot be followed.

2. *The probability distributions of important business events are often unknown.* Many finance theories are built on the notion of prices being affected by a large number of independent random events. Such situations lend themselves to models that produce smooth curves illustrating possible outcomes.[29]

In reality, much business success or failure is determined by a relatively small number of events that often can be discretely identified. For example:

- Getting a big contract, or not
- Hiring a talented manager who succeeds, or hiring one who fails
- Receiving regulatory approval to sell a new drug or other product, or not
- Receiving financing for a new investment at expected terms, or not
- Relying on key employees who remain healthy and on the job, or relying on those who do not
- Suffering under adverse government policies, or enjoying beneficial ones
- Such eternal worldly concerns such as bad weather, earthquakes, and fires

Statistical distributions exist that are similar to the assumed distribution of these types of events, such as the Poisson distribution that allows for a "jump" process, or the logistic distribution for modeling yes/no decisions. However, the uncomfortable fact is that managers and investors are confronted with a world in which *no* known probability distribution describes many of the risks they face. Without knowledge of such a distribution, they are essentially incapable of following the neoclassical investment rule, even if they wanted to do so.

3. *The future states of nature are affected by the entrepreneur's effort.* A standard assumption in statistics and finance is that states of nature are generated through a random process. However, for many businesses—probably most businesses—the value of the firm is affected by future states of nature that *are affected by the firm's managers.* Indeed, most events on the preceding list have outcomes that are clearly affected by the effort of the entrepreneur. Think of an entrepreneur rolling the dice . . . after shaping the dice as much as he or she can!

When an event is not random, the expected value of the outcome cannot be obtained by normal statistical means and may not exist in a well-defined sense.[30] An investor can still talk about what he or she expects to happen and rely on intuition, a small number of analogous situations, or professional judgment. However, reliance on any such techniques disproves, not confirms, the NPV rule.

When managers lack any one of these elements, they *cannot* follow the NPV rule. They must follow something else.

Failure 2: The Rule Ignores Option Value

A fundamental weakness in the NPV rule is that it ignores a powerful source of value: the *option to wait.* The ability to wait to make a decision is an essential part of actual markets, including both financial markets and real markets. As noted by one of the modern pioneers of the study of real options:

> The simple NPV rule is not just wrong, it is often *very* wrong. (Dixit and Pindyck, 1994, p. 136, emphasis in original)

A series of scholars writing in the late twentieth century established that following the NPV rule would mean that entrepreneurs *systematically* fail to make investments that were in their interests and would systematically make others that were not in their interests. Establishing that people following a specific economic theory systematically lose money is a devastating critique of that economic theory, because economists assume that rational people learn from their mistakes. Indeed, as we describe in Chapter 12, "Real Options and Expanded Net Present Value," a rational investor would often *not* follow the NPV rule given management flexibility and partial information about the future.

For centuries, mathematicians have known that the market price of a financial option is typically *not* equal to the expected net present value of the possible outcomes. Fibonacci, Bernoulli, and others wrestled with this problem in past centuries, as did such luminaries as John Neumann, Oskar Morgenstern, Paul Samuelson, and finally Myron Scholes and Fischer Black in the modern period.

Thus, to the extent that any business involves financial options (which could exist as assets, liabilities, or even features of the capitalization of the firm), the value of that firm cannot be a simple expected net present value of its future earnings.

Failure 3: The Rule Ignores Policy, Strategy, and Reputation

The NPV rule ignores the role of policy, reputation, and strategy. Successful organizations invariably follow some type of policy. By *policy*, I mean an established set of guidelines that govern the behavior of the organization or its members. Policies can include codified statutes, rules, and procedures, or just commonly understood precedents. Following a policy produces, among other things, a *reputation*. Reputation can be defined as the expectations of others about one person's future behavior, based on the precedence of past behavior.

Clearly, the reputation of a firm is critical to the business decisions of potential customers, investors, and workers. The neoclassical investment rule misses this completely, because it calls for the firm to undertake *only* investments that produce a positive expected net present value, using the firm's cost of capital as a discount rate. So, for example, if a firm had been successful selling top-quality goods in the past, a manager following the rule at that firm should immediately abandon this successful practice and sell cheaper, lower-quality products if it would produce a sufficient short-term profit. In reality, a firm that operated in such a manner would appear to be cavalier and unreliable to its customers and suppliers, as well as exhaust the patience of its employees.

In addition, *strategy* is an essential part of business. By strategy, we mean making decisions that depend on expectations of others' future actions and their expectations of ours. Strategy is as important to entrepreneurs as it is to military generals. It is hard to seriously discuss management, investment, or entrepreneurship without thinking about strategy.[31]

However, strategy is, strictly speaking, completely missing from the neoclassical model of the firm and the NPV rule. The hypothetical neoclassical firm would immediately use its capital whenever its management calculated a positive expected net return on a possible investment. Today, it may buy clothes to resell at flea markets; tomorrow it may purchase raw materials to produce cars; and the next day it may do nothing—depending on the outcome of the $E(NPV)$ equation. One cannot imagine that the resulting confusion would escape penalty in the marketplace.

Failure 4: Decision Makers Fail to Follow the Rule

Economics is not a subfield of mathematics. It is a social science.[32]

Furthermore, a theory that is beautifully expressed in math but fails to explain human behavior is a failed theory. Thus, we should consider the evidence that decision makers routinely do not follow the NPV rule.

There are several indicators of the failure of the NPV rule among investors. Recall the discussion in Chapter 1 under the section titled "Quandary 5: Managers Do Not Follow the Neoclassical Investment Rule." There we first stated the following observation about actual investor behavior:

> According to Brealey and Myers's Second Law, "The proportion of proposed projects having positive NPV is independent of top management's estimate of the opportunity cost of capital."[33]

Surveys of financial officers of large firms indicate that most such firms claim to have an investment policy requiring objective analyses of the expected net present value of proposed investments.[34] However, careful review of investment behavior suggests that managers in such firms *actually decide* using other criteria as well, and that the NPV rule is often *not* followed by investors and managers.[35]

Avanish Dixit and Robert Pindyck report the use of discount rates that are clearly different from those implied by orthodox finance theory, as well, as investment behavior that is at odds with standard neoclassical economics:

> The option insight also helps explain why the actual investment behavior of firms differs from the received wisdom taught in business schools. Firms invest in projects that are expected to yield a return in excess of a required, or "hurdle," rate. Observers of business practice find that such hurdle rates are typically three to four times the cost of capital. . . . On the other hand, firms stay in business for lengthy periods while absorbing operating losses, and price can fall substantially below average variable cost without inducing disinvestment or exit. This also seems to conflict with standard theory, but as we will see, it can be explained once irreversibility and option value are accounted for. (Dixit and Pindyck, 1994, p. 7)

But both academic research and anecdotal evidence bear out time and again the hesitancy of managers to apply NPV in the manner they have been taught.

How can such a discrepancy be explained? There are some obvious candidates:

- First, the use of investment committees indicates that professional judgment is essential and will override a mechanical rule.

- Second, numerous ways exist to adjust the numbers in a DCF analysis to push the calculated NPV higher or lower.[36] These include assuming a lower risk; assigning a lower capital requirement; projecting lower expenses, higher income, or higher terminal value; or extending the time frame.

- Third, organizational, regulatory, and professional reputation factors encourage companies to *report* the use of an apparently rigorous capital budgeting policy.[37] Given the ubiquity of the NPV rule in academic and professional literature, it is an obvious candidate for the basis of such a policy.
- Fourth, managers at such firms could realize that the earnings capability of the firm is not maximized by choosing only investments that pass a static NPV hurdle rate and rationally choose to make investments that are in their economic interest, regardless of any stated policy.

Among the reasons to reject the NPV rule, this could be the strongest: regardless of their technical sophistication and corporate policies and pronouncements, when it actually comes down to deciding how and when to invest money, smart people consistently rely on something other than a net present value calculation.

Failure 5: Liquidity Constraints Impinge on Both Firms and Investors

Much of corporate finance is focused on large, publicly traded firms that can issue both debt and equity securities or borrow from banks. For such firms, the concept of market rates of interest and the availability of multiple capital structure options are entirely relevant. However, such firms are the exception, not the rule.

For *most* firms, the capital with which they operate the business comes from a combination of household savings, long-term loans from family and friends, equity from partners and owner-operators, and possible venture capitalists. Many such firms, but not all, can borrow from banks using assets as security.

These firms face real liquidity constraints that prevent them from operating in the manner that the neoclassical investment rule presupposes. In particular, such firms often cannot invest in a new project, even when they believe such an investment would generate expected discounted future earnings that exceed the cost of the investment, because they cannot borrow or issue new stock on reasonable terms.

Liquidity constraints were noted by early modern economists, before the Modigliani-Miller propositions became the dominant paradigm in finance.[38] Such constraints are often assumed away in modern macroeconomic, microeconomic, and finance models. We need a valuation model that recognizes liquidity constraints and incorporates them in a manner that is consistent with business reality.

Failure 6: "Entrepreneurs Are Entrepreneurs"

Every year, tens of thousands of new businesses are started in the United States alone. All the available evidence indicates that *most of them* go out of business within the first five years of their existence.[39] This establishes an empirical basis for an extremely high discount rate on investments in new businesses.

Indeed, if we assume that half of a set of investments fail completely and the other half pay off completely, then a market discount rate for such investments would have to exceed 100 percent for that period, plus the risk-free rate, plus some additional risk premium, plus some allowance for underwriting or management profit.[40] For some of these firms, the only plausible market discount rate on an investment in the firm would be well above 100 percent per year, even if the risk-free rate (and inflation) were less than 5 percent per year.

Yet, even with such daunting odds, *entrepreneurs are still entrepreneurs.* Somehow, some way, they cobble together money and material to start businesses. Family, friends, and occasionally even banks lend them money to do it. Perhaps it is a good thing that most entrepreneurs lack an MBA, CPA, or advanced degree in economics. They have not been taught that the adventure they are about to begin has a negative $E(NPV)$, and that therefore they should stop. Their wisdom—and their drive—clearly comes from somewhere else . . . and we should all be thankful for that!

Other Failures

The preceding listing is powerful enough. However, there are additional reasons why the value of a business or an investment is not the expected net present value of future earnings. These include the following:

• *Utility is not time-separable.* An implicit assumption in the *NPV* and *E(NPV)* algorithms, and also in the Modigliani-Miller propositions, is that a dollar today is worth exactly the same (adjusted for discounting) as a dollar tomorrow and the next day. However, both informal and rigorous inquiry show this to be false.

We discuss this further and introduce an improvement known as *recursive utility* in Chapter 8 under the section titled "Incorporating Time Preference."

• *Companies face fixed costs and therefore have "inaction" regions.* Even under ideal conditions, businesses have costs that are essentially fixed during some time period. Managers of such firms prudently wait to make additional investments until the incremental revenue does not overcome the burden of the fixed or adjustment costs. Conversely, the same managers bunch expenditures when the fixed or adjustment cost thresholds are overcome.

Such behavior is entirely rational—but not consistent with the proposition that the value of a firm is the net present value of its expected earnings from operating assets that can be varied smoothly. (Examine Equation 3.1 again to see how fixed costs play havoc with Modigliani and Miller's Proposition I.)

Recently developed theoretical models of companies with adjustment costs illuminate this phenomenon. When such firms operate with an objective of maximizing net present value of profits (after adjustment costs) over time, and where stochastic shocks affect the state variables, they encounter *inaction regions* where the costs of adjustment exceed any gain or loss due to a proposed investment and where a better policy is to delay making investments.[41] These (theoretical) firms find it prudent to often not follow the neoclassical investment rule.

CONCLUSION: "A TOOL, NOT A RULE"

Here we summarize six failures of the NPV rule as a valuation principle:

1. *Decision makers lack* E(NPV) *information.* The information required to use the rule is often not available to decision makers at the time of their decisions, and no evidence suggests

that such information is regularly and strenuously sought by those same decision makers. This implies either that decision makers are irrationally ignoring the rule or that they have concluded that other rules are better.

2. *The rule ignores option value.* The rule ignores the option value of investments, including the option to wait. Because the values of options are important in any business, ignorance of this value means the rule is incorrect.

3. *The rule ignores policy, strategy, and reputation.* The rule partially ignores the benefits of a business policy and any resulting reputation and ignores completely the role of strategy. If these concepts are important to potential purchasers of business equity—and they certainly are—then the rule is incorrect.

4. *Decision makers fail to follow the rule.* Empirical evidence confirms that investment decisions are often, if not usually, not made using the rule. If a rule is not followed, then it is not a rule at all.

5. *Liquidity constraints impinge on both firms and investors.* The core analytical insight of the M-M propositions is that investors can synthesize a portfolio that captures the earnings of a firm in the same way that stocks (or stocks and bonds) do. However, this insight falls apart when liquidity constraints exists for either investors or firms.

6. *"Entrepreneurs are entrepreneurs."* The odds against the success of most new businesses are so high that any objective application of the $E(NPV)$ criteria for investing in it would rule out most businesses. Yet, thankfully, entrepreneurs still start firms. Who are economists, accountants, and finance experts to say they are all wrong?

As you consider these arguments, note that they are targeted to the reliance on the NPV *rule*, not the use of the NPV *algorithm*. Indeed, we continue the centuries-old tradition of finding the $E(NPV)$ algorithm to be a powerful tool when considering investment and other opportunities.

In other words: *NPV is a tool, not a rule.*

APPENDIX: ANTECEDENTS OF THE NPV RULE

Irving Fisher and John Burr Williams

Modigliani and Miller were on firm ground in economics. They were extending the work of two intellectual giants of the early twentieth century: Irving Fisher, whose magnum opus was *Theory of Interest* (1930), and John Burr Williams, whose *Theory of Investment Value* (1938) developed the modern tool of discounted cash flow analysis.[42] Unfortunately, these authors are often forgotten in intellectual history, and highlighting their work here both illuminates the development of the M-M propositions and suggests that earlier economists were less enthusiastic about turning the net present value tool into an investment rule.

Fisher and the "Investment Opportunity Principles"

There is no question, however, of the intellectual debt owed to Fisher. His *Theory of Interest* (1930) stated the following "Investment Opportunity Principles":

The Principle of Maximum Present Value

Out of all options, that one is selected which has the maximum present value reckoned at the market rate of interest.

The Principle of Comparative Advantage

Out of all options, that one is selected the advantages of which over any other option outweighs its disadvantages, when both these advantages and disadvantages—returns and costs—are discounted at the market rate of interest.

The Principle of Return over Cost

Out of all options, that one is selected which, in comparison with any other, yields a rate of return over cost equal to or greater than the market rate of interest.[43]

To be precise, Fisher preferred to use the term *interest* to apply to loans—including risky loans—but not equity investments.[44] Thus, Fisher's principles do not amount to a claim that business *equity* investments are valued in the same way as other investment opportunities.

John Burr Williams and the Conservation of Investment Value

John Burr Williams, also writing in the 1930s, developed many of the tools that are commonplace today. His *Theory of Investment Value* (1938) may have been the first systematic exposition of what is now called *discounted cash flow analysis*. In the preface of his book, Williams states that he wishes to "outline a new sub-science that shall be known as the Theory of Investment Value and that shall comprise a coherent body of principles." He describes the concept of "intrinsic value" that is the critical value above which an investor should not pay, which is determined by the present value of future dividends and returns of principal.

His "Law of Conservation of Investment Value" is similar to M-M Proposition I:

> If the investment value of an enterprise as a whole is by definition the present worth of all its future distributions to security holders, whether on interest or dividend account, then this value in no wise depends on what the company's capitalization is.[45]

This is, at least for investment value, the identical definition used in M-M Proposition I. Indeed, Modigliani and Miller felt compelled to note that others—including Williams— had attempted an "intuitive" argument for their Proposition I but had not specified how the equivalence was enforced. They then noted that their arbitrage argument (and, implicitly, their critical assumptions about riskless and uniformly priced debt) was unique.[46]

Irving Fisher and the Separation Theorem: A Historical Discussion

Some authors view Irving Fisher's separation theorem as the basis for the irrelevance finding of the M-M propositions. They argue that Fisher held that the firm's investment decision is independent of the preferences of the owner, and therefore independent of the financing decision.[47] The same line of thinking suggests that the production decision of an entrepreneur-owned firm is independent of the intertemporal consumption decision of the entrepreneur-owner.

Although M-M is clearly an extension of the work of Fisher, we do not conclude that the M-M propositions are implied by Fisher's work. We note that Fisher distinguished business loans from equity investments, frequently using the term *interest* for loans (including risky loans) and *profit* for equity investments. Fisher was also acutely aware that an entrepreneur's household finances directly affected his or her ability to finance a company (Fisher, 1930, part 4, chap. 17). Furthermore, Modigliani and Miller derived their propositions assuming that all interest rates are the same, and that debt is riskless two heroic leaps of faith that Fisher implicitly rejected.[48] Finally, the term *separation theorem* was not defined in Fisher's *Theory of Interest.*

II THE NATURE OF THE FIRM

4 THE NATURE OF THE FIRM

---

employees to rely on its promises, certain institutional requirements must be meant. Most importantly, these include private property and enforcement of contract.

WHAT IS A FIRM?

Key Questions About the Firm

If we are to discuss intelligently the value of a business, we must define rigorously what we mean by *business*. Such a definition should be consistent with a theory of the firm that covers all these topics:

1. Separation of Firms, Employees, and Investors: What separates a firm from an employee, an independent contractor, a stockholder, and a manager?

2. Motivation of Entrepreneur: What motivates entrepreneurs to start firms?

3. Intermediation: Do firms reduce the costs of transactions necessary to produce goods and services, when compared with a large group of independent contractors?

4. Aggregation and Scale: Why do firms not disaggregate into a large number of individual subcontractors, or, conversely, aggregate into a small number of megacompanies?

5. Ownership and Control: Does owning equity in a firm differ from controlling the management of the firm?

The Neglected Definition of a Vital Concept

In this chapter, we use the term *business* loosely to mean any entity that has businesslike operations or assets. We use the term *firm* to refer only to an entity that has the true economic significance of an operating business. What distinguishes these two is the subject of this section.

The definition of a firm has received surprisingly little attention in economics and finance. Even books that specifically discuss issues regarding business and valuation often leave the definition of the firm unstated. For example, no definition for *firm* or *business* appears among the more than 1,500 entries in *The Dictionary of Economics* (Bannoch et al., 1998), although *theory of the firm* is included. Similarly, neither term is included in the extensive glossary of *Valuing the Closely Held Firm* (2008),[1] nor are they mentioned in the "list of ideas" in *History of the Theory of Investments* (Rubinstein, 2006). Numerous books on business valuation ignore the topic or treat it as obvious.

A Common Definition of the Firm

Let us first attempt to answer this question with a definition that would cover most operating businesses in the United States: the common definition shown in Exhibit 4.1.

This definition, which represents many in regular use,[2] rules out government agencies, nonprofit organizations (including most churches, schools, and charities), and

---

EXHIBIT 4.1
Common Definition of a Firm

Common definition of a firm:

An enterprise with a motive to earn a profit.

---

nonoperating entities that exist as an accounting entity or tax fiction (such as most bank accounts, trust arrangements, and estates), as well as sham businesses.

This common definition would admit all the types of business entities recognized in the United States and the European Union (EU), including corporations, sole proprietorships, partnerships, and limited liability companies, to the extent they operated with a profit motive. However, it would also admit self-employed workers and independent contractors who file taxes as a separate business; many hobbyists, craftspeople, artists, and others who frequently or occasionally sell their work; writers working on a screenplay or novel that may never be published, alongside those who earn substantial royalties from bestselling works; and many others.

Abstractions and Definitions from Economics

In addition to the common definition, there are at least two candidates from the field of economics.

Neoclassical Abstraction: The Producer
Neoclassical microeconomics includes the concept of a producer. However, as we observe in Chapter 8, "Value in Neoclassical Economics," the organization of these producers is abstracted away in the neoclassical model. We assume that a large number of profit-maximizing firms are hiring a large number of workers and producing a large number of goods, somehow in perfect equilibrium. However, the firms themselves just spontaneously appear, and their interests and form of organization are assumed to match the profit-maximizing incentive assigned to producers in the model.

Thus, the neoclassical economic model does not provide a definition of a firm, but instead an abstraction for one.

Modern Neoclassical: Endogenous Entrepreneurs
Contemporaneously with the modern definition proposed in this book, American economist Daniel Spulber has proposed an ambitious revision of the neoclassical theory of the firm.[3] Spulber characterizes the neoclassical abstraction discussed previously (and in Chapter 8, "Value in Neoclassical Economics") as a model in which firms are treated exogenously, meaning they are out of the control of the consumers and workers in the model.

Spulber instead argues that entrepreneurs emerge from the broader class of consumers, and that the motivations of entrepreneurial-minded consumers can be modeled within an

---

EXHIBIT 4.2

Modern Neoclassical Definition of a Firm

Modern neoclassical definition of a firm:

A transaction institution whose objectives differ from those of its owners.

---

expanded neoclassical economics model.[4] Spulber follows the transaction cost theory of Ronald Coase, discussed shortly, in observing that firms coordinate production more efficiently than a large number of independent contractors making the same arrangements. Thus, in his model, the number of firms is dependent on the number of consumers, the size of the market, and the costs of transactions.[5]

Thus, what might be called a modern neoclassical model makes the emergence of entrepreneurs—and from them, firms—an endogenous variable in the economic model. We discuss this further later in the chapter.

Spulber's revision results in a modern neoclassical definition of the firm, shown in Exhibit 4.2.[6] This definition is based on two key criteria: *intermediation* and *separation*. Identifying these two factors, and also identifying a mechanism that gives rise to firms, breathes life into the concept of a firm within the neoclassical economics model.

A NEW DEFINITION OF THE FIRM

Defining the Firm: Three Essential Attributes

I define a "firm" as an *organization* with the following characteristics:

1. *Separate legal identity from its workers, managers, and owners.* In the United States, a separate legal identity is normally achieved by declaring that a company is a "person" under state laws.[7] Such a "person" can own property, incur debts, sue and be sued, and have imposed on it the responsibility to withhold and pay taxes.[8] In the EU, a firm is often called an *undertaking*.

For corporations, this means that equity owners (shareholders) have *limited liability*, generally limited to their equity investment. A similar arrangement in other countries, especially those that share the English legal tradition, is signaled by the use of the term *limited* after the name of a corporation. *Limited liability companies* are a more recent form of business organization that shares the separate legal identity and limited liability of shareholders.[9] The separate legal identity is usually, but not always, a bar to creditors of a company seeking the assets of an equity owner.[10]

2. *A motivation to earn profit for its investors.* Employees are motivated to earn wages, salaries, bonuses, benefits, and other forms of remuneration. A business, on the other hand, is owned by investors. One distinction between a firm's investors and its workers, is that the owners of the firm are motivated to manage it in a manner that earns a profit for the investors, rather than an increase in wages.

EXHIBIT 4.3
New Definition of a Firm

New definition of a firm:

An organization with:

1. A separate legal identity from its workers, managers, and owners

2. A motivation to earn profit for its investors

3. A set of replicable business processes

As an additional example, compare a person owning a winning lottery ticket with an entrepreneur. The lucky lottery player anticipates a stream of future earnings. An entrepreneur starting a business hopes to achieve a profitable year in the reasonably near future.

3. *A set of replicable business processes.* A business must have the capability to repeatedly produce, distribute, sell, or perform some type of service or product. Replicable business processes are the bases of these activities. By *business processes*, we mean practices that govern the work arrangements among people and materials that result in a salable product or service. Business processes include the production schedule; the invoicing and collection systems; the manner of building and the manner of selling; the practices of labeling or branding a product; and the practices of marketing, pricing, and selling the product.

This definition is summarized in Exhibit 4.3.

Distinctions Between a Firm and Other Activities

Profit Motive for Its Investors Does Not Mean Profit Maximization
The new definition clearly distinguishes businesses from nonprofit entities, government agencies, and many cooperatives and associations. Note that this definition does not include the embedded assumption that the managers of the firm always act in the interest of the shareholders, nor define "profit motive" as short-term "profit maximization."

Differences Among Definitions

Both the new and the modern neoclassical definitions differ from the common definition, and from each other. In particular:

- The common definition accepts any organization with a profit motive; the other definitions further restrict the subset of organizations that are "firms."
- The modern neoclassical definition includes separation and motivation criteria.
- The new definition includes separation, motivation, and replicable business practices criteria.

We discuss further two key differences shortly.

Profit Maximization or Just Profit Motive?

Another difference among these definitions involves the profit motive. Spulber's modern neoclassical definition identifies only objectives that differ from those of its owners. However, it further assumes that "separation implies the firm's objective is profit maximization" and that "the firm's owners unanimously prefer that the firm maximize profits."[11] This is completely consistent with the neoclassical model as a whole.

In contrast, the new definition includes the separation criteria, but assumes only a profit motive—not a profit *maximization* motive. As was noted among the quandaries posed in Chapter 1, "Modern Value Quandaries," there is strong evidence that entrepreneurs do not attempt to maximize profits in any one period.

Replicable Business Processes or Just Transactions?

Successful companies may have the ability to produce products or services that are differentiated from competitors; a more efficient manner of producing similar goods and services; proprietary techniques; specific products; particular locations; or other sustainable advantages or capabilities. The sustainable or *replicable* nature of these business processes is essential; without replicable processes, the business cannot operate over time and therefore cannot have any value.

The notion of replicable business processes is different from the intermediation role incorporated in the modern neoclassical definition. In particular, a business enterprise that can perform intermediation once but cannot sustain it is not a "firm" under the new definition. Thus, one limited-time arrangement (such as a contract to perform repairs during the next month, or a musical gig for a band, or the hiring of a subcontractor by a contractor for a particular project) in which intermediation occurs does not generate a firm.

COMPETING THEORIES OF THE FIRM: TRANSACTION COSTS AND RESOURCES

Although not sufficient as definitions of the firm, there are a number of important theories about the organization and rationale of the firm. These theories provide a basis for understanding what firms have value, why they are organized, and what criteria should be included in the definition of the firm.

The Transaction Cost Theorem

Ronald Coase introduced the leading theory on the purpose of the firm in his 1937 essay "The Nature of the Firm."

Coase's 1937 posed a provocative question to his fellow economists. He noted that microeconomic theory was based on supply-and-demand interaction in a market, with equilibrium prices being set to allow the markets to clear. The overwhelming consensus of economists was that such interaction allowed the most efficient allocation of resources, when compared with a planned economy in which decisions on resource allocation were imposed by a central authority.

Coase argued that companies were organized because it was too costly for individuals to contract for others to perform all the tasks that could be done by employees managed within a company. Coase argued that at some point, the benefits of free exchange of individual goods in a marketplace were outweighed by the benefits of a central person directing that exchange. This "transaction costs" argument explains why entrepreneurs can be successful in organizing a firm: they can produce goods and services more efficiently than consumers could on their own. As Harold Demsetz (1997a, p. 426) put it, Coase's theory is that "firms come into existence when the cost of consciously managing inputs (to achieve a given outcome) is less than the cost of using the price system."

However, Coase provided only a tentative definition of the firm, which focuses on the role of the business manager or entrepreneur in directing the efforts:

> A firm, therefore, consists of the system of relationships which comes into existence when the direction of resources is dependent on an entrepreneur.[12]

Coase acknowledges that this did not create a "hard and fast line" between a firm and other organizations. He did test this definition later in his essay by considering whether it properly distinguished between an employer and an employee, which of course it does. However, his definition incorporates only the intermediation element of the modern neoclassical definition.

The Other Coase Theorem

Ronald Coase was awarded the 1991 Nobel Prize in Economics for his "discovery and clarification of the significance of transaction costs and property rights." Perhaps the more famous Coase theorem is the one originated in his 1960 essay "The Problem of Social Cost." In that essay, he argued that disputes among property owners would be solved with little or no loss to social welfare, as long as property rights were protected, transaction costs were minimal, and the parties were allowed to negotiate with each other. This single essay was the birth of the law and economics field, and the term *Coase theorem* is strongly associated with it.[13]

The Resource-Based Theory of the Firm

Economist Edith Penrose proposed a resource-based theory of the firm in her seminal 1959 book *The Theory of the Growth of the Firm*.[14] Her original theory was focused on the *growth* of a firm, not its organization or size, as Penrose wrote in her first sentence:

> So far as I know, no economist has as yet attempted a general theory of the growth of firms. This seem to me so very strange . . .
> We shall be concerned with the growth of firms, and only incidentally with their size.
> (Penrose, 1959, p. 1)

For a theory of business value, this notion of firm growth is important. If we anticipate that future earnings will be part of a theory of value, then the ability of the firm to grow should be an essential part of the theoretical basis for business value.

Although the original theory does not attempt to define the firm, we examine it in search of insight into two questions: what makes a firm unique, and what makes some firms able to grow over time.

The resource-based theory of the firm asserts that there are three categories of produc-tive assets owned by a company:

1. Proprietary assets, such as architecture, reputation, and knowledge. These are intan-gible assets that are created by the firm itself.

2. Strategic assets, such as trademarks, technology, locations, and other assets that could have been purchased or developed internally.

3. Nonproprietary assets, which are owned by the firm but could be purchased by other firms as well.

Of these, only the proprietary assets are truly unique to the firm.[15] As Richard Caves (2007) puts it:

> Assets of this type are closely akin to product differentiation—the distinctive features of various sellers' outputs cause each competing firm to face its own downward-sloping de-mand curve. The proprietary asset might take the form of a specific property—a registered trademark or brand—or it might rest in marketing and selling skills shared among the firm's employees. (p. 3)

Proprietary assets could also include skill in innovations, know-how among employees, or other attributes in the "repertory of routines possessed by the firm's team of human (and other) inputs."[16] Other assets—while essential to the operation of the firm—are available for acquisition of development by competing firms.

Thus, this theory implies that certain proprietary resources are the defining characteris-tic of the firm. As a definition of the firm, this clearly fails (unless one is willing to declare every single worker and location unique). However, as an indicator of which firms can sus-tain their value, it is very important. In the new definition proposed in this book, the use of replicable business practices as a criterion is logically consistent with the resource theory of the growth of the firm.[17]

COMPETING THEORIES: AGENCY, SCALE, AND TEAM

Modern Agency Theory

Michael Jensen and William Meckling derived what has been called *agency theory* in the 1970s.[18] Agency theory begins with the assumption that firms can be theorized as a large group of contracts among individuals. These individuals include workers, managers, and stockholders. It then observes that the basic organization of the firm frequently creates a difference in the financial incentives for the *principal* (the stockholders) and their *agent* (the managers they hire).

As Jensen and Meckling quite properly noted, the concept of the principal-agent prob-lem in business was explicitly recognized at least as far back as Adam Smith:

> The directors of such [joint-stock] companies, however, being the managers rather of other people's money than of their own, it cannot well be expected, that they should watch over it with the same anxious vigilance with which the partners in a private copartnery frequently

watch over their own. Like the stewards of a rich man, they are apt to consider attention to small matters as not for their master's honour, and very easily give themselves a dispensation from having it. Negligence and profusion, therefore, must always prevail, more or less, in the management of the affairs of such a company. (Smith, 1776; cited in Jensen and Meckling, 1976, p. 1)

An entire literature has developed since the publication of the seminal work of Jensen and Meckling. However, given Adam Smith's statement of more than two hundred years ago, we should call this school of thought *modern agency theory*. Modern agency theory focuses on an element of both the modern neoclassical definition of the firm and the new definition: the separation between the firm and its employees and owners.

Efficient Scale Theories

We discussed earlier the observation of Edith Penrose in 1959, who lamented that economists were concerned about the size of the firm rather than its growth. Here we discuss that concern about size, hopefully in sufficiently brief fashion.

The common neoclassical abstraction of the firm as the producer allows for the specification of a *production function* for the firm in a model of the economy. A large number of inputs to the production function are required, and in order to efficiently produce such goods and services, an organization of a certain magnitude is required. This leads to the concept of *minimum efficient scale*. The intermediation role of the firm and the existence of transaction costs imply that there is a threshold below which it is too costly (in terms of contract expenditures, advertising expenditures, management scale, etc.) to produce certain goods and services.[19]

Minimum efficient scale is a critical concept for entrepreneurial firms, which often fail before achieving the scale that might have allowed them to remain in business. However, much as Penrose noted a half century ago, the existence of an efficient scale does not tell us much about why firms grow, or why they are organized.

Team Theories

In addition to those discussed previously, another class of theories bears noting: the "team" theories.

The central concept in these theories is that of the firm as a team. A *team* is a social organization as well as a functional one, in which there are roles for specific individuals, goals for the organization, identification for the organization and its members, and a management structure. The sports team is a handy metaphor, and sports culture is the primary donor of the language used in various team theories. Another metaphor is the army or other military organization.[20] I do not know who originated the concept and cannot identify a dominant version of it.[21]

Certain undeniable facets of human nature underlie these theories, starting with the social nature of humans. We can observe that people naturally congregate in groups in nearly all activities in life. This starts with couples and families and extends to tribes and clans; churches, parishes, sects, and religious organizations; clubs and chapters of associations;

political parties and committees that operate at local, state, and national levels; sports teams, clubs, and leagues; college conferences; neighborhood and block clubs; labor unions; trade associations; musical bands; arts communes and craft guilds; gangs, cells, "families," and other informal organizations; and affinity-based assemblages of all kinds.

Of course, humans have rigorous economic reasons to join groups, including groups that have business functions.[22] However, the role of solitary entrepreneurs in *starting* firms rules out social interaction within a group as a criteria for the existence of the firm. I conclude that one reason individuals organize firms and join them as employees, investors, or managers is that they like to join other people working toward a common goal. However, as other "teams" already exist, this social motivation cannot be the primary explanation for the existence of firms.

THEORIES OF THE SUCCESS OF THE FIRM

Other authors have developed rationales for the *success* of a firm operating in a competitive environment. To the extent success is important to the value of a firm—and quite obviously it is—we must consider these rationales as candidates for inclusion in a theory of the firm.

Rationales for the Success of a Firm

In recent decades, the attributes to which business success has been attributed—and for which there is a clear proponent that can be identified—include the following:

1. Strategy[23]
2. Comparative advantage in relevant markets[24]
3. Quality systems[25]
4. Innovation, "culture," and management[26]
5. Entrepreneurial spirits[27]
6. Personal interaction skills, friendly personality, and salesmanship[28]
7. Marketing, branding, "leadership," technology, and many others[29]

These attributes and others are often fodder for popular books, seminars, business school classes, and (apparently less frequently) actual empirical work.

Success Attributes and the Firm

Readers with a background in academic economics, finance, or accounting may be tempted to dismiss the success literature as little more than cheerleading. Based on the relative sales of books in this category, other readers may be tempted to similarly dismiss academic books on economics, finance, and accounting.

Given the incredible range of people who have become successful entrepreneurs, and the daunting statistics on business births and deaths across many countries, it should be clear that no one attribute guarantees the success of a firm or an entrepreneur. It should also be clear that *something* helps a successful entrepreneur persevere and eventually succeed, and these personal characteristics of an entrepreneur cannot be ignored. Thus, a definition of the firm, and an understanding of the value of the firm, must recognize the role of the individual entrepreneur.

INSTITUTIONAL REQUIREMENTS FOR A FIRM

The Institutions Necessary for Business and Investment

For true firms to function, other requirements exist that are normally outside the control of the entrepreneur. We call these *institutional requirements* because they describe the institutions that allow a business to function, and they govern the relationship among investors, workers, and managers. These requirements include the following:

1. *Private property rights.* People in the United States and other Western countries often take for granted one of the most hard-fought gains in human freedom: the right to private property. Although privately owned property is as old as property itself, the securing of the rights of citizens to private property is not universal even today. The adoption—with great reluctance—of Magna Carta by King John of England in 1215 was one milestone in the march to securing property rights.[30] The American Revolution and the adoption of the explicit protections of "life, liberty, and property" in the U.S. Constitution and the constitutions of the various states were other milestones.

The crumbling of the Iron Curtain in the recent past allowed for private property rights to be asserted—and sometimes secured—in many former Soviet countries. However, even today property rights are not secured in many parts of the world, and major difficulties in world trade and development stem from the lack of protection of private property in developing nations.[31]

2. *Enforcement of contracts.* Without contracts, there can be no free market economy. The ability to enforce those contracts is an essential role of governments and privately organized associations that govern some markets. Indeed, the enforcement of contracts is one of the major reasons asserted for the need for a central government among theorists who favor a *laissez faire* system of limited government.[32]

Recent mathematical financial research also notes the importance of enforcement of contracts for the existence of equilibrium prices under restrictive conditions, as well as recognition of the "bounded rationality" of investors who enter into contracts knowing that they cannot possibly anticipate all possibilities.[33] The vital nature of a legal system that enforces contracts is usually addressed in tracts on political economy or law and economics; it is refreshing to see the mathematical finance literature also recognize this requirement.[34]

3. *A system of accounting.* A system of accounting is necessary for the writing of contracts, for the recording and reporting of goods transferred in trade, for managers to understand the operations of the business, and for investors who entrust their capital to those managers and need reliable information on how that capital was used and what return on that capital

they should receive. In order for the separations and motivation criteria to be fulfilled, a system of accounting is essential. We discuss this in Chapter 6, "Accounting for the Firm."

Economics and Institutions: A Continuing Critique

Economics began with explicit thinking about institutions.[35] However, economics in recent decades often subordinated the examination of institutions in favor of the development of mathematical models. This critique of the field, however, has been voiced for at least a hundred years.[36] Economics remains slow to recognize how customs and institutions affect important economic decisions.[37]

In particular, economists in the last few decades have begun to understand how important these institutional factors are in allowing economic growth and alleviating poverty in underdeveloped countries.[38] Although there is no single measure for these institutional factors across nations, the *Index of Economic Freedom*, developed by the Canadian Fraser Institute, is one indicator with a consistent track record and defined methodology.[39]

Mathematics of the Firm and Institutions

The most insightful economists throughout history have observed how institutions affect people and their actions. The seminal article on modern agency theory begins by noting the importance of property rights and the primacy of private property rights, citing works by other authors writing in the early twentieth century and before.[40] However, many economics, finance, and business texts since then have relied heavily on mathematical formulations. Such formulations (some of which appear in this book) always rely on institutions for their validity. For example, it makes no sense to talk about debt and equity in a company if the equity and debt holders can have their interests confiscated at any time. Thus, thinking about institutions is not only important, it is *necessary*.

THE BUSINESS VALUE AXIOM

Why Firms Have Business Value

Individual workers can make money through both wages and other payments (such as reimbursements or commissions). These income flows appear similar to the profit on sales made by companies performing similar services. Clearly, owning a "business" that employs one productive worker could result in earnings to the "owner" that are very similar to the wages that same person would receive as an employee performing the same tasks. Indeed, this is the rationale behind most contract worker arrangements. Yet we conclude that a contract worker arrangement is *not* a firm.[41]

Furthermore, no other person would buy such a contract worker's "business." Even though such a business filed taxes, earned profits, and (assuming the worker expected to continue to work under the contract arrangement) could be expected to do so in the future, it has no value that can be transferred to an investor.

On the other hand, a contract-worker agency that had a record of contracting with both individual workers and companies may have a significant business value, because it both is

---

EXHIBIT 4.4
Business Value Axiom

Only firms have business value.

---

likely to continue to earn money in the future and has business practices that will allow it to do so. These observations motivate the business value axiom shown in Exhibit 4.4.

Other organizations can provide benefits that are social, political, educational, nostalgic, and governmental, but these benefits do not imply business value. A worker or investor can organize his or her affairs in a business entity that has legal standing, incurs tax obligations, and earns accounting profits; however, these attributes do not imply business value. This describes many instances in which sole proprietorships or contract workers earn considerable income from payments that are not labeled as wages or salary.

We define *business value* or *value of a business* as the fair market value of a *business enterprise*. Consistent with this definition and the definition of the firm as an enterprise that has the requisite separation of investors and workers, profit motive, and replicable practices, we adopt the following business value axiom: *Only firms have business value.*

The "Four Bars of Gold" Examples

Besides firms, other assets can have market value; a bar of gold is a good example. However, a bar of gold is not a business. Indeed, four bars of gold is not a business; it is merely something valuable. Four bars of gold on deposit at a brokerage firm is not a business; it is a portfolio. Four people with contracts to guard bars of gold is not a business; it is four jobs and something valuable. Forty thousand gold bars in a government vault in Fort Knox, Kentucky, is not a business; it is a government enterprise on tax-exempt land.

Four people who organize a company that hires workers to guard gold deposits—now that is a business!

5 THE ORGANIZATION AND SCALE OF PRIVATE BUSINESS

OUTLINE OF THIS CHAPTER

In this chapter, we examine the organization and scale of businesses in the United States. Any serious discussion of the value of businesses in a modern economy must be informed by data on those businesses, and we present such data in this chapter.

In particular, we present the available information on the following:

- The notion of "small" businesses, and a critical examination of the stylized facts about such businesses in the United States and a dozen other countries
- The available data on the largest privately held and publicly traded firms
- The number of businesses in the United States, and the number by size class
- The amount of revenue and the number of employees by size class
- The harsh statistics about births and deaths of firms in multiple countries, which indicate that most new firms fail within five years
- Different forms of business organization in the United States and other countries
- An estimate of the taxable business revenue of both public and private firms in the United States

The market capitalization of firms listed on the stock exchange is a subject of daily news. However, the market value of privately held firms is an obscure topic, and only recently has there been a direct estimate of the market value of such companies. Using the data on estimated taxable income, we present a revised estimate of the aggregate market value of privately held firms in the United States, noting that it exceeds the aggregate market value of publicly traded firms.

STYLIZED FACTS ABOUT BUSINESS IN THE UNITED STATES

Large Numbers of Small Businesses

What might be called the stylized facts about small business in America are repeated in an endless number of publications. An representative summary is the following conclusion of a U.S. Federal Reserve Board staff paper:

Small businesses—nonfarm entities with fewer than 500 employees—are an integral part of the U.S. economy. They account for about half of private sector output, employ more than half of private-sector workers, and have generated 60 percent to 80 percent of net new jobs annually over the past decade. (Mach and Wolken, 2006, p. A167)

Strong claims are packed into this short paragraph: Small businesses account for more than half of the private-sector output, employ more than half of the workers, and generate roughly three-quarters of the new jobs.

However ubiquitous, these stylized facts are difficult to confirm. The primary bases for them appear to be research by the U.S. Small Business Administration.[1] The SBA's 2006 *Annual Report*, among others, uses the "under 500 employees" definition for small businesses, noting that this threshold "means about 99.9 percent of employer businesses are small."[2] The report also notes that among the "maze" of federal statistics, it is difficult to find even a reliable estimate of the raw number of private firms.[3]

The SBA's observation about the paucity of data is a revealing indicator of the lack of attention paid to the topic of business formation and valuation among U.S. policy makers. It is also a signal that the stylized facts about small businesses should be subjected to a critical review before they are accepted. We critically examine the available data later in this chapter.

Huge Impact of Large Corporations

Despite the widespread acceptance of the claim that most businesses are small businesses, many people consider the dominant form of business in the United States—in terms of revenue, employees, and impact on society—to be the large, publicly traded corporation. It is at least mathematically possible to have a vast number of small firms, each contributing little to the economy, along with a small number of gigantic firms that generate the most value added in the economy.

It is tempting to accept this notion. Gigantic corporations are discussed daily in news reports about the stock market. They establish brands and products that are the subject of expensive advertising campaigns. They, and their products, are often familiar names to consumers across the country. Ford, Dell, IBM, Sun, Microsoft, Google, HP, Apple, Procter & Gamble, and General Electric are signal examples of such firms. Many readers can identify a specific product or brand from every one of these firms. Almost all readers in the United States (and in many other countries) can identify multiple products and services that were manufactured, branded, or serviced by such firms and their affiliates.

As we discuss shortly, very large corporations usually have revenues of more than a billion dollars annually and operate in multiple states and more than one country. Most of these very large businesses, but not all, have issued equity ("stock") that is traded on an exchange such as NASDAQ, AMEX, or NYSE. Usually, such stock can be purchased and sold by members of the public with relatively few limitations.

In general, we call companies whose stock is bought and sold among a large number of members of the public *publicly traded companies*. We distinguish these from privately held companies, as well as from government-sponsored enterprises.

THE LISTS: THE LARGEST PRIVATE AND PUBLIC FIRMS

The *Fortune* 500

Probably the best-known list of large firms is the *Fortune* 500, which has been published annually by *Fortune* magazine since 1955.[4] The 2010 list of America's largest corporations included the following as the top ten firms: Wal-Mart Stores, ExxonMobil, Chevron, General Electric, Bank of America, ConocoPhillips, AT&T, Ford, JP Morgan Chase, and Hewlett-Packard. Although the rankings change each year, the list of the very largest firms evolves slowly. Indeed, a look back at the 1985 list reveals that Exxon, General Electric, Mobil, Ford, IBM, and AT&T were in the top ten in that year as well.[5]

The top twenty-five of these firms reported profits of $150 billion on revenue of $3.2 trillion.[6] Just to get on the list of the top five hundred required revenues of more than $4.1 billion. To get on an extended list of the thousand largest firms required annual revenue of more than $1.5 billion.

The *Forbes* Global 2000

There are other ways to identify large companies. *Forbes* magazine, for example, compiles a Global 2000 list ranked by sales, profits, assets, and estimated market value.[7] The lowest-ranked of these two thousand firms (among those classified as a U.S. company) had revenues of $2.6 billion, assets of $8.5 billion, and more than 8,200 employees.[8] Other U.S. corporations that were included at the bottom end of this elite list typically had revenues well over $1.3 billion and between 4,000 and 8,000 employees. Most, though not all, of these large firms are publicly traded corporations.

Forbes 400 Largest Private Firms

Although most very large companies in the United States are publicly traded, some of these firms are privately held. In general, unless U.S. companies issue securities that are traded among members of the general public, they are not required to file financial data with the Securities and Exchange Commission.

Forbes magazine compiles a much-watched list of the largest privately held firms annually. The top ten companies on the 2009 *Forbes* list of the largest privately held firms were Cargill (with revenue estimated at $106 billion and 151,000 employees), Koch Industries, Chrysler, GMAC Financial, Bechtel, Mars, HCA, PricewaterhouseCoopers, Publix, and Ernst & Young (with revenue estimated at $21 billion and 144,400 employees).[9] The smallest of these firms generated annual revenue of $2 billion or more.[10] The figures for many firms were estimated by the magazine's staff from various sources, including various public disclosures.

Like the lists of the largest companies overall, the top tier of these firms changes relatively slowly. The 2006 *Forbes* list of largest private firms also included Koch Industries (revenue of $90 billion), Cargill (revenue of $70 billion), PricewaterhouseCoopers (revenue of $21 billion), and Publix Super Markets (revenue of more than $20 billion).[11]

Variation in Headquarters States

It is interesting to observe that the largest privately held firms appear to be more geographically dispersed than their publicly traded counterparts. Among the top twenty privately held firms, Michigan was the most common headquarters state (with three firms, only one of which was an automobile manufacturer[12]); New York was second (with two firms, both of which were accounting firms). Kansas, Minnesota, New Hampshire, Tennessee, and Utah proved just as successful as California and Texas, each placing one such firm on this elite list.[13] In contrast, the New York City area was the dominant headquarters location among the top twenty publicly traded firms.

Variation in Products

It is also interesting to note the variation in products and services among the largest public and private firms. Among the largest twenty private firms, agriculture and food services (Cargill, Publix, US Foods, C&S Wholesale, Mars) claim the most entries, along with retail and grocery (Meijer, Pilot Travel Centers, Love's Travel Stops). Financial services and accounting combined (GMAC Financial, Ernst & Young, PricewaterhouseCoopers) claim only three entries. In contrast, financial companies (Goldman Sachs, JP Morgan), oil companies (Conoco, Exxon) and major industrial or pharmaceutical firms (General Electric, Johnson & Johnson, Pfizer, Ford) occupy a very large share of the list of the top twenty publicly traded firms.

DATA ON U.S. BUSINESSES

The Number of Firms in the United States

We report in Table 5.1 the number of employer firms by size of employment and revenue, using data compiled by the U.S. Census Bureau. These data establish the scope of business enterprise in the United States: approximately 6 million companies that employ workers,

TABLE 5.1

Number of firms, size of employment, and revenue in the United States, 2007

Enterprise employment size	Number of firms	Number of establishments	Employment	Estimated receipts ($ thousands)
0–4	3,705,275	3,710,700	6,139,463	1,434,680,823
5–9	1,060,250	1,073,875	6,974,591	1,144,930,232
10–19	644,842	682,410	8,656,182	1,395,498,431
Subtotal: less than 20	5,410,367	5,466,985	21,770,236	3,975,109,486
20–99	532,391	723,385	20,922,960	3,792,920,977
100–499	88,586	355,853	17,173,728	3,612,050,221
Subtotal: less than 500	6,031,344	6,546,223	59,866,924	11,380,080,684
500+	18,311	1,158,795	60,737,341	18,366,661,220
Total	6,049,655	7,705,018	120,604,265	29,746,741,904

SOURCES: Compiled by author using data from the U.S. Census Bureau, *2007 County Business Patterns* and *2007 Economic Census*.

which involve approximately 7.7 million "establishments" (physical locations where operations are conducted by the business). The total revenue for these private-sector entities exceeds $29.7 trillion. Large and midsized firms (those with five hundred or more employees) account for most of this revenue, although the fact that they purchase goods and services from each other and from small firms makes this comparison only partially meaningful.[14]

Of the approximately 6 million employer firms in the United States during that year, only eighteen thousand had more than five hundred employees. As discussed further shortly, five hundred employees or fewer is a common government threshold for "small" firms. These data, therefore, establish the remarkable fact that approximately 99 percent of all businesses that employ workers in the United States are "small" businesses.

"Employer" and "Non-Employer" Firms

The U.S. Census Bureau and other statistical agencies often distinguish between "employer" and "non-employer" firms. Employer firms are those that employ at least one employee during the year. There are also a large number of taxpaying entities that employ no workers. Such entities are sometimes considered non-employer firms by the U.S. Census and other statistical agencies. Thus, the number of taxpaying business entities are a multiple of the number of individual operating businesses. For example, passive investment entities, most trusts and estates, some start-up firms, certain companies in bankruptcy whose assets are being liquidated, and other entities that are required to file tax returns or establish separate financial accounts could be counted as non-employer firms. In general, we do not consider such entities firms, as most would fail to meet the rigorous economic definition of a firm introduced in Chapter 4.

Evidence from Longitudinal Studies in the United States

Preliminary data from a longitudinal study of businesses, the Survey of Business Owners conducted by the U.S. Census Bureau in 2007, confirm some of the stylized facts presented here. These preliminary data indicate that there were approximately 27.1 million firms in the United States, of which 5.75 million had paid employees.

The employee firms accounted for $29.2 trillion in receipts.[15] Under the rigorous economic definition of the firm used in this book, almost all the non-employer firms would be considered contract workers. In total, they accounted for less than $1 trillion in receipts, much of which would be considered the economic equivalent of wages, salaries, and benefits.

For comparison purposes, in the same year U.S. GDP was approximately $14 trillion.

The Vague Notion of Midsized Firms

We cannot, from these data, distinguish between large, publicly traded corporations and midsized firms. Recall that a firm needed approximately $1.3 billion or more in revenue to make either of the 2010 lists of the largest U.S. corporations. Thus, a business with a few thousand employees and hundreds of millions of dollars in revenue would not have made the *Fortune* 1000 or *Forbes* Global 2000 for the year 2010. However, such a firm clearly cannot be considered *small*.

There is no widely accepted definition of a midsized firm. However, we adopt a working definition of *midsized* as applying to firms that are larger than the five-hundred-employee limit for "small" and not big enough to make it on the list of the largest corporations. This working definition would therefore identify businesses with between five hundred and, say, four thousand employees as midsized. This allows us to address the question of whether the largest firms contribute more to the overall economy than all other firms combined.

Data on "Large" Companies

A second view of the available data breaks out the employment for businesses in what the U.S. Census considers "large enterprise size." These data are shown in Table 5.2. Here again, we cannot distinguish between publicly traded corporations and privately held firms.

However, we wish to estimate the portion of employment, payroll, and revenue that is accounted for by the "big corporations" as described earlier, which are all publicly traded and have revenues in excess of about $1.3 billion. As a rough classification, we could use the data for all firms with more than five thousand employees to estimate the size of the "big corporation" group, although this is probably an overestimate.[16]

Using this conservative measure, the data reveal that small and midsize firms account for an impressive portion of all private-sector economic activity:

- At least 67 percent of the private-sector employment in the United States
- At least 63 percent of the private-sector payroll in the United States
- At least 57 percent of the revenue of all private-sector firms

TABLE 5.2
Employment, payroll, and revenue, midsized and large firms

Enterprise employment size	Number of firms	Establishments	Employment	Annual payroll ($ thousands)	Estimated receipts ($ thousands)
< 500	6,031,344	6,546,223	59,866,924	2,204,837,721	11,380,080,684
500–749	6,094	71,702	3,695,682	152,059,022	800,475,934
750–999	2,970	45,990	2,561,972	109,833,289	636,199,229
1,000–1,499	2,916	59,311	3,552,259	153,957,992	792,993,702
1,500–1,999	1,542	46,221	2,664,416	120,606,441	695,739,349
2,000–2,499	942	36,388	2,094,728	94,001,450	544,038,807
2,500–4,999	1,920	118,282	6,687,266	320,640,371	1,979,674,138
5,000–9,999	952	115,222	6,628,415	324,791,017	2,263,012,551
10,000+	975	665,679	32,852,603	1,546,050,929	10,654,527,510
Total	**6,049,655**	**7,705,018**	**120,604,265**	**5,026,778,232**	**29,746,741,904**

MEMO

Firm size categories and share of:	Employment	Payroll	Receipts of firms
Less than 5,000 employees	67%	63%	57%
5,000 employees or more	33%	37%	43%

SOURCES: Compiled by author using data from the U.S. Census Bureau, *2007 County Business Patterns* and *2007 Economic Census*.

If these indicators are correct—and they are at least approximately correct—then the private-sector economy in the United States is dominated by privately held firms, almost all of which are small and midsized.

Sensitivity Test: The Definition of *Large*

These conclusions depend critically on the classification of midsized firms as those with between five hundred and five thousand employees. To see how robust our conclusions are to this definition, consider the following sensitivity test:

- Expanding *Large*: If we redefined *large* to include all firms with more than a thousand employees (almost eliminating the midsize category), then such firms would be shown to dominate the U.S. economy in terms of output. However, this is a most unsatisfactory construction, as most of these large firms would be privately held, which would clearly not fit the popular conception of big corporations.

- Shrinking *Large*: On the other hand, if we redefined *big corporation* to be all firms with more than ten thousand employees, we would have approximately the thousand or so largest firms in the United States. This definition of *big* could be termed "*Fortune* 1000 big" and would indeed represent the largest publicly traded companies in the nation. The share of the economy these big firms represent would be substantially smaller than those reported previously for *large*.

In addition, note that much of these data are collected by tax authorities and government statistical agencies that do not hold to any economic definition of a firm. We make a rough adjustment for this by including only employer businesses in the data reviewed earlier.

Total Business Receipts and GDP

Gross domestic product (GDP) is *not* equal to the sum of receipts of all businesses, even if GDP is adjusted for net exports and government expenditures. The receipts of businesses in an economy, because they buy products and services from each other, sum to a total that is much larger than the private-sector output portion of gross domestic product. In concept, GDP should count the market value of the products from an industry as the same amount, regardless of whether it was produced by a handful of tightly integrated firms or by a large number of small companies.

This conceptual difference explains how large businesses (using the five-thousand-employee threshold) can account for a majority of business receipts yet a minority of GDP. Large businesses frequently purchase products and services of small and medium-sized businesses and in turn resell them (with some value added) to end users. Thus, some of the value added from those smaller firms is included in the receipts that accrue to the largest businesses.

Small Business and GDP

It is not possible to quickly apportion GDP into that produced by small businesses and that produced by others.[17] However, the U.S. Small Business Administration estimates that approximately 51 percent of U.S. GDP from nonfarm enterprises is produced by small businesses, meaning those with fewer than five hundred employees.[18] Their researchers found little variation across years, with small-business shares ranging between 49 percent and 52 percent during the last few decades. As "midsized" businesses also represent some share of GDP, this implies that the dominant large corporation represents only one-third to one-quarter of private-sector GDP.

THE ENTREPRENEURIAL CYCLE

The Entrepreneur and the Birth of a Firm

When does a business start? Usually, the start date recorded by the government agencies that compile data on businesses is the year that the fledgling firm first files a tax return as a separate entity or files articles of organization with the state government or similar entity.

In our experience, this is often well *after* the entrepreneur actually begins working in the business. Early-stage entrepreneur tasks can include forming the legal organization and filing the necessary registration documents for tax and legal purposes; developing products or services; lining up financing; creating or revising a business plan; designing marketing materials, brand names, logos, and other advertising and marketing materials; seeking customers; recruiting employees; and finding office or production space, as well as beginning to sell goods and services.

However, in the United States and most other countries, the regular operation of an employer business requires a formal registration or organization as well as the filing of tax returns. Thus, data on business operations that begin with the formal year of registration or organization are a reasonably good indicator of when a firm begins hiring workers, incurring tax liabilities, or both.

U.S. Small Business Association Data on Births and Deaths

The U.S. Small Business Association (SBA), relying on census and IRS data, estimates the number of firms that organize and go out of business in the United States each year. These "births and deaths" data should be considered with a few additional observations in mind. First, as noted earlier, they depend on formal registrations, which some entrepreneurs delay for some time after their business begins operating. At the same time, businesses that cease operating frequently must continue to pay taxes and remain registered with the relevant government entity as they wind down their affairs. Thus, the data probably exaggerate the number of firms that actually operate for the entire calendar year, while undercounting enterprises that operate informally or have not yet formally organized under the relevant statute. Second, the data cited here are for *employer* firms, meaning firms that declare that they have an employee who is paid wages. This rules out a segment of the entrepreneurial population that has not yet hired a worker separate from the entrepreneur, including those that may never do so.

With these notes in mind, Table 5.3 reports SBA data on business starts and closures in 2004–2008. These data are strikingly consistent across multiple-year periods.[19] From these data, we draw three critical conclusions:

TABLE 5.3
Openings, closings, and bankruptcies of U.S. companies

Category	2004	2005	2006	2007	2008
Births	628,917	644,122	670,058	663,100	627,200
Closures	541,047	565,745	599,333	571,300	595,600
Bankruptcies	34,317	39,201	19,695	28,322	43,546

SOURCES: Compiled by author using data from the U.S. Department of Commerce, Bureau of the Census; Administrative Office of the U.S. Courts; U.S. Department of Labor; and Employment and Training Administration.

1. Approximately one business starts for every business that closes in the United States.

2. Only a small fraction of the companies that cease operating do so through bankruptcy.[20]

3. Among employer firms, the number of business births and deaths annually is approximately 10 percent of the total number of businesses.

The Birth of Small Businesses

Ninety-five percent of these firms (closing and opening) had fewer than twenty employees in the first year of the period. It is interesting to note that the same data indicate that 320 large firms (with five hundred or more employees) began operations during that period, and 330 ceased operations. Both the number of new firms and the direction of the net change in firms vary widely year to year.

This demonstrates again that most firms are small and that most *new* firms are small. It further suggests (but does not prove) that many new firms, maybe more than half, go out of business within a decade or less. We consider this question in Table 5.3.

Survival Rates for New Firms

For many years, it has been commonly asserted that most new businesses fail in the first several years of operation. Until recently, it was difficult to confirm or dispute this assertion with reliable data. However, the U.S. Census Bureau began releasing longitudinal data from a large panel of firms several years ago, allowing for direct observation of firm entry and exit over time.

A recent summary of these Business Dynamics Statistics (BDS) data concludes the following:[21]

- The one-year survival rate for firms organized in 2004 was 76.4 percent. The one-year rate has fluctuated around this level since 1977, but has remained steadily between 70 percent and 80 percent since the early 1990s.

- The five-year survival rate for firms organized in 2000 was 50.7 percent. This has also fluctuated, although it was slightly less than 50 percent for much of the 1990s and has never been much higher than 51 percent since the data were first reported for 1977.

- Both survival and exit rates are affected by the business cycle.

- The *entry rate* for new businesses (the share of new employer businesses that are newly registered in a year) has been relatively stable, in the range of 12 percent plus or minus 1 percent from the 1990s through the mid-2000s. The *exit rate* is slightly lower, meaning the number of firms has increased over time.

New Jobs from Small Firms

Another interesting analysis from these data highlights the role new businesses in the United States play in creating new jobs. The BDS data show that new firms hire workers at a much higher rate than old firms—if they survive:

> For example, establishments belonging to very young firms (age 1) have a net employment growth of about 15% conditional on survival, whereas those belonging to older firms (age 29+) have a net employment growth rate of about 4% conditional on survival. However, younger firms experience much more employment loss due to establishment exit, nearly 20% at very young firms, than do larger firms. ("High Growth and Failure," 2009, p. 2)

These data indicate that the commonly stated observation about new firms creating most jobs is probably correct.[22] However, these data also indicate that the exit of new firms destroys many jobs as well. We consider the international data on this issue later in this chapter, under the section titled "Types of Businesses: Publicly Traded Corporations."

The Odds Against Entrepreneurs

If the preceding statistics are to be believed—and our experience suggests that they should—the odds against business survival for an entrepreneur are long. Indeed, professional artists, inventors, and other creative geniuses have often been viewed by society as pursuing dreams rather than careers—a metaphor richly embroidered by writers throughout history.[23]

Less prosaic scholars, including the great neoclassical economist Alfred Marshall, have added scholarly weight to the notion that innovators, artists, and inventors often attain very little wealth:

> In this connection we may divide employers and other undertakers into two classes, those who open out new and improved methods of business, and those who follow beaten tracks. The services which the latter perform for society are chiefly direct and seldom miss their full reward: but it is otherwise with the former class. (Marshall, 1890, 1920, VI.VII.3, 5)

Marshall goes on to write that those that "pioneered new paths" often confer on society "benefits out of all proportion to their own gains" and that at least sometimes they have "died millionaires." Thus he acknowledges both the tremendous gains that entrepreneurs can provide to themselves and others and the long odds against success.

BUSINESS SIZE, ENTRY, AND EXIT IN OTHER COUNTRIES

Other countries with developed economies have collected data allowing for international comparisons of the number of small businesses and their relative output compared with the GDP of the country, as well as firm entry and exit. The data issues we discussed for the United States are magnified when dealing with international comparisons. Furthermore, institutional, cultural, legal, and tax differences strongly affect business organization in various countries. Nonetheless, these comparisons provide an excellent indicator of how business activity among U.S. entrepreneurs compares with those in other countries.[24]

Number of Small Businesses and Share of Employment

International data confirm the finding from the preceding U.S. data: *Small business*, using any reasonable definition, accounts for most private-sector businesses and employment in developed countries. In particular:

- Statistics Canada reports 1.1 million employer businesses in the country, out of a total of 2.3 million business establishments. Of these, more than 99 percent are in the range of 1–499 employees. These employ 64 percent of Canada's workers.[25]

- New Zealand found that about 89 percent of the enterprises in the national business directory had five employees or fewer in 1998, and less than 1 percent had fifty employees or more.[26]

- The same New Zealand study compared the share of total employment in "smallish enterprises" among Organization for Economic Cooperation and Development (OECD) countries and found that the share of employees in firms with fewer than a hundred employees ranged from 38.9 percent (United States) to 73.5 percent (Italy).[27]

- Other OECD cross-country analyses suggest that small and medium enterprises (SMEs; firms with fewer than 250 employees) account for more than 99 percent of establishments and more than 60 percent of the employment in such countries as Turkey, Switzerland, Sweden, Spain, and Portugal.[28]

- The 2009 European Union report on SMEs reports that there were more than twenty million enterprises in the EU in 2008, of which only forty-three thousand were large-scale enterprises. This implies that more than 99 percent of the EU business enterprises were SMEs. The same 2009 EU Report also calculates that 67.4 percent of employment in the nonfinancial private sector occurred in SMEs.[29]

Entry and Exit Rates; Survivorship

Data on firm entry and exit ("births and deaths") and survivorship over time should be considered along with the fact that many European countries have larger government sectors than the United States, and that cultural, regulatory, and tax differences affect whether individuals are likely to start a business and operate it formally (meaning registering and paying taxes) in various countries.

The international data summarized next suggest that the United States enjoys a somewhat higher entry rate than most other OECD countries. Among developed countries, the United States also seems to have the highest survivorship rate.

A 2003 OECD study found that firm entry rates during 1989–1994 were approximately 12 percent in the United States, which was exceeded by one or two percentage points by

France and Portugal. Italy, Denmark, Western Germany, and Finland had entry rates of approximately 9 percent.[30]

The same OECD study examined survivorship rates across countries at two-, four,- and seven-year intervals. After adjusting for international comparisons, they found that the two-year survivorship rate was the highest in the United States (at approximately 80 percent) and lowest in Canada (at approximately 60 percent). After seven years, about half of the firms in the United States and Portugal remained; about 40 percent remained in Italy, West Germany, and Finland; and less than 40 percent remained in France and Canada.

Share of GDP

The share of GDP produced by small private firms is an especially important indicator of the contribution of such firms. The 2009 EU Report on SMEs provides data on the larger (twenty-seven-country) European Union. These data indicate that 58 percent of the value added in the nonfinancial private EU economy comes from SMEs, and only 42 percent comes from large firms. This matches the dominance of SMEs in overall revenue (*turnover*) at 58 percent and the number of people employed at 67 percent.

New Zealand estimated the contribution to GDP of enterprises in finely distributed employment size segments. It estimates that 26 percent of the country's GDP comes from firms with five employees or fewer, and 60 percent comes from firms with ninety-nine employees or fewer.[31] These results, though not exactly comparable, are not inconsistent with the U.S. estimate of approximately 51 percent of GDP coming from small firms (less than five hundred employees).

TYPES OF BUSINESSES: PUBLICLY TRADED CORPORATIONS

Recap: Defining Characteristics of a Firm

We devoted considerable effort in Chapter 4, "The Nature of the Firm," to a rigorous definition of a firm. In particular, we defined a firm as an organization with three characteristics:

- A separate identity from its workers or managers
- A motivation to earn profit for the investors
- A set of replicable business processes

In this section, we review forms of organization available to a business. We start with the forms available in the United States and then briefly consider similar forms available in other countries.[32]

The C Corp

Publicly traded firms in the United States generally fall into one large category: the C corporation. General Motors, Ford, IBM, Microsoft, General Electric, Coca-Cola, Intel, and many other well-known companies use the C corporation form.[33] Indeed, the C corp is what many people commonly call a corporation. The C corp is distinguished by equity shares that can be held and traded by domestic or foreign persons; the ability to have multiple classes of stock; limited liability for shareholders; and the application of federal income tax to the earnings of the firm itself.

In the United States, corporations are typically established under state laws that establish the corporation as a separate "person" under the law, which can own property, employ workers, and sue and be sued and is responsible for paying taxes. These state laws, as well as federal laws governing relations with investors, typically establish the obligation of directors or managers to act in the interests of shareholders. Delaware is a common state in which to domicile publicly traded corporations because of the depth of the corporate law in that state. Thus many firms that primarily do business in other states are Delaware corporations.

Corporations in Other Countries

The corporate form is powerful and has been adapted in countries around the world. Some examples of similar corporate forms from other countries are shown in Table 5.4.

Corporations are normally chartered, licensed, or otherwise designated by national or state (provincial) governments. The provisions governing such charters vary considerably among jurisdictions and change from time to time. For example, the UK adopted the Companies Act 2006 only recently. Chapter 2 of the act identifies the *Ltd.* (for private limited companies) and *Plc* (for public limited companies) forms as well as a special provision for Welsh companies that can end their name with *cwmni cyfyngedig cyhoeddus* or *c.c.c.* A portion of the act is excerpted in Exhibit 5.1.

TABLE 5.4
Corporate forms in other countries

Country	Form	Abbreviation	Comment
United Kingdom	Private Limited Company	Ltd.	Emphasizes limited liability of shareholders
	Public Limited Company	Plc	Emphasizes both public nature and limited liability
			These same terms are often used in other countries that share the English common-law tradition, including the United States
Spain	Sociedad Anónima	S.A.	Emphasizes the corporate (society) aspect; notes that individual stockholders can remain largely anonymous
India	Limited	Ltd.	Based on English law tradition
Italy	Società a Responsabilità Limitata	S.r.l.	Similar to limited liability companies
	Società per Azioni	S.p.A.	Similar to public corporations
Germany, Austria	Aktiengesellschaft	AG	Similar to public corporations
	Gesellschaft mit beschränkter Haftung	GmbH	Similar to limited liability companies
Brazil	Sociedade Limitada	Ltda.	Similar to limited liability companies
	Sociedade Anônima	S.A.	Similar to public corporations

EXHIBIT 5.1

The UK Company Act of 2006 (Excerpt)

Limited and Unlimited Companies

(1) A company is a "limited company" if the liability of its members is limited by its constitution.

It may be limited by shares or limited by guarantee.

(2) If their liability is limited to the amount, if any, unpaid on the shares held by them, the company is "limited by shares."

(3) If their liability is limited to such amount as the members undertake to contribute to the assets of the company in the event of its being wound up, the company is "limited by guarantee."

(4) If there is no limit on the liability of its members, the company is an "unlimited company."

Private and Public Companies

(1) A "private company" is any company that is not a public company.

(2) A "public company" is a company limited by shares or limited by guarantee and having a share capital—

(a) whose certificate of incorporation states that it is a public company, and

(b) in relation to which the requirements of this Act, or the former Companies Acts, as to registration or re-registration as a public company have been complied with on or after the relevant date.

TYPES OF BUSINESSES: PRIVATELY HELD COMPANIES

The Privately Held Corporation

The privately held business in the United States is typically organized in one of a handful of forms. As noted previously, the C corp is the dominant form of organization of publicly traded firms in the United States. However, many private firms are also C corps. Some have some shares traded in informal or thin markets. Some later become publicly traded companies. In addition, a fraction of publicly traded companies each year become privately held.

In contrast to the shares in a C corp, interests in S corporations, most partnerships, limited liability companies, and sole proprietorships cannot, in general, be publicly traded in the United States. These forms are discussed next.

The Limited Liability Company (LLC)

The limited liability company (LLC) is a relatively recent form of ownership that combines key advantages of the C corp and the partnership. These are formed under laws that create LLC or LLP (limited liability partnership) business forms or similar designations.

The key factor borrowed from the corporation is limited liability for the investors. The key factors borrowed from partnerships are straightforward equity shares and pass-through tax treatment.

Under U.S. tax laws, LLCs can often choose to file as partnerships or S corps. In either case, the LLC reports the earnings of the firm, which are then imputed to the equity owners (typically called *members*) of the firm in proportion to their fractional ownership. Such entities are therefore known as *pass-through* entities for tax purposes.

The Partnership

A partnership is an association formed by agreement among persons that agree to share, subject to specific rules, the costs and benefits of a business enterprise. Partnerships are a very old form of business; Fibonacci discussed the distribution of profits and losses in a partnership in his *Liber Abaci* (1202).

Because it is an association, the partnership technically ends and restarts as a separate entity every time a partner enters or leaves. In general, partners in a partnership do not enjoy the limited liability that shareholders in a corporation enjoy, unless they are formally designated as *limited partners*. The partnership and the partners in it are usually liable for the actions of each partner. For these reasons, partnerships are often the preferred form of business organization only when the members are quite closely associated and have clear shared interests. Often, every partner is actively involved in the same business and comes from the same profession.[34]

In general, partnerships are pass-through entities for U.S. income tax purposes. Most partnerships are privately held. However, there are a limited number of publicly traded partnerships, or PTPs (sometimes called *master limited partnerships*) in which units are traded on exchanges, like shares of stock.[35] The owners of these units generally become limited partners in that their risk of liability is limited to their ownership interest in the partnership.

The S Corp

An S corp is a corporation taxed under a provision of the Internal Revenue Code known as *subcategory S*. It files a tax return very similar to that of a C corp. Furthermore, an S corp typically shares the characteristic of limited liability for shareholders. However, unlike C corps, an S corp is restricted in terms of both number and type of shareholders.[36] In addition, an S corp is a pass-through entity in terms of federal income taxation. This means that the earnings of the company are imputed to the shareholders in proportion to their equity ownership.

Some noncorporations such as LLCs may also elect to be taxed as an S corp. Thus, the term *S corp* is often used ambiguously to mean both form of organization and tax filing form.

The Sole Proprietorship

The sole proprietorship is the classic entrepreneur and home-based business form. In effect, any business enterprise that is not organized formally is a sole proprietorship.[37]

The "proprietor" of the sole proprietorship is the owner and manager. He or she may have employees, sign contracts, borrow money, and sue or be sued. However, in general the person who is the proprietor is liable for all the obligations of the business, and any earnings from the business are treated like wages for tax purposes.

Remark: U.S. Taxes

Under U.S. income tax laws, the net business income from the sole proprietorship is taxed as if the earnings were wage and salary earnings of an employee. This carries two important implications:

1. The taxation of *net* business earnings (rather than gross revenue) means that the business can deduct many business expenses.

2. The net earnings are taxed for both income taxes and payroll taxes such as FICA (Social Security) and Medicare.[38]

Given the potential for creative use of these provisions to evade or reduce taxes, it is not surprising that the IRS in the United States scrutinizes sole proprietorships more than wage-and-salary earners.[39]

VALUE OF PRIVATE FIRMS IN THE UNITED STATES

Census and Tax Data on Business

We have summarized above the available data on the number of employer businesses in the United States. We have also considered several forms of organization and the most important tax implications of each form.

In this section, we attempt to use this information, along with records from tax filings, to estimate the number of bona fide firms operating in the United States for a year for which tax, survey, and census data are available. With these data, we compare the income, and the likely market value, of privately held and publicly traded firms in the United States. (Because we use data from multiple sources, the number and scale of operations reported for each segment may differ somewhat from the statistics used elsewhere in this chapter.)

Number of Business Tax Filers

Table 5.5 reports the number of business tax filers by type of organization. One can compare these data with the data in Table 5.2. Note that the number of C corp, S corp, and partnership returns exceeds the number of employer firms reported by the U.S. Census. This is consistent with the observation that some companies file multiple returns, including specific returns for wholly owned subsidiaries.

Note also the large number of sole proprietorship returns filed. This is also consistent with the notion that many such filers are, in fact, reporting income that is similar to

TABLE 5.5
*Number of firms and business tax returns in the United
States, 2002*

C corporation returns filed	2.1 million
S corporation returns filed	3.2 million
Partnership returns filed	2.2 million
Nonfarm sole proprietorship returns filed	18.9 million
Total "business" returns filed	26.4 million

SOURCES: U.S. Department of the Treasury, Internal Revenue Service, *SOI Bulletin.*

wage-and-salary earnings, passive investment earnings, or other income that arises from activities that fail to meet our rigorous definition of a firm.

Taxable Income from All Firms

Although publicly traded firms in the United States and other countries typically report their revenue, income, and other financial data to a regulatory authority, privately held firms typically do not. Thus the general public has detailed and voluminous data on publicly traded firms but very little on their far more numerous private counterparts.

Indirect estimates of the value of private and public firms come from two related sources: the Federal Reserve Board's Flow of Funds and Survey of Consumer Finances. The latter is based on consumer responses to survey questions and represents consumer perceptions of the value of their investment assets, including stock in private and public firms.

The 2009 publication of "The Value of Private Firms in the United States" by *Business Economics* (Anderson, 2009) provided a direct estimate of the revenue and income of privately held and publicly held firms in the United States. The same article used aggregate data on IRS tax filings by form of business organization as the basis for apportioning income among private and public businesses as well as nonbusiness activities. We show these data for the year 2002 in Tables 5.6 and 5.7.

We can highlight the following observations about these data and the comparable figures for the year 2007:

- Total business net earnings for the year 2002 were just under $1.1 trillion, on business receipts of just under $21 trillion. (In 2007, receipts were in excess of $30 trillion and taxable income was over $2.9 trillion.)

- C corporations accounted for $258 billion in net earnings in 2002 (and $1.1 trillion in 2007). C corps can be publicly traded or privately held. Using the apportionment scheme from Anderson (2009), we apportion most C corp revenue and earnings to publicly traded firms. This is consistent with the evidence from the *Fortune* 500 and *Forbes* Global 2000 suggesting that the largest corporations have a disproportionate share of the revenue and income among C corps.

- S corps had $3.8 trillion in receipts in 2002 (and $6.0 trillion in 2007). Taxable income from these firms topped $183 billion in 2002 (and $400 billion in 2007). All the S corps are privately held firms, and therefore we apportion all of the reported S corps earnings to privately held firms.

TABLE 5.6

Business receipts and net income by form of business, 2002

Type of organization	Business receipts ($ millions)	Net income ($ millions)
C corporations	13,455,844	258,674
S corporations	3,841,281	183,479
REITs and RICs	255,898	154,371
Partnerships (general, limited, LLC)	2,414,187	270,667
Sole proprietorships (nonfarm)	1,029,692	221,113
Sum of net income	**20,996,902**	**1,088,305**
MEMO: *Comparison with alternate measures*		
IRS: All business returns	$20,741,004	$1,088,304
Ratio to total of all business taxpayers	101%	100%
NIPA: Corporate profits with IVA and CCA	n/a	872,200
Ratio to total of business income		80%

SOURCES: Anderson, "The Value of Private Firms in the United States" (2009); U.S. Bureau of Economic Analysis; Internal Revenue Service.

NOTES:
• Base data on taxable income is from Internal Revenue Service, Integrated Business Data.
• Methodology and apportionment are from Anderson (2009).
• "Nonbusiness" income includes wage and salary earnings and passive investment income reported on business tax returns.
• Net income is reported as "Net Income Less Deficit" in IRS SOI source data.
• BEA NIPA data are for adjusted corporate profits. IVA is inventory adjustment; CCA is capital consumption allowance.

TABLE 5.7

Net income by type of organization, 2002

Type of organization	ESTIMATED NET INCOME BY TYPE OF ORGANIZATION ($ MILLIONS)		
	Nonbusiness	Publicly held	Privately held
C corporations			
Apportionment: public (70%)		181,072	
private (30%)			77,602
S corporations			
Apportionment: private (100%)			183,479
REITs and RICs			
Apportionment: nonbusiness (100%)	154,371		
Partnerships (general, limited, LLC)			
Apportionment: private (100%)			270,667
Sole proprietorships (nonfarm)			
Apportionment: nonbusiness (65%)	143,724		
private (35%)			77,390
Sum of net income	298,095	181,072	609,138

SOURCES: Anderson, "The Value of Private Firms in the United States" (2009); U.S. Bureau of Economic Analysis; Internal Revenue Service.

NOTES:
• Base data on taxable income is from Internal Revenue Service, Integrated Business Data.
• Methodology and apportionment is from Anderson (2009).
• "Nonbusiness" income includes wage and salary earnings and passive investment income reported on business tax returns.
• Net income is reported as "Net Income Less Deficit" in IRS SOI source data.
• BEA NIPA data are for adjusted corporate profits. IVA is inventory adjustment; CCA is capital consumption allowance.

- The partnership category is more complicated. Many LLCs report their taxable operations on partnership returns. The partnership category includes general and limited partnerships and LLCs filing partnership returns. (Some LLCs file as S corps, and some as sole proprietorships, so it is likely that some LLC income is in these categories.) Taxable earnings from partnerships was $271 billion in 2002. We apportion this and all the $683 billion in 2007 taxable earnings from partnerships to privately held firms.

- For sole proprietorships, we apportioned most of the revenue and earnings to nonbusiness activity such as implicit wage and salary earnings. There is no way of knowing precisely how much sole proprietorship revenue flows to organizations that fit the economic definition of a firm. We assign the remainder to privately held firms.

- We excluded REIT income from either business category, under the assumption that most of it is passive investment activity. However, some fraction of this income is certainly business income, and the assumption used in the table is conservative.

Implications from Earnings Data

Looking at these data, using a consistent apportionment scheme for two years that are a half decade apart, is instructive. The following are the most obvious implications:

- Business income is clearly affected by the business cycle, as macroeconomic theory and ample evidence outside this analysis dictate. The year 2002 was one of modest recovery from a mild recession in the United States. The year 2007 was the peak year before the Great Recession started in 2008.

Picking out one category illustrates this. For example, revenue at S corps grew from $3.8 trillion to $6.0 trillion from 2002 to 2007, a 58 percent increase. Income, however, more than doubled, a 118 percent increase for the same time period.

- The assumptions and methodology used here imply that between two and three times as much business earnings went to private firms as public firms during these years. See again Tables 5.6 and 5.7.

Implied Value of Privately and Publicly Held Firms

The data just described, for two different years, represent the taxable income of aggregate classes of firms. Market capitalization data exist for many publicly traded firms, as do summary statistics (such as price/earnings [P/E] ratios) for subsets of those firms. However, for privately held firms, which constitute most of the firms and account for most of the earnings, no separate market value observations are available.

Anderson (2009) provided a direct estimate of the aggregate value of privately and publicly held firms in the year 2002. The base data for this estimate was an allocation of taxable income among business entities in the United States. Using the same methodology and apportionment scheme as in the 2009 article, we estimate the aggregate value of public and private firms for the year 2007 in Table 5.8.

An income approach method, appropriate to large aggregates, was used to derive these estimates. Stock market data on publicly traded firms provide a strong empirical basis for

TABLE 5.8
Estimated market value of U.S. public and private firms, 2007

	PUBLICLY HELD ($ MILLIONS)		PRIVATELY HELD ($ MILLIONS)	
	Taxable income and ratio	*Implied value*	*Taxable income and ratio*	*Implied value*
C corporations				
Taxable earnings	742,554		318,237	
P/E ratio	18.9		18.9	
		11,031,261		6,014,684
S corporations				
Taxable earnings			400,730	
P/E ratio			18.9	
				7,573,802
REITs and RICs				
Taxable earnings			—	
P/E ratio			18.9	
				—
Partnerships (general, limited, LLC)				
Taxable earnings			683,367	
P/E ratio			18.9	
				12,915,644
Sole proprietorships (nonfarm)				
Taxable earnings			98,195	
P/E ratio			10.0	
				981,950
Totals		**14,034,264**		**27,486,080**

MEMO
Market capitalization,
  domestic equities: NYSE, end 2006 $ 15,421,168
                 NASDAQ, end 2006 $ 3,865,004
                 Wilshire 5000, mid-2006 $ 13,600,000
Survey of Consumer Finances (2007): $ 14,344,200
  implied household business equity ownership

SOURCES: Anderson, "The Value of Private Firms in the United States" (2009); Internal Revenue Service; World Federation of Exchanges; Wilshire Associates; Survey of Consumer Finances. See Table 5.7 for additional source notes.

NOTE: Exchange-reported equity market capitalizations include some foreign corporations and other noncomparable entities.

the use of a P/E ratio to describe the relationship between the market price of an aggregate of traded equities and the reported (or expected) earnings of the underlying firms. Of course, for any individual company, numerous other factors come into play. Furthermore, the P/E ratio is properly considered a descriptive statistic, not a causal factor.

The results of the analysis are striking. Privately held firms, taken as a group, are far more valuable than their better-known publicly traded counterparts. This arises directly from a natural source: there are more of them, and they produce a lot more earnings. Furthermore, this result is robust across approximately a half decade of data.

Another observation is that the government statistics on household holdings of private business equity appear to substantially underestimate the amount actually held by consumers. Indeed, sources such as the Federal Reserve Board's Flow of Funds and the Survey of Consumer Finance appear to provide an order-of-magnitude estimate of the market value of publicly traded stocks, but only a fraction of that of private firms.[40]

Limitations of the Methodology

The methodology used in this exercise is subject to significant limitations, all of which are worth noting:

- As noted in the original article, the range of error around the estimate of the market value of private firms is *huge*. Even a 5 percent margin of error on the 2007 market value estimate is a swing of more than $1 trillion! However, the purpose of the exercise was not to arrive at a point estimate of market value, but instead to derive a reliable indicator of market value *relative to* the observed market capitalization of publicly traded firms.

- For consistency, we present here an estimate of 2007 market values using the same apportionment scheme and implied aggregate P/E ratios as in the original estimate using 2002 data. Certainly, there was some variation in the actual apportionments and P/E ratios between the years and among the categories.

- The apportionment of REIT and sole proprietorship income to business income is quite conservative. On the other hand, a small portion of partnership income may be interpreted as belonging to the publicly held category, given the existence of a small number of large partnerships that have some type of active market in partnership interests.

- The difference between taxable income and accounting income introduces some bias, although the amount of that bias is difficult to assess. The use of taxable income in the P/E ratio probably biases the value estimate in a conservative direction. Corporations have an incentive to reduce taxable income, but their managers have an incentive to report higher accounting income. Most of the published information on P/E ratios is based on accounting income, so using a similar P/E ratio for taxable income probably underestimates the implied value.

- The use of a P/E ratio for any firm carries inherent limitations. One of the most obvious is that many firms *lose* money in any given year. However, such firms do not usually lose all their value. Thus, for any large aggregate of firms, there are some for which a standard P/E ratio is meaningless. A second limitation is the choice of earnings to use in the ratio: should it be last year's or this year's (expected) earnings?

In addition to the limitations listed here, there are also a raft of differences between the market structure for private firms and that of their publicly traded counterparts. The implications of this for valuation methods are discussed at several other places in this book.

6 ACCOUNTING FOR THE FIRM

This chapter focuses on the history, proper role, and limitations of accounting. Elements of this chapter include the following:

- The vital role of accounting in business
- Why accounting is *not* the same as valuation, management, or finance
- The history of accounting, including a discussion of the great Italian Renaissance-era mathematician Pacioli and the little-known (in the West) ancient Indian sage Kautilya
- Principles of accounting, starting with the most important one: ethics
- The role of the historical cost principle in accounting and an introduction to its use in the traditional "asset" method of valuation
- A brief overview of the key accounting statements for a firm
- An introduction to accounting concepts used in traditional valuation methods

I believe an understanding of the principles and role of accounting is more important than a detailed description of financial statements, so this chapter concentrates on the former rather than the latter.

A BRIEF HISTORY OF ACCOUNTING

Pacioli, the Renaissance, and the *Summa*

Modern double-entry accounting is generally credited to the Italian mathematician Luca Pacioli in the fifteenth century.[1] Pacioli's 1494 masterpiece, *Summa de arithmetica, geometrica, proportioni et proportionalità*, presented mathematical knowledge of many forms. Pacioli credited Euclid of Alexandria (c. 300 BC), and Leonardo of Pisa (Fibonacci, c. AD 1170–1270) for some of his work on mathematics. He also discussed games of chance. One of Pacioli's friends was the great Leonardo da Vinci, who illustrated a later book of Pacioli's, the 1509 *Divina proportione.*[2]

Today, the best known of Pacioli's contributions is the section of his book that summarized the double-entry accounting used by Venetian trading firms. Pacioli's work was re-presented (and often extended) in other Italian works, and also in Flemish and English works, by the middle of the 1500s.[3] Although Pacioli did not claim to invent double-entry accounting, he clearly codified a practice in a manner that came to dominate the world of commerce. Thus, I consider the *Summa* to be one of the most influential books ever written.

Trade, Private Property, and the Spread of Accounting

Economists generally point to the trade across the Mediterranean Sea as the critical driver for this development in accounting, because the buyer and seller often did not come face-to-face. However, there are obviously other factors at work that bear noting today. The Association of Chartered Accountants in the United States describes the development as follows:

> In attempting to explain why double entry bookkeeping developed in 14th century Italy instead of ancient Greece or Rome, accounting scholar A. C. Littleton describes seven "key ingredients" which led to its creation:
>
> • Private property: The power to change ownership, because bookkeeping is concerned with recording the facts about property and property rights.
>
> • Capital: Wealth productively employed, because otherwise commerce would be trivial and credit would not exist.
>
> • Commerce: The interchange of goods on a widespread level, because purely local trading in small volume would not create the sort of press of business needed to spur the creation of an organized system to replace the existing hodgepodge of record-keeping.
>
> • Credit: The present use of future goods, because there would have been little impetus to record transactions completed on the spot.
>
> • Writing: A mechanism for making a permanent record in a common language, given the limits of human memory.
>
> • Money: The "common denominator" for exchanges, since there is no need for bookkeeping except as it reduces transactions to a set of monetary values.
>
> • Arithmetic: A means of computing the monetary details of the deal.
>
> Many of these factors did exist in ancient times, but, until the Middle Ages, they were not found together in a form and strength necessary to push man to the innovation of double entry. Writing, for example, is as old as civilization itself, but arithmetic—the systematic manipulation of number symbols—was really not a tool possessed by the ancients. Rather, the persistent use of Roman numerals for financial transactions long after the introduction of Arabic numeration appears to have hindered the earlier creation of double-entry systems.[4]

It is interesting to note how complementary these "key ingredients" are to the items we listed in our definition of the firm, including the institutional factors (such as private property) we discussed in Chapter 4.

Of course, businesses existed before modern accounting, but the development of those businesses was greatly hampered by the absence of accepted practices of accounting. Thus, along with science, literature, and art, the flowering of the Italian Renaissance also gave much of the world a system of accounting.

Ancient Precursors to Accounting: Kautilya

The development of modern accounting since Pacioli is well documented in history. However, there are ancient precursors that bear noting.

One of the earliest texts on the organization of an economy, the Indian sage Kautilya's *Arthashastra* (c. 250 BC) devotes much thought to the development of trade and to the proper custody and recording of public funds. There is an argument that Kautilya's work, rather than Pacioli's *Summa* (written 1800 years later!), was the first treatise on systematic accounting.[5]

However, the question is doubly blurred: First, both Kautilya and Pacioli wrote primarily about topics *other than* accounting. Pacioli's work is primarily about mathematics, and Kautilya's is primarily about the management of a state by a powerful ruler.[6]

Second, the definition of accounting itself comes into play in the debate over its creation. In particular, Pacioli describes accounting techniques in the modern sense, including double-entry accounting techniques, and their use in business. Kautilya attempts nothing of this type, yet describes more than a millennium earlier the (more important) concept of honest accounting being essential to a society and government.[7] It is not clear that Pacioli saw accounting as a distinct discipline from mathematics; it is not clear that Kautilya saw it as distinct from economics.[8]

This question cannot be completely resolved by historians. In my view, if accounting is primarily a set of techniques and a scheme of records, then Pacioli is history's clearest progenitor. However, if it is a moral and institutional basis for society, Kautilya is a much earlier scholar on the topic.

PRINCIPLES OF ACCOUNTING

Ethics

There are numerous arithmetic and conceptual principles in accounting. However, I agree with the accounting authorities Kermit Larson and Paul Miller, who identified *ethics* as the fundamental principle in accounting:

> Accounting must be done ethically if it is to be an effective tool in the service of society. This is, perhaps, the fundamental principle of accounting. (Larson, Miller, and Garrison, 1993, p. 6)

Larson and Miller note that people rely on accountants to decide how to recognize income and costs, which results in wealth being transferred from one person to another. They also work with confidential information, including salary, tax, and business plan information.

Accountants rely on a large body of standards and laws to guide their decisions. However, without ethics, all the other rules and standards lose meaning. Indeed, as recurring scandals in too many walks of life prove, following rules while ignoring fundamental ethical principles leads to misrepresentation, breach of fiduciary duty, and often fraud.[9]

The essential purpose of accounting is to present the condition of a business in a manner that informs, rather than misleads, others. Conventions, rules, and standards help achieve that goal because they pressure disparate entities (and those with competing incentives) to conform their reporting. Violating the ethics principle means that such "rules" are merely technical constraints to be manipulated, avoided, or disregarded.

Fundamental Principles of Accounting

A bewildering array of accounting standards exist; in fact, it would be more correct to say an array of *sets* of accounting standards, because each country (and some international organizations or industries) often use more than one set.

However, there is a relatively short list of fundamental accounting *principles*. Larson and Miller, the authors of the long-running *Fundamental Accounting Principles* textbook, identify eleven such principles.[10] We list these, along with comments, below:

1. *Business entity principle:* A business must be accounted for separately from its owner or owners. Recall that one of the elements of our definition of a firm was "separate legal identity"; see Chapter 4, "The Nature of the Firm."

2. *Objectivity principle:* Information in financial statements must be supported by evidence. The Financial Accounting Standards Board describes a related concept as *neutrality*:

   To be neutral, accounting information must report economic activity as faithfully as possible, without coloring the image it communicates for the purpose of influencing behavior in *some particular direction*. (FASB, *Statements of Accounting Concepts No. 2*, 1980, para. 100)

3. *Cost principle:* Information in financial statements must be based on costs actually incurred in business transactions. This is often called the *historical cost* principle. We will discuss this further under the section titled "Historical Cost."

4. *Going-concern principle:* Accountants prepare financial statements under the assumption that the business will continue operating.

5. *Revenue recognition principle:* Revenue should be recorded or "recognized" on the income statement according to three guidelines:

   a. Revenue should be recognized at the time it is earned. (This is often distinct from the time a sales contract is signed.)

   b. Revenue of many forms can be recognized (including cash and credit sales that result in an account receivable for the selling firm).

   c. The amount of revenue recognized should be the actual cash received, or the cash-equivalent fair market value of any other consideration.

6. *Time period principle:* The activities of a business occur during specified time periods. Financial reports should show the results of operations for each period.

7. *Matching principle:* Expenses should be reported in the same accounting period as the revenues that were earned as a result of the expenses.

8. *Materiality principle:* In the reporting of activities of relatively small size or effect, accounting principles may be ignored if the effect on the financial statements is unimportant to their users.

9. *Full disclosure principle:* Financial statements should contain all relevant information about the operations and financial position of the entity.

10. *Consistency principle:* A firm should use the same accounting methods period after period.[11]

11. *Conservatism principle:* Where conditions are uncertain, the accountant should report in a conservative—but not pessimistic—manner.

Remark: Considerations That Are Not Principles of Accounting

It is interesting to note a few concepts that are *not* included in the fundamental principles of accounting. These omissions are not accidental. They include the following:

• *Certainty.* The principles recognize that some accounting entries will require estimates, and others judgment.

• *Precision.* A false claim to precision undermines the usefulness of any statement, including financial statements.[12] The accounting profession wisely chose usefulness over precision for that reason.

• *Prediction of market value.* Financial statements record the transactions of the firm, normally relying on the principle of historical cost. Valuation of the firm is not a goal of accounting, or even a by-product.

• *Substitution for management.* Managers of firms use accounting information to manage; investors use it to invest; tax collectors and tax preparers use it for tax purposes. The key point here is that *using* the information for such purposes is different from the purposes themselves. The accounting profession recognizes this by, among other things, developing types of accounting practices designed to serve certain users. Cost accounting and managerial accounting are two examples.

Remark: Other Statements on the Principles of Accounting

The preceding descriptive list, which draws heavily on accounting practice in the United States, is one of a number of statements on the principles of accounting. Other organizations also promulgate standards of practice that often substantially overlap those listed here. These include the following:

• The Financial Accounting Standards Board (FASB), which outlined the principles of accounting in a series of "statements of concepts," the first two of which are excerpted in this chapter.

• The International Accounting Standards Board (IASB), which dates from a multinational agreement signed in 1973 by the United Kingdom, the United States, Canada,

Germany, Japan, and other nations. It maintains a set of International Financial Reporting Standards. An IASB statement is excerpted later in this chapter.

• Various boards and agencies that establish accounting standards for particular types of organizations or for regulatory purposes. Two of the more visible of these are the Government Accounting Standards Board in the United States and the Bank for International Settlements (BIS), which has promoted international banking standards under the direction of its Basel Committee.[13]

Historical Cost

Of the principles of accounting that affect valuation, perhaps the most important is that of *historical cost*. In general, transactions occur at one point in time, and that transaction at that time establishes the cost attached to the item that was purchased or the revenue associated with the item that was sold. This is the historical cost principle, and it allows accounting statements to be prepared over multiple time periods with confidence and comparability.

> The information provided by financial reporting largely reflects the financial effects of transactions and events that have already happened. Management may communicate information about its plans or projections, but financial statements and most other financial reporting are historical. For example, the acquisition price of land, the current market price of a marketable equity security, and the current replacement price of an inventory are all historical data—no future prices are involved. (FASB, *Statements of Accounting Principles No. 1*, 1978, para. 21)

Of course, market values change over time for almost all assets. This includes financial assets such as stocks and bonds as well as tangible assets such as inventory, property, equipment, and real estate. Intangible assets such as trademarks and patents also fluctuate in market value. Estimating the market value of all these assets at any one time would be an impossible task for most enterprises. Hence, the historical cost principle is a useful convention that allows the information to be presented on a consistent basis.

Remark: "Fair Value" and "Mark to Market" Requirements

In a deviation from the historical cost principle, accounting or regulatory authorities may require some firms to report an estimate of market value for certain balance sheet items. Examples of this, for publicly traded firms, include certain stock options given to managers. A related example is the recognition of gains or losses due to currency fluctuations. These are sometimes called *mark to market* requirements, and the market standard is often *fair value*.[14]

To the extent these requirements allow an investor to understand the true financial picture of a company, these are beneficial requirements. However, investors should also recognize that stating most of a firm's assets and liabilities on one standard, and some under a different standard, may cause an "apples and oranges" problem.

IMPORTANT ACCOUNTING STATEMENTS

Principal Financial Statements

We only briefly discuss specific accounting statements in this section, with a focus on the relevance of these to the value of firms.

The Financial Accounting Standards Board explains the primary purpose of financial statements, and the most important of those statements, as follows:

> Financial statements are a central feature of financial reporting. They are a principal means of communicating accounting information to those outside an enterprise. Although financial statements may also contain information from sources other than accounting records, accounting systems are generally organized on the basis of the elements of financial statements (assets, liabilities, revenues, expenses, etc.) and provide the bulk of the information for financial statements. The financial statements now most frequently provided are (a) balance sheet or statement of financial position, (b) income or earnings statement, (c) statement of retained earnings, (d) statement of other changes in owners' or stockholders' equity, and (e) statement of changes in financial position (statement of sources and applications of funds). (FASB, *Principles of Accounting Concepts No. 1*, 1978, para. 16)

The International Accounting Standards Committee adopted a similar statement of the elements composing a "complete" set of financial statements, which include statements of end-of-period financial position and a retrospective financial position; statements describing comprehensive income, changes in equity, and cash flows during the period; and notes.[15]

We will discuss explicitly three of these: the balance sheet, the income statement, and the statement of changes in financial position, commonly called the *cash flow schedule*.

The Balance Sheet

We discussed earlier in this chapter the origin of modern accounting. Of all the financial statements, the balance sheet is probably the clearest expression of this particular masterpiece of thought from the Italian Renaissance. It is a device that came to dominate the entire world of commerce.

The balance sheet is a snapshot of the assets of a firm, taken at one time, with the claims against the firm arrayed against its assets. It illustrates the fundamental accounting identity: *assets equal liabilities plus equity*. Indeed, the statement is called the balance sheet because the two sides of the firm's finances must balance. The connection between the transactions that generated the assets and liabilities, which generally show up on the income statement, and the balance sheet is the logical feature of double-entry accounting first codified by Luca Pacioli in the late fifteenth century.

Balance sheets are described in detail in numerous accounting references, and summary statements for a set of representative firms are shown in Appendix C, "Description of Subject Companies."

The Income Statement

The income statement (also called a *profit and loss* or *P&L* statement) records the sum of transactions during a specific time period. Recall the matching and time-period principles of accounting; these together with the historical cost principle enforce the collection of transaction data reflecting the operations of the firm during a time period such as a month, quarter, or year.

There are various conventions for reporting revenue and costs. The common presentation calculates first a *gross profit* or *gross margin* as the net of revenue from the sale of goods less the cost of producing those goods. This is different from the operating profit, which is the gross margin less other operating costs.

The profit available to distribute to investors is usually called the *net profit* and is the amount left after all operating costs (including interest expenses) and income taxes are paid. Of course, most firms do not distribute all their net profits to investors each year.

The Cash Flow Statement

The net profit of a firm—the *bottom line*—is often considered the acid test of a firm's success or failure. Indeed, it may be the test that the entrepreneur views as most important. However, the accounting net income is rarely the actual cash surplus of the firm. Almost all operating firms have some differences between cash surplus and net profit. These are due to the following factors:

• *Noncash charges.* A firm must sometimes record expenses that were not paid in cash that year. Probably the most pervasive of these are capital depreciation charges. A firm must typically depreciate, rather than expense, capital expenditures. Following the matching principle of accounting, this approximately matches the useful life of the asset with the cost of the asset. However, it is immediately clear that the firm actually *paid* for the capital expenditure at a different time than the depreciation was recorded.

• *Financing of sales.* Many firms cannot insist that their customers pay cash on the date of delivery of their products and services. Thus, they implicitly finance those sales by accepting promises to pay within a certain time period.

• *Timing of other payments and receipts.* In addition to the financing of sales, firms may have other payments or receipts that do not arrive at the same time as the recognition of the income or expense on the accounting income statement.

• *Financing of the firm.* A firm is financed by a mixture of debt and equity, meaning that lenders are due periodic principal payments and equity investors some form of dividends or other distributions. Such payments are quite real, but are not expenses of the firm that are shown on the income statement.

The cash flow statement reconciles the accrued revenue and expenses of the company with the cash flow of the firm.

Remark: Varying Definitions of Cash Flow; Differences in the Literature

Note that the cash flow of the firm, as defined by generally accepted accounting principles (GAAP) or other accounting principles, may be different from other measures of operating cash flow. In particular, it is generally different from earnings before interest, taxes, depreciation, and amortization (EBITDA), and certain definitions of cash flow that are sometimes used for valuation purposes.

This is one area of considerable difference in the literatures of finance, economics, and accounting. Economics texts often rely on an abstract notion of the profit of a firm, sometimes failing to distinguish even between stock corporations and the more common partnerships and limited liability companies. On the other hand, many accounting and finance texts devote as much space to technical discussions of cash flow and income measures as they do to how the firm actually makes money. Even careful readers can be easily confounded by these differences in both style and purpose.

ACCOUNTING CONCEPTS USED IN TRADITIONAL VALUATION METHODS

Concepts Used in the Asset Approach

We describe the traditional asset approach to valuation in Chapter 13, under the section titled "The Asset Method." The asset method relies on the accounting identity as a principle of valuation. Of course, accounting is *not* valuation, and accounting statements are generally prepared using the historical cost principle rather than the market value principle. Therefore, the asset approach has inherent limitations.

However, timely preparation of accounting statements provides good information for valuation. In particular, the accurate recording of asset purchases, as well as properly recording expenses and depreciating assets, gives an investor or potential purchaser a fair view of the firm's assets. The traditional asset method relies on this information as the primary basis for the value of the company.

Concepts Used in the Income Approach

We describe the traditional income approach to valuation in Chapter 13, under the section titled "The Income Method." The income approach relies on the principle that value is dependent on expected earnings to the owners of the firm. In this chapter, we already observed that accounting statements provide multiple possible definitions of income and cash flow. Practitioners of traditional income methods often use another, distinct set of definitions in their calculations. Two such commonly used definitions of cash flow are used in traditional income approach valuation methods:

1. *Net cash flow to equity.* The net cash flow to equity is the net income, adjusted for noncash items in a similar manner as in the cash flow statement, and also adjusted for the use of working capital within the firm. This measures the earnings that could actually be distributed to owners.

This is also called *free cash flow to equity* (FCFE), although a number of authorities discourage the use of this term.

2. *Net cash flow to the firm.* Net cash flow to the firm measures the total cash flow to all financial stakeholders, including both equity holders (stockholders, partners, and members

TABLE 6.1

Cash flow measures used for income-method valuation

FREE CASH FLOW TO THE FIRM FROM NET INCOME	
Net income	$ 500
+ Depreciation	600
+ Interest expense * (1 − tax rate)	100
− Investment in fixed capital	650
− Investment in working capital	125
Free cash flow for the firm (FCFF)	$ 425

FREE CASH FLOW TO THE FIRM FROM CASH FLOW FROM OPERATIONS	
Cash flow from operations	$ 975
+ Interest expense * (1 − tax rate)	100
− Investment in fixed capital	650
Free cash flow for the firm (FCFF)	$ 425

FREE CASH FLOW TO EQUITY FROM FREE CASH FLOW TO THE FIRM	
Free cash flow to the firm	$ 425
− Interest expense * (1 − tax rate)	100
+ Net borrowing	200
Free cash flow to equity (FCFE)	$ 525

FREE CASH FLOW TO EQUITY FROM NET INCOME	
Net income	$ 500
+ Net charges	540
− Investment in fixed capital	650
− Investment in working capital	125
+ Interest expense * (1 − tax rate)	60
+ Net borrowing	200
Free cash flow to equity (FCFE)	$ 525

FREE CASH FLOW TO EQUITY FROM CASH FLOW FROM OPERATIONS	
Cash flow from operations	$ 975
− Investment in fixed capital	650
+ Net borrowing	200
Free cash flow for the firm (FCFF)	$ 525

of a limited liability company) and debt holders (long-term and short-term lenders). Preferred stockholders and holders of other types of securities that blur the distinction between debt and equity are also considered. As with cash flow to equity, adjustments are made to convert accrual income to cash flow, and also to adjust for working capital needs. This is also called (less precisely) *free cash flow for the firm* (FCFF), or *cash flow to invested capital.*

The main difference between cash flows to equity and those to the firm are interest expense less the implied tax shield, if any, of interest payments.

Note on Definitions

The precise definitions of these terms vary somewhat, depending on the authority. Shannon Pratt and colleagues (2000, chap. 10) and Aswath Damadoran (2002) provide commonly used definitions in applied valuation work; Jay Abrams (2001) provides a more thorough analysis that takes into account additional transactions that provide or consume cash. Table 6.1 provides an example set of calculations.

III   ECONOMIC THEORIES OF VALUE

7 VALUE IN CLASSICAL ECONOMICS

This chapter begins our tour of ten different valuation theories. We start with the oldest theory of value in the field of economics. In this chapter, we do the following:

- Review the economic theory of value that dates as least as far back as Adam Smith and the eighteenth century and may have independently been articulated by Kautilya in the third century BC.

- Observe that the labor theory fails to explain the actual determination of prices in a modern market economy. Conversely, we observe how such a long-discarded economic theory appears to motivate, though not quite determine, the price of many services even in the modern economy.

- Begin our testing of each theory of value by attempting to apply the labor theory to estimate the value of three representative firms.

THEORIES OF ECONOMIC VALUE: CLASSICAL THOUGHT

Adam Smith and the Labor Theory

The economic study of value can be traced at least as far back as the *labor theory of value* that originated with Adam Smith and was developed by David Ricardo and many others. The labor theory is simple, intuitive, and compelling. Although it has been supplanted in formal microeconomics, it continues to form the basis for pricing of many services as well as compensation for labor.

Adam Smith described the theory as establishing value on the amount of human toil required to acquire the commodity. In Smith's famous example of the beaver and the deer, the relative labor inputs required for a commodity largely determine its relative worth:

> If among a nation of hunters, for example, it usually costs twice the labour to kill a beaver which it does to kill a deer, one beaver should naturally exchange for or be worth two deer.

It is natural that what is usually the produce of two days or two hours labour, should be worth double of what is usually the produce of one day's or one hour's labour. (Smith, 1776, Book I, p. 54)[1]

Indeed, Smith goes on to make the point that "the real price of everything" is the "toil and trouble of acquiring it."

The real price of everything, what everything really costs to the man who wants to acquire it, is the toil and trouble of acquiring it. What everything is really worth to the man who has acquired it, and who wants to dispose of it or exchange it for something else, is the toil and trouble which it can save to himself, and which it can impose upon other people. What is bought with money or with goods is purchased by labour as much as what we acquire by the toil of our own body. That money or those goods indeed save us this toil. They contain the value of a certain quantity of labour which we exchange for what is supposed at the time to contain the value of an equal quantity. Labour was the first price, the original purchase-money that was paid for all things. It was not by gold or by silver, but by labour, that all the wealth of the world was originally purchased; and its value, to those who possess it, and who want to exchange it for some new productions, is precisely equal to the quantity of labour which it can enable them to purchase or command. (Smith, 1776, Book I, chap. 5)

David Ricardo Revises the Labor Theory

Although compelling in principle, the theory had important weaknesses that were recognized long ago. In particular, the measure of value was the quantity of labor required. However, this definition raises several questions. Would one count the quantity in terms of time spent, time adjusted by productivity, or wages? What about using tools to increase productivity of labor? How can it explain varying prices for similar commodities over time, such as high food prices during a drought?

Smith's theory was further developed by David Ricardo, another English economist, in a manner that both addressed and highlighted these inconsistencies. Ricardo's 1817 *Principles* attempted to incorporate into the labor theory three vital concepts: scarcity, utility, and productivity. Here is Ricardo's statement in his first chapter, "On Value":

The value of a commodity, or the quantity of any other commodity for which it will exchange, depends on the relative quantity of labour which is necessary for its production, and not on the greater or less compensation which is paid for that labour.

It has been observed by Adam Smith, that "the word Value has two different meanings, and sometimes expresses the utility of some particular object, and sometimes the power of purchasing other goods which the possession of that object conveys. The one may be called value in use; the other value in exchange. The things," he continues, "which have the greatest value in use, have frequently little or no value in exchange; and, on the contrary, those which have the greatest value in exchange, have little or no value in use." Water and air are abundantly useful; they are indeed indispensable to existence, yet, under ordinary circumstances, nothing can be obtained in exchange for them. Gold, on the contrary, though of little use compared with air or water, will exchange for a great quantity of other goods.

Utility then is not the measure of exchangeable value, although it is absolutely essential to it. If a commodity were in no way useful—in other words, if it could in no way contribute to our gratification—it would be destitute of exchangeable value, however scarce it might be, or whatever quantity of labour might be necessary to procure it.

Possessing utility, commodities derive their exchangeable value from two sources: from their scarcity, and from the quantity of labour required to obtain them. (Ricardo, 1821, chap. 1, sec. 1)

These passages recognize factors that determine a market price. However, putting them together does not create a coherent theory of value. This is evidenced from reading Ricardo's later restatement of the labor principle, in which productivity results in "considerably modified" values:

The principle that the quantity of labour bestowed on the production of commodities regulates their relative value, considerably modified by the employment of machinery and other fixed and durable capital. (Ricardo, 1821, chap. 1, sec. 4)

Other flaws were observed in the decades following the publication of the important works of Smith and Ricardo. In particular, the difference between the "invariant" or *intrinsic value* of a commodity and its *value in exchange* for other goods was a key contention of critics by the mid-1800s.[2] However, the classical Smith-Ricardo labor theory of value was the dominant theory of value, at least in the English-speaking world, until the late 1800s.[3] Since then, the dominant value paradigm became the neoclassical notion we discuss in Chapter 8, "Value in Neoclassical Economics."

The Continuing Relevance of the Discarded Labor Theory

The labor theory of value is no longer considered a valid basis for microeconomics, and its influence in macroeconomics has waned considerably since the collapse of the Soviet Union. However, no matter how irrelevant it may appear in academic thought, one can easily observe how it maintains a relevance in everyday life and commerce.

For example, every time an artisan explains the price of her handwork on the basis of "the work that has gone into it," she is using the labor theory of value. Every time a professional person charges for his services on the basis of the number of hours worked multiplied by a rate, he is relying on the labor principle of value. The common practice of paying higher wages for people with greater skills is completely consistent with the adaptation of the labor theory for "productivity" that Ricardo introduced nearly two hundred years ago.

It seems the classical economists were incorrect on the determination of value in the market. However, the labor theory they produced was based on a sound insight into human nature.

Historical Note: Kautilya's *Arthashastra*

The Indian sage Kautilya wrote a text on the management of the state, known as the *Arthashastra*, around 250 BC. This book was largely lost for fifteen hundred years, resurfacing in the nineteenth century and being translated into English only in the twentieth century. Thus, the classical-era economists could not have been aware of it.

Nonetheless, Kautilya specifies a setting of prices that is based on a labor theory of value, albeit one that appears to be "considerably modified" by productivity.[4] For example, his "superintendent of weavers" sets wages as follows:

> Wages shall be fixed according as the threads spun are fine, coarse (*sthúla*, "big") or of middle quality and in proportion to a greater or less quantity manufactured.[5]

Similar statements appear for the wages paid to other craftspeople and workers. On the other hand, Kautilya also invokes supply and demand as the basis for the prices of some commodities.

Although the precise interpretation is dulled by twenty-two centuries of history and a translation from an ancient language, Kautilya lays out convincingly the manner in which a ruler should enforce wages and prices on the basis of the productive work performed. Kautilya's similarities with the classical economists of Europe is reinforced by his discussion of the proper role of taxation. Adam Smith, without knowing it, repeated many of these in 1776.

As striking and original as Kautilya's work is, I would stop short of calling it a statement of an economic theory of value. Kautilya primarily gives advice to a powerful monarch rather than explaining how free individuals buy and sell. Thus, he is better compared to Niccolò Machiavelli than to Adam Smith.

Distinction from Marxist "Labor Theory of Value"

The labor theory of value has a peculiar place in the "Marxist economics" school of thought.[6] We distinguish the Marxist from the classical labor theory in two respects:

1. First, Marx proposed a change in the ownership and control of property, if necessary by violent revolution.[7] This is fundamentally different from the assumption of classical economists (and the neoclassicists after them) that businesses are, and will be in the future, managed by private owners. Partially on this basis, many economists reject Marx's work almost entirely as a theory of "economics."[8]

2. Second, private property rights are antithetical to the socialism that Marx proposed. As we noted in Chapter 4, under the section titled "Institutional Requirements for a Firm," private property is an essential institution for the development of business and the security of business value.[9]

VALUATION APPLICATION: CLASSICAL LABOR THEORY

Testing Each Valuation Method

We examine multiple valuation methods in this book, first from a historical and theoretical perspective, and then from a practical one. To address the latter, we attempt to estimate the value of sample companies using each of these methods.

Of course, valuing a company requires consideration of a range of topics about a firm, its customers, management, finances, and the economic environment within which it works. We provide a summary of each firm in Appendix C, "Description of Subject Companies."

Practical Valuation Tests: Three Example Companies

We conclude in this chapter that the labor theory of value is not a sound basis for determining the market value of a privately held firm, but that the theory had some insight into human behavior. Following are the results of testing the theory on three representative firms.

S. H. Importers

S. H. Importers has two primary sources of income: selling or renting antiques, and producing antique replicas. If we were to attempt to value the firm using the labor theory of value, we might conclude that because more labor is devoted to reproducing antique furniture, according to this theory, it should be more valuable than furniture pulled from inventory or purchased secondhand. However, antiques are generally more expensive and considered more valuable than reproductions.

Thus, the labor theory of value fails to even explain why the company charges different prices for different services or goods. Scarcity, as Ricardo pointed out, influences overall value. While labor inputs are useful in economic discussion, they do not determine value or provide much help toward estimating the value of the overall company.

A & A Consulting

A & A Consulting relies heavily on the direct products of its labor force to turn a profit. The company's billing practices are similar to those of a law firm, in which each employee has his or her own rate schedule and clients are billed by the hour. Employees detail what they do for a project and for how long. Projects are budgeted based on the amount of time each team member is expected to spend. At a glance, the historical performance metrics indicate the firm is much more profitable when the number of billed labor hours is high than when it is low.

For this particular firm, labor inputs play a large part in predicting profitability. Furthermore, the profit of the firm divided by the number of hours varies considerably and could be negative. Thus, although useful, the labor theory fails as a basis to estimate the company's overall value.

Exxon

Exxon is a large publicly traded corporation and a dominant oil producer. Its stock price on major stock exchanges in different countries can be tracked relatively easily.

The labor theory of value provides little basis for predicting the market capitalization or share price of such a firm. Indeed, it is difficult to arrive at a labor-theoretical stock market pricing model, because the labor that went into creating a publicly traded company appears to have little relationship with the market capitalization or stock price.

8 VALUE IN NEOCLASSICAL ECONOMICS

OUTLINE OF THIS CHAPTER

This chapter continues our tour of valuation theories, examining what is familiar to genera-tions of college students and probably the most commonly articulated theory of economic value. In this chapter, we do the following:

- Review the emergence of the neoclassical or "marginalist" school of economics in the late nineteenth century.

- Describe the formal elements of the neoclassical microeconomics model, including a recapitulation of the notions of supply, demand, price, and commodities.

- Observe that the basic theory is powerful and essentially unchallenged in describing the mechanics of price-setting for commodities in an open marketplace.

- Review elements of the theory that are not settled: utility, risk aversion, and time preference. We also further discuss some observations about human nature that have recently been organized into a "behaviorist" school that challenges some of the neo-classical model's tenets.

- Discuss the weakness of the neoclassical model of the operation and even existence of businesses.

- Test the usefulness of the neoclassical theory as a basis for estimating the value of three representative firms.

THEORIES OF VALUE: NEOCLASSICAL ECONOMICS

The Introduction of the Marginalist School

The modern formulation of value is based on neoclassical economics, which is the origin of such common ideas as the notion that prices are set when "supply equals demand." For many people, the *only* formal economics they know is neoclassical economics.

Neoclassical thinking was pioneered by the French economist Léon Walras, the English economist William Jevons, and the Austrian economist Carl Menger, all of whom authored seminal books in the 1870s.[1] An identified neoclassical school arose around the beginning of the twentieth century. I attribute its popularization throughout the Western world to Alfred Marshall, and in particular to his *Principles of Economics*, first published in 1890.[2] Indeed, the *neo-* prefix in *neoclassical* is clearly established by the great care with which Marshall distinguishes the "marginalist" thinking of Jevons, Walras, and himself from the classical economists Adam Smith, David Ricardo, and Thomas Malthus.[3]

In general, neoclassical economics rests on three principles:[4]

1. People have rational preferences about possible outcomes, including work, leisure, and purchases. These preferences are often modeled in a "utility" function.

2. People act to maximize their utility, and firms act to maximize profits.

3. People act independently on the basis of the information available to them.

The neoclassical school is sometimes called the "marginalist" school because it relies on the decision tool of comparing the incremental or *marginal* utility of an action with its marginal cost. *Marginal* refers to the next unit (or last unit) in a transaction. As Alfred Marshall wrote in the preface to the first edition (1890) of *Principles of Economics*:

> Under the guidance of Cournot, and in a less degree of von Thünen, I was led to attach great importance to the fact that our observations of nature, in the moral as in the physical world, relate not so much to aggregate quantities, as to increments of quantities, and that in particular the demand for a thing is a continuous function, of which the "marginal" increment is, in stable equilibrium, balanced against the corresponding increment of its cost of production.[5]

Price-Setting in the Marginalist Setting

The neoclassical school dismisses the labor theory (from the "classical" economists such as Ricardo and Smith) as a determinant of value. Instead, *prices* are set in a marketplace, by the interplay of supply and demand. Here, *supply* and *demand* are the collective wishes, decisions, and intentions of many individual business managers, investors, workers, and consumers.

Prices are set in such a market when the marginal unit of demand matches, at a specific price, the marginal unit of supply. Other suppliers may wish to supply more (at a higher price), but the buyers will not pay the higher price. Similarly, marginal buyers may wish to purchase more, but at a price too low to attract suppliers. Thus, the marginalist school solves the paradox that bedeviled the classical economists: why are diamonds more expensive than water, when water is vital to life itself? To the neoclassicists, it is the marginal demand and supply in a specific market, at a specific time, that sets the price. This is the case regardless of the intrinsic value of the commodity or how much labor was expended to get it.

The Firm and Price in the Neoclassical Model

The supply-and-demand explanation of price-setting in a marketplace does not explicitly contemplate the firm that produced the good. Furthermore, it does not include any explicit allowance for the wages of the salesperson, rent for the shop owner, payments to farmers or other suppliers, or taxes to the government. Indeed, if demand for a specific good or service is low enough (meaning that nobody in the marketplace is willing to pay enough to cover all the costs of production and distribution), the neoclassical model indicates that the market price will be below the cost of producing it.

Thus, at first glance, price-setting in the marginalist school treats the firm just as it treats all persons in the chain of events that result in the goods being brought to the market: it largely ignores them. As we see shortly, that does not mean that the *costs* of production and distribution are ignored, just that they are treated in an abstract and limited way.

Of course, businesses cannot remain in operation unless they are able, over time, to make a profit on the sale of their goods and services, which rewards and motivates the owners of the firm. The neoclassical model relies on an abstraction for this, by assuming that the cost of production for firms in a competitive market include the cost of financing the firm at market rates of return for capital investment. Anything over this market rate of return on capital investment is considered *rent*, or supranormal returns, which is assumed to attract other businesses into the market until the rent disappears.

With this abstraction, we can draw neat supply-and-demand charts that show how a market-clearing price is set where the supply curve meets the demand curve. We can also show—with a little more effort—how this same point is where the firm's marginal cost equals its marginal revenue. This is the one-period profit maximization model that is familiar to generations of economics students. Indeed, it is essentially the same model that the pioneers of the neoclassical school outlined almost a century ago.[6]

Additional information on the formal mathematics of the neoclassical model is discussed in Appendix B, under the section titled "Mathematics."[7]

Two Assertions About the Neoclassical Model

Given this brief summary, we now offer two assertions to be tested later: first, an endorsement of the neoclassical model for a particular purpose, and second, a provocative condemnation of its inadequacy for a different purpose.

1. *Superiority of the neoclassical model of the retail market.* The abstractions about the firm incorporated in the neoclassical model make sense in a one-period model that establishes the basic market dynamic for *price-setting* in the retail market for common goods and services. If we are interested only in this important topic, the neoclassical model has no superior.

2. *Inadequacy of the neoclassical model of the firm.* The same model makes little sense when our focus is the *firm*. In particular, the neoclassical model is grossly inadequate when we consider a multiple-period market involving considerable risks (including risks of bankruptcy) for the firm and its workers; one in which the ability to obtain capital investment

at "market" rates (or to earn "market" rates of profit) are tenuous concepts or unsupportable assumptions; or one in which technology, regulation, taxation, and market conditions change regularly.

CONSUMER WELFARE AND PREFERENCES

Microeconomic Foundations: Preferences and Utility

The microeconomics of consumer welfare is the basis for our understanding of work, leisure, and trading among human beings. The neoclassical model, especially when considered together with newer developments, is the dominant model for these aspects of human behavior.

Microeconomics begins with a small set of axioms about consumers. We summarize the essential axioms next. (A reader with knowledge of microeconomics may note that we deliberately avoid assuming certain characteristics that sometimes appear in theoretical economic models.) We state these axioms using informal language. Certain mathematical properties are stated more formally in Appendix A, under the section titled "Microeconomics; Utility." Additional resources are also described in Appendix B, under the section titled "Mathematics."

Consumer Preference Axioms

1. *Consumers prefer some things to others.* Consumer preferences are the basis of consumer decisions. Among the decisions consumers make are choosing to spend money or save it and choosing whether to work (called *labor*) or to not work (called *leisure*). Such decisions are *trade-offs*, because, for example, a consumer trades off some leisure time to work and therefore earn money; the same consumer may trade off some savings to purchase a vacation.

We say that these preferences indicate that certain activities give them greater *utility*, meaning pleasure, usefulness, and other desirable features. In particular, consumers *prefer* one bundle of commodities and other choices over another. The utility function is a mapping of these preferences.

2. *Consumers have rational preferences.* Elements of "rational" preferences include the following:

- *Consumers prefer more, rather than less, of any commodity that benefits them.* For example, four days of vacation is more desirable than three; two new shirts are worth more than one. Note that consumers do not necessarily prefer bigger or more expensive items; they may prefer a smaller car, for example, along with more money for vacation. However, given the choice between a desirable small car plus one week of vacation, and two small cars and two weeks of vacation, they prefer the latter.

- *Consumers benefit in decreasing amounts as the number of units they consume of any commodity grows.* This is perhaps best illustrated by food; people insist on enough food for subsistence, and work hard to ensure that they have enough to eat. Given the opportunity, they work harder to purchase more food as well as delicacies. However, at some point they will not work harder just to eat more, or more expensive, food.

- *Consumers prefer less risk about the future to more risk.* This concept is known as *risk aversion*, and ignoring it can have serious implications for business valuation. We discuss the topic further later in this chapter, under the section titled "Risk Aversion."

- *Consumers prefer to receive income now rather than later.* By receiving income, we mean receiving the power to acquire goods to use immediately or reserve for future consumption. Food is a good example. First, when you are hungry, you much prefer eating food now rather than later. Second, if you can stock your pantry with food for the next month, you would rather have it stocked right now than to have a promise from the store that it will give you the goods next month. Indeed, for subsistence items such as food, you *must* consume some amount now in order to survive to the next time period. We discuss this topic in some detail later in this chapter, under the section titled "Incorporating Time Preference."

3. *Consumers make decisions based on information available with reasonable effort.* Consumers form expectations about the future based on information they have in the present. This is quite obvious from a real-world perspective. Acquiring additional information has a cost, and consumers consider this cost in relation to the risks and benefits they perceive about the underlying decision.

For example, a person may spend a lot of time researching home prices and pay a broker's fee for some assistance in evaluating many available properties. The same person may stop at the first fast-food restaurant he sees on the way home from seeing a house. There is no contradiction here; the home buyer knows that it is costly to sell one home and buy another, and devotes his limited time to that decision rather than researching the available restaurants.

4. *Consumers act on their preferences.* At first blush, this is just logical housekeeping. It makes no sense to assume consumers have a strong desire to do something, but never do it. Furthermore, we want to look at the *actual behavior* of people, rather than mysterious (and unobservable) utility functions.

This led to the formulation of an axiom that consumers reveal their preferences by their actions. There is a formal name for a common version of this axiom: the *weak axiom of revealed preference*, or WARP.[8] However, the axiom has come under fire from behavioral economists, in particular those contesting the unprovable connection between thought and action.[9]

Commonsense Observations About Human Nature

Note that we do *not* assume a number of restrictive concepts that sometimes appear in models used in finance or economics or implicitly embedded in some valuation practices. In particular, unless there is a specific reason for the contrary, we reserve the following assumptions about human nature:

- *People are different.* Not all consumers have the same preferences. As a corollary, a "representative consumer" or "representative investor" may not indicate the average or aggregate behavior of a group of people.

• *People change their minds, and life happens to all of them.* Consumers not only *may* change their preferences over time, they almost certainly *do*. This includes their preferences regarding risk, the value of leisure time, the desire to pass along gifts and bequests to others, and the importance of moral, social, or group values relative to pecuniary interests.

• *People care about risk.* Consumers are not *risk neutral*, meaning that they are likely to be willing to pay something other than the expected value of a future earning opportunity. (We discuss risk aversion in more detail later in this chapter, under the section titled "Risk Aversion.")

• *People have a certain regard for government and other institutions—and a healthy skepticism as well.* People do not assume that all government policies are unchanging; they may attempt to avoid or evade some taxes and other government strictures; and they may distrust institutions such as banks and regulatory agencies. Implications of this commonsense assumption include: people often hold precautionary reserves against the possibility that some institution does not fulfill its promises; and people may anticipate that future government policies will require them to pay additional taxes. (See the section later in this chapter titled "Incorporating Time Preference.")

• *People consider the cost of acquiring information and the risk of not having it.* In the standard neoclassical model of a single-period market, consumers are assumed to have complete information and to obtain this information costlessly.[10] Such an assumption may be close to true in certain markets at certain times, but it is clearly not the case for major macroeconomic variables or general business conditions.[11]

These commonsense reservations have been extended into an entire subfield of economics, which we discuss shortly.

INCORPORATING TIME PREFERENCE

Recognition of Time

We can incorporate into a theory of the consumer a recognition of time and a preference for events along the time spectrum.[12] This is called the *time preference* of consumers. As we discussed earlier, we assume consumers rationally prefer to receive consumption items now, rather than later. In particular, we assume that consumers apply a *discount* to the future price of a commodity when they determine the amount they would be willing to pay today.

The discount rate, the gross rate of return on assets, and the interest rate are all related, though not identical, concepts. We review the conventions we use for these in Appendix A, under the section titled "Consumer Budget Variables: Payoffs, Returns, and Discounting."

Rationales for Time Preference

The neoclassical economist Irving Fisher, in his 1930 book *Theory of Interest*, devoted significant effort to explaining the time preference of consumers and investors:

When present capital wealth, or capital property, is preferred to future, this preference is really a preference for the income expected to flow from the first capital wealth, or capital property, as compared with the income from the second. The reason why we would choose a present fruit tree rather than a similar tree available in ten years is that the fruit yielded by the first will come earlier than the fruit yielded by the second. The reason one prefers immediate tenancy of a house to the right to occupy it in six months is that the uses of the house under the first leasehold begin six months earlier than under the second. In short, capital wealth, or capital property, available early is preferred to the capital wealth, or capital property of like kind, available at a more remote time simply and solely because the income from the former is available earlier than the income from the latter.

Thus all time preference resolves itself in the end into the preference for comparatively early income over comparatively remote, or deferred, income. Moreover, the preference for early, or prompt, income over late, or deferred, income resolves itself into the preference for early enjoyment income over deferred enjoyment income. (Fisher, 1930, chap. 4, sec. 2)

Indeed, Fisher described six "personal characteristics" that affected a person's time preference, or "impatience":

We have seen, therefore, how a given man's impatience depends both upon the characteristics of his expected income stream, and on his own personal characteristics. The rate of impatience which corresponds to a specific income stream will not be the same for everybody. . . . Impatience differs with different persons for the same income and with different incomes for the same person. The personal differences are caused by differences in at least six personal characteristics: (1) foresight, (2) self-control, (3) habit, (4) expectation of life, (5) concern for the lives of other persons, (6) fashion. (Fisher, 1930, chap. 4, sec. 9)

We shall return to these important considerations later in this book because they have broad implications for the value of private businesses, and because they are too often neglected in contemporary treatments of finance and valuation.

The Consumer's Savings Problem: First Glance

The fundamental consumer optimization problem is often shown as Equation 8.1. Here the consumer attempts to maximize the discounted sum of lifetime utility, which is determined by decisions involving consumption and work effort made in each time period. A discount factor (between zero and one) is multiplied by the satisfaction from each period. Although not shown, the standard model also allows for some savings across periods, and for some income as well.[13] This is sometimes called the *consumer's savings problem*, because it often boils down to a question of how much to save and how much to consume.

Many income-approach valuation models also implicitly adopt this assumption. This includes Equation 3.1, M-M Proposition I, the neoclassical investment rule described in Chapter 3, "The Failure of the Neoclassical Investment Rule," and Equation 3.2, M-M Proposition II.

Equation 8.1 Consumer's Optimization Under Time-Separable Utility

$$\max_{c,n\in\Gamma} U_t = \sum_{t=0}^{\infty} \beta^t [u(c_t, n_t)]$$

where:

β = discount factor, $0 < \beta < 1$

t = time index

c_t, n_t = consumption and work effort at time t

U_t = lifetime utility

Γ = allowable consumption and labor choices given
           budget constraint and physical limitations

However ubiquitous this assumption in finance, it is clearly *not* correct for investors and entrepreneurs in many (if not most) cases in which they face major investment decisions. We illustrate this with an example and discuss two causes—risk aversion and aggregation across time—in more detail.

TIME-SEPARABLE AND RECURSIVE UTILITY

Time-Separable Utility

It is common in the finance, economics, and professional valuation literature to evaluate the current market value of a financial asset using a net present value algorithm of some type. Such net present value formulas (and expected net present value formulas) usually imply that the benefits of receiving income on different dates are different only because of the underlying discount factor. Such models incorporate an implicit assumption of *time-separable utility*. As the name implies, this means that you can separate the benefits of receiving income on separate dates and then add the benefits together.[14]

In general, neoclassical economics holds that the fundamental consumer optimization problem is to maximize his or her lifetime utility. Traditionally, this assumption was transferred to finance in a form that presumed time-separable utility. Thus, many of the valuation theories presented in this book, including the traditional income approach, are implicitly based on time-separable utility.

Recursive Utility

An alternative specification is known as *recursive utility*.[15] This specification includes a separate *aggregator function*, which governs how expected utility in one period is aggregated with expected utility in another. The aggregator function encodes the outcome of future expected (and possibly uncertain) outcomes in the form of a current-period equivalent. Such an aggregator takes into account time and may also take into account risk.[16] Note that simply allowing the discount rate to vary over time is not the same as recursive utility, and fails to capture certain important dynamics related to an entrepreneur's behavior.

We assume, even with our commonsense reservations about preferences, that consumers choose between two possible nearly identical courses of action based on the fact that one results in a larger payoff (or costs less) in the short term. However, there are many reasons why an investor, consumer, or worker would *not* choose between two possible courses of action solely on the basis of their expected net present value of the future payoffs. For entrepreneurs and investors, particularly relevant reasons for this include risk aversion (such as aversion to bankruptcy) and the importance of timing of income and expenses when the financing of the firm arises primarily from household resources.

Differences Among Valuation Approaches

The ten valuation approaches presented in this book fundamentally differ on the presumed form of function utility. In particular:

- The value functional approach and the modern recursive equilibrium explicitly adopt recursive utility.

- The traditional income and asset approaches, the classical and neoclassical economics approaches, and modern portfolio theory are explicitly based on time-separable utility.

- The traditional market and real options ("expanded net present value") approaches represent something of a mixed answer or an agnosticism to the question. With the market approach, one may interpret the question as moot, as value is determined by what the market will pay in any current time period. Similarly, the real options approach often involves adding (in a time-separable manner) the estimated value from an income-approach method to one arising from an option valuation, with the latter method possibly relying on recursive utility.

- The complete-market approach relies on time-separable utility in its concept of the law of one price and assumption about portfolio formation. However, the complete-market assumption makes the question moot to some extent.

We return to this topic in Chapter 16, "The Value Functional: Applications," under the section titled "State and Control Variables in the Value Function Approach."

RISK AVERSION

One aspect of utility functions bears further attention: the treatment of risk.

In general, consumers, workers, and investors are not indifferent to risk, because they are people. As people, they take chances when driving, dating, voting, and investing; they sometimes gamble for entertainment or purchase lottery tickets that they know are likely to expire worthless; and occasionally they lend money to friends who they believe are unlikely to repay it. All these—not just the "investment" activities—reflect attitudes about risk.

Common sense indicates that people prefer less risk to more risk, at least when they are thinking about their own income, assets, and other indicators of welfare. This explains why people purchase life insurance and put aside savings for a "rainy day" while at the same time purchasing lottery tickets and gambling at casinos. The first set of actions reflects a reasonable prudence and precaution about basic comforts of life, in which the consumer forgoes income in order to achieve some peace of mind. The second set of actions reflects a desire for entertainment and the indulgence of a handful of risky bets. If the amounts of money involved in the second set of actions are small relative to the consumer's current income, then any associated losses could be considered entertainment expenses, even if they are imprudent entertainment expenses.[17]

The Interesting Case of Risk-Neutral Behavior

We noted in Chapter 3, "The Failure of the Neoclassical Investment Rule," that the standard neoclassical investment or NPV rule relies on the expected net present value of future earnings. Using the expected net present value as the basis for decisions does not mean the investor is ignorant of risk; indeed, he or she could be very sophisticated about risk. However, it implies a *risk-neutral* attitude, meaning that the investor intends to pay neither more nor less for an investment that exhibits a higher amount of risk (measured by the variance in returns).

Other mathematical models, which are discussed in detail in Chapter 10, "Arbitrage-Free Pricing in Complete Markets," extend this in a formal way to all securities purchased in a complete market, provided a new set of "probabilities" can be defined and used. At this point, we simply note that consumers are generally *not* risk neutral in their attitudes, and any risk-neutral valuation model should be considered carefully.

Specifying Attitudes Toward Risk

Sometimes, in both empirical and theoretical work on investment behavior, one must specify the form of the utility function in a manner that subsumes an attitude about risk. As motivated by the preceding discussion, one indication of those attitudes is the relationship between the amount of money at risk and the amount of total income (or assets) a person has. These have been formulated in both a relative and absolute sense as parameters known as the *coefficient of absolute risk aversion* and the *coefficient of relative risk aversion*, as well as a parameter for *prudence*.

Additional information is available from the resources listed in Appendix B, under the section titled "Mathematics."

Common Attitudes Toward Risk

A common attitude toward risk can be described by example. Consider a reasonably conservative homeowner who occasionally gambles away a small portion of his paycheck, but avoids risky investments and risky behaviors. Such a person exhibits an aversion to risk that is larger for large bets than for small bets and an attitude of indulging in gambling only after all of life's key expenses are already covered. Such a person is said to exhibit *decreasing absolute risk aversion*. Together with a general risk aversion (implied by purchasing insurance and maintaining household savings), this implies that a person is prudent in the economics sense.

THE NEOCLASSICAL MODEL AND THE ACTUAL WORLD

Observations on the Neoclassical Model

The neoclassical model is built on some critical assumptions and abstractions. Observe the importance of the following assumptions in the management of an actual firm:

1. *The revenue and cost functions are differentiable in every action.* This is a standard assumption in many mathematical derivations; without the assumption one cannot use many of the modern tools of comparative statics. However, many of the important actions in an actual firm are extremely "lumpy" in either the time or quantity dimension. For example, hiring workers cannot be done instantaneously; productive work often cannot be purchased in small increments; the scale of a facility is difficult to change in the short term; advertising and other services often require contracts that extend over a specific time period; prices and wages cannot be quickly changed.

This means that even if the manager of the firm could reduce the revenue and cost functions to a defined equation, that equation probably could not be differentiated at many points. Thus, the optimization rule "marginal cost equals marginal revenue" technically falls apart, because nobody can compute a marginal cost or revenue with respect to numerous important actions.

2. *The revenue and cost functions are known.* In fact, the revenue and cost functions of operating businesses are impossible to know completely. Managers often use short-term approximations and rules of thumb based on their own experience. However, even in well-managed firms with expensive management information systems, the total and marginal costs of each item produced are at best an estimate and often a rough guess.

For example, consider service providers. What is the cost of producing, say, next month's auto mechanic services at an auto dealer, this week's advertising at a radio station, or the management of the local bank, dentist's office, or creative artist's enterprise this quarter? For most of those firms, accounting data could be used to estimate the direct costs of some services, but for the indirect costs, the firms rely on estimates and cost allocation methods that are approximations at best.

Are these flaws just examples of imperfect information or a stake through the heart of the neoclassical model? We consider this again in Chapter 15, "The Value Functional: Theory."

3. *The maximization takes place in one period.* In the neoclassical model, the entire profit maximization occurs in one time period of undefined duration. Of course, the neoclassical model synthesized by Debreu (1959) and others contemplates time, discounting, and interest. However, the firm's optimization occurs in one period, and the discounting process is largely used for consumers and their budget constraint.

This is a critical difference from the actual business environment. In nearly every actual business, decisions in one period affect the results in the next. Thus, the entrepreneur cannot maximize profits in one period without affecting the next. As Vickers (1987, chap. 1) noted, even Alfred Marshall "at the high tide of neoclassicism" had complained of "the great importance of the element of time . . . the source of many of the greatest difficulties in economics" and noted similar observations about the weakness in the model by Walras, Robinson, and others.[18]

We return to this observation in Chapter 15, "The Value Functional: Theory."

4. *Firms are managed without agency problems or asymmetric information.* The neoclassical model not only assumes the profit maximization objective; it abstracts out of the equation the people that are supposedly maximizing. Over the past half century, much effort has gone into identifying two dimensions of difference between the firm and the people managing it. These two dimensions—agency and asymmetric information—are dealt with explicitly in this text.

5. *Firms are managed without uncertainty.* The fundamental equations of the static neoclassical model do not include factors that are uncertain.[19] This, among other assumptions, allows a neat equilibrium to result between the desires and budget constraints of consumers and the profit maximization of the producer, with the market system doing the matchmaking.

The neoclassical model has been modified to allow uncertainty about future certain variables in the cost or revenue functions. Many of these models incorporate a restrictive assumption about known distributions of those outcomes. Although this is a movement toward reality, it is not the reality of the manager of the firm; the assumption about perfect foresight has been replaced with one of perfect knowledge of distributions.[20] Debreu helped extend the model to include a certain kind of uncertainty, that of multiple possible states of nature, in which prices could be different.

6. *There is no bankruptcy for the firm or limited liability for investors.* In the neoclassical model, the financing and organization of the firm is essentially ignored, as are the institutional factors of bankruptcy and limited liability. We can observe implications of this: employees, suppliers, investors, lenders, and customers ignore things such as the firm's reputation, management, and financing. They can do so because, under the assumptions of the model, there is no risk to contracting with them. We can also observe the lack of concepts for risky start-up firms or distressed firms. On top of that, the neoclassical model implicitly assumes that the costs related to organizing, managing, and financing a firm involved in producing a product are the same among different producers.

Does the Neoclassical Model Describe the Actual World?

These assumptions are clearly violated in actual markets, even in the most efficient markets involving publicly traded firms and goods that are close to simple commodities. Furthermore, these violations are not merely technical, or of little importance. In particular:

1. The revenue and cost functions are probably not known and are not differentiable in every action. Even if they can be roughly approximated in well-established firms (for example, by a equation of fixed cost plus variable cost per unit), they are almost certainly "lumpy."

2. Firms are systematically operated with agency problems and asymmetric information. The existence of such problems is known by investors and managers.

3. All the important functions of the firm involve uncertainty. Furthermore, neither the future values of important variables nor their distributions are known with certainty.

4. The objective function of the firm must be different from profit maximization, and the inputs to the objective function cannot be simply cost and revenue.

5. The maximization of the objective function takes place over multiple periods.

6. Bankruptcy and limited liability are features of the marketplace for investment capital, labor, materials, and products. Employees, investors, customers, and suppliers consider the risks that a firm will go out of business when they make contracts with the firm. Thus, the costs for a new entrant to a market are usually much higher than for existing entrants.

All in all, the neoclassical model does not stand up well under these conditions.

Historical Criticism of the Neoclassical Model of the Firm

The failures of the neoclassical model of the firm have not been wholly ignored over the past century. For example, the great American thinker Herbert Simon (1916–2001) noted that the theory of the firm was "classically, the theory of a monolithic entrepreneur" back in 1964.[21] More recently, Harold Demsetz, summarizing decades of research since the publication of Ronald Coase's theory, noted newer research had only partially filled in three gaping holes in the neoclassical concept of the firm.[22]

Accounting researcher Mike Lucas (2003) summarized dozens of studies involving accounting and econometric methodologies, concluding that "the empirical evidence supporting neoclassical price theory is not strong and much of the research that generated it is methodologically flawed."[23] Lucas associates this modern "reality gap" with the "marginalist controversy" of the 1950s within the field of economics, in which competing explanations were offered to explain the apparent failure of firms to act as the neoclassical model expected them to act.[24]

These criticisms confirm my own observation about entrepreneurs: they do not attempt to maximize current-period profits. The neoclassical model simply does not fit them.

A Counterexample: The Oil Industry

Before we accept the preceding bold claims—that *none* of the assumptions about firms embedded in the neoclassical model hold in reality—let us look for at least one industry in which they might be approximately true.

The best candidate for such a counterexample would be one that sells similar products across the globe, so that the products would be similar to the "commodity" in the neoclassical model. It would also be convenient if the commodity in question has been in use for many decades and is essential to the economies of most nations. Furthermore, we would like to see an industry in which the commodity can be sourced from multiple countries and traded on well-developed markets. Finally, we would like to find an industry in which many such companies issue publicly traded securities that are duly followed by investment analysts from a diversity of investment brokers.

And—if it is not asking too much—we would like these firms to use similar technology for producing and distributing their products. Going still further, beyond a reasonable request, it would be convenient if there were some kind of cartel that either controls or dampens the fluctuations of prices.

Unbelievably, we have such an industry: global petroleum producers. If the neoclassical model of the firm were ever going to work, it should work here.

It does not.

The cost functions involve considerable risks of exploiting certain fields, not to mention political risks. These cannot be hedged easily or at all. Even when reserves are known, the ability to ramp production up or down is limited by the costly drilling platforms and distribution system. Considering that a supertanker can carry a half million long tons of cargo, it is difficult to add or subtract, say, a few thousand gallons of gasoline to your capacity.[25] Clearly, none of these firms engage in single-period profit maximization. Their management and investment structures involve significant agency problems and information asymmetries. Even with insurance and other risk hedging offered by the deep market for petroleum products, a large producer can sustain potentially ruinous damage, such as through outright confiscations of its property, a tanker disaster, additional taxes, or breakup of its operations.[26] This, along with other business risks, has resulted in occasional bankruptcies even in an industry that claims some of the largest firms in the world.

Even in this industry, which is as close to the ideal as any of which I am aware, every single one of the neoclassical assumptions about the firm is violated.

Conclusion: The Failure of the Neoclassical Model of the Firm

The evidence just cited clearly demonstrates the failure of the neoclassical model of the firm to adequately describe the price mechanism as well as other decisions of the firm. That does not mean that managers are indifferent to profits or that they do not attempt in some way to maximize them within narrow constraints. However, it does mean we must find another basis for a theory of firm value.

THE BEHAVIORIST SCHOOL

Bounded Rationality and Rational Expectations

Two important advances in the economic theory of information, and the use of this information in forming expectations about the future, have been developed in recent decades. One important theory is called *rational expectations* in a specific sense in macroeconomics.[27] Another is called *bounded rationality* in the microeconomics sense.[28] Both these theories call into question certain implications drawn from common models of neoclassical economics (and, in particular, finance) and macroeconomics.

We touch on only some of this research—much of which is still being debated—in this book. However, we can motivate its relevance by asserting that consumers use available information to make decisions, consider the cost and benefits of acquiring additional information, and care about risk. These are all included in our list of commonsense reservations about human nature.

In general, we assume that actual investors, managers, and consumers exhibit bounded rationality and a weak form of rational expectations about macroeconomic conditions and government policy.[29] However, many of the standard models of economic behavior do not include these assumptions, so we attempt to distinguish between theoretical models and those intended to describe actual behavior.

The Behaviorist Critique

A recent critique of the neoclassical school arises from what is loosely called the *behaviorist critique*. Although this critique is too new to have a coherent model or neatly defined set of principles on which nearly all adherents agree, some consistent themes bear noting. The following are three recurring themes in behavioral finance and economics:

1. *Heuristics.* People often make decisions based on approximations, rules of thumb, and other shortcut methods that appear to stray far from the mathematical models of formal neoclassical analyses. One aspect of this is called bounded rationality, and we discuss it explicitly under the topic of profit maximization.

2. *Framing.* The way a problem or decision is *framed*, or presented to the decision maker, affects the decision. In economics, decisions often involve much information, some of it misleading, almost all of it incomplete. Furthermore, decision opportunities are frequently presented to consumers and investors by interested parties.

3. *Market inefficiencies.* Some observed market outcomes appear contrary to predictions of the neoclassical model, especially when the neoclassical analyses are based on rational expectations and market efficiency. These include apparent mispricing of financial assets.

This organization of thought should be considered tentative, as the definition of behaviorist thought is contested.[30] However, all three themes appear in this excerpt from an essay by Joe Pomykala (2004):

> For more than a century the canonic model of decision making in economics had been based upon a rational economic agent *homo economicus* who simply maximized expected utility or happiness given a preference ordering over different states of the world, and thus human behavior could be reduced to an optimization problem solvable by differential calculus (given cardinality, but only ordinality is sufficient). Behavioral economics considers human decision making to be more complex. People have limitations in knowledge and cognitive ability. Rationality may be considered bounded by such constraints.
>
> The normative assumptions in economics describing human behavior had become increasingly challenged by descriptive models and empirical evidence showing that behavior was inconsistent with the canonic model, such being labeled as "irrational." For example, choices between identical states of the world depend upon reference points generating

framing and endowment effects or inconsistent and non-transitive preferences. Systematic bias or error exists in the decision making process as agents apply heuristics to economize on the decision making process. (Pomykala, 2004)

Differences Between the Behavioral and Classical Approaches

A clear distinction, and one that both enthusiasts and critics would accept, is that the behaviorist school emphasizes research that is quite different from much of neoclassical economics. In particular, it focuses on experimental research, often uses survey methodology, and draws insight from psychology. What is sometimes called *game theory* is frequently employed, including experiments that use game theory concepts to attempt to elicit responses that illuminate consumer or investor preferences, as well as ways of learning and patterns of acting.

Frequent topics in behavioral finance include the *equity premium puzzle* and the discount on closed-end mutual funds.[31] Both of these involve empirical data on widespread market behavior that fails—consistently—to match the standard neoclassical finance model's predictions.

Prospect Theory

One of the clearest insights from behaviorist school is *prospect theory*, which seeks to explain how people make decisions.[32] Prospect theory postulates that people display the following characteristics when considering a risky proposition: reference dependence (thinking about a gain or loss in reference to a specific level); loss aversion (more concern with losing money than with gaining it); and diminishing sensitivity (less concern with highly unlikely events).[33] Such attributes of human nature seemingly defy the expected utility theory formulation of John von Neumann and Morgenstern (1944), on which much of modern finance is based.

References on Behavioral Economics and the Classical Reassertion

The reliance of neoclassical economics on axioms of revealed preference imply that decisions are made in a way that drastically simplifies human considerations. Of course, any drastically simplified model of human behavior fails some empirical tests. Prospect theory provides a set of alternative models of choice that explain some decisions the traditional models do not.

Is this a failure of the neoclassical model, or simply an improvement within the same framework? That debate continues.

There is a small literature on both behaviorist finance and reassertions of neoclassical finance in the face of behaviorist criticism. In addition to the sources cited earlier, the behaviorist approach in economics is represented in the Nobel Prize lecture given by Daniel Kahneman in 2002 and the *Microeconomics* text by Sam Bowles (2005); behavioral finance papers are collected in the volume edited by Richard Thaler (2005). A forceful reassertion of neoclassical finance against these critiques was authored by Stephen Ross (2005). We see Ross's exposition of the neoclassical model again in Chapter 10, "Arbitrage-Free Pricing in Complete Markets," under the section titled "The 'No Arbitrage' Principle."

VALUATION APPLICATION: NEOCLASSICAL EQUILIBRIUM

We conclude that neoclassical theory is not a sound basis for determining the market value of a privately held firm because no such firm actually fits within the neoclassical model. To illustrate this, we examine our three representative firms described in Appendix C, "Description of Subject Companies," and describe how each firm contradicts a significant assumption of the neoclassical theory.

S. H. Importers

S. H. Importers does not engage in single-period maximization, because focusing on single-period profits would go against common sense. Unless its managers were anticipating closing the company's doors, they would plan for additional time periods.

A & A Consulting

A & A Consulting relies on its labor force to provide consulting services to its clients. However, its cost of operations is difficult to know completely. As with most firms, managers at A & A Consulting rely on estimates and cost allocation methods to approximate project budgets. Given that A & A Consulting tailors much of its services to its clients' requests, costs are not fully known until the project is completed. Additionally, even if a project is well managed, it can become more expensive and involved than projected.

These unknown costs are a fact of life for this firm. The neoclassical model fails to take it, and other matters, into account, and therefore would not be a good valuation principle for A & A Consulting.

ExxonMobil

Very large publicly traded firms do often behave, in aggregate, in a manner that is roughly consistent with the neoclassical model. Such firms often have adequate access to financial markets and professional management and are large enough to ride out bad economic times. They also have the management resources to attempt to calculate such concepts as marginal cost for key products.

However, the neoclassical model fails completely in describing the company's actions to develop future reserves. These are real options that the firm must purchase now to remain valuable in the future. Such purchases (particularly because they cannot be adequately valued using the neoclassical investment rule) would appear irrational within a strict neoclassical microeconomics model, because they violate the profit-maximization principle.

9 MODERN RECURSIVE EQUILIBRIUM AND THE BASIC PRICING EQUATION

INTRODUCTION TO MODERN RECURSIVE MICROECONOMICS

Rejecting the Neoclassical Model of Valuation

We summarized three foundations of microeconomics, including consumer preferences and utility, time preferences, and risk aversion, in Chapter 8, "Value in Neoclassical Economics." However, the neoclassical model was essentially a one-period model, which is clearly inadequate for valuation purposes. Moreover, despite the ubiquity of the neoclassical investment rule in valuation and finance literature, we demonstrated that it systematically leads to incorrect business decisions and is routinely overruled by actual managers and investors.

Motivating the Modern Recursive Model

The recursive microeconomic model is an extension of the neoclassical model that directly addresses the time preference and aggregation inadequacies of the neoclassical model. It also indirectly addresses issues of risk aversion that are not handled properly in the neoclassical model.

We motivate this extension by stating the consumer's savings problem across multiple periods. This can be done concisely using a few mathematical equations, although these equations differ in a specific and crucial aspect from those of the neoclassical model. We derive a solution for the consumer's saving problem that can be used as the basis for almost all contemporary theories of investment behavior—including the mean-variance framework, CAPM, factor models, and numerous variants. This is an ambitious target, and carefully setting out the manner in which consumers make decisions in this setting is critical to achieving it.

Key Topics in This Chapter

In this chapter, we review the mathematics of modern recursive microeconomics, with a focus on valuation and finance. This does not do justice to the recursive model as a setting for evaluating a large universe of problems. However, it does provide an excellent basis to discuss key topics in valuation, including the following:

- The consumer's savings problem in a modern, multiperiod form. This problem establishes a recursive form of decision making that is the basis for both the modern microeconomic model and the value functional approach to business valuation presented in Chapter 15, "The Value Functional: Theory."
- The basic pricing equations (BPE) that result from solving the multiperiod consumer's savings problem.
- The widespread applications of the BPE in understanding asset pricing models.
- A pervasive and powerful interpretation of the basic pricing equation: the existence of the stochastic discount factor (SDF).
- Recursive optimization.
- An introduction to the formal mathematics of states of nature and the state-preference theory of pricing.

Using these tools, we present advanced valuation techniques in later chapters.

Remark: Is the Recursive Method a New "School"?

For the purpose of identifying valuation principles, we distinguish between the neoclassical model and the modern recursive model, implying that the recursive model is significantly different from those of the neoclassical school that have dominated economics for more than a century. However, this separation is novel at this point. In particular, the recursive model has only recently become defined enough—and described sufficiently in reference texts—to separate it from its neoclassical roots.[1] Readers should consider whether the recursive method presented here, and further developed in Chapter 15, "The Value Functional: Theory," warrants such consideration.

RECURSIVE DECISION MAKING: CONSUMER SAVINGS

A Second Glance at the Consumer's Savings Problem

The consumer's savings problem consists of maximizing utility across multiple time periods; in each period, the consumer decides how much to save and how much to consume. Variations of the problem include allowing uncertainty about future earnings and asset prices, exploring different forms of utility functions, and incorporating government policies and their effects on after-tax real income, prices, and consumer behavior.

We presented a similar version of this classic model in Chapter 8, "Value in Neoclassical Economics," under the section titled "Incorporating Time Preference." This version, however, subtracts a separate labor income variable, adds a market for lending and for investing, and explicitly assumes random variation in income and therefore the need for consumers to form expectations about the future.

We express the objective function, discount factor, time index, and control variables as follows:[2]

1. The objective of the consumer is to maximize expected utility over multiple time periods, where utility arises from consumption and where a discount factor is applied to future consumption. Of course, the amount of consumption in any period must be feasible, so the amount of consumption in any one period must fall within a budget constraint. This objective is stated in Equation 9.1.

Equation 9.1 Consumer's Savings Problem: Objective

$$\max_{c \in \Gamma} U_0 = E_0 \sum_{t=0}^{T} \beta^t [u(c_t)]$$

where:

β = discount factor, $0 < \beta < 1$

t $= 0 \dots T$

c_t = consumption at time t

$u(c)$ = utility from consumption

Γ = feasible consumption given income and savings

2. The utility function fulfills the classical assumptions as well as most (but possibly not all) of the commonsense reservations listed in Chapter 8, "Value in Neoclassical Economics, under the section titled "Consumer Welfare and Preferences." At this point, it is unnecessary to state a particular form.

3. The consumer receives earnings from a stream of dividends on stock holdings, which may be stochastic. The price of a share (net of the dividend) is p_t and the dividend is y_t at time t. For such investments, we denote the number of shares of stock owned as N_t.

4. The consumer can also borrow from or lend to others at a known gross rate of return. Denote the gross payout on bonds issued (meaning borrowing) or purchased (meaning lending) by L; L is negative if the bonds are issued. The issue price of bonds is $1/R * L$, where R is the gross rate of return.

5. The consumption, savings, and lending decisions in each period determine the amount of their assets in the next period. This asset value process is expressed in Equation 9.2.

Equation 9.2 Consumer's Savings Problem: Asset Value Process

$$A_{t+1} = L_t + (p_{t+1} + y_{t+1})N_t$$

6. Each period, the consumer faces a *budget constraint* that prevents him or her from spending money that is not available. Reflecting market reality, we also impose a limit on borrowing and lending. The budget restraint can be expressed as an inequality, in which the total expenditures on consumption, together with any lending and purchasing of stock, cannot exceed the total amount of assets A_t. Consumption that meets the budget constraint is considered part of the feasibility set Γ (see Equation 9.3).

Equation 9.3 Consumer's Savings Problem: Budget Constraint

$$c_t + R^{-1}L_t + p_t N_t \leq A_t$$

where:

c_t = consumption

A_t = total asset value; $A_t > 0$

L_t = net bond purchases (lending)

N_t = net shares purchased

p_t = price of shares

c_t is feasible $\Leftrightarrow c_t \in \Gamma$

7. There are a set of easily incorporated additions to the model, which we do not include here, such as a predictable stream of labor earnings, a variation in an exogenously determined gross rate of return, and many government fiscal and monetary policies. These, in general, do not affect the key results.

Solving the Problem

We now have a concisely stated problem. It would be relatively easy to solve if it involved no uncertainty and only one period. Indeed, this is the standard neoclassical model.[3]

However, we have allowed an indefinite number of periods and a stochastic stream of earnings. We also allowed consumers multiple choices, including borrowing, selling stock, lending, buying stock, and consuming either the income from each period or the income from previous periods. On top of all that, we charged consumers with forming an expectation about future events, gave them a budget constraint that would not allow them to borrow without prospect of repayment or consume what they cannot purchase, and saddled them with a utility function that makes them work strenuously to avoid consuming all their earnings and therefore facing starvation.

To solve this problem, we use a *recursive* technique. We develop this further in Chapter 15, "The Value Functional: Theory," under the section titled "Introduction to Dynamic Programming."

Recursive Utility Maximization

Consider the problem of maximizing utility in only two periods, rather than an indefinite number. The consumer has the following *control* variables that he or she can change: L and N, which are the amounts of the two types of investment assets the consumer owns. The consumer's problem is to maximize the utility from consuming a long, discounted stream of earnings that arise from both random stock dividends and known rates of return on bonds, as expressed in Equation 9.1.

If we narrow this down to just two periods, we can use differential calculus to find the maximum. The solution to the maximization problem is summarized in Equation 9.4. Each equation describes a trade-off between the gain from the earnings stream on one of the assets (determined by one of the control variables) and the loss of utility from forgoing consumption.

Equation 9.4 Euler Equations for the Consumer's Savings Problem

$$u'(c_t)R^{-1} = E_t \beta u'(c_{t+1})$$
$$u'(c_t)p_t = E_t \beta (p_{t+1} + y_{t+1}) u'(c_{t+1})$$

These equations are known as *Euler equations* in mathematical finance. They express the condition of a stationary value of a function, in terms of balanced changes (differentials) in an integral value, caused by changes in one or more variables.[4] In this case, the small change made by consumption in time t must balance the small change made by the (expected, discounted) change due to consumption in time $t + 1$.

Because the problem has been formulated as a two-period one, the same problem repeats in the next time period (with the trade-off at that point between *that* period's immediate consumption and the future earnings that would come from forgoing it). This repeated analysis of similar considerations, in which the result from one iteration feeds directly into the next, is known as a *recursive* model.

THE BASIC PRICING EQUATIONS

The following are symbols used in text of this section:

β subjective discount factor

m_{t+1} stochastic discount factor (SDF)

x_{t+1} payoff at time $t + 1$

B_t price of pure discount bond at time t

Deriving a Stochastic Discount Factor

The Euler equations represent consumer behavior derived from first principles. Note that we did not discuss portfolios, efficient markets, arbitrage, CAPM, profits, betas, martingales (neither the bird nor the mathematical concept), separating hyperplanes, diffusions, or Brownian motion; used only one Greek letter; and somehow found an equation that specified how much a consumer would pay for an investment asset. This result is quite powerful . . . but the rest of finance still has some relevance!

This Euler equation relates the price we would pay today for an asset to the payoff it will produce tomorrow.[5] In the discussion of this model, we confine the term *asset* to assets that can be readily converted to a monetary equivalent each period. These may be termed *investment assets*. To derive this, start by rearranging the second Euler equation so that the price the consumer would pay is on the left side and the expected returns are on the right side. Then rearrange the terms so that all the factors based in the consumer's own preferences are separated from those that arise from the payoffs of the asset, as shown in Equation 9.5.

Equation 9.5 Deriving the Stochastic Discount Factor (SDF)

$$u'(c_t)p_t = E_t\beta(p_{t+1} + y_{t+1})u'(c_{t+1})$$

$$p_t = E_t\beta(p_{t+1} + y_{t+1})\frac{u'(c_{t+1})}{u'(c_t)}$$

$$p_t = E_t\left\{\beta\frac{u'(c_{t+1})}{u'(c_t)}(p_{t+1} + y_{t+1})\right\}$$

Now adopt the convention that the *payoff* of an asset is defined as the selling price and any attached dividend, and denote the payoff at time $t + 1$ as x_{t+1}. Similarly, define the combination of the subjective discount factor β with the ratio of marginal utilities for next period and this period as the *stochastic discount factor*, and denote this by m_{t+1}, as shown in Equation 9.6.

Equation 9.6 Payoffs and the Stochastic Discount Factor

$$x_{t+1} \equiv p_{t+1} + y_{t+1}$$

$$m_{t+1} \equiv \beta\frac{u'(c_{t+1})}{u'(c_t)}$$

Basic Pricing Equation

Substitute into Equation 9.5, deriving the stochastic discount factor (SDF) using the terms we just defined. We now have a useful representation of asset prices, derived almost entirely from first principles. We call this the *basic pricing equation* (Equation 9.7):[6]

Equation 9.7 Basic Pricing Equation (BPE)

$$p_t = E(m_{t+1}x_{t+1})$$

This powerful equation relates the payoff from *any asset* to the current price a consumer would be willing to pay for it. Of course, many of the terms embedded on the right side of the equation (such as subjective discount factors and the marginal utility of consumption in the next period) are not directly observable. However, even if the terms are indirectly observable, the equation is a powerful tool.

Basic Pricing Equation: Application to Risk-Free Bonds

We can apply this tool to a theoretical risk-free government bond and see if the equation correctly prices it. The price of a pure discount bond today is B_t, which generates a payoff of B_{t+1} in the next period. Because it is a risk-free, pure discount bond, we already know the price in the next period will be the gross risk-free rate of return multiplied by the price today.

Using the fact that the future payoff is known, and the definition of the gross risk-free rate of return, we can confirm that the basic pricing equation correctly prices the government bond (Equation 9.8).

Equation 9.8 The Risk-Free Rate in the Basic Pricing Equation

$B_t = E(m_{t+1}B_{t+1}) = m_{t+1}B_{t+1}$, as the bond payoff is known

$B_{t+1} = B_t R^f = B_t(1 + r^f)$, where r^f is the risk-free interest rate

Furthermore, we can derive the relationship between the risk-free rate and the stochastic discount factor (Equation 9.9):

Equation 9.9 Risk-Free Rate: Price of Purchasing One Unit with Certainty

$B_t = m_{t+1}[B_t(1 + r^f)]$ (substituting for the future bond payoff)

$1 = m_{t+1}R^f$

Summary of the Modern Recursive Model

The findings in this section and the basis for them are important enough to summarize:

1. Consumers maximize utility, which is a function of consumption.

2. They maximize it over multiple periods, subject to a budget constraint that may involve prices set exogenously (outside their control). However, these multiple-period time spans can be broken into a series of two-period decisions.

3. They may have an income (or "endowment") stream, which may vary over time.

4. Uncertainty about the future requires them to form expectations about income, prices, and their needs with partial information; they form these expectations using only the information they have at the time.

5. They "discount" expected future earnings, using a factor that is larger than zero but (typically) smaller than one. This discount rate is based on the consumer's own preferences. Nothing requires this discount rate to be equal to a specific interest rate in the market, or to be equal to anybody else's discount rate, or to be the same over time, or to be "risk neutral."

6. They may defer consumption in one period, which can be interpreted as "saving" money. If so, they can "lend" it to another person by buying bonds or invest it in stocks. Either option earns them a payoff that they can use to fund consumption in a later period.

7. By applying a technique of calculus, we determined that the optimum consumption path for a consumer-investor would be secured by balancing the pain of the loss of

consumption today with the pleasure of the discounted future earnings from saving the money involved. We termed the equations that expressed these relations *Euler equations*.

8. A useful encapsulation of the Euler equations, with respect to investment assets, can be derived by combining the subjective discount rate of the consumer with the consumer's marginal utility functions for consumption in this period and the next. The product of the discount rate and the ratio of these marginal utilities can be termed the *stochastic discount factor*.

9. Using the stochastic discount factor, an expectation operator, and a future payoff, we can express the current price of any investment asset through the *basic pricing equation*.

CLASSICAL INVESTMENT THEORIES

This section presents classical theories about investment behavior and asset pricing, which are firmly grounded in the axioms of consumer behavior. Although these theories have strong bases in both theory and evidence, they are often omitted from texts in mathematical finance or valuation or relegated to footnotes or obscure references. I present them here because they describe human behavior, including the behavior of humans that start businesses and invest in them.

Investment as Precautionary Savings

The fundamental budget constraint of individual consumers gives rise to a basic theory of investment: precautionary savings.

Consider a consumer-investor with a stream of earnings, a stream of expenditures, and the ability to invest some of the excess of earnings over expenditures in one period. Such a consumer makes a consumption-savings decision each period, knowing that saving today means the ability to consume more tomorrow. This, to be clear, is not a theory about behavior; it is merely the budget constraint.

Now allow uncertainty about the future earnings stream; even a little uncertainty is enough to demonstrate the point. Does the consumer consume all the earnings in each period?

Although we have introduced the concept of a utility function to model consumer preferences, we need not make much use of math here. People like to eat. They take great pains to ensure that they and their families will have something to eat in the future.[7] If you recognize that there is some uncertainty about earnings in the future, you can expect that people will save something to ensure they will eat in the future.[8] We could observe that proverbs such as "Save for a rainy day" have a firm basis in utility theory; to be more correct, we should observe that utility theory matches the proverbs!

Given this simple model of consumer behavior, we see a clear interest for *precautionary savings*, or savings in one period to allow for future consumption in a later period. This is one motivation for investment.

Milton Friedman's "Permanent Income" Theory

The famous permanent income theory of Milton Friedman provides another, expanded basis for savings and investment behavior.[9]

Friedman theorized that consumers would recognize that their expenditures were largely under their own control, whereas their earnings were partially outside their control. The reasons for this lack of control are extensive; they include macroeconomic variations (the "business cycle"), changes in technology, management changes, health, interpersonal relationships, weather, and numerous other factors. Based on this, Friedman theorized that consumers would plan their household budgets based on their expectations about *permanent income*, which is the income they expect to receive on a regular basis. Income sources that were irregular and surprising (such as an unexpected bonus, gift, tax refund, prize, inheritance, or other windfall) would be viewed as outside the permanent income, and a part would be saved. On the other hand, an unexpected reduction in income (such as the unfortunate complement of any item in the previous list) would be viewed as temporary and not affecting the underlying household budget except by a relatively small amount.

Extensive empirical testing has confirmed Friedman's insight, and some form of permanent income effect on consumer behavior is incorporated in most sophisticated macroeconomic models. We note it here because of its importance in understanding investment behavior. If savings is identical to investment at the consumer level, then a part of the investment pool available at any time to purchase equity interests in businesses (or lend them debt) is dependent on factors related to consumers' preferences to smooth their consumption overtime.

Irving Fisher's Theory of Investment

Irving Fisher wrote the *Theory of Interest* in 1930, which established the basis for much of what later became modern finance. Fisher's terminology is more primitive than the finely sliced terms we use today, but his admonition to readers bears repeating:

> Many people think of interest as dependent directly on capital. As already suggested, it will help the reader to proceed in the following analysis if he will try to forget capital and instead think exclusively of income. Capital wealth is merely the means to the end called income, while capital value (which is the sense in which the term capital is ordinarily used by interest theorists) is merely the capitalization of expected income. (Fisher, 1930, chap. 4, sec. 1)

Here Fisher states two important points: First, he identifies the primacy of income, which he describes at some length as including "enjoyment income" and the income necessary to purchase the basic goods of life. Capital wealth, which we would probably call *capital investment* today, is merely a means to an end; the end is the ability to secure enjoyment income. Second, he states that "capital value . . . is merely the capitalization of expected income." We dispute the modern overextension of this notion into the "NPV equals value" rule, but there is no doubting the fundamental notion that the value of an investment is based on expected future benefits.

Robert Lucas's Asset Pricing Theory

Another influential model of investment was created by Robert Lucas, Jr., who, like Milton Friedman, was awarded the Nobel Prize in Economics.

Lucas (1978) created what is sometimes called the *endowment model*. In it, consumers were given a stream of endowments (income) and a desired consumption pattern. Given this stream of income and the availability of both consumption goods and investment assets, they adjust the asset prices to an equilibrium. This equilibrium is the point that maximizes the sum of current utility and future discounted utility from consumption.[10] This forces the consumer to balance the benefits of investing (and earning a return) that secures future consumption against the greater enjoyment of consumption today.[11] It incorporates the logic of the Euler equations (see Equation 9.4) into a restriction on asset returns.

The Lucas model is the basis for much theoretical and some empirical investigation into why asset prices change, and introduced the recursive approach to mainstream economics. Note that "asset prices change" means that asset *returns* also change.[12]

The Lucas model originated a series of models that are generally classed as *consumption-based models* because they begin at the beginning: consumers' desires for consumption.

BUBBLES, PUZZLES, AND TROUBLES

The Equity Premium Puzzle

An important example of research on consumption and investment behavior is the paper by Mehra and Prescott (1985), in which they attempted to compare the expected rate of return on equity investments among American investors with their implied discount rate on consumption, using a variation of the Lucas model. Relying on a number of assumptions about the type of utility function of consumers and their risk aversion, they produced a curious result: the *risk premium* on equity investments appears to be much too high for the implied discount rate on consumption.

This apparent deviation has been dubbed the *equity premium puzzle* and has been the subject of many empirical and theoretical efforts at unwinding the result.[13] The data underlying the puzzle seem to be a convenient platform from which to contest a number of controversial topics in economics, including behavioral economics critiques, the question of whether the underlying macroeconomy (and the attitude of consumers within it) has changed over time, whether the specifications of the underlying equations are correct, and whether we are using the proper data.

Asset Pricing and "Bubbles"

One may wonder where in these theoretical models the notion of a "bubble" exists. One may assume that bubbles are completely irrational moments in financial history, epitomized by the infamous Dutch tulip bulb mania of the seventeenth century. Dutch traders at the time bid up the price of tulip bulbs (from the tulip flower) to spectacular highs, and then watched them crash.

In fact, economists have difficulty allowing too many "irrational" incidents to clutter up their world, because recurring human behavior must be, in order to fulfill the axioms of the field, in some sense rational.[14] There must be some basis for episodes in which—in retrospect, of course—everyone agrees that the market was wrong.

We do not need to look back at Holland three centuries ago for just such an episode; the memory of the dot-com bubble still resonates in U.S. financial markets. Although the phenomenon is too recent (and painful for some) to define precisely, experts nearly universally accept that a technology stock market bubble existed in the United States in the late 1990s. During that period, stock market prices for shares in firms whose business plans involved selling something on, in, or via the Internet diverged sharply upward from a plausible earnings-related basis.

Are bubbles only an irrational excess—or are there fundamental reasons why investors participate in them?

In fact, we can derive bubble behavior for rational investors, at least in some circumstances. In particular, the no-arbitrage assumption that is the basis for many modern asset pricing theories—and, tempered by search and transaction costs, modern investment behavior—assumes that some investors participate in bubbles. In some circumstances, a motivated and prepared speculator should make a low-risk investment in a security that has an upward-trending price.[15] Also, a market that includes a large number of stocks with an extremely high price/earnings ratio may be called a "bubble," even when many of the stocks had little historical earnings on which to calculate a P/E ratio. Thus, a bubble that crashes could be a case of firms with rapidly growing—but greatly uncertain—earnings, with the uncertainty resolved toward lower permanent earnings rates.[16] The careful investor notes the ambiguity in the use of the term *bubble*.[17]

Models that explicitly incorporate bubbles are described, for example, in Ljungqvist and Sargent (2004, sec. 13.3) and Cochrane (2001, sec. 20.1).

Consumer Behavior vs. Business Investment Models

The insights gained from the classical theories of precautionary savings and permanent income provide the basis for a critique of naive theories of the value of businesses.

Consumers' interest in saving money (and therefore the size of the investment capital pool) primarily depends on *their* situation. Consumers assess the risks inherent in the future, and form their attitudes toward that risk, based on their own information and preferences. It is reasonable to assume that their interests in such topics as sophisticated investment models, company strategic plans, and portfolio advice are subordinated to their desires to adequately secure their future consumption. It is also reasonable to assume that their attitudes toward risk are not adequately captured by such convenient assumptions as von Neumann–Morgenstern utility functions, that they have limits to their borrowing power, and that they operate in incomplete markets.

If this is the case, what does it mean for classical models of business value?

At first glance, it is clear that the factors listed here directly affect the pool of investment capital available for publicly traded and privately held firms. Furthermore, these are acute factors for entrepreneurs, who often finance some of their business efforts, either implicitly or explicitly, from household savings. Thus, the models that bypass these primary concerns of consumer-investors and consumer-entrepreneurs cannot adequately explain business value.

This does not bode well for the neoclassical investment rule, nor for CAPM and related portfolio models (which rely on specific assumptions about wealth and risk preferences), nor for the neoclassical microeconomics model, nor even for a modern recursive model that fails to capture these factors. This observation should motivate a close reading of the models presented in Chapter 10, "Arbitrage-Free Pricing in Complete Markets"; Chapter 11, "Portfolio Pricing Methods"; and Chapter 15, "The Value Functional: Theory."

VALUATION APPLICATION: MODERN RECURSIVE EQUILIBRIUM

Although the modern recursive equilibrium extends the neoclassical model by addressing its inadequacies, including time preference, it is not suitable for determining the market value of a privately-held firm. Just as in Chapter 8, "Value in Neoclassical Economics," no value would be determined by applying this theory to the subject companies described in Appendix C. In particular, the restriction of the model to what we termed investment assets (those that can be readily converted to cash in any period) rules out the financing structure used by approximately 99 percent of businesses.

To be specific, refer again to the most comprehensive formulation of the consumer's savings problem presented in this chapter, shown in Equation 9.2 and Equation 9.3. Suppose a consumer wants to buy (or sell) a unit of stock in one period. Of the three sample companies we consider, only one would have equity shares that could be purchased in anything close to this manner. And for that one, the consumer must accept the "market price." Furthermore, if the consumer is also an investor in a closely held business, then the equations do not separate the financing, operating, and consuming decisions of the entrepreneur-consumer.

However, parts of this theory provide the basis for other valuation theories. In particular, the consumer's savings problem establishes a recursive form of decision making used in the value functional approach, which is described in Chapter 15, "The Value Functional: Theory."

IV FINANCE THEORIES OF VALUE

10 ARBITRAGE-FREE PRICING IN COMPLETE MARKETS

In this chapter, we discuss one of the breakthrough concepts of modern finance: the use of the *no-arbitrage* principle in complete markets as the basis for the powerful mathematics of *risk-neutral* or *equivalent martingale* pricing. The field of study that now surrounds these principles is sometimes called *neoclassical finance*. This model relies on two intertwined assumptions: the existence of complete markets and the assumption that market participants act to ensure that no arbitrage profits are possible.

Elements of This Chapter

This chapter covers the following topics:

- The origin, simplicity, and elegance of the no-arbitrage principle
- The importance of the complete-market assumption and its connection to the no-arbitrage principle, including the "first fundamental theorem of finance"
- The portion of the world's markets in which the assumption of complete markets is approximately correct, and the remainder where it is clearly not correct
- The serious difficulties in applying the technique in incomplete markets
- The mathematics of the neoclassical finance model, beginning with the notion of state-contingent prices
- The related concepts of risk-neutral discount rates, martingales, and equivalent martingale prices
- The pricing of assets in complete markets

We conclude that equity in private businesses is almost always traded in incomplete markets. However, the reality of incomplete markets does not mean that complete-market valuation is confined to academic use; the serious student of valuation must understand its underlying principles.

THE NO-ARBITRAGE PRINCIPLE

No Arbitrage as a Staple of Finance

If there is one staple of modern finance, it is the following: there shall be no persistent arbitrage in traded markets.[1] Conceptually, *arbitrage* is buying something and reselling it for a profit, without taking any risk. If you can make something from nothing, merely by trading, and incur no risk in doing it, you have found an arbitrage.

Metaphorically, this is an extension of the "no free lunch" rule in microeconomics and the "no perpetual motion machine" rule in physics. Mathematically, as we will see, the no-arbitrage assumption can have powerful effects—although it requires significant assumptions.

A nice summary of the meaning and role of the no-arbitrage assumption is the following from Fonseca's *History of Economic Thought*:

> An asset market is, naturally, the "place" where assets are traded and, consequently, purchase prices are determined. The determination of asset prices is one of the main concerns of financial theory and there are a handful of competing theories. However, one of the central features of asset pricing theory, or, as some claim, "the one concept that unifies all of finance" (Dybvig and Ross, 1987), is the stipulation that, in equilibrium, asset prices are such that "arbitrage" is not possible.
>
> It might be useful to clarify at this point what is meant by "arbitrage." Intuitively, many people would associate arbitrage with "buying low and selling high." More formally, an arbitrageur purchases a set of financial assets at a low price and sells them at a high price simultaneously. (Fonseca, 2008)

This central assumption has been a key to many innovations in finance. This includes, of course, the no-arbitrage pricing model, but also the Modigliani-Miller theorem, the Black-Scholes model of option pricing, and the intertemporal capital asset pricing model. Indeed, the no-arbitrage assumption has become ubiquitous enough to earn its own acronym (NA) in finance texts.

The Antecedents of No Arbitrage in Finance

The notion of risk-neutral pricing originated with Kenneth Arrow (1953, 1970) and Jacques Drèze (1971), although many authors cite Stephen Ross (1978) as the originator of the modern variation. The identity of the precise originator(s) of the theory is a subject of minor dispute.[2]

Many of the breakthrough techniques were developed in the 1970s.[3] However, the central and nearly constant assumption in such models is the no-arbitrage assumption, based on the powerful insight that participants in active markets do not allow others to make riskless profits through arbitrage among different securities. However, the antecedents of the no-arbitrage principle in finance appeared earlier.

State pricing or state-contingent securities were developed by Arrow (1953).[4] This powerful concept became one of the bases for mathematical microeconomics, neoclassical finance, modern recursive equilibrium microeconomics, and the value functional theory. However, I believe that the work of Arrow and Gerard Debreu should be viewed as establishing the modern synthesis of neoclassical microeconomics, rather than the no-arbitrage principle of neoclassical finance.

Assertion, Overreach, and Counterattack

The review of classical and neoclassical microeconomics we completed in the previous chapters does not reveal any clear antecedents to the no-arbitrage principle as the cornerstone of a pricing model. That is not to deny that the neoclassical model of supply and demand presumes a market in which like commodities are sold for a like price. However, the existence of a market and a market-clearing price does not mean no arbitrage. Furthermore, the intersection of price and demand is *not* a market discipline formed by any application of the no-arbitrage principle.[5]

Thus, the neoclassical finance model should be seen as a *bona fide* breakthrough in recent intellectual history. However, because the neoclassical finance model is so new, it suffers from the weaknesses of any new theory. One of those weaknesses is the tendency of its adherents to assert the application of the theory well outside its proper boundaries. We discuss shortly whether this has occurred with neoclassical finance. In particular, we discuss an intellectual counterattack from what is currently called the behavioral school. The boundaries of neoclassical finance, and the degree to which the criticisms of it are valid, are much in dispute today.

STATE-CONTINGENT PRICES IN COMPLETE MARKETS

In this section, we use the wonderfully concise presentation of Stephen Ross (2005, chap. 1) as a guide to pricing in the neoclassical finance model. However, I have added a number of explanatory and historical notes, particularly where different authors approach the topic from different perspectives.

States of Nature

The neoclassical model of finance incorporates powerful tools for modeling uncertainty in the real economy. The fundamental concept is that there are multiple possible *states of nature* or simply *states*. Formally, there is a state space, Ω, that includes a finite number of possible states of nature (Equation 10.1).

Equation 10.1 States of Nature

$$\Omega = \{\theta_1, ..., \theta_m\}$$

The state space includes m mutually exclusive states of the world that can occur at a specific time, such as $t = 1$. At that time, uncertainty is resolved; the world is in one and only one of the m states of nature.

State-Contingent Securities; Portfolios

Assume that a finite number of traded assets exist in a complete market. In particular, assume n traded assets with a set of prices captured in a *price vector* at a specific time. Given these prices, an investor constructs *portfolios* consisting of certain amounts of each asset. The elements of the portfolio vector η are sometimes called the *weights* (Equation 10.2).

Equation 10.2 Price and Weights Vector

$p = [p_1, ..., p_n]$ price vector

$\eta = [\eta_1, ..., \eta_n]$ weights vector

$i = 1, ..., n$ index of securities

The cost of a portfolio is a weighted sum of the individual elements of the price vector, with the weights being the amounts of each security. In vector terms, the cost is the dot product of the portfolio weight vector and the price vector (Equation 10.3).

Equation 10.3 Portfolio Construction and Cost

$$p\eta = \sum_i p_i \eta_i \quad (i = 1, ..., n)$$

State-Contingent Prices

Now, with the n securities and m possible states of nature, we can construct a matrix of possible prices at time $t = 1$. These prices can be considered *security payoffs* in the sense that they either produce a cash payoff (such as a dividend) or can be sold for the market price.

A security that pays off in a specific state is sometimes called an *Arrow security*; the matrix of payoffs in different states is called the *Arrow-Pratt tableau*, after Kenneth Arrow and John Pratt, two pioneers of the field. The tableau includes m rows that represent the states of nature and n columns that represent the asset prices (Equation 10.4).

Equation 10.4 Arrow-Pratt Tableau of State-Contingent Prices

$$G = \left[g_{ij} \right] = \text{payoff of security } i \text{ in state } j \ (\theta_j)$$

$$G = \begin{pmatrix} g_{11} & \cdots & g_{1n} \\ \vdots & \ddots & \vdots \\ g_{m1} & \cdots & g_{mn} \end{pmatrix}$$

The Complete Market

In this introduction to the complete-market model, we made two broad generalizations that we note here:

1. We specified a limited number of traded assets. Such assets could include what we call securities (stocks, bonds, etc.) that can be frequently traded. In actual markets, this could also include land, buildings, nonstock business equity interests, and commodities for which there is no active market.

2. We also specified a limited number of states. However, thus far we made no connection between the n states and the m securities.

In fact, an important property is largely determined by these factors; it is called market *completeness*. Intuitively, market completeness means there are traded securities with enough variety that they represent in their prices all investment risks. Another intuitive description of a complete market is one in which all risks can be insured.

We discuss this topic more extensively later in this chapter, under the section titled "Complete and Incomplete Markets." The question of whether markets are sufficiently complete for private firms is an important one throughout this book.

THE NO-ARBITRAGE ASSUMPTION

Arbitrage Defined

Within this model, we can formally define *arbitrage* as a portfolio with no negative payoffs and with a positive payoff in some state of nature. An arbitrage is like a bet that can be made in which it is not possible to lose while still possible to win.

Mathematically, an arbitrage is a portfolio, η, with the properties described by Equation 10.5.

Equation 10.5 Definition of Arbitrage

$p\eta \leq 0$

and

$G\eta > 0$

In an arbitrage, there is a strict inequality for at least one component of the budget constraint. Thus, an *arbitrage portfolio* is a portfolio with the following characteristics:

- It is formed using current prices to purchase and sell securities, so the net cash outlay (cost) is zero or less than zero.

- Given the tableau of possible payoffs (future prices), the portfolio does not lose money under any state of nature.

- It has a positive payoff in at least one state of nature.

In other words, it is a no-cost portfolio with no negative payoffs, and with a positive payoff in some state of nature.

The economic intuition is that given an opportunity to purchase such a portfolio (and earn money with no risk), investors would hurry to exploit it. Intuitively, this rush to fill the vacuum would eliminate true arbitrage opportunities quickly, as prices and quantities adjusted. Thus, almost all mathematical finance models—and many other models—assume no arbitrage.

COMPLETE AND INCOMPLETE MARKETS

Complete Markets

Stephen Ross (2005, chap. 1) defines a complete market as follows:

> one in which for every state θ_i there is a combination of the traded assets that is equivalent to a pure contingent state claim, in other words, a security with a payoff of the unit vector: one unit if a particular state occurs, and nothing otherwise.[6]

This rigorous mathematical definition benefits from some supplementary intuition. A complete market is one in which *all* the market risks are priced in traded securities. For example, a complete betting market would be one in which you could always bet in favor of, or against, your favorite sports team. Note that "complete" *does not mean* "good" prices or "low" prices. Indeed, in complete markets some risks are priced extremely high—but they are priced!

One may think of a complete market as one in which you could buy insurance for every possible risk, even if the price of that insurance was very high. Returning to the sports-betting example, in a complete market you could always find someone to bet for, and against, every team in the league, on every game.

The Assumptions Behind No Arbitrage

It is worth considering the critical assumptions embedded within the notion of a complete market. Here are a few:

1. *There are few (or no) transaction costs.* Note that significant transaction costs would prevent a speculator from making profits from exploiting small differences in prices. Recall the inequalities in Equation 10.5. If transaction costs are introduced, then the payoff to the seller of a security differs from the amount paid by the buyer.

2. *Traded assets are available to a wide class of investors.* The complete-market model assumes that all risks that affect securities prices are traded in an open market. Now consider assets that are not commonly traded, where the factors underlying their value (such as earnings of a company, or supply and demand for a commodity, or other natural or market conditions) vary over time. The payoff from such a security would be difficult to represent in the tableau presented in Equation 10.4.

In addition, consider assets that are not available to certain investors but are available to others. The tableau of payoffs now differs depending on the investor. Hence, the fundamental pricing model no longer works for some investors, some assets, or both.

3. *There are constant returns to scale in the investment opportunity set.* In theoretical models, it is easy to assume an investor can purchase any amount of a security and borrow any amount of money to do so.[7] For investors with substantial liquidity operating in widely

traded markets and comfortably within the band of credit constraints, this is probably correct most of the time. However, it is clearly *not* correct for many investors all the time, and for all investors some of the time.

In particular, it is generally *not* true for most investors in privately held firms, for at least two institutional reasons: the firms themselves do not have open trading in their equity; and the investors rarely have the ability to borrow against the equity.

Other assumptions could also be seen as corollaries to those given here: that security prices are set in a market that is not effectively controlled by managers of the underlying companies; that securities are well defined and separate from labor earnings of employees of the underlying firms; and that default and counterparty risks are either absent or explicitly included in the span of the securities offered.

We discuss the applicability of these restrictive assumptions further later in this chapter, under the section titled "Incomplete Markets and the Firm."

Mathematics of Complete Markets

In mathematical terms, a complete market can be represented by a tableau of payoffs G that is of *full-row rank*. In linear algebra, *rank* is a measure of the number of linearly independent columns or rows in a matrix.[8] Intuitively, we can think of a complete market as one in which every portfolio can be represented by a sum of the security payoffs in the market; such a sum is a linear combination.

If we attempt to establish a linear relationship between the price vector p and the tableau G, we find the following equation for prices as a linear combination of payoffs (Equation 10.6).

Equation 10.6 Prices as a Combination of Payoffs

$p = qG$

When G has full rank, this equation has a unique solution (Equation 10.7):

Equation 10.7 Unique Price in a Complete Market

$q = pG^{-1}$

This existence of a unique solution in a complete market is the basis for many models of pricing assets.

Incomplete Markets

It is easy to see that an *incomplete* market is one in which you cannot buy or sell certain risks. For example, all of the following would be examples of incomplete markets:

- A gambling market in which nobody was interested enough to bet for or against certain teams, or wager on the outcome of certain games

- An insurance market in which one could not purchase insurance for certain risks, such as the risks of a person failing to get a job in her chosen field
- A market for investment capital in which you could not find investors willing to purchase securities in some companies
- A market for houses in which, even if a seller were willing to drop the price, he would be unable to find an immediate buyer

One may get the notion, from reading economics books, that markets are nearly complete. On the other hand, attempting to buy or sell household items or insure against everyday risks provokes the suspicion that we actually live in a world full of incomplete markets.

Mathematics of Incomplete Markets

When the tableau *does not* have full rank, the equation has many possible solutions. Thus, in an incomplete market, there is *no unique pricing vector.*

Stripped of its mathematics, this means that the theory provides *no justification for a specific price for any security* in an incomplete market. This holds even if you have excellent information about future payoffs and the likelihood of future states!

We return briefly to incomplete markets later in this chapter, and discuss the implications in the section titled "Incomplete Markets and the Firm."

PROBABILITIES AND RISK-NEUTRAL PROBABILITIES

Motivating Risk-Neutral Probabilities

We may wish to use familiar net present value mechanics to value an uncertain stream of future earnings. A clear manner of doing this is to combine two powerful mathematical tools:

1. The time-discounting mechanism of present value
2. The probability-weighting mechanism of expected value

Indeed, we introduced this mathematical notion as *expected net present value.* In this setting, pricing using an expected net present value calculation requires a known set of possible future payoffs, a known probability of states that would produce these payoffs, and a known discount rate. With such knowledge, we could calculate the expected net present value of the payoffs. However, the real world rarely provides unambiguous discount rates and known probabilities. This is a problem.

Risk-Neutral Probabilities in Complete Markets

Turning the Problem on Its Head
To motivate the powerful technique of risk-neutral pricing, we turn this problem on its head:

1. Start with *known* prices and payoffs. This leaves two unknowns: the probabilities and the discount rate.

2. Simplify the problem further by assuming that the appropriate discount rate is the risk-free rate, because the purchaser will not be accepting any risk. Now the discount rate, prices, and payoff set are known.

3. Use the $E(NPV)$ formula to supply "probabilities" that make the current price equal the "expected" value of the future payoffs, when discounted at the risk-free rate.

These latter probabilities are unusual. They are *not* expressions of the likelihood that the events (states of nature) will actually occur.[9] Instead, they are fractions that weight the potential outcomes, so that the weighted-and-discounted sum of the payoffs equals the current price. These fractions are called in the literature *risk-neutral probabilities* or *twisted probabilities*. They meet the critical mathematical features of probabilities; they sum to one, and they are all positive. Thus, they are mathematically *equivalent* to the actual probabilities.[10]

Formal Definition

Risk-neutral probabilities are defined as a set of probabilities that price an asset as the expected value (using these probabilities) of the discounted future payoffs, where the discount rate is the risk-free rate. In simpler terms, they are ratios that match up the prices in the market to the payoffs on securities, along with the risk-free rate. We use a symbol for these probabilities such as $\tilde{\pi}_i$. Here we use a *tilde* (which looks like a twisted bar) to denote the use of the risk-neutral measure; perhaps for this reason, some authors describe the *twisted expectation* as the expectation taken with respect to the twisted probabilities.

Formally, consider an asset with payoffs in the next period that vary by state (Equation 10.8):

Equation 10.8 Payoffs Across States

$$z = (z_1, ..., z_m)$$

Then the risk-neutral pricing operator $V(z, \pi, r)$ establishes the value of the uncertain future payoffs as the probability-weighted sum of the risk-free-rate-discounted future payoffs (Equation 10.9):

Equation 10.9 Risk-Neutral Pricing

$$V(z, \pi, r) = \frac{1}{1 + r^f} \tilde{E}(z) = \frac{1}{1 + r^f} \sum_{i=1}^{m} \tilde{\pi}_i z_i$$

or

$$V(z, \pi, r) = R_f^{-1} \sum_{i=1}^{m} \tilde{\pi}_i z_i$$

where:

$$R_f^{-1} = \frac{1}{1 + r^f}$$

Here the summation is taken across m states of nature, with the risk-neutral measure being the basis for the probability. The arguments of the pricing operator include the payoffs, the probabilities, and the discount rate.[11] The second version of the formula uses the convention R^{-1} as the inverse of the gross discount rate.

State Prices and the Pricing Kernel

We can define the complementary notions of *state prices* and *state pricing density* to determine prices in complete markets, using the same logic as before. The state price density, or the *pricing kernel*, is a vector of factors for *states* (Equation 10.10):

Equation 10.10 Pricing Kernel or State Price Density

$$\phi = (\phi_1, ..., \phi_m)$$

Intuitively, the density or kernel is a measure across states that we can use to sum (or integrate) possible outcomes. Using the state price density and the actual probabilities allows us to price an asset (that has specific payoffs in these states) as an expected value. This expected value uses the state price density to weight the payoffs and uses the actual probabilities to weight the outcomes across states (Equation 10.11):

Equation 10.11 State Price Density Formula

$$V(z, \pi, \phi) = E(\phi z) = \sum_i \pi_i \phi_i z_i$$

Here again, the expectation of the future values is taken across the m states. Note that the pricing kernel ϕ already captures the discounting process for next-period payoffs.

State Prices and the Basic Pricing Equation

Recall that by definition, complete markets contain enough securities that one can form a contingent claim for every possible state. These Arrow securities have a *state price*, because they are claims contingent on a specific state or outcome.

Using the state prices and state price density allows us to reuse the basic pricing equation. Consider again the expectation in Equation 10.11. Using the actual probability measure, it weights the payoffs under different states. However, it also scales these payoffs using the state price density; this captures the subjective assessments of other investors.

Equation 10.12 makes the equivalence between the stochastic discount factor and the pricing kernel (*state price density*), for a specific asset i, explicit.

Equation 10.12 Basic Pricing Equation, SDF, and Pricing Kernel

$$V(z, \pi, \phi) = E(\phi z)$$
$$p_t = E(m_{t+1} z_{t+1})$$
$$m_{t+1,i} = \phi_i$$

THE THEOREM OF ARBITRAGE-FREE ASSET PRICING

"The Fundamental Theorem of Finance"

If the complete-market assumptions stated previously are fulfilled, an extremely powerful theorem describes the price of all assets in the market. This theorem has become known as the *fundamental theorem of finance*.[12] We consider later whether it deserves this truly august name. Stephen Ross (2005, p. 5) formulates the theorem as follows:

Fundamental Theorem of Finance (Ross)
The following three conditions are equivalent:

1. No arbitrage (NA)

2. The existence of a positive linear pricing rule that prices all assets

3. The existence of a (finite) optimal demand for some agent who prefers more to less

Because Ross is one of the originators of the approach, his formulation deserves considerable weight. However, certain ambiguities in his formulation could easily give rise to misunderstanding.[13] Therefore, we present the same theorem in an alternative version attributable to Cvitanic and Zapatero (2004, chap. 6):

Fundamental Theorem of Finance (Alternative Version)

No arbitrage = existence of at least one equivalent martingale measure

Consider a discrete-time financial-market model with finitely many possible random outcomes. If there exists a martingale measure with positive probabilities, then the market is arbitrage-free. Conversely, if the market is arbitrage-free, then there exists a martingale measure with positive probabilities.

Market completeness = existence of a unique equivalent martingale measure

Consider a discrete-time financial-market model with finitely many possible random outcomes. If there exists a unique martingale measure with positive probabilities, then the market is complete and arbitrage-free. Conversely, if the market is arbitrage-free and complete, then there exists a unique martingale measure with positive probabilities.

The concepts of completeness, equivalent martingale measure, and unique measure are all essential to the application of this theorem. They also sharply limit the application of the theorem.

THE LAW OF ONE PRICE

The Law of One Price in Complete Markets

The *law of one price* (LOP) or *single-price law of markets* is a concept closely related to the risk-neutral pricing in complete markets. Just as the foregoing has been presented in different ways, so has the law of one price. We start with the complete-market version (Equation 10.13):

Law of one price: In a complete market, the price of an asset will equal the price of a repli-cating portfolio of state claims.[14]

Equation 10.13 LOP in Complete Markets

$$P_i = \sum_s p_s X_{is}$$

$s \quad = 1, ..., S$ (states)

$i \quad = 1, ..., n$ (securities)

$p_s \quad =$ state price for state s

$X_{is} =$ payoff of security i in state s

Note that the sum here is taken across states of nature, and the factors p_s are known as *state prices*, or the price of a *state claim*. A state claim is a claim to receive one dollar (or other unit of money) if, and only if, the specific state occurs in the future.

Relationship Between LOP and Risk-Neutral Pricing

Thus, the LOP in complete markets requires the price of each security to equal a particular kind of expected net present value of the future payoffs: the kind where the expectation (about future random events) and the discount rate (for the net present value) are repre-sented by state claim prices. The LOP formulation for complete markets should seem to be reminiscent of another formulation useful in complete markets: the risk-neutral pricing presented earlier in this chapter, under the section titled "Probabilities and Risk-Neutral Probabilities." That is because the formulas are fundamentally equivalent and require the same complete-market, no-arbitrage assumption.

Which approach is superior? Consider the following critique.

Sharpe's Critique of Risk-Neutral Probabilities

A critique of the risk-neutral approach was offered by Nobel laureate William Sharpe. Sharpe's statement of the LOP in Equation 10.13 makes the *state price* the explicit factor that weights payoffs in order to determine a market price, rather than using the mysterious risk-neutral probabilities. His explanation is worth reading, especially for those who wish to either use this approach to price securities in nearly complete markets or fully understand the mathematics of complete-market pricing:

In our version, p_s is the price that must be paid today to receive 1 unit at the future date if and only if state s occurs. The sum of all these state prices is the amount that must be paid today to receive 1 unit at the future date with certainty . . . denote this d. Now, imagine that you wish to receive \$1 at the future date if and only if state s occurs. You can borrow p_s dollars to buy the state claim, which will require you to pay p_s/d at the future date, whether state s occurs or not. This amount is called the *forward price* (f_s) of a claim for dollar in state s. . . . Many financial engineers use this approach, calling each forward price a "risk-neutral probability," although this obscures the underlying economics. While the forward prices will sum to 1 . . . they will typically differ from true probabilities. Moreover, the world is not one in which people are neutral to risk. Nonetheless, the procedure is harmless enough, and those who use this version share our goal of understanding the determinants of state prices. (Sharpe, 2007, sec. 4.9.1)

The LOP in Partially Complete Markets

It is convenient that the LOP holds in a complete market. However, the market for private firms is incomplete. You cannot buy and sell securities that cover every risk or contingency, including those present in privately held firms. So we look at the LOP from the perspective of a *payoff space* that is smaller than the set of all possible contingencies.[15] Recall that, as presented earlier, if the number of states is more than the number of unique securities, then the market is incomplete.[16] We restrict the payoff space to a finite number of securities and a finite number of risks.

Here the payoff space for the securities we are examining (the set of all possible payoffs of securities that can be purchased) is a proper subset of all the possible payoffs under all states. We call the payoffs for an individual security x_i, the payoff space $\underline{X}$, and the set of all possible payoffs in all states $\mathbb{R}^s$, as shown here:

$\mathbb{R}^s$ set of possible payoffs in all states

p_s state prices for state s

$\underline{X}$ payoff space

x_i payoff of individual security

We make an important further assumption: investors can make portfolios out of any combination of traded securities using a simple linear equation, such as half a share of Microsoft and fifty shares of Green Bay Packers football club stock.[17] Or, as Cochrane (2001, sec. 4.1) puts it: "The price of a burger, shake, and fries must be the same as a Happy Meal." Note that this is not a trivial assumption; bid-ask spreads, commissions, and borrowing constraints would violate it. These two assumptions (a finite real payoff space and portfolio formation) within a payoff space are summarized in Equation 10.14.

Equation 10.14 Law of One Price Assumptions

Finite Real Payoff Space

$$\underline{X} \equiv \text{payoff space}$$

payoffs $x_1, x_2, ..., x_h \in \underline{X}$

$$\underline{X} \subset \mathbb{R}^s$$

Portfolio Formation Assumption

$$x_1, x_2 \in \underline{X} \Rightarrow (ax_1 + bx_2) \in \underline{X}$$

Given these assumptions, we have the following version of the law of one price (Equation 10.15):

Equation 10.15 Law of One Price in Payoff Space

$$p(ax_1 + bx_2) = (a[p(x_1)] + b[p(x_2)])$$

This version of the LOP is more realistic than a blanket assumption of complete markets. However, it applies *only* to securities that are actually traded, fulfill the portfolio formation assumption, and are within the payoff space available to other investors. Here is a formulation in words:

> Law of one price: Assume there are no transaction costs and no bid-ask spreads. . . . If a combination of assets (a portfolio) produces the same payoff vector as another combination of assets (another portfolio), then the two portfolios cost the same. (Lengwiler, 2004, sec. 3.2)

LOP, Linear Pricing, and the Discount Factor

Recall the basic pricing equation, derived from first principles in Chapter 9, "Modern Recursive Equilibrium and the Basic Pricing Equation," under the section titled "The Basic Pricing Equations." This equation states that the price of an asset today (p_t) is equal to the expected payoff x_{t+1} (including the selling price and any dividend) multiplied by some stochastic discount factor m_{t+1} (Equation 10.16).

Equation 10.16 Basic Pricing Equations

$$x_{t+1} \equiv p_{t+1} + y_{t+1}$$
$$m_{t+1} \equiv \beta \frac{u'(c_{t+1})}{u'(c_t)}$$
$$p_t = E(m_{t+1} x_{t+1})$$

The LOP implies that a unique discount factor m_{t+1} exists for all securities within the payoff space. Furthermore, it implies that the discount factor is a linear combination of the other payoffs within the payoff space.

Remark: Mathematics of the Law of One Price

Mathematically, the existence of one price to all assets (at least within the payoff space) is a consequence of the *Riesz representation theorem*. This theorem asserts that bounded linear functionals can be represented by inner products.[18] In this case, the discount factor is an inner product of the functional incorporating preferences of the market participants with the payoffs within the market.

Notes on the LOP

The combination of the basic pricing equation and the LOP seems magical; indeed, it is a wonderful theory and application. However, it has serious limitations worth noting:

- The entire theorem is limited to the payoff space; there are clearly many risks outside the payoff space.

- In virtually all markets, the portfolio formation assumption is incorrect to some degree. The assumption is completely violated for most relevant equity markets involving private firms. Indeed—as we noted earlier—it was even violated in the example we gave in the text!

- The theorem holds that a unique discount factor exists in the payoff space. It says nothing about discount factors outside the payoff space. Unless markets are complete, there are many possible stochastic discount factors m that solve $p = E(mx)$.

- Note that the portfolio formation assumption allows a kind of weak completeness within the payoff space; if investors can form portfolios and reap the returns from them, they can also capture any arbitrage profits that may occur. If the portfolio formation assumption is *not* true, then the ability of investors to capture these goes away, and the LOP falls apart as well.

TECHNICAL REHABILITATION OF COMPLETE MARKETS

Earlier in this chapter, under the section titled "Probabilities and Risk-Neutral Probabilities," we present complete markets by crafting the Arrow-Pratt tableau of payoffs for a finite number of securities in a finite number of states. We define a complete market as one in which every state risk could be insured. This, in linear algebra, can be summarized as a rank condition: the number of independent securities within the payoff space must be at least as large as the number of possible states.

Such a market, with such a rank condition, is a theoretical ideal that is not attained in almost all markets. However, a number of technical mechanisms have been proposed that rehabilitate complete market pricing methods in markets that do not appear to fulfill the rank condition. We examine these briefly next.

1. *Spanning securities.* Complete markets can be synthesized when sufficient securities exist to span the payoff space, meaning that a linear combination of the existing securities (sometimes called *basis securities*) can be used to produce the payoffs of all securities.[19]

2. *Long-lived securities with continual trading (dynamic completion).* Complete markets can be synthesized in cases in which there are long-lived securities with continual trading opportunities, and in which such securities cover the risks not represented in the other security prices.[20] This idea is an elaboration of one proposed originally by Arrow (1953).

A plausible example of this would be a "weather security" for a farming economy. A constantly traded weather security could cover risks such as hot weather and low rain to farmers, without requiring individual separate securities for each weather condition.

3. *Quasi-completeness with idiosyncratic risk securities.* A number of authors have conceived models in which individuals could hedge their own ("idiosyncratic") risk of future income through some type of security. In some of these models, there is also a set of call options on the total amount of future income. In such a *quasi-complete market*, the social welfare

benefits of a complete market arise through mutual trading of risks.[21] We discuss this further below.

Unfortunately, none of these are sufficient to rehabilitate complete markets for private firm equity. In particular:

- There are inadequate securities to span the "human capital" risks that are important in entrepreneurial firms, as well as in more established firms where key personnel are important to the firm's leadership, image, or ability to innovate.

- Privately held firms, by definition, do not have long-lived equity securities that incorporate the risks that are otherwise missing from the market. Furthermore, there are no other securities that, through regular trading and price movements, incorporate these risks.

- While hedging idiosyncratic risks would have broad benefits, very few financial market options exist for owners of private firms to do so.

Remark: Social Benefits of Completing Markets

We focus in this book on the incompleteness of financial markets and of the real markets in which private firms operate. However, a similar discussion should be held about many other real markets in which workers and their families operate, in which they are exposed to risks of unemployment, natural resource costs, adverse government policies, war, human capital deficiencies, and many, many others. There are clear benefits to allowing people to purchase and sell securities that lower their overall risks; the incompleteness of most markets effectively prevents them from doing so. The relatively few exceptions (such as life, health, and property insurance) are widely accepted.

The economist Robert Shiller has proposed that securities be created that allow individuals to trade on risks that are important to them.[22] For example, an oil-price security (tradeable in lots of appropriate size to a household or small business) would allow a family that drives a lot to hedge the risk of an oil-price hike, or offset part of the cost of purchasing a fuel-efficient vehicle, by appropriate buying and selling of such securities. Unfortunately, such securities would be difficult—but not impossible—to create. One recent positive development has been the growth of microfinance and small exchanges in recent years, which has greatly expanded the possibilities for entrepreneurs to make use of some such securities.[23]

WHY ARE THERE ARBITRAGEURS IN A NO-ARBITRAGE WORLD?

The Paradox of the Ubiquitous Assumption

The no-arbitrage assumption is often accepted without question in the finance literature—and then later challenged in practice when the facts appear to fulsomely contradict it. Why, one may ask, can economists assume no arbitrage when buildings are full of traders who are professional arbitrageurs? This is the kind of paradox that occurs when a powerful theory is defined in precise terms, but popularized in a careless fashion.

The answer to the paradox lies in the distinction between what I term *mathematical arbitrage* and *practical arbitrage*. A truly risk-free profit—a mathematical arbitrage—is rare in financial markets. All kinds of market participants eliminate those; we can consider many active investors to be mathematical arbitrage policemen. What *practical* arbitrageurs seek is low-risk profits. In modern financial markets, many experienced traders (including some professional arbitrageurs) seek low-risk trades that are likely to produce small profits. To execute these, they must bear transaction costs, residual risks (such as counterparty risk and trading execution risk), and the cost of operating.

Low Risk Is Not the Same as Zero Risk

As investors learn and then apparently forget with numbing frequency, *low risk* is different from *no risk*. Painful examples of this discovery include Black Monday of October 1987,[24] the collapse of the trading firm Long Term Capital in 1998,[25] and the more recent collapse of Fannie Mae and Freddie Mac.[26]

The Weak Law of No Arbitrage

Momentary examples of arbitrage profits do occur but cannot last. Stephen Ross acknowledges that his own involvement in a mortgage-finance arbitrage firm resulted in the discovery of transient, nonscalable opportunities for low-risk trades that produced significant profits. However, the search for these, and their execution, involved considerable search and transaction costs. He describes these costs and the resulting limited number of profitable trading opportunities as establishing a "market equilibrium" for arbitrageurs.[27]

Although the term *arbitrage* is used less often outside financial markets, a similar no-arbitrage discipline occurs in markets for certain tangible goods such as real estate, houses, and cars.[28]

From observing markets such as these, and thinking carefully about what the assumption of no arbitrage really means, I propose what might be called the *weak law of no arbitrage* (Exhibit 10.1):

EXHIBIT 10.1
Weak Law of No Arbitrage

In any traded market, mathematical arbitrage is nearly absent, but practical arbitrage is ubiquitous.

INCOMPLETE MARKETS AND THE FIRM

The Problem of Incomplete Markets

We now make quite explicit a serious limitation of the application of risk-neutral pricing to private firms. Recall that a complete market is one in which every risk can be hedged (or insured); this requires that securities exist that span the risks in the market. In such cases, the no-arbitrage assumption implies a positive linear pricing operator.

However, actual markets are usually *incomplete*, meaning many risks cannot be hedged. In the following discussion, we focus on the market for equity in private firms, although the general incompleteness of markets extends well beyond this.

The Causes of Incomplete Markets for Private Firm Equity

There are several reasons why the market for equity in private firms should be considered to be incomplete:

Unspanned Risks

1. *Unspanned internal risks of private businesses.* Owners of equity interests in privately held firms often face risks that are not spanned in the market. These include the internal risks of almost all private businesses, meaning risks arising in their key personnel, products, and business operations.

For much larger firms, one may assume (and perhaps test empirically) that the risks are a combination of a large number of relatively small risks, summed together, and such risks in the aggregate are approximated by a normal distribution.[29] Such a claim could be advanced for large firms (or, with more support, for a large number of large firms over a long time frame). However, it is clearly insupportable for small and medium-sized firms, and perhaps all privately held firms. Of several risks, we can identify three important internal risks that are generally not spanned in the investment market:

   a. *Entrepreneur risk:* The role of the entrepreneur in founding companies is vital. Their role in nurturing and growing them is critical. At some point in a new firm's growth, the founding entrepreneur's role becomes less than critical and, eventually (given continued growth and the passage of time), less important. Until then, the firm's investors bear the risk inherent in the mortality, health, interest, and personality of the entrepreneur.

   b. *Key-person risk:* Most firms have one or more key people for whom the observations about entrepreneur risk stated previously apply in some proportion. The existence of *key man insurance contracts* addresses one aspect of this risk (mortality) but not the others. Privately held firms are likely to suffer more from key-person risk than publicly held firms.

   c. *Labor income risk:* We have listed the risks to the firm inherent in key people and the founding entrepreneurs. We can also note the risks *to the entrepreneur* of investing time and effort into a company.

2. *Unspanned risks in external cash flows.* The cash flows from operations in a privately held firm, as well as the operational expenses of such a firm, cannot be easily replicated by using traded assets. For example, service firms rarely can replicate the earnings (or revenue) from their expected professional work over the next three months. Although some large firms can partially hedge the price of commodities such as corn, pork bellies, or wheat, most cannot hedge the costs of rent, taxes, payroll (including benefits), and other significant expenses.

Transaction Costs

3. *Transaction costs and other market imperfections.* Even very active markets have imperfections such as transaction costs, minimum lots for trading, and barriers to entry for investors. For private firms, these are often significant.

In particular, investors in private firms often cannot borrow easily, short-sell private equity interests or otherwise write options on them, or purchase fractional amounts. The portfolio formation (the "Happy Meal" rule) is almost always violated for equity in private firms.

Lack of Observed Prices

4. *Lack of observable prices for private firm equity.* There are often *no* observable prices for the equity in most private firms for significant time periods. That does not mean the firm has no value during that period or that interested buyers and sellers did not negotiate (and even consummate) transactions. What it does mean is that the assumption of an observable price vector is not a tenable one. We discuss this more shortly.

Other Limitations to Complete Markets

5. *Bounded rationality and costly information.* We assume people are rational in that they act in their self-interest and use information to inform themselves about potential future events. However, we also assume they are bounded in their rationality, meaning that they attach a cost to information.

In the case of privately held firms, this cost of information can be significantly higher than for publicly traded firms (especially for mutual funds provided by large national financial service firms). This is an impediment to buying and selling equity in private firms.

6. *Large asymmetries in information.* Information asymmetry cannot be assumed entirely away, even when dealing with large publicly traded firms subject to disclosure and registration requirements. However, for privately held firms, potential investors must overcome much larger barriers to understanding the firm. These may call into question, along with other factors such as controlling interests, the no-arbitrage assumption.

Discussion of Two Specific Causes

Lack of Traded Price Data

In general, prices of the equity of privately held firms (and therefore returns, volatility, covariance, and other key statistics) are available only intermittently. In modern portfolio theory (MPT) and common financial practice, such investments are typically ignored or implicitly treated as noninvestment assets, similar to equity in a home.[30]

Labor Income Risk

For privately held firms, especially those that are started and run by an entrepreneur, the importance of labor income is often the most important nonmarket risk. Many entrepreneurs work extraordinary hours during the years in which they start and run their business. This work is usually their main source of income, and often the main source for their households.

Thus, labor income is an important basis for their welfare; unfortunately, with limited exceptions, labor income cannot be insured. Therefore, for firms in which the founders, partners, or other owners earn both labor and investment income from the firm, labor income risk is a significant violation of the assumption of a complete market. Cochrane (2008) described this recently:

> Strangely, though it has been included almost from the start in portfolio theory, hedg-ing non-market income is as rare as hedging state variables in practice. Steel workers, and their pension funds, do not short the Steel industry portfolio, or even the Auto industry. One would expect a class of money managers to have emerged that developed expertise in this hedging, understanding portfolios of traded assets that can hedge common sources of outside income, and selling these individual-specific tailored-portfolio services for fees. This has not happened. Academic research in asset pricing has focused almost entirely on finding "priced" factors, alphas for the one investor who has no outside income, and has ignored finding and characterizing nonpriced factors that, by providing free insurance, are potentially the most important for typical investors. Incorporating outside income is also hard, especially when markets are incomplete, and perhaps this is why it is overlooked. (Cochrane, 2008, p. 5)

Remark: Insuring Parts of Labor Income Risk

Some limited labor income risks have common insurance options, including the fol-lowing:

1. Life insurance, which can provide income to a surviving household if a wage earner dies.

2. Disability policies, which provide some income in the case of a temporary or per-manent disability. However, as of the time of this publication, the disability policies commonly offered in the United States usually insured income far less than that enjoyed by managers.[31]

Note that these are far fewer risks than an entrepreneur (especially one with a family) actu-ally faces. This alone creates a significantly incomplete market for him or her.

Conclusion: Private Firms Operate in Incomplete Markets

Complete markets are those in which the risks inherent in *every* state can be insured. How-ever, there are important risks for privately held firms that *cannot* be insured in the market. Moreover, the causes of incomplete markets extend well beyond minor imperfections (such as modest bid-ask spreads and transaction costs) that occur in every market. Furthermore, various technical mathematical constructs that can complete theoretical markets clearly do not exist in actual markets for privately held firms.

Therefore, we conclude that equity in privately held firms is *generally traded in an incom-plete market*. As we can see immediately, this has important consequences.

CONSEQUENCES OF INCOMPLETE MARKETS

The Elegant Simplicity of Complete Markets

We presented earlier in this chapter the fundamental theorem of finance, which, given the assumption of complete markets, guarantees the existence of a *unique* market price enforced by arbitrage.

Unfortunately, the results of the fundamental theorem do not apply to what are called incomplete markets in the literature of mathematical finance. The observation of Koopmans (1974) is worth repeating: the Arrow-Debreu model "is in the nature of a magnificent *tour de force*, enriching our insight, but with a somewhat strained relationship to reality."[32]

Consequences of Incomplete Markets for Neoclassical Finance Models

If markets are not complete, much of the mathematics summarized in the equations presented earlier in this chapter still work. However, they work in ways that are much more limited than in complete markets.

No Unique State Prices or Well-Defined Pricing Formula

Within the state-preference pricing model used in this chapter, the following implications result from abandoning the complete-market assumption:

1. *The state prices ("Arrow prices") are not unique, even in an equilibrium.* This means that more than one set of prices can be observed in a market in which all participants have concluded the trades they are capable and willing of executing.

In the terms of the basic pricing equation $p = E(mx)$, complete markets and the law of one price imply a unique, positive discount factor m. If we assume that there is no (mathematical) arbitrage but that markets are incomplete, then an unlimited number of discount factors m could complete the equation and price the asset with payoffs x.[33]

2. *There is no well-defined formula for pricing new assets that are not in the "span" of current assets.* The "span" of the market includes all risks already priced in the market. (Recall the rank condition for complete markets.) If a new security is introduced into a complete market, and it is *redundant* in the sense of being a linear combination of the others, nothing much changes. However, if a new security that is not in the market span is introduced, it cannot be priced using the mechanisms developed for complete markets and may also disturb the equilibrium price of the other assets.[34] For example, a mutual fund made up of a simple combination of traded stocks could still be priced using the existing information in the market. However, a mutual fund that included securities dependent on untraded risks could not.

3. *The interests of people who invest in firms and manage them no longer unanimously determine the firm's production plans.* We noted the paucity of the theory of the firm in neoclassical economics. Much of the results of welfare economics depend on a greatly simplified model of the firm, operating in a simplified product market. If we abandon the complete-market assumption, then other welfare implications of the neoclassical model fall apart. In particular, conflicts erupt among shareholders, managers, and employees of a firm, because these people have different interests.

In the neoclassical model with complete markets, they could trade all risks and adjust their prices to an equilibrium that matched the profit maximization assumption for the firm. However, in incomplete markets, managers, employees, and shareholders of the firm face risks they cannot insure through market trades, and therefore they pursue different (and conflicting) interests in their work and investment.[35]

Of course, the existence of principal-agent and manager-employee conflicts is no surprise. What could be a surprise to many readers is the extent to which the neoclassical model with complete markets essentially assumes those away.

EXAMPLE: EXPECTED NPV, ARBITRAGE, AND PRICES IN DIFFERENT MARKETS

Introduction

Let's consider the example of the community basketball, as seen by various individuals. We considered this earlier in Chapter 2, "Methods and Theories of Value," when we discussed standards of value. We previously illustrated how value is different under different standards, and how different individuals estimate value differently. Using the same facts, we now illustrate how NPV and $E(NPV)$ calculations can lead to value estimates that are wrong in practice.

We also illustrate the effect of arbitrage on a market.

The Basketball Example: Market, Intrinsic, and $E(NPV)$

In this example we attempt to estimate a basketball's fair market value by calculating its intrinsic value, its accounting book value, and its expected net present value. This example is summarized in Table 10.1.

In this example:

1. Frank is willing to pay $20 to play with his own basketball (or, actually, his association's basketball), and has high confidence that he will be playing. His expected net present value matches the intrinsic value he assigns to it. Both are well above the actual market value of a new one in surrounding communities, which we assume we know from observing many transactions.

2. Sally thinks the basketball may be useful as a prop, conversation piece, or occasional diversion. She thinks exactly like Frank—they just derive different benefits from it.

TABLE 10.1

Comparison: Expected net present value and other value standards

Person and interests	Fair market value ($)	Intrinsic value ($)	Accounting book value ($)	$E(NPV)$ ($)
Frank the aspiring basketball player	15	20	10	20
Sally the aspiring actress	15	5	10	5
Tom the golfer	15	0	10	5
Pooja the astronaut	15	−4	10	−10

3. Tom sees no benefit to any sports equipment other than golf equipment. However, one of his regular foursome may like to use the ball sometime, so it has some expected value over the next season to him.

4. Pooja has places to go. She sees no need for the ball and would pay to have it removed. However, if nobody disposes of it, she thinks there is a 20 percent chance that she will be charged $50 to clean up the sporting goods when the association disbands. Therefore, her expected NPV is 0.20 * –$50 = –$10.

What do we observe from this exercise? First, none of the individuals calculated an expected net present value that was equal to the market value of the ball. One even estimated a *negative* E(NPV), meaning she would pay to have it removed! Clearly, even if we have near-perfect information and functioning markets, expected net present value does not equal market value.

Second, and just as powerful, the group of expected NPVs neatly surrounds the actual fair market value—at least among those that consider the asset to be worth something.[36] Indeed, if we interviewed dozens of individuals in the market, we might find that the distribution of answers produced a good indication of fair market value.

Nearly Complete Markets with Practical Arbitrage Illustration

Now extend the example to introduce practical arbitrage. Suppose that the sale of the basketball was forced, and for some reason the person in the example who placed a high intrinsic value on the asset was gone from the market. Would the price fall to near zero?

Probably not; we might find an arbitrageur who would purchase basketballs at distressed prices and then resell them as soon as possible to others. Such people would not rely on E(NPV) formulas; they would only consider the ability to resell quickly to others who *did* place an intrinsic value on the asset.

In fact, let's meet another local resident known as Barb the Arb. Barb has little use for basketball as a sport. Her sport is arbitrage. When the community puts the basketball up for sale and finds no takers at the offering price of $15, Barb is quick to purchase for $13. She knows that these assets have been trading hands around $15, and she quickly finds Frank, who places an intrinsic value of $20 on the ball. He happily buys for $16 what he "values" at $20.

Table 10.2 shows the net cash receipts and expenditures for all individuals as well as how the total receipts and expenditures match. Note that we now have two market transactions: one for $13 and one for $16. These bracket the $15 market price we identified earlier. This is an example of how arbitrageurs police the market and keep transaction prices near the market price. It is also an example of how bid-ask spreads exist in the market and how arbitrageurs get paid.

Note on Practical Arbitrage in This Example

We must note here that Barb's activities in the market fall short of theoretical arbitrage, in at least two areas: first, Barb took some risk that the price of the basketball would fall during the time she held it, and that there was a buyer available at a higher price. Second, some transaction costs were involved (at least the search costs for Barb to find Frank).

TABLE 10.2
Arbitrage and the basketball example

Person	Sell price ($)	Purchase price ($)
Community	13	—
Barb	16	−13
Frank	—	−16
Total	**29**	**−29**
Memo: Markup charged/paid	3	−3

Such market imperfections are common when interests in private businesses are involved. In the lexicon of the weak law of arbitrage, Barb is a practical arbitrageur. Her efforts required some risk and expense, but earned her a small profit and stabilized the price.

Incomplete Markets Illustration

A good example of how nearly complete markets differ from incomplete markets can be illustrated with the same basketball example. We already observed how four different people with four different interests would consider the purchase of one or more basketballs. Their differing interests were encapsulated in the intrinsic value they placed on the marginal basketball. We noted how the addition of one more person, Barb the Arb, also changed things. Barb had no interest in basketballs, but she liked to make money.

Now consider the same people in two different neighborhoods. In the first, a nearly complete market exists in basketballs. That is, there are active markets for balls, which can be purchased, sold, and even "sold short." The second neighborhood involves a large number of people who do not know what a basketball is. It is an incomplete market with few actual transactions. Table 10.3 summarizes the market value for a basketball in each neighborhood.

In the column labeled *Interest*, we express the interest of each person. Note the key difference between the consumers and the arbitrageur. The consumers are interested in buying a basketball and probably would do so at the right price. The arbitrageur is interested in buying as many basketballs as possible, given the opportunity to earn a risk-free profit by immediately selling them.

Observations on the Difference

Complete-Market Neighborhood

In the complete-market neighborhood, the high intrinsic value of a basketball to Frank means he will go to nearby stores and ask neighbors to find a ball to buy. Frank is not foolish; he'll buy one at the lowest price available, consistent with his taste in basketballs. The other consumers have a much lower intrinsic value; only Sally might buy one, and only then at a garage sale.

However, Barb has a strong influence on the market. She buys all the balls she can get that appear on the market for less than $14 and immediately sells them in another neighborhood for $16. She keeps track of the markets for this type of commodity and knows how much of a spread she must earn to cover her transportation and other costs.

TABLE 10.3
Comparison: Market value in complete and incomplete markets

Person and interests	Interest	Memo: Intrinsic value ($)	Action in incomplete markets	Action in nearly complete markets
Frank the aspiring basketball player	Buy 1 at $15	20	Buys one, even if price is high	Buys one, at market price
Sally the aspiring actress	Buy 1 at $5	5	Might buy one, at garage sale, as a prop, if price is really low	Nothing; no interest in paying a market price
Tom the golfer	No interest	0	Nothing; needs garage space for extra clubs even if price is zero	Nothing; no interest in paying a market price
Pooja the astronaut	No interest	–4	Nothing	Nothing
Barb the Arb	Buy many at $14 Sell many at $16	None	Does not participate	Actively buys and sells
Market value	—	—	Multiple market prices	About $15

What is the market price here? The completeness of the market encourages arbitrageurs, and the fact that one is active means the market price fluctuates in the narrow band of $14 to $16, which we characterize as "about $15." In such a market, Frank buys one, and nobody else buys one. Everybody is happy—at least on the basketball court.

Incomplete-Market Neighborhood

In the incomplete market, Frank will pay a high price to obtain just one ball, because he likes to play. Sally does not particularly like to play but would buy one at a garage sale for much less than Frank would pay. The other two consumers have no interest in purchasing a ball at all and probably would not even if it were nearly free. So if one is on the market for less than $20, Frank will buy it; if not, he cannot play. Frank is not really happy with this; he has to wait to find a ball and (based on his extensive knowledge of markets in other neighborhoods) knows he is paying an extravagant price for the single ball he buys.

What is the market price here? There is no single market price. In any given time period, there may be transactions at $20, $15, or $4; there could also be no market transactions because only one person really wants one; or there may be basketballs simply given away.

ANALYSIS OF THE SAMPLE FIRMS

In this book, we test each of the identified theories of valuation by attempting to use them to value three sample firms described in Appendix A, "Description of Subject Companies."

For the neoclassical finance theory, we have the following result:

• *S. H. Importers.* S. H. Importers, a private company, issues no publicly traded securities. The assumption of complete markets cannot be made. Given these factors, the neoclassical finance model offers no pricing capability.

- *A & A Consulting.* A & A Consulting similarly issues no publicly traded securities. However, given the company's history of regular cash distribution to its members, and record of occasional transactions among equity holders, at some price its equity would become very attractive to qualified investors. The complete-markets model does not tell us this price.

- *ExxonMobil.* ExxonMobil is one of the largest firms in the world, with securities that are widely traded. Thus, derivative securities for both ExxonMobil's stock and the price of its major asset, oil reserves, are traded in certain submarkets. In such submarkets, it may be possible to create a nearly replicating portfolio of securities for ExxonMobil stock. This will not be a true complete market. However, it may be nearly complete and therefore allow complete-market pricing formulas to provide a useful guide to the stock price for the firm.

11 PORTFOLIO PRICING METHODS

OUTLINE OF THIS CHAPTER

This chapter describes the most common analytical approach to valuing business investments assembled as part of an investment *portfolio*. The idea of focusing on the portfolio, rather than on any individual investment, is a powerful one with ramifications that extend beyond the pricing of individual investments.

In particular, we discuss the following:

- The mean-variance framework, as outlined by Harvey Markowitz in the 1950s. This framework has significance in and outside its original focus of portfolio investment.

- The relationship between portfolio models and the basic pricing equation we derived in Chapter 9, "Modern Recursive Equilibrium and the Basic Pricing Equation."

- The most familiar of the portfolio investment models: the capital asset pricing model (CAPM). We present it here in a recursive form that, while still relying on at least one heroic assumption, matches much of what we know about household investment behavior.

- The Roll critique of the CAPM and similar models that presume that household wealth exists primarily in the form of tradeable securities. This critique is especially telling given the fact that approximately 99 percent of firms are not publicly traded, and that much of household wealth is in the form of nontradeable assets.

- The prevalence of an *ad hoc* empirical CAPM in applied work.

- An effort to use portfolio theory to estimate the value of the three example firms we use repeatedly in this book.

Completing this chapter will provide the reader with an understanding of the use and the limitations of portfolio models in business valuation.

PORTFOLIO MODELS AND THE BASIC PRICING EQUATIONS

Returning to the Basic Pricing Equation

Recall the basic pricing equations from Chapter 9, "Modern Recursive Equilibrium and the Basic Pricing Equation," under the section titled "The Basic Pricing Equations." These describe how consumer-investors choose to save in the multiple-period setting of the modern recursive model.

These equations encapsulate a simple and powerful logic: the future expected payoffs of any investment (including the future asset price x and any dividend y) are related to the current price p through a stochastic discount factor and an expectation operator. See Equation 11.1. Unless we are wrong—really wrong—about what consumers want, any useful investment asset pricing method should logically fit these equations.

Equation 11.1 Basic Pricing Equations

$$p_t = E(m_{t+1}x_{t+1})$$
where:

p_t = price at time t

$x_{t+1} \equiv p_{t+1} + y_{t+1}$ = payoff at time $t + 1$

$m_{t+1} \equiv \beta \dfrac{u'(c_{t+1})}{u'(c_t)}$ = stochastic discount factor

Although the logic is strong, the practicality of the equation has not been demonstrated. In particular, the equation does not say *how* the stochastic discount factor is determined, nor how expectations are formed. Thus, a wide variety of consumer preferences, forms of risk aversion, beliefs about future payoffs, and so forth could conceivably fit within these equations. Furthermore, the equations deal only with investment assets that can be readily converted to cash in each period.

Portfolio Models and the Basic Pricing Equations

In this chapter, we present the mean-variance framework, factor models, CAPM, and its variants as special cases of the basic pricing equations. We call these *portfolio methods* because they all focus on portfolio investment—investment in a specific set of securities selected from a universe of possible securities—rather than on the discipline of the no-arbitrage assumption to derive prices.

Recall that in complete markets, we can determine the specific prices of *every* security. A focus on portfolios is less important if every security has a unique price determined in complete markets. However, investment markets are usually not complete, and households have strong reasons to consider their savings in terms of a portfolio.

Assumptions; Distinction with Neoclassical Finance

Modern portfolio theory does not start with the assumption of complete markets, which is a useful distinction from the neoclassical finance models we discussed in Chapter 10,

"Arbitrage-Free Pricing in Complete Markets." However, portfolio models do presume a large number of securities, each with known prices and frequent opportunities to trade. They also presume a large number of investors and very small transaction costs. For some investors and some sets of securities, the complete-market conditions may be approximately fulfilled. Many portfolio models also rely on strong assumptions about the form of utility function and risk aversion of investors, as well as the distribution of returns among investments. Finally, some portfolio models implicitly rely on an assumption that household wealth is primarily in the form of tradeable securities. We note in this chapter where violations of these assumptions have strong consequences

LINEAR FACTOR MODELS

Linear Restrictions Within the Basic Pricing Equation

The basic pricing equation $p = E(mx)$ does not define the stochastic discount factor m, in terms of observable or known qualities. Furthermore, aside from the multiplication of the SDF and the payoff, the equation says nothing about the interaction between the two.

Most portfolio models impose a simple linear structure on this interaction. For this reason, we consider them *linear factor models*, as illustrated in Equation 11.2.

Equation 11.2 Linear Factor Pricing Models

$$p_t = E(m_{t+1}x_{t+1})$$

where:

$$m_{t+1} = a + b'f_{t+1}$$

a, b = parameters to be estimated

f_{t+1} = economic, business, and other factors

Linear factor models condense the information investor-consumers use to determine how much they will pay for an asset into a linear combination of other variables they can observe. These factors could include economic variables (such as GDP growth, inflation, or interest rates), business variables (such as retail sales or demand in a specific industry), and other factors such as government policies, perceived riskiness of the world or nation, or life considerations such as beginning a new career, having a child, or saving for college.

As we will see, the specific factors used, the manner of estimating them, and other empirical questions have created fodder for thousands of different variants.

Conversion of Basic Pricing Equation to Return-Beta Models

Readers of standard corporate finance books may not have seen the basic pricing equation or the term *stochastic discount factor*. However, they will have certainly seen terms such as *beta* and models in which returns are modeled as a regression equation with a β in them. However, such return-beta models are not separate and distinct ideas about how consumer-investors act, but are a special case of the basic pricing equation. Indeed, it is not too hard to see the basis of the CAPM in Equation 11.2.

We describe briefly how these return-beta models can be derived from the following basic pricing equation. The details of such derivations and useful notes on the inherent limitations imposed by some of the assumptions are covered in Cochrane (2001, sec. 6.1–6.2) and a handful of other references. Additional information on derivations of various models from the basic pricing equations is described in Appendix B, "Guide to the Solutions Manual," under the section titled "Mathematics."

The algebra of the derivations is important to financial economists, but the underlying principle is important to anyone dealing with financial markets: *the fundamentals of consumer welfare provide a basis for all valid models of investor behavior.* The corollary to this principle is also important: models that violate the fundamentals of consumer welfare probably do not describe how consumers actually act.

Derivations of Return-Beta Models

Many asset pricing models can be derived from the basic pricing equation $p_t = E(m_{t+1}x_{t+1})$. Such derivations often rely on the following assumptions and calculations:

- $E(m)$ must be positive, if there is an absence of arbitrage. This also rules out dividing by zero in the equations.
- If we would like to work with linear models, then the statistical formula for the expectation of a product of two random variables provides a crucial assist. Think of the stochastic discount factor m and the gross returns on securities as random variables. Then, the product of their expectations produces a linear model: $E(mR) = E(m)E(R) + \text{cov}(m, R)$.

A general derivation of return-beta models, attributable to Cochrane (2001, sec. 6.1), is shown in Equation 11.3. In reviewing these equations, note the following:

- Readers familiar with the more common presentation of "beta" models can confirm that the β factor here is a ratio of a covariance to a variance, just as in the classic CAPM model.
- The λ and γ terms are variables expressing market and subjective discounting information. The equation expresses the expected return on a security as the sum of two factors: an intercept and the product of a market information variable and a β factor. The selection of the market information variable or variables is a contentious issue within finance.

Equation 11.3 Derivation of Return-Beta Model

$$p_t = E(mx_{t+1}) = E[m(p_{t+1} + y_{t+1})]$$

$$1 = E\left[m\frac{(p_{t+1} + y_{t+1})}{p_t} \right] \text{(dividing by } p_t)$$

$$1 = E[mR] = E(m)E(R) + \text{cov}(m, R)$$
      (using definitions of return and expectation)

$$E(R_i) \quad = \frac{1}{E(m)} - \frac{\mathrm{cov}\,(m, R_i)}{E(m)} \quad \text{for security } i$$

Define $\gamma \equiv \dfrac{1}{E(m)}$ and multiply right term by $\dfrac{\mathrm{var}(m)}{\mathrm{var}(m)}$

$$E(R_i) \quad = \gamma + \beta_{i,m} \lambda_m$$

where:

$$\beta_{i,m} \quad = \left(\frac{\mathrm{cov}(m, R_i)}{\mathrm{var}(m)} \right)$$

$$\lambda_m \quad = \left(-\frac{\mathrm{var}(m)}{E(m)} \right)$$

Also note that the basic pricing equation we used here implies a simple two-period model, which is commonly used in finance even though it rarely describes actual household savings behavior. Using the recursive form of the consumer's savings problem, as in Equation 11.4 (see later in chapter), allows for an explicit consideration of consumer wealth as well as income and allows for some asset pricing models to be extended to multiple-period settings.

THE MEAN-VARIANCE FRAMEWORK

Modern Portfolio Theory

A revolution in finance began in the middle of the twentieth century with the establishment by Harry Markowitz of the mean-variance framework for explaining investors' asset purchase preferences.[1] This led to the celebrated capital asset pricing model (CAPM) of William Sharpe and John Linton.[2] These innovations became the basis for modern portfolio theory and many common tools for analyzing prices in traded markets. The later development of the arbitrage pricing model of Stephen Ross and the intertemporal capital asset pricing model of William Merton extended our understanding of how investors place relative values on assets in traded markets.[3]

As Ross noted in a recent review of neoclassical finance, all these developments were based on the insight that the relationship between risk and the prices investors would pay for an asset rely on observations about the risks in the portfolio, not just the risks of the particular asset itself.[4] For this reason, mean-variance portfolio analysis, the CAPM, APT, factor models, and related innovations from 1950 to 1980 are sometimes called *modern portfolio theory.*

Valuation Premise in Mean-Variance Models

In the mean-variance framework, investors attempt to earn investment returns to secure consumption in the future. They have normal utility functions and in particular prefer more consumption to less consumption and less risk to more risk.[5] These premises are widely incorporated in economic and financial models and are not unique to the mean-variance framework or modern portfolio theory. Another critical premise—shared with the complete-market models of Chapter 10 — is that "investment behavior" is largely confined to transactions involving traded securities and money accounts.

Accepting this, it is useful to break the fundamental premises of the mean-variance models into three propositions:

1. Investors recognize that there is uncertainty about the returns on future investments. A half century ago, Markowitz called uncertainty "a salient feature of security investment" and noted:

   Only the clairvoyant could hope to predict with certainty. Clairvoyant analysts have no need for the techniques in this monograph. (Markowitz, 1959, introduction)

2. Investors care about returns on their entire investment portfolio and understand that prices of individual investments are correlated.

3. The metrics that are used by investors to choose investments are those of the first two moments of the distribution of returns: the mean and the variance. The mean return metric is used by investors to forecast the expected payoffs available to support their future consumption, and the variance metric allows them to consider the variability in those payoffs.

The first two propositions are common to many financial models—although the universe of potential investments, and their availability to investors, is a contentious issue. (We discuss one pointed and influential critique later in this chapter, under the section titled "Limitations of CAPM and Factor Models.")

The third premise generates the most questions about the applicability of the approach, and also provides the basis for significant advancements in our understanding of investment behavior.

THE CLASSIC CAPM

Introduction: The Elegance of the CAPM

The CAPM is an elegant and instructive model of investor behavior. It depends critically on a set of assumptions about consumer preferences, investment returns, other income to investors, the universe of investments, and the terms for investing. One reason for the durability of the CAPM after four decades is its simplicity; it provides an easily digested theory about a complex subject. Another is the relative plausibility of the underlying assumptions, at least with regard to investor behavior involving portfolios of traded securities.

We test shortly that "relative plausibility." However, we first derive the CAPM from the basic consumer welfare principles stated in Chapter 8, "Value in Neoclassical Economics," and in particular the basic pricing equations. We present multiple theoretical derivations, plus an explanation of what I term the *empirical CAPM*. Contrary to the normal practice, we present the most difficult derivation first, because it is the closest to how consumer-investors actually think about investments over time.

Recursive Form, Derived from Fundamentals

Recall the consumer's savings problem of Chapter 9, "Modern Recursive Equilibrium and the Basic Pricing Equation," under the section titled "Recursive Decision Making: Consumer Savings." In this problem, we introduced the notion of *recursive* decision models, in which a person breaks a multiperiod problem into a series of two-period decisions.

Using this recursive formulation and very few assumptions about consumer preferences, we can write the consumer-investor's utility function as a combination of the utility from current consumption, and the expected discounted value of the wealth of the consumer in the next time period. This is shown in Equation 11.4.

Equation 11.4 Recursive Consumer Utility Function

$$U_t = u(c_t) + \beta E_t \left[V(W_{t+1}) \right]$$

where:

U_t = consumer welfare at time t

$u(c_t)$ = consumer welfare from consumption at time t

$V(W_{t+1})$ = value of wealth at time $t+1$

β = subjective discount factor $(0 < \beta < 1)$

Note on the Value Function; Fundamental Tension

Note the introduction of the *value function* $V(W)$, which produces a satisfaction to the consumer-investor in terms equivalent to the utility derived from immediate consumption. (The related concept of the value functional equation is described in Chapter 15, "The Value Functional: Theory," under the section titled "The Idea of a Functional Equation.") People clearly feel satisfaction (or anxiety) about the value of their wealth (including money in the bank, cars, houses, etc.) given their future plans to spend money.

This important equation summarizes much of what we know about consumer-investors and rules out a number of behaviors that are inconsistent with human nature. In particular, consumer-investors here do not foolishly think only about their consumption today; they also plan for the future. Indeed, the fundamental tension here is *not* choices *among investments*, but the choice *between time periods*. The consumer first decides whether to consume today or save for tomorrow.

Maximizing Condition

Equation 11.5 states the first-order condition for maximizing total utility in the model:

Equation 11.5 Consumer Optimization in the Recursive Savings Problem

$$p_t u'(c_t) = \beta E \left[V'(W_{t+1}) x_{t+1} \right]$$

Here we have the straightforward Euler equation for the consumer-investor: the marginal value of consumption today is set to the discounted marginal value of expected wealth tomorrow.[6] Using the same logic as the derivation of the stochastic discount factor in the basic pricing equations, we next derive the SDF in this model (Equation 11.6):

Equation 11.6 SDF in the Recursive Consumer Utility Function

$$m_{t+1} = \beta \frac{V'(W_{t+1})}{u'(c_t)}$$

The Quadratic Value Function

Now we introduce a crucial restriction in the model: the quadratic value function. The quadratic value function, like the variance of a distribution, is based on squared deviations from a specific level. In this particular form, we assume that the consumer tries to minimize the squared deviation from a subjectively determined desired level of wealth.[7] Equation 11.7 is one useful type of quadratic value function.

Equation 11.7 A Quadratic Wealth Value Function

$$V^{\text{quadratic}}(W_{t+1}) \equiv -\frac{\eta}{2}(W_{t+1} - W^*)^2$$

W^* = subjectively determined desired level of wealth

$E(W_{t+1}) \geq W^*$ (for "most" t)

W_t > 0 (for all t)

η > scale factor

Here the consumer highly values wealth that is close to the desired level of wealth, which is sometimes known as a *bliss point*. The consumer-investor wishes to maximize value and does so by making the squared deviations from the bliss point smaller.

There are two important points to note here:

1. We are using *value* as if it were equivalent to *utility*. However, the arguments of the functions $u(c)$ and $V(W)$ are quite different. Wealth is not the same as consumption; wealth is useful only because it secures future consumption. (Recall the fundamental rule of investor behavior: *real investors optimize their welfare, not their discounted cash flows.*) We discuss this transition from utility-to-value shortly.

2. Quadratic utility functions imply human preferences we know to be incorrect. In particular, they imply improbable risk aversion and stability of consumption and earnings over time.[8] Thus, quadratic utility (and value functions based on quadratic utility) are not a proper basis for modeling investment behavior outside the conditions outlined later in this chapter, under the section titled "Limitations of CAPM and Factor Models."

Readers interested in learning more on these points should consult the resources listed in Appendix B, "Guide to the Solutions Manual," under the section titled "Mathematics."

The Quadratic CAPM

Using the quadratic value function and the recursive form of consumer-investor utility produces the basis for a theoretically sound CAPM, relying on the crucial assumption of quadratic utility. (Another assumption, not discussed here, is that investment returns are stable over time.) All that remains is the regression equation that forms the basis of the stochastic discount factor. Because the standard regression equations (which are called *ordinary least squares* for good reason) use a quadratic formulation, this is straightforward empirically.

Other CAPM and Factor Model Derivations

There are other ways to derive the CAPM, each of which requires severe assumptions and restrictions.[9] These include the following:

- Two-period, quadratic-utility investors
- Exponential-utility investors, with normally distributed investment returns
- Logarithmic-utility investors

In addition, multiple-factor models (such as arbitrage pricing theory [APT]) can be derived using similarly severe restrictions, but with multiple factors representing conditions in the economy and financial markets included in the specification. This is contemplated in the general derivation shown in Equation 11.3.

The Empirical CAPM

I report a common variant of CAPM and factor models in this subsection. It is included last among the portfolio models because it is the least rigorous of the models presented here, is often misused, and is significantly divorced from theory. However, variants of it are widely disseminated among corporate finance texts, business primers, accounting texts, and other places. I call it the *empirical CAPM* because it uses a bit of theory, ignores a lot more, and relies on a lot of data.

The Construction of the Common Empirical CAPM

We can construct an empirical CAPM (and, optionally, certain factor models) using the following argument:

1. Assume the first three premises of the mean-variance framework. This is good theory and a good start on a model. Matters, however, are about to go downhill.

2. Assume that the wealth portfolio is represented by publicly traded stocks on a major exchange and a risk-free security that can be purchased or sold by any investor. Ignore trading costs, limits on the ability to borrow, and all other securities, including those of privately held firms. These are all incorrect, but for some investors, the resulting errors are probably small.

3. Using only the data on publicly traded stocks in the United States, estimate a regression of the standard CAPM equation. Observe that the regression equation appears to fit very well, given these data. Conclude that the underlying theory and assumptions have been largely validated.

   This is one error heaped on another. Much stock market data suffers from survivor bias; no stock market data represent total household wealth; and "goodness of fit" only implies correlation.

4. *Optional:* Observe that the regression results can be improved by adding additional factors—even if they make no sense—and conclude that a multifactor model may be even better than the CAPM, because it improves the goodness of fit. This is a pure statistical artifact.

This, unfortunately, is an all-too-common abuse of CAPM.[10] It begins well enough, starts downhill, and ultimately crashes in pieces. However, many an investor (or analyst) does not know about the crash, because the regression will nearly always produce excellent goodness-of-fit statistics that appear to validate the model.[11] It may be entertaining for investors and may help them pick undervalued stocks. However, it is not a true model of investment behavior but instead an assemblage of factors that, together during some time period, helped predict aggregate stock market returns.

Remark: No Rehabilitation for the Empirical CAPM

No scholar or professional should confuse the steps listed here with any rigorous model. That the CAPM or factor model deviates from reality is not a stinging criticism in and of itself; every model simplifies and therefore deviates from reality. However, the empirical CAPM deviates from reality *and* from theory.

LIMITATIONS OF CAPM AND FACTOR MODELS

The Serious Limitations of CAPM

The CAPM is a wonderfully instructive model. Furthermore, the mean-variance framework was an epochal improvement in our understanding of investor behavior. However, the CAPM is *not* a complete model of consumer-investor behavior and has little to offer for understanding investor-manager behavior involving private firms.

Assumptions for the CAPM

Standard assumptions used in CAPM (and often other models) include the following:[12]

1. No transaction costs exist.
2. All assets are infinitely divisible.
3. Investors consider the first two moments of the distribution of returns (the mean return and the variance in the return).
4. All investors can borrow and lend without limit at a uniform market rate of interest.
5. There exists a riskless asset and a riskless interest rate.

6. There are only two time periods, implying that all holdings can be liquidated at the end of the period, at a market price.

7. All elements of household wealth are represented by traded securities.

8. Individuals cannot affect the price of a security by buying or selling.

None of these assumptions are correct. We consider a few of these assumptions to find out how damaging these violations of assumptions are.

First Problem: Wealth Portfolio Not Empirically Available

The basis for the CAPM is a theoretical linear relationship between expected returns and the returns on the "wealth portfolio" of all available investments. This raises the immediate question: are all the elements in the wealth portfolio available to investors?

Missing Equity and Lending Investments

Let us consider the actual elements of the wealth portfolio of investors in developed countries: stocks and bonds in traded markets; equity investments (such as partnership interests and equity in closely held firms); lending to low-risk and high-risk borrowers; option contracts; real estate investments; collectibles (such as art and classic cars); and "sweat equity" in a start-up firm. Are most consumer-investors given the opportunity to invest in all these?

The answer is clearly no. Most consumer-investors cannot invest in instruments that require significant capital investment in order to achieve the necessary scale, such as commercial real estate and private business equity interests. They cannot lend easily to high-risk borrowers and may also have difficulty lending to low-risk borrowers.

In general, consumers can borrow via a variety of sources, including mortgage loans, high-cost consumer loans, and auto loans. However, they have limited ability to borrow or lend at the risk-free rate. Some consumers, with a significant bid-ask spread, can borrow and lend at low-risk rates.[13]

The most glaring problem for our purposes is the omission of private-firm equity from the data on the wealth portfolio available thus far to researchers examining the CAPM and related models.

Stock Markets as Poor Proxy

In empirical work—and often inadvertently in theoretical work—the wealth portfolio is proxied by the public stock markets.[14] However, if we believe the fundamental premises of the mean-variance framework, investors are still investors, and they invest to secure consumption. Furthermore, they dislike risk, especially risk that is highly correlated with their existing investments. For investor-managers who hold some share of their assets in private firms, the omission of private-firm equity in the wealth portfolio used in the empirical CAPM is a therefore a serious matter.

Second Problem: "Fishing" and the Roll Critique

The CAPM has been extensively tested, with mixed results. However, there is a serious problem with such tests involving returns on publicly traded stocks. Economist Richard

Roll noted in 1977 that the actual wealth portfolio includes other investments, as we discussed earlier. In addition to the theoretical problem this presents, it causes an unavoidable empirical problem: the tests of CAPM using the stock market as the "wealth portfolio" were actually joint tests of the definition of the market as a whole and the CAPM model.[15]

A problem that extends beyond the CAPM is the *fishing* or *data snooping* problem: given a large amount of data, some models appear to work solely because of random variations. Researchers have strong incentives to discover models that work well with the data. Given the number of empirical tests of various factor models, there is undoubtedly some fishing going on.[16]

Another problem is the *survivor bias* in many datasets of stock prices; for obvious reasons, these datasets are composed largely of firms that remained listed on the public exchange for the entire time period, and some datasets consist solely of survivors. Although some efforts have been made to reduce this bias, it remains in much empirical work.[17]

Third Problem: Asymmetrical Risks of Private-Firm Equity

A third problem with the CAPM is that the risks faced by investors in private firms do not match those of stock market investors. This is especially the case for entrepreneurs who start up firms. These risks are quite asymmetrical, meaning that the mean-variance framework misses a salient feature of the risk distribution.

A related problem involves the self-selection bias in both privately and publicly traded firm data. Most entrepreneurs *chose* to take the risks of starting businesses, and many put a substantial part of their overall wealth into that effort. Their behavior is probably not well represented by that of investors who chose *not* to take similar risks and instead invested in publicly traded stocks.

Conclusion: The Brilliant but Flawed CAPM

The three preceding observations demonstrate serious flaws in the CAPM (as estimated using stock market data) when applied to private firms and the entrepreneurs that start them.

VALUATION APPLICATION: MODERN PORTFOLIO THEORY

In this section, we attempt to use MPT methods to estimate the value of the three example firms described in Appendix A, "Description of Subject Companies."

S. H. Importers

The observations for A & A Consulting below also apply to S. H. Importers.

A & A Consulting

A & A Consulting, a privately held, profitable service firm, clearly has market value. However, it has no publicly traded securities. Data exist on revenue, earnings, distribution to investors, and historical prices for a small number of equity purchases. However, we cannot calculate, at least not in good conscience, a "variance" for returns in the manner assumed by the MPT approach. Similarly, it is difficult to correlate the equity value in the firm with that of other firms with equity traded in the stock market.

Furthermore, the Roll critique of the CAPM cuts deeply against MPT methods involving this and other private firms. Investors in such firms often have a significant portion of their wealth in the firm's equity. The exclusion of such investments from the data used in CAPM and factor models is a serious problem. Finally, although some equity transactions have occurred with the firm, relatively high transaction costs make them difficult to compare with stock market prices.

ExxonMobil

ExxonMobil, a publicly traded firm, is part of many investment portfolios that are largely guided by tenets of modern portfolio theory. Because ExxonMobil is such a large company, with an enormous market capitalization, many (probably most) of its investors are portfolio investors. By *portfolio investors*, we mean people who first choose to invest in a portfolio of a certain size, and regard the choice of securities as a distinctly secondary decision. If they are investing in large amounts in the stock market, they probably have some exposure to ExxonMobil. MPT can help them narrow the list of candidate stocks or mutual funds, or help reduce the overall risk in the portfolio. MPT techniques provide guidance on the likely market price of ExxonMobil stock, given data on other large energy companies.

MPT is less helpful in establishing the value of ExxonMobil as a takeover target or the value of any individual businesses within it. It also largely fails to address the portion of the company's value that is essentially real options on natural resource leases. However, given the huge scale of the company, these issues are probably less important for Exxon than for most publicly traded companies.

12 REAL OPTIONS AND EXPANDED NET PRESENT VALUE

- A recently proposed synthesis of traditional income methods and real options analysis, which we call *expanded net present value* (XNPV), to distinguish it from the $E(NPV)$ algorithm that is the heart of traditional income approach methods.

REAL AND FINANCIAL OPTIONS

Options and Opportunity

An option, generally speaking, is an opportunity. Having, or *holding*, an option implies that you have an opportunity. People like opportunities, even if they choose not to exercise them. Thus, a person who holds an option holds something of value. We should expect that options also provide value to businesses.

An *option contract* formalizes a business opportunity. In such a contract, the person who provides the opportunity to the other party is the *writer* of the option. Normally, the writer of an option contract receives compensation for providing the opportunity to the *owner* of the option and for shouldering the responsibilities that may come with that contract. The other party to any option contract is known as the *counterparty*.

Real and Financial Options

There are two broad classes of options, known as real and financial options. Both are mechanisms of opportunity.

In general, we describe options based, or *written*, on financial instruments (such as stocks and bonds) as *financial options*. The securities on which the financial options are written are known as the *underlying securities*. Financial securities on which option contracts are written are often widely traded, and well-developed options markets exist for standardized financial option contracts. Many such contracts can be traded with relatively small transaction costs and counterparty risks.

We call options written on real assets (such as land, natural resources, and agricultural products) *real options*. Because real assets usually do not have regularly observed transaction prices for standard quantities, the term *underlying security* is not accurate. We adopt the convention of calling such assets simply the *underlying*. Aside from a narrow group of specific option contracts, real options are usually not traded on well-developed markets, are not standardized, and are subject to considerable transaction costs and counterparty risks. We note shortly that the distinction between real and financial options is not always clear.

A Canonical Example: The Pure Call Option

Let us consider a canonical example of a financial option. A *call option* is the right, but not the obligation, to purchase an underlying asset at a specified price during one or more specified time periods. This price is known as the *strike* price. If the underlying security or asset is priced above that strike price on the exercise date, then the owner of the call option receives a net payoff equal to the difference between the strike price and the market price. (This payoff could be in the form of a payment from the writer of the option, or of buying the underlying at the strike price and immediately reselling it at the market price.) If not, he or she receives nothing.

The complement to a call option is a *put option*, which gives the owner the right (but not the obligation) to sell a security at a specific strike price, during one or more specific time periods.

The value of a pure put and call option at maturity is shown in Equation 12.1.

Equation 12.1 Call and Put Option Value

$$C_T = Max\left[(S-K),\ 0\right]$$
$$P_T = Max\left[(K-S),\ 0\right]$$

where:

S = spot price (current market price) of underlying security

K = strike or exercise price

C_T = value of European call option at $t = T$

P_T = value of European put option at $t = T$

t = 0, ..., T is a time index

"In the Money" Options

A call option at an exercise price lower than the current price of the underlying security is called *in the money*; conversely, a call option on stock that is currently priced well below the strike price is "out of the money."

European and American Options

A *European option* is one in which the option is exercised at a specific time: the expiration date of the option. In contrast, *American options* can be exercised during an extended time period before the expiration. The pure put and call options described earlier were European options.

Exotic Options

In addition to the put and call options, many exotic financial options exist. Among these are *Asian options*, which are based on the average price of the underlying security during a specific period. *Bermuda options* have specific times at which the option can be exercised. In *lookback options*, the lowest (or highest) price of the underlying security establishes a transaction value. Other variations include *swaps*, which are combinations of puts and calls, and *swaptions*, which are options on swaps.

Indications of Value for Options

Recall the value of a pure put or call option at maturity, which was expressed neatly in Equation 12.1. A much more difficult question is the value of options *before* maturity. Intuition suggests that an option is valuable even if you do not exercise it; this suggests that options are valuable even if they are not currently in the money. In fact, even pure financial option contracts that are out of the money typically have some market value.

Even under ideal conditions, the market value of financial options is affected by all the following factors:

1. The difference between the strike price and the current (*spot*) price of the underlying security
2. The time between now and the expiration of the option
3. The market rate of interest
4. The volatility of the underlying security

When conditions are not ideal, other factors (such as the risk that the counterparty will not fulfill the contract, risks related to the underlying assets, and transaction costs) also affect the value. We discuss these factors further later in this chapter, under the sections titled "The Search for the Price of Financial Options" and "Real Options."

Net Present Value Does Not Predict Option Value

Recall the algorithm of expected net present value: it is the mathematical expectation (across a random set of events) of the net present value of future cash flows. This $E(NPV)$ algorithm thus captures three of the four factors that affect option value under ideal circumstances. However, it does not capture the fourth: volatility.

Therefore, even under ideal conditions, the expected net present value algorithm (and any discounted cash flow analyses based on it) will not accurately predict the market value of an option contract.

Futures and Forwards

Two related contracts bear discussing: forward contracts and futures contracts. These are sometimes lumped together as *forward commitments*, meaning commitments to do something in the future. They are sometimes considered option contracts, although they are different from pure call and put options.

Forward Contract

A *forward contract* is a contract to deliver a specific commodity to a specific buyer at a future (forward) date for a specified price. Forward contracts typically have the following characteristics:

- Require the delivery (or payoff) of one party to the other
- Are not standardized and are difficult to exchange on a secondary market
- Require each party to bear the credit risk of the other
- Are often private transactions
- May involve real commodities such as agricultural products or financial instruments such as a foreign currency

Futures Contract

A *futures contract* is similar to a forward contract but is standardized in its terms. Futures are traded on an exchange and are commonly regulated by a government agency. Futures contracts typically have the following characteristics:

- Carry an explicit or implicit guarantee from an exchange and may have the exchange be the issuing party, allowing the contracts themselves to be traded on a secondary market relatively easily
- Are marked to market daily
- Allow or require the counterparties to make payments through a clearinghouse on a regular basis

There are reasons for both futures and forwards. Futures contracts provide liquidity and trading capability that are desirable to investors wishing to hedge against risks that are represented in the futures market. Forwards may provide a manner to directly manage a specific risk, if an appropriate counterparty can be found and if the counterpart risk is acceptable.

Are Forwards and Futures Options?

We intuitively described holding an option as having an opportunity but not an obligation. Strictly speaking, both parties to forward and futures contracts have an obligation; one must deliver a commodity and the other must receive it and make payments. This is qualitatively different from a pure option, as evidenced by the fact that parties to a forward or futures contract may not pay or receive anything at the time of the contract.

Furthermore, forwards (and some portion of futures) require delivery of the underlying asset, whereas many financial options require only a financial payoff. In addition, the underlying asset may or may not be a real commodity. Finally, parties to forward contracts typically bear significant counterparty risk.

Forward commitments of various types have traditionally been traded alongside financial options and are commonly discussed in the same texts. However, for the reasons stated here, it is difficult to classify them neatly as either real or financial options.[1]

BRIEF HISTORY OF OPTION CONTRACTS

Two Thousand Years of Option Contracts

Option contracts, broadly defined, have existed for at least two thousand years. Such contracts originated in ancient times and expanded drastically in the seventeenth and eighteenth centuries, with dramatic consequences in Europe, Asia, and the Americas. Against this sweep of history, the explosion of trading in financial options appears as a recent phenomenon.

Ancient Roots

Some scholars trace the introduction of options to ancient Egypt. Others assert that ancient Phoenician, Greek, and Roman traders used option contracts to reduce the risks of maritime commerce. There is indisputable written evidence of some type of option contracts dating back at least three thousand years.[2]

One oft-told story is of the ancient Greek philosopher Thales of Miletus, who paid earnest money to secure the rights to use olive presses in advance of the harvest. According to the story, Thales then rented the presses to others during the harvest season, at much higher prices. The teller of this tale was the great philosopher Aristotle, in his book *Politics* (c. 350 BC).

Early Modern Option Contracts in Asia

Option contracts existed in Asia at least as far back as the seventeenth century. The house of a wealthy rice merchant named Yodoya in Osaka, Japan, became a regular meeting place for traders in *rice tickets* as early as 1650 and is sometimes identified as the first formal futures exchange in the world. These were a contract to receive a certain amount of rice from a warehouse at a future date. By 1710, formal *rice coupon* futures contracts were traded.[3]

Along with the rise in commerce and financial markets in Europe after the Middle Ages, option contracts are recorded in a number of European countries, including Holland, England, France, and Germany, beginning in the seventeenth century.[4] In some cases, these option contracts were known as *privileges* and were closer to commercial trade contracts than true financial options. Options were traded on the stock of the East India Company at least as far back as 1719.[5]

Early Modern Options in Europe; Confusion de confusiones

In 1688, the Spanish businessman and poet Joseph de la Vega wrote a treatise on the financial markets in Amsterdam titled *Confusion de confusiones*. This book, perhaps the first one to describe the modern stock market, discusses trading in option contracts and laments the influence of emotions, guile, and even trickery that existed even then. Two centuries later, the London broker Charles Castelli wrote a pamphlet in 1877 that explained options trading in multiple markets. Indeed, he illustrated it with an example of arbitrage profits earned by exploiting differences between the London Stock Exchange and the Constantinople Bourse.[6]

Contemporary Expansion

The Chicago Board of Trade was established in 1848, and the rival Chicago Mercantile Exchange was founded in 1919. These exchanges regularized forward and futures contracts involving agricultural commodities such as grains. Sometime around 1900, options trading on stocks began to grow in major financial centers such as Paris and London.[7]

A turning point came in the 1970s with both the founding of the Chicago Board Options Exchange in 1973 and the nearly contemporaneous publication of the famous Black and Scholes option pricing article. Within several years, financial options trading spread to major exchanges in multiple countries and, soon afterward, to de facto worldwide trading through major markets. Today, the use of derivative securities and option contracts is integrated into financial and currency markets across the globe—with great consequence to investors in those markets.

The Nature of Ancient and Early Modern Contracts

Optionlike contracts date back more than two thousand years, but the characterization of ancient and early modern contracts as *options* is problematic. Many were primarily forward contracts (requiring delivery and involving product quality terms) rather than pure puts or calls.[8] If you were to fully diagram the underlying payoff and risk characteristics of such contracts, you might find many of them *more* complicated than a standard exchange-traded financial option, because they involved counterparty risks, operated in incomplete markets, lacked standardization, and were based on unusual underlying securities or commodities. Many of these contracts would be classified today as real options, others as forward commitments.

Thus, we should understand the history of option contracts, broadly defined, as one in which forward commitments and optionlike agreements have been struck for more than two millennia, and in which financial options have been traded for approximately one century.

THE SEARCH FOR THE PRICE OF FINANCIAL OPTIONS

Solving a Mystery

The celebrated Black-Scholes formula solved one of the longstanding problems in modern finance: the correct value of a pure call option on a share of stock under strict market conditions. The search for this formula consumed years of the time of some of the era's best minds. The discovery and publication of the formula itself spawned a vast literature on financial options and, later, a smaller literature on real options.

The pioneers in this search included two individuals who created precursors to modern option pricing models. The books by the London broker Charles Castelli (1877) and the French mathematician Louis Bachelier (1900) both provide an early modern attempt to describe the proper pricing of such a contract.

Nearly a half century passed before the advent of unpublished papers by Paul Samuelson (1955) and the dissertation of James Boness (1964). Boness, in particular, anticipated the 1973 Black-Scholes-Merton pricing formula for pure financial options. It is interesting to note that he had translated Bachelier's dissertation from the original French.

Honors for Black, Scholes, and Merton

The famous Black-Scholes-Merton formula earned Myron Scholes and Robert Merton the 1997 Nobel Prize in Economics, and had Fischer Black not passed away before then, he would have been similarly honored.[9] Sadly, aside from the celebrated accomplishments of Black and Scholes (and, properly, Merton), little attention is paid to any of the other pioneers in the contemporary literature, and relatively little acclaim was given to them in their own time.[10]

The Black-Scholes-Merton Formula

This celebrated formula prices a pure call option on a non-dividend-paying stock as the difference between a factor based on the current market value of the underlying stock, and a factor based on the volatility of that stock and the remaining time to expiration of the option contract. This captures the two dynamics of an option: the *intrinsic value*, and the *time value*:

- The intrinsic value for a pure call option is the simple difference between the actual (spot) price and the strike price, if the difference is positive.
- The time value is a probability-weighted, discounted sum that reflects the likely result of future random movements of the underlying security. Because some out-of-the-money options may end up in the money because of such random variations, the time value can be positive even when the intrinsic value is zero.

These factors are calculated using the cumulative normal distribution $N(y)$, meaning the probability that a variable with a standard normal distribution $N(0, 1)$ will be less than y. The two $N(y)$ factors therefore take values between zero and one. See Equation 12.2.

Equation 12.2 Black-Scholes-Merton Formula

$$C = c(S, K, t, r, \sigma)$$
$$= SN(x) - KN(x - \sigma\sqrt{t})e^{-rt}$$

where:

C = value of a European call on a non-dividend-paying stock

S = current (spot) price

K = strike price

t = time until expiration

r = interest rate

$\dfrac{dS}{S}$ = $\sigma dt + \sigma dz$ (α = drift; σ = volatility; z is an increment of standard Brownian motion)

x = $\dfrac{\ln(S/K) + \left(r + \frac{1}{2}\sigma^2\right)t}{\sigma\sqrt{t}}$

$N(y)$ = cumulative normal distribution

Motivating the Formula

A number of excellent texts derive this formula from the underlying stochastic differential equation of the stock price process. Since we are interested primarily in real options, we do not attempt to duplicate that derivation here.[11] However, we do want to observe the following to motivate the formula:

- The B-S-M formula does not involve a expectation about future earnings of the company issuing the underlying security, and furthermore does not have any risk preferences for the buyer of the option embedded in it.
- Indeed, the formula contains no standard mathematical expectation; instead there are two risk-neutral expectations embedded in the factors $N(x)$ and $N(x - \sigma t^{-1/2})$.

Recall the assumption of a complete market and the existence of a risk-free security; this allows for the use of complete-market methods of neoclassical finance.

- If the spot price S is very large compared to the strike price K, the call option is almost certain to be exercised. Then $N(x)$ and $N(x - \sigma t^{-1/2})$ would be the cumulative normal distributions of large number (because S/K is very large). Thus, they converge toward one. If both the $N(y)$ factors are equal to one, the formula becomes $C_+ = S - Ke^{-rt}$, where the $+$ sign indicates a deep in-the-money call option. This is the same as a forward contract on an investment asset that pays no income.[12]

- If the stock price is very low compared to the strike price, the two $N(y)$ terms converge toward zero (because $\ln(S/K)$ is very low).

- Consider the results of using the formula in a world with no volatility in the stock, in which case $\sigma = 0$. Given the assumption that the stock price is a geometric Brownian motion (GBM), it grows steadily. Again, assuming that the discipline of complete markets forces riskless securities to be priced using the risk-free rate, we have the expected payoff at time t of $\max(Se^{rt} - K, 0)$. This matches our intuition that if there is no uncertainty, a call option on a stock should be the discounted value today of the simple difference between the future stock price and the strike price.

Standard Assumptions; Reservations

The Black-Scholes-Merton formula relies on a set of assumptions that have become standard in the study of pricing financial options. These assumptions include the following:

- The underlying stock pays no dividends, is regularly traded, and has a known spot price.

- The underlying stock follows a stochastic process (known as geometric Brownian motion) that produces a lognormal distribution of prices (and normally distributed returns). An important further assumption is that the volatility of this diffusion is known and constant, at least for a short time period.

- A risk-free security is traded in the market of the same duration as the option contract, and it establishes a risk-free interest rate; this risk-free rate is usually also assumed to be constant for at least a short time period. As with the preceding observations, observe that S, K, r, and σ are all arguments to the B-S-M formula shown in Equation 12.2.

- There are no commissions, insurance payments, or other transaction costs.

- The underlying security can be immediately liquidated if necessary.

- There is no counterparty risk (the risk that the writer or owner of the option will not immediately make payment or otherwise perform the obligations under the contract), or such risk is completely covered by collateral or insurance.

These assumptions often hold approximately for certain financial options traded among certain market participants, during many time periods. Relaxing some of these restrictions (such as opening up the restriction on when the option can be exercised, or whether dividends are paid, or varying the basis for the exercise of the option) results in pricing models that are much more complicated and in many cases cannot be solved using closed-form equations.

Practical Difficulties: Financial Option Pricing

Black and Scholes did not claim that their formula would value options accurately in practical market conditions, and for good reason. We can immediately observe some problems in applying the B-S-M formula in practical settings:

- The B-S-M model assumes complete markets, the absence of transaction costs, the lack of counterparty risk, and the ability to borrow without binding constraints. For some financial markets in certain time periods, and some market participants, this would be approximately correct. However, in unusual market conditions (such as those that occurred during the Great Recession of 2008–2009) these conditions did not uniformly hold even for very large market participants.

- The formula assumes that a volatility parameter is known and constant, at least for a short time period. However, available information can be used only to estimate this parameter, even under near-ideal situations. Indeed, many practitioners use *implied volatility*, which is calculated by using *actual* prices in a specific model to estimate parameter values for a model.[13]

- The model assumes that a risk-free security can be traded at exactly the desired interval, and that the return on this security is known in advance (or does not change). However, the prices on actual risk-free securities (such as U.S. Treasury bills) change frequently.

- The B-S-M formulas were elegantly derived using stochastic calculus, which focuses on very small changes occurring in very small time increments. Therefore, the results of the formulas also change frequently as market conditions change.

Because of these factors, using the B-S-M formula naively in the derivatives market could be a direct ticket to pauperhood!

THE OPTION MODEL OF FIRM VALUE

Introduction: Equity as a Call Option on a Firm

In their 1973 article, Black and Scholes touched briefly on the idea that stocks and bonds issued by corporations could be considered options on the market value of the firm. In particular, they observed that the equity in a corporation could be viewed as a call option on the value of the firm, with the strike price being the value of the debt. We examine this concept, which has important implications for the value of firms, in this section.

Black and Scholes noted that under common bankruptcy law in the United States and many other countries, equity holders have the residual claim on the firm's assets in the case of bankruptcy. Thus, if the firm is liquidated, the proceeds first pay off all bondholders, and anything left goes to the equity holders.

Thus, equity ownership for a profitable, well-capitalized firm is like a deep-in-the-money call option, with the underlying being the earning ability of the firm, or the firm's assets. Equity ownership in a risky, but still solvent, firm is like a just-in-the-money call option.

The Option Value Model of the Firm

The classic option value model of the firm relies on certain heroic assumptions about markets, the company, and investors. However, even a dramatically simplified model demonstrates how option valuation is essential to business valuation.

Characteristics of the Model

Assume the following structure of the firm, markets, and institutions:[14]

• The firm is a publicly traded corporation operating in a country with the basic law structure that exists in the United States, England, and many other countries, including limited liability and bondholder preferences in case of bankruptcy.

• The firm finances its operations using two securities: a stock and a bond. The accounting identity of the firm forces the book value of its assets to be the sum of the book values of its liabilities (the bond) and its equity (the stock).

• The bond issued by the company is a zero-coupon (pure discount) bond with a specific face value of L, maturing at time T.

• The stock issued by the company pays no dividend. However, investors can earn capital gains by selling at time T, if it makes a profit from its operations and either holds cash to distribute later or reinvests it profitably. This is a similar assumption to that made by Modigliani and Miller and implies a complete market and no arbitrage in the firm's securities.

• The company is subject to random events as well as the normal underlying economic trends. The current market value of its expected future earnings, A_t, follows a geometric Brownian motion process. Such a process is characterized by a constant-proportion drift and diffusion.[15] Note that this means the assets will never become zero before T.

We could call this the "assets" of the firm, although they are *not* assets in the accounting sense, nor do they approximate the assets of most operating companies. Recall that the B-S-M model for financial options on stock assumed the *stock* followed a GBM process; here we assume the "assets" follow such a diffusion.

• The company also faces a risk of bankruptcy, meaning that the value of its assets could drop below the value of the debt. There are no transaction costs, and in the event of bankruptcy the assets can be immediately liquidated at market value.

• There also exists a risk-free bond and other securities that allow for the payoffs of the "asset" security A to be replicated in the market. This market is therefore complete.

• Market discipline forces the market value of the firm's stock to be the difference between the market value of its "assets" and that of its liabilities.

Under these assumptions—including the institutional assumptions of limited liability and bondholder preference under bankruptcy—the firm's stock is effectively a call option of the "assets" of the firm. See Equation 12.3.

Equation 12.3 B-S-M Option Model of the Firm

Accounting Identity

$$A_t \equiv L_t + S_t$$

where:

L_t = market value of bond at time t

$\bar{L}$ = face value of bond at time T

S_t = market value of stock at time t

Asset Process

$$dA_t = \varphi A_t dt + \sigma A_t dz(t)$$

φ, σ constants; $z(t)$ a stochastic process

$A_t > 0$, all t

$t = 1, \dots T, \dots$ a time index

Value of Equity and Debt at Maturity

$$V(L_T) = \min(A_T, \bar{L})$$
$$V(S_T) = \max(A_T - \bar{L}, 0)$$

The Option Model of Firm Value: Implications

Implications: Price of a Stock

Following this logic—and it is good logic—we come to a startling conclusion: securities issued by firms in this simplified world must have some "option value," because *they are options.*

Under the strict market and institutional conditions just described, including complete markets and limited liability for stockholders, the market value of the stock and bond can be calculated directly as the value of a financial option (Equation 12.4).

Equation 12.4 Price of Stock in Complete Markets with Limited Liability

Market Value of Equity

$$S_t = \tilde{E}_t[e^{-r(T-t)} \max(A_T - \bar{L}, 0)]$$

where:

$\tilde{E}_t$ = expectation under risk-neutral measure

r = riskless borrowing rate

A_t = market value of assets

t is current time; T is time of expiration

Market Value of Debt

$$V(L_t) = A_t - S_t$$

Implications: Validity of Traditional Theories

This has strong implications for the validity of traditional theories of business valuation. In particular:

• The value of a firm will be different from the expected net present value of its future earnings from existing operations, even under the most favorable assumptions about markets and institutions. To the extent that these deviations are significant, the neoclassical investment rule will be incorrect and income-approach valuation methods will be flawed.[16]

• The difference between the market value of a call option on the firm's assets (the stock) and the expected net present value of the firm's earnings will become larger when the assets are volatile or when the firm is not strongly capitalized.

Thus, we should expect that the implicit error for ignoring option value would be relatively large for growing, small, midsized, privately held, and distressed firms. In other words, it will be relatively large for nearly all firms *except* large, publicly traded, stable, well-capitalized firms in industries with relatively little technological change.

• An evaluation of the capitalization of a company *always* has some relevance for its value, because the capitalization of the firm is essential to the evaluation of the implied option value of equity in the firm.

• Recognizing the serious risks of failure and high degree of volatility for start-up firms, the decision to invest in such a firm cannot be viewed solely through the lens of the expected value of its future earnings. The same observation could also apply to any firm with significant volatility in expected earnings or significant risk of insolvency.

REAL OPTIONS

Real Options and Managerial Flexibility

One failure of the neoclassical investment rule was outlined in the seminal 1994 book by Avanish Dixit and Robert Pindyck, *Investment Under Uncertainty*. Following the findings of McDonald and Siegel (1986) and Myers (1977), they outlined how the existence of managerial flexibility renders the neoclassical investment rule incorrect. Thus, making proper business investment decisions—by which we mean using the available information in a rational manner—*requires* a valuation technique that recognizes the value of embedded options.

Real-World Assumptions About Real Options

Unfortunately, integrating real options into a valuation framework is not easy. Real option valuation must work in a much more difficult environment than Black, Scholes, and Merton assumed in their derivation of a financial option pricing formula.

In particular, we must deal with the following real-world conditions:

1. The "underlying" is usually not a security and often does not have a regularly observed market price. Instead, the underlying could be equity in a closely held business, a controlling share of such a business, parcels of real estate, natural resource leases, new technologies or promising drugs, operating facilities, or intellectual property.

2. Markets are usually incomplete, and therefore there is no unique pricing rule enforced by a no-arbitrage condition.

3. Transaction costs (and costs of due diligence) exist and are probably significant.

4. The market rate of interest for the relevant investors is typically not the risk-free rate.

5. The subject company, investor, or entrepreneur may have borrowing constraints.

6. Counterparty risk exists, although it may be partially ameliorated with contract provisions and insurance.

What "Real Options" Exist for Firms?

A variety of bona fide real options can be identified for operating firms. These include the following:

1. Growth options
2. Option to defer
3. Option to abandon an investment (*scrap*)
4. Option to learn
5. Option to expand
6. Option to shut down

Some authors further classify real options into *operative* options and *strategic* options, with the latter involving potential operations and the former current operations.[17] The dividing line between these is not clear.

We directly evaluate growth options, options to defer investments, and options to abandon and shut down.

Growth Options

One of the most common real options, and one deserving of special notice, is the *growth option*. Stewart Myers (1977) first proposed that the value of the firm could be decomposed into the value generated by its existing operations and the value of its "growth options" for future expansion. From a purely financial perspective, the growth options of a firm are the complement to bankruptcy risk. Both represent the potential of the company to achieve market results that are outside the natural growth of its existing activities, and could result from a handful of risky business decisions.

Probably the easiest demonstration of growth options is the value of a start-up firm with no history of earning a profit. If such a firm has *any* market value, it is probably due to the firm's growth options.

Option to Defer

The option to defer an investment exists whenever a firm can take advantage of a business opportunity in the current period and in some subsequent period. As with other options, there may be a cost to the firm to secure this option.

Options to Scrap or Shut Down

Two of the most common real options are the options to scrap and shut down. Often, a firm has the opportunity to exit a particular line of business, shut down an operation, abandon an investment, or sell a license or patent that it is underutilizing, and to do so on reasonable terms. In a large share of such occasions, the firm's management decides not to exercise this option. However, that does not mean that the option has no value.

Frequent Ignorance of Scrappage Options in Traditional DCF Models

The option to scrap is commonly ignored in traditional income models. For example, when an income approach model includes a terminal value that is the perpetual capitalization of then-current earnings, the option to scrap is probably being ignored. Indeed, the use of a perpetual-capitalization formula such as the Gordon growth formula implies that no options are exercised that cause the firm to deviate from its growth path in the future.

However, it is probably not the only option to be ignored. Sometimes the effect of ignoring the option to scrap is partially offset by ignoring the growth options embedded in continuing in the same line of business.

Idiosyncrasy of Real Options

Unlike standardized financial option contracts, real options are usually specific to the firm and dependent on the firm's business model and strategy. This distinction, sometimes overlooked in contemporary discussions of real options, was implied by Stewart Myers when the concept was first introduced into the literature in 1977:

> Thus part of the value of a firm is accounted for by the present value of *options* to make further investments on possibly favorable terms. This value depends on the rule for deciding whether the options are to be exercised. (Myers, 1977, pp. 148–149; emphasis in original)

This idiosyncrasy concerns not just the risks the company faces, but also what we call the "policy" the firm follows in the value functional approach described in Chapter 17, "Applications: Finance and Valuation."

Caution on Separating Real Options from the Business

One must be careful to not assume that a valuable, incremental real option exists in a business when the exercise (or refusal to exercise) of that option is already embedded in the general operation of business. Because real options are usually idiosyncratic and related to the firm's operations in some manner, the distinction is not easy to draw.

Similarly, failing to take into account the consequences of exercising a real option—or counting them twice—can cause major errors in valuation. One must consider whether the management and financiers of a firm are willing to support the exercise of options, as well as bear their cost, before simply adding the value of a real option to the current-operations value of the firm. We return to this issue below.

REAL OPTION VALUATION: METHODS

The Need for Robust Option Valuation Tools

The search for the price of a pure financial option, under ideal conditions, took more than a century. There are now plenty of analytical models that, for a variety of standard financial options, can quickly provide an estimate of market prices (usually under strict assumptions). However, we are still looking for a truly robust valuation tool that will estimate the market value of real options. Next, we outline a dozen methods in a handful of categories and provide some practical comments on the applicability of each.

Possible Methods

Closed-Form and Analytic Models

The following models can be employed to directly calculate option values in the narrow set of cases in which the assumptions of the model are approximately fulfilled.

1. *Black-Scholes-Merton model.* The B-S-M model discussed earlier has produced many variations, which can sometimes be used for financial options under near-ideal market conditions. However, real options involve complications that cannot be assumed away and therefore rarely are solvable using this model. One should be particularly cautious of simply plugging an implied volatility parameter into a standard financial option model in an effort to produce a desired outcome.

2. *Binomial models, including the Cox-Ross-Rubinstein (C-R-R) model.* The binomial model first proposed by Cox, Ross, and Rubinstein (1979) is a discrete-time model of random price movements in an underlying security. The model contemplates a stock whose price can go up, or down, at specified time intervals. The binomial distribution converges to a normal distribution as the number of trials goes toward infinity. Recall that a normal distribution assumption was a basis of the original B-S-M formula for financial options. Because of this, for pure European options, the Black-Scholes-Merton and the Cox-Ross-Rubinstein models converge to the same result.

Because the C-R-R model can be extended to more situations than the classic B-S-M and can be programmed to work quickly, it is often the basis for practical option pricing work today.

3. *Lattice models.* The binomial model underlying C-R-R can be expanded to trinomial and more complicated models sometimes known as *lattice* models.[18]

Representing future events by a series of up or down movements, these models create a lattice of possible outcomes. Lattice models are often visualized as a sideways-facing tree and are therefore similar in structure to the decision trees described earlier. These models can also incorporate assumptions such as varying volatility that are impossible to use in the standard binomial model.

4. *Model-specific closed-form equations.* For a handful of models involving specific functional forms (including the statistical process producing the underlying prices, the form of the option, and the type of regular earnings or payments), closed-form equations have been developed. These equations provide, under these limited assumptions, a solution to a specific option pricing model.

Nearly-Complete-Market Models

The following techniques rely on the assumption that markets are nearly complete but no closed-form solution is known.

5. *Contingent Claims Analysis (CCA).* Contingent Claims Analysis is based on the assumption that complete markets include securities that price the risks involved in the subject real option. CCA has often been proposed as a method for real options involving natural resources such as oil and coal, as well as facilities that extract or refine raw materials. For a number of these commodities, the price of a newly extracted standard unit is regularly priced in an open market, and some form of traded security reflects this price.

In such cases, it may be possible to construct a *contingent claim* that produces a set of payoffs that nearly replicate or hedge those of the real options investment. The discipline of complete-market pricing models can then be asserted as a pricing mechanism. The result hinges on the assumption that a nearly risk-free portfolio should, in theory, earn the risk-free rate in a nearly complete market.

6. *Good deal bounds.* John Cochrane and Jesús Saá-Reuquejo proposed in 2000 an innovative application of certain techniques often used in complete markets, for use in markets that are only partially complete.[19] The technique makes use of the intuition that an investor will want to be compensated for risk, and that such an investor will therefore consider the additional expected return promised by a risky investment relative to the additional risk it carries. A good metric for this is the *Sharpe ratio* of excess return to excess risk, which is a dimensionless number.[20]

The developers of this technique suggest that investors will consider investments that can be approximately hedged by other ("basis") assets. This reduces, but does not eliminate, the unhedged risk. The allowable market price for a risky investment (after considering the portion of the risk that can be hedged) should be within the bounds set by the best and worst deals available. If, in fact, an investor could choose between a large set of risky investments that could be neatly categorized by numerically precise measures of risk and return, this "bounding the pricing kernel" approach could have substantial merit.

There are difficulties in implementing this approach, starting with the fact that the variance and covariance of expected returns in a real options problem are hard to define and may be impossible to measure. This is a promising angle for future development.

Monte-Carlo Methods

The term *Monte Carlo* in statistics and related fields refers to simulating the outcome of numerous random events using a mathematical model that uses randomly generated numbers and then examining the outcomes of the simulated events to infer the distribution of outcomes of actual events. The Monte Carlo approach is generally attributed to Stanislaw Ulam, the brilliant Polish mathematician who co-developed the hydrogen bomb with physicist Edward Teller and also worked with the mathematician John von Neumann on the Manhattan Project. In a telling example of serendipity, Ulam originally developed the method to simulate the outcome of a card game and then realized it could be used to simulate the effects of atomic collisions.[21]

7. *Monte Carlo models of option pricing.* An approach to pricing options that have no known closed-form pricing model is to construct a model of the contract's behavior and use Monte Carlo trials to simulate the outcome. This technique can be quite useful when there are multiple sources of uncertainty that may interact or where the underlying price process is unusual. Of course, the technique requires modeling correctly the behavior of the underlying events and properly generating random equivalents of those events. If that is possible, the analyst can then evaluate the outcomes as a whole, including the average or median result as well as the dispersion of results.

The Value Functional, Stochastic Control, and Similar Methods

A separate approach is to recast the problem as a recursive decision problem, solving a Bellman equation or similar functional equation. Such a mathematical approach is at the heart of the value functional approach. Variations of this method are sometimes called *stochastic control, impulse control,* or *Markov decision problems.*

8. *Optimization with stochastic control.* This approach models the objective of the holder of the option as solving a recursive problem. The model includes the actions the holder can choose, which can be as simple as the binary choice "exercise | do not exercise." The model also includes a transition function for the state of nature, which can involve stochastic elements. Such a tool can deal explicitly with options to wait, costs to scrap, and other managerial decisions embedded in the value of a project or a firm.[22]

Stochastic control algorithms are novel and described only in a relative handful of other texts.[23] We propose them for use in business valuation in Chapter 15, "The Value Functional: Theory," and provide applications in Chapter 16, "The Value Functional: Applications."

9. *Markov decision problem.* Many real options problems, especially when they involve interactions among operations and different real options, can be transformed into a particular form of value functional equation known as *Markov decision problems* (MDPs).[24] Such problems are characterized by a discrete set of states and actions. We discuss MDPs within the broader value functional approach in Chapter 15, "The Value Functional: Theory."

Decision Tree Analysis

10. *Decision tree analysis.* Decision trees, or more properly event trees, are used in a number of algorithms. In particular, binomial and lattice models implicitly create trees of possible outcomes, as do some value functional and Markov decision problems. We reserve the term *decision tree analysis* (DTA) for the use of a model-specific event tree with model-specific decision points, probabilities, and payoffs to examine a problem. However, the nomenclature varies considerably, and numerical models such as the C-R-R binomial model are sometimes called implementations of decision tree analysis. For many real options problems, a decision tree is the most straightforward representation. It is often a useful step in visualizing the problem even if DTA cannot be used to solve it.

A serious methodological problem for DTA involves the selection of a discount rate. Simply using a single discount rate estimated for a typical firm in the industry (especially if stock market data are the basis for the estimate but the firm is privately held) will almost always be incorrect if the risks incorporated in the tree do not reflect (at every node) the typical business risk in the industry. In my experience, this can be a minor problem or a major problem, depending primarily on whether the various branches of the tree reflect risks that are asymmetrical or are substantially different from each other.

11. *Decision tree analysis supplemented with Monte Carlo simulations.* One advanced technique can be useful when real options are compounded, random events are expected to dominate future decisions, or both. The technique involves creating a decision tree and then using Monte Carlo simulations to estimate the values of certain nodes on the trees.

Professional Judgment

12. *Professional judgment.* In my experience, the most common method of estimating the value of real options in business is to use professional judgment. This is probably due to the lack of robust tools to estimate the value of real options, a certain degree of ignorance about the existence of some tools, and a reluctance to explicitly abandon traditional methods even when they are inappropriate for the task. However, in cases where the analyst has useful data on the firm and on the available real options, and that data is supplemented by advice from a person with substantial experience, it can be the best available method.

Sometimes, an anticipated exercise of real options (particularly growth options and abandonment options) is directly incorporated into discounted cash flow schedules, which are then presented as the results of a traditional income method of valuing the current operations of the company. (Unfortunately, the use of such terms as *two-stage DCF* and *three-stage DCF* can camouflage this fact.) This may create the similar discount rate problem as identified earlier for DTA and may also create the more serious problem of failing to identify the relevant assumptions and techniques used by the analyst.

Note on Software

The software necessary for various real options methods varies widely. Since this field changes rapidly, see the resources discussed in Appendix B, "Guide to the Solutions Manual."

REAL OPTIONS AND MANAGERIAL FLEXIBILITY: EXAMPLES

Key Definitions

The direct study of real options requires a careful distinction between two concepts:

- We describe the *value of an investment* or value of an asset at a certain time as the amount the investor would pay to purchase that investment, at that time, as implied by the definition of *fair market value.*

- We define the *value of the investment opportunity* at a certain time as the amount a person would be willing to pay for the *opportunity* to make the investment.

These definitions allow us to analyze the value of an opportunity and distinguish it from the value of an underlying asset.

The Manufacturing Plant Example

The following example illustrates how the standard discounted cash flow methods can generate the wrong signal to a manager or investor. The numerical analysis is based on an example from two of the pioneers of the field, although I have expanded the presentation of institutional and economic factors.[25]

Idealized Investment Opportunity Conditions

Consider the following idealized investment opportunity:

- A large firm has the opportunity to construct a new manufacturing plant. The plant would produce a product that the company knows how to build, distribute, and sell.

- The cost of building the plant includes the cost of hiring employees, obtaining raw materials, and beginning production. There is a predictable rate of price inflation that affects all costs similarly, except for one specific commodity.

- There is at least one similar company in the same industry with traded stock or another traded security that depends on the same factors. The production technology and production costs in the industry are stable and reasonably competitive. All the relevant firms are able to borrow money and issue stock at market rates.

- In addition, the firm has a good estimate of its cost of capital for an investment of this type, and a risk-free security exists. The cost of capital is above these rates of interest and above the inflation rate. All these rates are constant and known.

- The plant would produce a product that is in constant demand. However, the market price of the product is subject to significant random variation.

Specific Prices and Probabilities

Now assume, under these ideal conditions, that the company uses available information and financial experts to accurately estimate the likely costs of constructing the plant and the expected profits (or losses) from producing the product and selling it at market prices in the future. These same experts identify only one contingency: the price of an important commodity that affects the future demand for the product and therefore its value to all firms in this industry. Even for this contingency, however, they have assigned a probability distribution of outcomes for both the plant and the related security.

- The price of acquiring the rights to build the plant, building it, and hiring the workers to operate it is $I = \$104$. There is an implicit cost of delaying the decision to build, which is the (predictable) rate of inflation.

- We ignore here the fact that the company could escrow the money not spent in a risk-free security during that time, or assume that any such interest earnings are equivalent to an option premium paid to retain the rights to build in the future.

- Depending on the future price of the important commodity, the value of the plant to the firm could be $V_1 = \$180$ or $V_2 = \$60$ with equal probability one year from now. Similarly, the market price for the traded security could be $S_1 = 36$ or $S_2 = 12$. The information on those prices will arrive after $t = 0$, although in time for decisions to be made at $t = 1$.

- The risk-free interest rate, which we also assume is the borrowing rate for the firm and the underlying rate of price inflation, is $r = 8$ percent, and the expected return on equity in the industry is $d = 20$ percent, which we accept as the company's discount rate on capital investments of this type.

An event tree illustrating this two-period problem is displayed in Figure 12.1.

Very Optimistic Assumptions

These assumptions are *very* optimistic in terms of information, management capability, ability to predict future costs and demand, and access to financial markets. In such favorable situations, we would expect a standard finance tool to work quite well. Let us see whether it does.

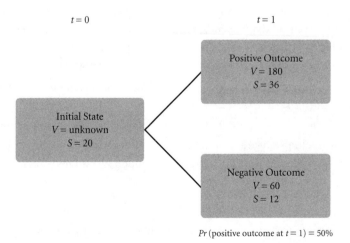

Figure 12.1   Manufacturing investment example: Event trees

Manufacturing Plant Investment: DCF Analysis

Consider the following standard DCF analysis of the investment opportunity:

1. Building the plant is an irreversible decision, and once the decision to build is made, the plant is worth only the net present value of its future earnings.

2. The value of the investment is uncertain, primarily because the selling price of the product to be manufactured there varies, and therefore the earning power of the plant varies.

3. The company follows the standard capital budgeting rule, using its cost of capital as a discount rate. The gross $E(NPV)$ of making the investment today is calculated by discounting the prospective cash flows and weighting them by the probability of each alternative. The expected net present value of those cash flows is a neat $V_{DCF} = \$100$. This means the expected net gain from the investment ($V_{DCF} - I$) is a negative \$4.[26]

Thus, the classic $E(NPV)$ decision rule says *no*. Indeed, it says *no* with near-complete information about costs of capital, future raw material prices, future operating costs, and future demand for the product.

The basic assumptions and the DCF calculations are shown in Table 12.1.

TABLE 12.1
DCF analysis of the manufacturing investment

Real Options: Manufacturing Plant Example

	Year 0	Year 1 (positive outcome)	Year 1 (negative outcome)
Value of plant (V_0, V^+, V^-)	Unknown	$ 180	$ 60
Value of security (S_0, S^+, S^-)	$ 20	$ 36	$ 12
Probability of outcome (p, $1 - p$)		50%	50%
Cost to Build Plant (I)	**$ 104**		
Discount rate for firm (d)	20%		
Borrowing discount rate (r)	8%		
Risk-free discount rate (r_f)	8%		
Asset price inflation rate	8%		

DCF Analysis of Building Plant at t = 0
(Solve for $E(NPV)$ – given V^+, V^-, p, d)

	Year 0	Year 1 (positive outcome)	Year 1 (negative outcome)
EV of outcome [$V^+ \times p$, $V^- \times (1 - p)$]		$ 90	$ 30
Discount factor: $1/(1 + d)^t$		83%	83%
NPV of outcomes		$ 75	$ 25
E(NPV) of returns	**$ 100**		
Gross cost of investment (I)	−104		
Expected discounted return	**$ (4)**		

Decision under standard E(NPV) Rule: Do not build

SOURCE: Author's illustration of example from Trigeorgis and Mason (1987, 2001).

Manufacturing Example: Real Options Analysis

We now use the same information and assumptions to conduct a real options analysis of the same investment opportunity. However, we make use of the subtle distinction between the *opportunity* to build the plant and actually building one.

This is not a significant change to the problem stated earlier. Firms building structures and planning to hire workers usually can acquire the land but not build, or acquire the land and build but not hire the workers, if economic or other events get in the way of successfully completing the project. Such decisions impose their own costs, but management almost always has some flexibility, and even in this idealized example we noted that delaying construction imposed an inflation cost.

We conduct two types of real options analysis: an application of decision tree analysis augmented with standard discounted cash flow tools, and a contingent claims analysis that requires a crucial additional assumption and some additional tools.

Real Options Analysis I: Climbing the Decision Tree

Decision tree analysis (DTA) is based on outlining the logical structure of events and actions over time, identifying the decision points along the way, and then weighting the possible outcomes by probability and likely costs or revenues. Decision trees as a method for analyzing investment behavior are described in Trigeorgis (2003); Damadoran (2002) also describes the technique, as do Koller, Goedhart, and Wessels (2007). The collected papers edited by Schwartz and Trigeorgis (2001) discuss this and related approaches to real options valuation.

Difficulties in Using Decision Tree Analysis

DTA presents three main difficulties:

1. The first difficulty in using decision trees is distilling the decision points to no more than a handful of discrete nodes on the tree. Such distillation is usually the first difficulty with *any* decision process; the primary strength of DTA is making this step explicit and visualizing it.

2. The second difficulty is accurately capturing the discrete changes in value (for both the subject opportunity and related state variables) that would occur at each node. In DTA (and in other approaches such as value functional and CCA), the most important state and decision variables can be highlighted at each node, whether or not a related accounting schedule is prepared.

3. The third difficulty is properly assigning a discount rate to each stage or to the entire opportunity. This latter problem has consumed much of the attention of some of the real options pioneers, perhaps because it arises quickly when comparing the use of DTA with that of CCA.

Application to Manufacturing Example

We use the method to analyze the manufacturing investment example as follows:

1. Create a decision tree that breaks out the information available at each time period and identifies decisions that can be made at each time period.

2. Note that the market price of the product is a natural state variable (summarizing the state of affairs or market conditions) and that the value of the plant itself can be considered a function of that state variable. These variables (the value of the investment and the price of a *twin security*) summarize the state of the investment at any time. Associate these state variables with each leaf on the tree, as shown in the section titled "Real Options Analysis II: Contingent Claims Analysis."

3. Recalculate the expected net present value of the opportunity to invest at each decision point (node) of the tree. Observe how the expected net present value changes as information about state variables unfolds over time.

4. Using this decision rule and the same probabilities of events and cost of capital, allow the investor one year to decide whether to build the plant. Calculate the $E(NPV)$ of the investment using that rule at each node, as follows:

   a. At the first node ($t = 0$), the $E(NPV)$ is negative, as calculated previously.

   b. At $t = 1$, if the outcome of the random event is negative, the value of the plant is deeply negative.

   c. At $t = 1$, if the outcome of the random event is positive, the value of the plant is deeply positive.

   Therefore, if we can defer the decision to $t = 1$, the $E(NPV)$ is an expected *gain* of $28. This occurs even assuming that the price of building the plant increases in the interim.[27]

5. Use the decision rule of exercising the option to *build the plant* only if all available information indicates that the value of the plant exceeds the cost of the investment. Given the results, choose to *acquire the rights* to build the plant at $t = 0$ and then build at $t = 1$ only if commodity prices move in the positive direction.

This analysis uses the same information as the traditional DCF method yet produces the opposite conclusion.

Real Options Analysis II: Contingent Claims Analysis

A contingent claims analysis (CCA) requires one additional critical assumption: that the risks of the investment (and the resulting payoffs) can be replicated with other securities. To illustrate the use of this method for the manufacturing investment example, assume that a traded security exists that replicates the payoffs from the construction of the new plant. This allows for a contingent claims analysis to be done as follows:

1. Using the assumption that the payoff can be perfectly replicated with another security and related assumptions (including a lack of transaction costs), create a replicating portfolio of securities or other asset investments and contracts.

2. Observe their prices and also observe the risk-free interest rate.

3. Assume that the requisite borrowings (potentially short-selling and acceptance of counterparty risk) can be accomplished without significant additional costs.

4. Use the risk-neutral pricing methods presented in Chapter 10, "Arbitrage-Free Pricing in Complete Markets."

TABLE 12.2

Contingent claims analysis of manufacturing investment

CCA Analysis of Building Plant at $t = 0$

(Using replicating payoffs from S and risk-free discount rate, solve for risk-neutral probabilities. Requires complete markets and payoff-replicating security S).

SOLVE FOR RISK-NEUTRAL PROBABILITIES

Replicating portfolio: $E = nS^- B$

Formula for pr: $pr = [(1 + r_f) \times S_0 - S^-]/(S^+ - S^-)$

Value for "risk neutral" probability of (+) outcome pr: 40%

CALCULATE RISK-NEUTRAL E(NPV) AT $t = 0$

	Year 0	Year 1 (positive outcome)	Year 1 (negative outcome)
Risk-neutral EV of outcome		$ 72	$ 36
Risk-free discount factor: $1/(1 + r_f)^t$		92.59%	92.59%
Risk-neutral NPV of outcome		$ 66.67	$ 33.33
"Risk-neutral" expected net present value (discounted at risk-free rate)	**$ 100**		
Gross cost of investment (I)	−104		
Expected discounted return	**$ (4)**		
Decision under risk-neutral, one-period E(NPV) rule:	*Do not invest*		

CCA Analysis of Right to Building Plant at $t = \{0, 1\}$

(Use payoffs calculated above; generate real option choices at possible exercise points. Requires complete markets and payoff-replicating security S).

	Year 0	Year 1 (positive outcome)	Year 1 (negative outcome)
Value of plant (V_0, V^+, V^-)		180	60
Gross cost of investment (I)		$ (112.32)	$ (112.32)
Net proceeds before option		**$ 67.68**	**$ (52.32)**
Max(Proceeds, 0)		**$ 67.68**	—
Risk-free discount factor: $1/(1 + r_f)^t$		92.59%	92.59%
Risk-neutral probabilities pr		40%	60%
Risk-neutral NPV		**$ 25.07**	—
Expected discounted return		**$ 25**	
Decision under risk-neutral, multi-period real options rule:	*Do not build*	*Exercise right to build*	*Do not build*

SOURCE: Author's illustration of example from Trigeorgis & Mason (1987, 2001).

Using these methods and relying on these assumptions produces a net value of the investment of $25. See Table 12.2.

Because we do not expect such complete-market conditions to occur often for business investments, we do not reproduce all the calculations here.[28] We can observe, however, that the value of the investment opportunity estimated using a decision tree analysis that did not require heroic assumptions is reasonably close to the CCA estimate based on a complete-market assumption.

Observations; Application to Real-World Investments

We can immediately observe two important results from this example:

1. The CCA and DTA methods produced nearly identical recommendations: maintain the right to build, but *do not exercise it* unless the key uncertain event (commodity

prices moving up) occurs. Thus, the real option is valuable but should not necessarily be exercised immediately.

2. Both recommendations *contradict* the standard capital budgeting rule. This contradiction occurs even under favorable assumptions about information on costs, financing, and probabilities.

These results support the key principle of real options: when management has flexibility, and where some decisions are irreversible, there are often opportunities to substantially increase or reduce investment payoffs by exploiting that flexibility.

There is also a third result: even in simple cases, methodological issues arise. In this case:

1. There was a small difference between the CCA and DTA results at $t = 1$, though both indicated the same decision. That difference is rooted in the use of a risk-neutral probability measure and risk-free rate with CCA, under the additional assumption of complete markets. In most cases involving real options, a true replicating portfolio is not available. However, even the availability of a partially replicating portfolio of alternative investments provides investors with useful price information and the possibility of hedging some risks.

2. We did not ignore the cost of maintaining the option to build in this example, because we included an inflationary cost and ignored any offsetting interest gains from delaying investment. In practical situations the ability to preserve an option is likely to impose costs that should be explicitly considered.

Real Options Example: The Growing Statewide Franchise

Another example of the practical use of real options is the following analysis of an actual company, performed by the author and his colleagues in a case involving a breach of contract.

Key Facts in the Case

- The company was a franchisee that represented a nationally known brand of services to business and leisure travelers.

- The franchisee had a solid operating track record, with consistent revenue increases and steady profitability. The revenue largely tracked the growth of population and tourism activity in its state but also was affected by the occasional opening of successful locations in parts of the state that were just developing.

- The franchisee had a first-right-of-refusal provision for its entire state in its franchise agreement, which it had vigorously defended in the past. It also had a management policy to be the first mover and aggressively entered new markets in the state whenever a business opportunity presented itself. This was costly in the short run, and some but not all of these new locations proved profitable.

- A breach of contract by the franchisor affected both current operations and the opportunity to enter new markets.

Valuation Method

The valuation approach taken in this case was affected by methodological, legal, and evidentiary matters. We present only the methodological issues here:

1. Extensive analysis of historical accounting records showed a consistent pattern of expenses relative to revenue and an approximate allocation into fixed, variable, and semifixed categories.

2. Using a practical income method, the company's lost earnings *from current operations* was estimated using the expected growth trend of revenues from those operations, less the marginal changes in costs estimated using the cost factors identified previously.

3. In addition to these lost earnings from current operations, *lost growth options* were estimated by using the actual incremental revenues from a set of newly opened locations. Because not all of these locations remained open, we estimated the lost growth options using an implicit discount on the potential earnings from the likely number of new locations that would have been opened in the next decade or so. That discount reflected the risk of these *new* business operations, not the discount rate associated with the firm's current operations.

4. Care was taken to not double-count the earnings or expenses from the current operations and growth options analyses and to be consistent in the assumptions regarding the two. In particular, the firm's policy of aggressively pursuing new locations had at least two effects: higher operating expenses and higher revenues. It would have been incorrect to naively incorporate one effect but not the other.

5. The valuation and damages estimate required, of course, significant analyses of industry conditions, past analogues of the breach-of-contract events, and company-specific issues that are not summarized here.

This general approach is consistent with the proper use of what is sometimes called *expanded net present value*, discussed in the next section.

AN EXPANDED NPV VALUATION THEORY

Historical Precedents

The idea of returns to investment as more than a simple discounted cash flow was recognized by Irving Fisher in his 1930 *Theory of Interest*:

> I have generally avoided the term productivity of capital because it may be used ambiguously to mean physical productivity, or value return, or return over costs; and because it suggests that capital produces income value instead of the reverse; and because it attributes the value of manufactured things to the cost of production, instead of to their discounted future services.
>
> I prefer the term investment opportunity. It has some of the demerits as well as the merits belonging to any new term. It is unfamiliar and therefore requires precise definition. The

concept of investment opportunity rests on that of an "option." An option is any possible income stream open to an individual by utilizing his resources, capital, labor, land, money, to produce or secure said income stream. An investment opportunity is the opportunity to shift from one such option, or optional income stream, to another.

It includes all possible opportunities to invest—those that can yield only negative returns upon the investment as well as those which are capable of yielding very large surpluses over the amount of the investment or cost.[29]

As noted in Chapter 3, "The Failure of the Neoclassical Investment Rule," Fisher's work strongly motivated that of Modigliani, Miller, Dean, and others that produced the net present value rule of capital budgeting around the middle of the twentieth century, and the complete passage above shows he was close to proposing it himself. However, he explicitly notes something that is missing from the net present value rule and from the related M-M proposition on the value of a firm: investment opportunities are like options.

Expanded Net Present Value (XNPV)

Modern finance has an unresolved tension regarding the value of a firm, as noted in Chapter 1, "Modern Value Quandaries." On one hand, it teaches legions of business school students the Modigliani-Miller propositions, the neoclassical investment rule, and the frequent use of discounted cash flow analysis. On the other hand, it also recognizes both real and financial options. The tension cannot be ignored: either the value of the firm is the net present value of its future earnings from current operations, or it isn't.

One attempt to salvage the M-M propositions and much of traditional finance has been to modify the concept of future earnings, creating a notion of *expanded net present value*. The idea originated at least as far back as Myers (1977), who suggested that the true value of a firm consisted of the discounted prospective earnings of its current operations plus the value of its real options. Dixit and Pindyck (1994) also argued that the orthodox theory of business value, based on the use of an $E(NPV)$ rule, was incorrect, and that an improved theory should incorporate value arising from both real options and current operations.

This concept has been variously described as *strategic net present value*, *dynamic net present value*, and *expanded net present value*. We use the latter term, which is probably the most commonly used in the literature, and abbreviate it *XNPV* to distinguish it from the $E(NPV)$ rule underlying the orthodox income approach to valuation.

An Expanded Net Present Value Scheme of Firm Value

Alexander Vollert (2003, sec. 2.2) proposed a particularly detailed scheme of firm value components that illustrates the XNPV concept. He outlines four sources of firm value:

1. *Static firm value*, determined by *assets in place*, for which standard discounted cash flow analysis can be used, assuming "the firm adopts its originally chosen strategy without taking flexibility into account."

2. *Strategic real options*, reflecting managerial flexibility to undertake additional investments, develop new intangible assets, or pursue future business opportunities.

3. *Operating real options*, reflecting the ability to "improve the returns from existing assets."

4. *Financial real options*, reflecting the ability to change the capital structure of the firm. Here, Vollert makes the interesting observation that maximizing the value of equity alone will lead to different decisions than maximizing the value of the entire enterprise.

Vollert calls the sum of these sources of firm value the *dynamic firm value*, although we will use the term *expanded net present value*.

A Caution: Separating Existing from New

In both practice and theory, it is difficult to separate the effects of the different sources of firm value in Vollert's scheme, as he acknowledges. This is particularly the case when one attempts to distinguish the value of assets in place from those from new investments in the same industry or in process improvements. Vollert explicitly segregates operating real options from static firm value. Other authors implicitly combine these two.

COMPARISONS WITH INCOME AND VALUE FUNCTIONAL METHODS

Comparison: XNPV and Traditional Income Methods

These methods are similar in their treatment of the operating assets of the firm. Indeed, XNPV, by definition, uses traditional DCF to evaluate the value of existing operations. However, the two are different enough to warrant the following comparison:

- DCF practitioners have little theoretical guidance about the inclusion of state and action variables, leading to the common error of simply extrapolating recent results to produce a forecasted cash flow schedule. At least for the real options portion of an XNPV analysis, the state and action variables can be stated explicitly.

- The existence of growth options is one motivation for one of the many variations of the income approach, known as the two-stage or three-stage discounted cash flow models. In such models, the practitioner assumes that a company will grow at different rates during different future time periods. Such an assumption is usually a blunt adjustment for the likelihood that the firm exercises some growth options during the next several years. As noted previously, it is an error to use the same discount rate for both continuing operations and possible future operations subject to specific contingencies. A skilled practitioner will seek a focused, explicit manner of dealing with significant growth options when they exist.

Comparison: XNPV and Value Functional Approaches

We present the value functional approach in Chapter 15, "The Value Functional: Theory." However, it is worth pausing here to note how that approach compares to the notion of the value of the firm as the expanded net present value of its future earnings.

• *Existence and value of real options.* Both these approaches incorporate the view that the value of the firm is *not* the NPV of earnings from its current assets, based partially on the existence of management flexibility.

• *Importance of state and action variables.* The value functional approach highlights state and action variables, in contrast to the focus on the accounting income statement typical of the income approach. Real options analysis does the same (with the action variable typically restricted to the exercise of the option), although restricting the analysis to the specific investment opportunity.

• *Mathematics: The XNPV method relies on a simple sum.* The XNPV approach is based on a notion of the value of the firm as the *sum* of two quantities: the expected net present value of future earnings from current or existing operations, and the real options available to the firm that are in addition to the value from current operations. Solving the XNPV equation is not difficult, provided that the value of the real options can be quantified and that the possible interaction between current operations and real options is properly handled.

• *Mathematics: The value functional method relies on a functional equation.* The value functional approach is based on the notion that management decisions integrate current operations and real options in a recursive fashion every time period. Mathematically, this requires a *functional equation*, which is a different mathematical construct than the sums used in DCF and XNPV.

• *Use of numerical techniques.* Solving a value functional equation is inherently difficult and often requires numerical techniques. Some real options problems require similar levels of

TABLE 12.3
Real options methods: Recommendations by industry

Valuation task	Likely usefulness of real options	Underlying risks	Possible replicating portfolios or "twin securities"
Retail businesses (operating)	Limited for operating; medium for real estate–related costs	Expansion; competition; interest rates and other real estate development and operating costs	Competing firm equities; real estate investment trusts (REITs)
Service businesses (operating)	Limited	Expansion; competition; technology	Competing firm equities; technology risks very difficult to replicate
Natural resource reserves	High	Underlying resource value; technology changes; political risks	Some resource prices could be hedged; technology and political risks are difficult or impossible to hedge
Technology businesses (operating, R&D)	High, but difficult	Technology; distribution channels	Competing firm equities; distribution channel interests; R&D and technology licensing entities
Intellectual property; product R&D	Very useful	Technology; innovation; commercialization	Replicants listed above; distribution and commercial interests

TABLE 12.4
Real options methods: Recommendations by type of problem

Type of problem	Recommended methods (primary; secondary)	Notes
Investment opportunity in a familiar industry, with business risk related primarily to overall industry demand or market-wide prices	DTA, MC, XNPV; VF, CCA, Good deal bounds	DTA, Monte Carlo, and XNPV are likely to work with the typical information set, if used properly. Other methods require data on state variables or twin securities. Note that standard DCF will often fail when real options are present.
Purchase opportunity for rights to natural resources or commodities	All real options methods could be considered.	Best method will depend on the quality of the data on state variables, the availability of twin securities with small transaction costs, and the ability to model the likely future value of the rights given possible state variable paths. With excellent information on these, CCA or MC may be the best methods. With limited information, VF, DTA, or XNPV may be more reliable.
Major business decision involving a change in management, policy, industry, or scale	DTA; VF, DCF	Since the proposed change would place the company outside its historical experience, historical operating data cannot be the primary basis for projections of future results. Management instincts and subjective judgment will probably be important factors in the decision, so analytical tools should support the use of this information
Change in financial structure or leverage; issuance of debt or equity	DTA, VF, CCA; DCF, XNPV, financial options	Note that standard DCF analysis assumes a static capital structure, and standard financial options formulas assume no borrowing constraints. Changes in financial structure directly contradict these assumptions. Therefore, consider other methods first.
Opportunity for technology investment or R&D expenditure	DTA, MC, XNPV; VF; CCA (if twin security available)	As with natural resource rights, the availability of information is critical. Value functional or CCA, if possible, is probably the best method. If these are not possible, consider DTA and Monte Carlo. Properly used, XNPV may be the best method when solid information is available on the risks and rewards of the potential investment.
Impending gain or loss of key person, franchise, or license	Value functional (if related to policy of company); CCA (if twin securities available), XNPV, DTA	Recursive decision structure of the value functional approach matches the company's problem well. If loss or gain can be replicated in the market, the simpler CCA method may be used.

NOTES: CCA = contingent claim analysis; DTA = decision tree analysis; MC = Monte Carlo simulation; VF = value functional approach; XNPV = expanded net present value

computing effort, such as Monte Carlo techniques. On the other hand, solving DCF equations is quite easy.

• *Usage in incomplete markets.* The XNPV and value functional approaches can normally be used in incomplete markets, although some real options techniques require complete or near-complete markets.

RECOMMENDATIONS ON REAL OPTION APPLICATIONS

Recommendations by Industry

Possible real options approaches for investments made by private firms vary considerably. In this section, we summarize advice on the first methods to consider by looking at typical problems by industry, and then by characteristics of the problem itself.

We start with considering the likely real options applications for certain industries, as shown in Table 12.3. Note that for some industries, real options techniques are difficult to apply, often because no replicating portfolio of securities exists that provides pricing guidance or hedging opportunities.

Recommendations by Type of Problem

Table 12.4 summarizes advice on the options that should be considered for analyzing management decisions and their effect on the value of companies. Note that I recommend DCF analysis as a backup in many situations; remember the conclusion that net present value is "a tool, not a rule," and even in cases of managerial flexibility, it has its uses.

V TRADITIONAL AND VALUE FUNCTIONAL THEORIES OF VALUE

13 TRADITIONAL VALUATION METHODS

ELEMENTS OF THIS CHAPTER

Introduction: Business Valuation in Disparate Literatures

In this chapter, we introduce the three traditional methods of valuing a business: the market approach, the asset approach, and the income approach. These methods appear in nearly every contemporary text in the professional literature, and often in the legal and taxation literature as well. Thus, they will be quite familiar to those whose background is in accounting, taxation, or forensic economics. Indeed, I argue that these are too often the *only* methods presented in books and articles intended for valuation practitioners.[1] The converse lament is similarly true; one or more of these traditional methods are frequently absent in much of the finance and economics literature.

An Outline of Traditional Methods

Three traditional methods deserve study because they have some theoretical basis, and because they are regularly employed in actual valuation work. The three "generally accepted" traditional methods are the following:

1. The *market approach*, which is based on the market value of similar firms

2. The *asset approach*, which is based on the excess of the value of a firm's assets over its liabilities

3. The *income approach*, also sometimes loosely called the discounted cash flow (DCF) approach, which is based on the net present value of the expected future income of the firm

In this chapter, we examine each of these approaches and consider the following:

- The underlying valuation principles
- The manner in which the method is used in practical work

- The deficiencies of the approach
- The use of subjective adjustments by practitioners to reconcile differences between the result of a straightforward use of the methodology, and the practitioners' actual opinion of value

Finally, we show valuation estimates for each of the three firms described in Appendix C, "Description of Subject Companies," using the asset and market approaches. In doing so, we demonstrate how subjective adjustments can become the dominant factor in a traditional-methods valuation.

Cracks in the Wall of Tradition

As demonstrated further shortly, certain commonly used methods in both the asset approach and the income approach are vulnerable to serious, fundamental critiques. Some authors have noted that "cracks are starting to develop in this easy categorization" of these three as the "generally accepted approaches."[2]

We outline the three approaches and note some fundamental weaknesses in Table 13.1.

TABLE 13.1
Three traditional business valuation approaches

Approach	Principle	Best use	Weakness
Market	Value of firm indicated by actual market transactions. Comparable firms with market transactions can be used as the basis for valuing a different firm.	Business interests that are commonly traded. Publicly held companies in industries with multiple similar firms.	Private firms rarely have well-traded equity interests. Difficulties in finding comparable firms. Vulnerable to weak claims of "synergies" when used for acquisitions.
Asset	Value of firm indicated by value of assets of firm, less the value of the liabilities. "Marking to market" the balance sheet reveals the value of the firm.	Natural resource firms where value is largely dependent on reserves. Distressed or bankrupt firms; purchase negotiations between similar firms.	Value is not indicated by historical cost. Circular reasoning in valuation premise; multiple individual items must be valued to arrive at value of firm. True firms have value because of their ability to earn future profits, not because of the value of their individual assets.
Income	Value of the firm indicated by ability to earn future income for owners. By capitalizing the expected future income flow (discounting future cash flows), one can estimate the current market value.	Operating firms with well-established business patterns. Damages analyses for such firms.	Valuation premise ignores management control, other management benefits. Is inadequate when "real options" are important or substantial strategic decisions are impending. Forecasting income and discounting it are difficult and require professional judgment.

THE MARKET APPROACH: THEORY

Valuation Principle

The valuation principle of the market approach is straightforward, and is a direct reflection of neoclassical economics: the value of a firm is based on the prices of other similar firms in the marketplace. To the extent that firms—or shares in a firm's equity—are commodities traded in open markets, this is a solid basis indeed.

The glaring weakness of the market approach is the fact that equity in most firms is *not* commonly traded in a marketplace. As a result, practical use of this approach normally requires a search for a comparable company, then adjustments for the type of company and also its scale. These fundamentals are captured in Equation 13.1.

Equation 13.1 Market-Approach Value Equation

$$V_{market} \approx (V_{comparable} + adjustments) \bullet scale\ factor$$

When truly comparable firms are traded in the marketplace, the market approach is often the most solid guide to business valuation. For publicly traded firms with extensive trading histories—such as those listed on the most active stock exchanges—this is the most common practical valuation approach.

Common Market Methods

Three methods are commonly used for employing available market data:

1. *Prior sale of company's shares.* This method can be useful if a firm's shares had been sold in prior time periods. The prices and sales terms should indicate the value of the business at that time.

2. *Guideline transaction.* This method uses available transaction data, usually involving mergers or acquisitions, that reveal the price agreed on by a buyer and seller for a business similar to the subject company. If either the buyer or seller is a publicly traded company, some information is usually disclosed in the firm's public filings.

Some data are also available from privately maintained databases that cover thousands of small business transactions. In some cases, a practitioner can calculate one or several ratios of sales-price-to-important-company-variable from comparable transaction data and then apply these to the subject company's data to arrive at a value estimate.

3. *Guideline publicly traded company.* This method requires identifying publicly traded companies similar to the subject company and then using the former's quoted share price to estimate the market value of the subject company.

Market Capitalization of Publicly Traded Firms

A market-approach value estimate can be easy to apply for many large firms. Publicly traded firms, meaning firms with stock that is traded among a large number of potential investors, have an implied market value.

The value of the equity in a publicly traded firm can be estimated from actual market transactions as the number of outstanding shares multiplied by the closing price of a share on a public market (Equation 13.2). Exchanges generally have minimum market capitalization requirements for listing a company, so this method is available only to firms that meet the size requirements and are listed on an exchange.[3]

Equation 13.2 Market Capitalization of a Publicly Traded Firm

$$V \equiv N * P$$

where:

V = market capitalization

N = number of shares outstanding

P = market price of one share

This equation defines the *market capitalization* of a firm, which is the implied market value of a firm's equity.

Vagaries of the Market Cap

Certain vagaries of the market cap should be recognized, including those originating in both parts of the equation:

1. *Vagaries about the price.* The market price is not established precisely by every transaction, because of the existence of bid-ask spreads, transaction costs (such as commissions), and other factors. For widely traded stocks, this creates a relatively small zone of uncertainty; for thinly traded stocks, these factors may be more important.

2. *Vagaries about the shares.* Classic finance theories are often based on the assumption that firms are financed by only two categories of claimants: stockholders and lenders. Many large, medium, and small firms actually have multiple classes of claimants, each with specific provisions governing their claims. These include different classes of stock (common stock, preferred stock, restricted stock) and different types of loans (commercial paper, commercial loans, corporate bonds).

In addition, the market cap is an indication of the market value of equity alone. For firms that are in or near bankruptcy, or for firms whose shares are not actively traded, this may not provide a true indication of the value of the firm's assets and liabilities or of the firm as an ongoing entity.

Rarely Observable Values of Private Firms

The fair market value of private firms is rarely observable, even within a small zone of uncertainty. This lack of market value data occurs for at least six reasons.

1. Typically there is no active market in the equity of privately held firms. This does not mean that there is no market demand or supply, only that there are insufficient transactions to describe a market price.

2. Some of the potential buyers and sellers are subject to pressure, compulsion, related activity requirements, or other concerns.[4] In contrast, a person may purchase stocks in large publicly traded firms without any additional requirements beyond those imposed by the exchange or broker.

3. Prospective buyers find it quite difficult to obtain even rudimentary financial information about most privately held firms.[5]

4. The bid-ask spread and transaction costs (including the costs of performing due diligence) are much higher for interests in privately held firms than for interests in publicly traded firms.

5. Private buyers and sellers often do not report the transaction prices, or do so only to income tax authorities.

6. Equity interests in private firms are often purchased in large chunks at a time, thus making transactions less frequent, less transparent, and more complicated.[6]

The lack of observable data on private-firm equity prices has strong implications for the techniques available for estimating firm values.

THE MARKET APPROACH: PRACTICE

Introduction: Three Valuations of Three Subject Firms

In this section and in similar sections in other chapters, I report estimates of the value of three actual firms, which are described in Appendix C, "Description of Subject Companies." Only the information relevant to specific valuation methods is shown in each chapter.

Note that these descriptions were prepared by different valuation practitioners and only lightly edited by the author of this book. Therefore, they are not uniform in terms of style, nor completely consistent in terms of assumptions and methods. I have highlighted in each case the role of professional judgment, including the judgment of which methods to use.

S. H. Importers

The valuation analyst for S. H. Importers observed that there were no arm's-length sales of the company's shares during the past ten years, so comparable market transactions were sought through a search through a transaction database. The search, for SIC#5932 Antiques/Antique Dealers, and NAICS#453310 Antique Dealers, yielded no comparable transactions for the period January 1, 2000, through June 30, 2010, in California or in the entire Pacific region. The practitioner concluded that given the lack of data on comparable businesses, it would be inappropriate to use the guideline transaction market method.

However, a search under NAICS#442110 for Furniture Store resulted in several possible comparables, only four of which were remotely close to S. H. Importers' line of business:

- Pier 1 Imports, Inc.
- Cost Plus, Inc.

TABLE 13.2
S. H. Importers: Comparison companies

June 30, 2010	Pier 1	Cost Plus	Haverty	Bed Bath
Closing price per share	$6.79	$3.14	$11.73	$37.62
Fiscal year end	2/28/2010	1/31/2010	12/31/2009	2/28/2010
FY sales ($ millions)	1,291.0	869.5	588.3	7,828.8
FY net profit ($ millions)	86.8	−63.3	−4.2	600
FY earnings per share (EPS)	0.86	−2.87	0.2	2.3
Market capitalization ($ millions)	795	69	209	9,927
FYE EPS	0.61	−1.42	0.25	2.48
P/E ratio	11.13	−2.21	46.92	15.17
S. H. Importers pps at comps' P/E	88.48	−17.57	373.01	120.6
Total Value of S. H. Importers Shares	**$88,484**	**−$17,570**	**$373,014**	**$120,602**

SOURCE: Comparable firm data compiled from *Yahoo! Finance* data; analysts' calculations

- Haverty Furniture Companies, Inc.
- Bed Bath & Beyond, Inc.

All four companies are considerably larger than S. H. Importers and primarily engage in retailing furniture and furnishings, both domestic and imported. None of the companies' descriptions listed antiques or any type of design or refinishing services, so the practitioner deemed their lines of business to be incomparable to S. H. Importers.

Using the Method Without Adjustment

The analyst completed a market-method valuation, for illustration purposes, without making any adjustments to the four comparable companies' data. These are shown in Table 13.2.

To calculate these estimates, the analyst multiplied the earnings per share (EPS) by the price/earnings (P/E) ratio for each stock, yielding the closing price per share for the day. For Pier 1 for example, an EPS of $0.61 times a P/E ratio of 11.13 yields a per-share price of $6.79. Using an average P/E ratio of the four comparables of 17.75 times earnings per share of $7.95 yields an implied per-share price for S. H. Importers of $141.08. This implies a total market value, based on one thousand shares outstanding, of $141,080.

Conclusion

The individual P/E ratios of the four comparable companies yield four widely variant results. The analyst concluded that this demonstrated the inappropriateness of this market valuation method to determine an opinion of value for S. H. Importers, given the available data.

A & A Consulting

The valuation analyst for A & A Consulting noted that there were a handful of actual market transactions involving fractional equity interests in the firm over the past several years. These suggest an implicit value of the firm between $1.6 and $2.3 million, with no discount for minority interests or premium for control.

TABLE 13.3
A & A Consulting: Comparison publicly traded companies

	CRA International	LECG Corporation	Navigant Consulting	FTI Consulting, Inc.
Symbol	CRAI	XPRT	NCI	FCN
Previous CLS	$22.77	$2.95	$12.62	$42.66
52-week range	$19.70–$31.47	$2.28–$4.29	$11.32–$15.59	$36.10–$56.41
Earnings per share (ttm)	0.7	−2.9	0.44	2.7
P/B	0.96	0.78	1.47	1.78
P/S	0.85	0.41	0.89	1.37
Revenue ($ millions)	$294.66	$263.20	$707.24	$4,400.00
EBITDA ($ millions)	$27.09	−$8.45	$100.65	$317.01
Market cap ($ millions)	$251.40	$108.80	$631.00	$198,000.00
PEG ratio	1.44	2.05	1	0.83
P/E	**32.48**	**N/A**	**28.62**	**15.82**

SOURCE: Compiled using *Yahoo! Finance* data

TABLE 13.4
A & A Consulting: Price ratios for three comparables

	CRA International	Navigant Consulting	FTI Consulting, Inc.	A & A Consulting
Revenue ($ millions)	$294,660,000	$707,240,000	$4,400,000	$1,670,721
EBITDA	$27,090,000	$100,650,000	$317,010,000	$129,033[a]
Price	$22.77	$12.62	$42.66	—
Price/sales	0.85	0.89	1.42	—
P/E	**32.48**	**28.62**	**15.82**	—
Market cap ($ millions)	$251.38	$631.00	$198,000.00	—

[a] Operating Profit
SOURCE: Compiled from *Yahoo! Finance* data and private firms' financial statements

No publicly traded firms of the same size exist. Among large firms, there are a small number of comparable firms in terms of services provided. Among these firms and the subject firm, some useful metrics for comparison purposes include the following:

- Enterprise value/revenue
- Enterprise value/EBITDA

The analyst prepared a market-approach estimation of value for A & A Consulting as of May 2010, using the data on comparison firms and relevant ratios shown in Table 13.3.

Out of these four firms, one has not been profitable. A & A has been profitable over the past five years, and therefore the outlier of the group (LECG) was removed.[7] Table 13.4 shows how the company compares to the other three firms used in this market approach valuation.

Marketability Adjustment

The analyst noted that when estimating the value of a privately held company on the basis of ratios implied by the market capitalization and share prices of publicly traded companies, an adjustment for the relative lack of marketability in the form of a discount from the

TABLE 13.5
A & A Consulting: Market approach valuation estimate

| | VALUATION IMPLIED BY | | |
	CRA International	*Navigant Consulting*	*FTI Consulting, Inc.*
Price/sales valuation estimate (adjusted)	$1,420,113	$1,486,942	$2,372,424
P/E valuation estimate (adjusted)	$4,190,996	$3,692,928	$2,041,304

implied value is normally applied. Table 13.5 shows the estimated value of A & A Consulting, using the market approach, comparable publicly traded companies, and a substantial marketability discount of 19.5 percent.

Conclusion

For this firm, a range of estimates could be produced, but only with substantial subjective adjustments. By taking the average of the three valuation estimates shown and observing actual sales prices in the past, the analyst arrived at the following estimates of A & A Consulting:

- Implied by price/sales ratio: $1.76 million
- Implied by price/EBITDA: $3.31 million
- Implied by actual sales prices for this firm's equity: $1.6 to $2.3 million

ExxonMobil

ExxonMobil has a market capitalization and a share price established by numerous transactions. Furthermore, the company has at least a small handful of competitors of similar size and global reach. The importance of the company's stock to investors worldwide means that substantial analyst coverage is available on the firm as well.

Traditional methods often perform quite well for companies like this. In particular, the market method—since so much market information is available—is a relatively easy method to use. The valuation analyst concluded that the market method was preferable and did not complete an income method analysis.

THE ASSET APPROACH

The Accounting Identity

The valuation principle behind the asset approach is based on a fundamental accounting identity; the book value of the assets must equal the book value of the sum of equity and liabilities. In the Asset Approach, this identity becomes the basis for a valuation opinion, rather than the basis for accounting records.

The accounting process normally follows the production cycle in a typical firm: first production of the product, then sales, and later collection of the accounts receivables from those sales. Each of these transactions results in changes in assets and liabilities. At the end of a time period, the result of all these transactions is summarized in an income statement. The income or loss then flows through to the balance sheet.

The balance sheet provides the (book) value of equity by ensuring that the recorded amounts of assets balance (equal) those of liabilities and equity.

Accounting Identity as a Valuation Tool

When the same identity is used as the basis for a valuation opinion, the flow of logic is different. The balance sheet itself is the starting point, with the value of each individual asset (or category of assets) considered separately. This is summarized in Equation 13.3.

Equation 13.3 Asset-Approach Value Equation

$$V_{\text{asset method}} \equiv \text{Assets}_{fmv} - \text{Liabilities}_{fmv}$$

where:

$$\text{Assets}_{fmv} = \sum_{i=1}^{I} \text{Assets}_{i,fmv}$$

$$\text{Liabilities}_{fmv} = \sum_{j=1}^{J} \text{Liabilities}_{j,fmv}$$

fmv	= fair market value of individual assets and liabilities
i	= 1, ..., I index of firm's assets
j	= 1, ..., J index of firm's liabilities
$V_{\text{asset method}}$	= value of firm's equity using asset method

The assumption that the market value of a business is the difference between the market value of its liabilities and assets is not a general principle of economics. However, variations of this principle have been used in influential finance models.[8]

Note on GAAP and Other Accounting Standards

GAAP (generally accepted accounting principles) and other accounting standards are intended to provide a consistent methodology to report financial statements to investors. These accounting standards are normally based on the historical cost principle, as we discussed in Chapter 6, "Accounting for the Firm." The resulting accounting statements are *not* an attempt to estimate the current market values of either assets or liabilities. It is worth recalling Statement of Accounting Principles No. 1:

> Financial accounting is not designed to measure directly the value of a business enterprise, but the information it provides may be helpful to those who wish to estimate its value. (FASB *Statement of Accounting Concepts No. 1*, 1978)

Thus, accounting statements should be properly considered as an *aid* to the estimation of a firm's value but not an estimate of value themselves.

Practical Use of the Assets Method

Practitioner's Definition

The asset-based approach is defined in *The International Glossary of Business Valuation Terms* as follows:

> A general way of determining a value indication of a business, business ownership interest, or security using one or more methods based on the value of the assets net of liabilities. (AICPA, 2007)

Flaws in the Accounting Identity Approach

However compelling the logic behind the accounting identity, there are serious weaknesses in using it as the basis for valuation of the firm. We consider two:

1. *Circular reasoning.* The asset-approach valuation equation requires market-value estimates of the debt of the firm and of individual assets. Presuming these are available, we are presented with a tautology: value is defined as . . . value.

2. *Omission of the essential attributes of a firm.* The firm, as we define it in this book, is an *organization* in which *people* pursue profit, using a replicable set of *business processes.* The asset-approach valuation equation excludes people, profit motive, and business practices. It also abstracts away the organization. Thus, the approach ignores the essence of a business, at least as it is defined here.

An illustration of this weakness is presented next.

An Illustration: The Bars-of-Gold Example Reconsidered

Recall the bars-of-gold example at the end of Chapter 4, "The Nature of the Firm." There we considered an entity that owned four bars of gold, although four hundred bars of gold would work just as well. We noted that these assets would have a clear book value: the historic cost of acquiring the gold. A warehouse of such bars could be the assets of a business.

How would the asset-approach value equation assist us in valuing this business? At first glance, we would conclude that the approach would be a reliable basis on which to report the balance sheet of this business. However, it is unlikely that any owner would simply sell the gold at its historic cost if the market price had risen, so the balance-sheet entries would have to be marked to market for a valuation estimate. At that point, an asset-approach method would likely produce a reliable estimate of the market value of the *warehouse* and its contents.

However, this same approach cannot distinguish between the warehouse full of gold and the gold-trading operation that owns the warehouse. The latter may have considerable value in excess of its current inventory and real estate. This is a natural consequence of misusing an accounting identity designed centuries ago to *account* for the assets and liabilities of a firm. Such an identity is not a valid basis for an estimate of the *future earning ability* of a human organization.

Practical Uses Given Weaknesses

The weaknesses just identified for this approach are serious. However, there are a set of practical uses for the asset-based approach in valuation. Subject companies for such a practical use of this approach include the following:

- A non-operating business, or one expected to be liquidated in the near future.
- A business in which separate operating units can be separately valued, along with any attached liabilities.
- A business in which the returns from specific assets are the essence of the operation. This is often the case with passive investment vehicles.

In these situations, the logical flaws in applying the approach to an operating business are less important.

Note on Business Value Axiom

Recall the axiom "only a firm has value as a business," and the related definition of the firm, both introduced in Chapter 4, "The Nature of the Firm." The practical uses of the asset approach illustrate the importance of this axiom: when a business is no longer a firm, then its value is reduced to simply its net assets. Otherwise, its value is often much more than its assets.

VALUATION APPLICATION: ASSET METHOD

S. H. Importers

The valuation analyst for S. H. Importers presented a hypothetical net asset valuation of the firm as of June 30, 2010. The analyst concluded that a straightforward net asset valuation, based on the accounting balance sheet, would not yield a good prediction of market value. Hence, significant adjustments were made based on professional judgment, as further described shortly. Table 13.6 presents S. H. Importers' book value balance sheet with various adjustments applied. This adjusted net assets method exercise estimates the company's value at $1,004,600.

The analyst adjusted the following categories of assets:

- Accounts Receivable: S. H. Importers does not carry any reserve for uncollected receivables, and management advises that historically, uncollectible receivables have never amounted to more than 0.1 percent of annual sales in any year. *No adjustment is therefore necessary.*
- Inventory: ABC Appraisers, professional appraisers of fine art and antiques, conducted an inventory appraisal as of June 30, 2010. Their opinion was that the fair market value on a liquidation basis as of that date was $1,650,000. *A positive adjustment of $272,834 was therefore made.*
- Fixed assets: A fully depreciated delivery van has a book value of $0 but a blue book value of $18,500.

TABLE 13.6

S. H. Importers: Adjusted net assets as of June 30, 2010

	Book value	*Adjustment*	*Fair market value*
ASSETS			
Current assets			
Cash	$ 49,142		$ 49,142
Accounts receivable	44,109[a]	—	44,109
Inventory	1,377,166[b]	$ 1,377,166	1,650,000
Other current assets	1,720		1,720
Total current assets	$ 1,472,137		$ 1,744,971
Fixed assets	239,584		239,584
Accumulated depreciation	(162,534)		(162,534)
Net fixed assets	$ 77,050c	$ 29,800	$ 47,250
Total assets	$ 1,549,187		$ 1,792,221
LIABILITIES			
Current liabilities	95,368		—
Long-term debt	—		—
Due to principals	692,234		$ 692,234
Other LTD	—		—
Total LTD	$ 692,234		$ 692,234
Total liabilities	$ 787,602		$ 787,602
Net assets	$ 761,585		$ 761,585
Adjusted net assets	$ 1,004,619		$ 1,004,619

[a] Uncollectible receivables
[b] Reflect appraised value
[c] Reflect appraised value and abandoned leasehold

- Woodworking and office tools and equipment had been expensed as acquired and hence showed no book value. S. H. Importers relied on a professional appraiser to estimate the fair market value of all woodworking, office, and computer equipment as of June 30, 2010, to be $28,750.

- Leasehold improvements with a net book value of $77,050 would be abandoned in the event of a liquidation. There would be no penalty for abandoning the lease on the showroom, warehouse, and woodworking facilities, except that no deposits would be recovered.

A total negative adjustment of $29,800 ($18,500 + $28,750 − $77,050) therefore must be made to net fixed assets.

A & A Consulting

A & A Consulting is an operating firm that is profitable. However, the valuation analyst considered the asset approach using two methods: without adjustments as an operating company, and assuming its assets were sold.

A & A does not have a great deal of tangible assets or debt. The accounting net worth of A & A consulting does not represent a good indication of its market value. The company's strong reputation continues to attract a variety of clients, which an acquiring firm could potentially use. The services the firm provides and the talent it harnesses would be its largest asset, which is not captured using the asset approach.

Should it hypothetically liquidate, it would have depreciated office equipment such as computers, desks, and chairs to sell. The price of office equipment less the cost to dispose of these items, and the remaining lease payments, does not provide any basis to estimate the company's value as an operating firm. The name *A & A Consulting* could potentially be sold for some amount, although it would be worth much less if one or both of the *A* names were not involved. We viewed any estimate based on the scrap value of the firm's assets as unduly speculative.

Overall, the analyst concluded that this method fails at estimating the value of this firm.

ExxonMobil

The valuation analyst concluded that asset methods generally fail completely for firms like ExxonMobil, in which the most valuable assets are often natural resource leases, intellectual property, or other intangibles. The accounting (historical cost) basis of valuable natural resource leases typically bears little resemblance to their actual market value. Hence, the firm's standard balance sheet is a poor indicator of its market value. Furthermore, the existence of market data on the firm's shares suggests that the market method would generally be preferable.

THE INCOME METHOD

Valuation Principle of the Income Approach

The valuation principle of the income approach is straightforward: the value of the enterprise is the sum of the expected future income, discounted at the company's cost of capital. This is the basis for the neoclassical investment rule and is also the premise that underlies the Modigliani-Miller theorems and much of their progeny.

This principle, of course, has considerable merit when used properly in a nearly complete market. For securities that are widely traded and produce a regular stream of earnings, it is one of the building blocks of valuation in practice.

Value Equation in the Income Approach

Next we present equations that capture the principle of the income approach and are used in practice to value firms. Equation 13.4 estimates earnings with the net present value formula for a set of discrete time periods. Equation 13.5 estimates value for an indefinite number of time periods. An initial set of time periods are represented as in the previous equation. In addition, a *terminal value* is determined by the perpetuity formula and the values of the last discretely forecasted time period. These formulas use time indexes only for the income variables. They assume that discount rates do not vary over time and that a trend growth rate can be forecasted for the perpetuity.

Equation 13.4 DCF Value Equation: Discrete Periods

$$V_{dcf} \equiv E_t \left[NPV \left(\sum_{t=1}^{T} \pi_t \right) \right]$$

$$= E_t \left[\sum_{t=1}^{T} \frac{\pi_t}{(1+d)^t} \right]$$

where:

$\pi_t = rev_t - costs_t$ is a measure of distributable profits or cash flow

$t = 1, ..., T$ is a time index to a terminal period T

$d > 0$ is a net discount rate

$E_t \left[\bullet \right]$ is the expectation operator given information at time t

Equation 13.5 DCF Value Equation: Discrete Periods Plus Terminal Value

$$V_{dcf} \equiv E_t \left[NPV \left(\sum_{t=1}^{T} \pi_t + TV_T \right) \right]$$

where:

$TV_T = \pi_T \dfrac{1+g}{d-g}$ is a terminal value at time T

g is a trend growth rate in profits

d is a net discount rate

$\{g,d\}$ assumed to remain constant in perpetuity

$0 < g < 1, \quad 0 < d < 1, \quad g < d$

The DCF Equations Versus a DCF Schedule

These equations are much shorter than a DCF schedule of the type shown in many valuation and finance texts. Scheduling the revenue and cost and running out the results over several periods of time would result in data presented as an accounting income statement. Although these equations are much more compact than a detailed income statement, their logic is the same.

The Classic Dividend Discount Model

The dividend discount model (DDM) could be viewed as the root of all income-approach business valuation methods. Consider an equity interest (a *share* of stock) in a firm that pays a regular dividend. The firm's earnings are distributed to investors through a dividend. Investors can also earn (or lose) money when they buy or sell shares; such earnings or losses are considered *capital gains*. For now, focus on the dividend stream and consider how much an investor would pay for the right to earn this stream of dividends in the future.

Equation 13.6 uses the income approach principle, and an assumed institutional arrangement of a corporation paying a regular dividend to investors, to derive a value estimate.

Equation 13.6 Constant Growth Dividend Discount Model

Stock price $= S_0$

$$S_0 = F\left[\frac{Div_1}{1+d} + \frac{Div_2}{(1+d)^7} + \cdots + \frac{Div_t}{(1+d)^t} + \cdots\right]$$

$$= E\left[\frac{Div_0(1+g)}{1+d} + \frac{Div_0(1+g)^2}{(1+d)^2} + \cdots + \frac{Div_0(1+g)^t}{(1+d)^t} + \cdots\right]$$

$$= \frac{Div_0(1+g)}{d-g}$$

Assume g, $d =$ constants; $g < d$

Key Assumptions in the Dividend Discount Model
Serious assumptions are embedded in the DDM:

1. The company will continue to earn enough money to pay constantly increasing dividends. This assumption alone should be considered heroic in most circumstances.

2. The discount rate is constant and known.

If these assumptions are not tenable, a different model should be used. One common variant is the *two-stage DDM*, in which the growth rate of dividends is discretely forecasted for a certain set of periods, and then a constant-growth DDM model (with a growth rate assumption that is close to nominal GDP growth) is used as a terminal value. This is analogous to the discrete-period-plus-terminal-value DCF method shown in Equation 13.5.

Additional Observations About the Dividend Discount Model
We can observe the following about the dividend discount model:

1. The model is based on *dividends that are distributed*. Companies first have to earn income, then decide whether to distribute part of the income. Thus, the dividend discount model assumes both *earnings* and a *dividend policy*.

2. The dividend *policy* is always important. Many large publicly traded firms have an announced policy, and the stock market often reacts negatively to deviations from that policy.[9] However, most firms do not fit into this category. In general, any dividend policy can be changed by the manager of a firm, at least with the acquiescence of a majority of the investors, directors, or members.

3. The use of the term *dividend* is not restrictive. Any cash distribution of earnings from a business (such as a distribution to partners or members of a limited liability company) can be used in the dividend discount algorithm, if the benefits to the investor are the same as in the classic dividend from a corporation.[10]

The importance of the dividend policy and who sets it motivates the discussion of the *agency problem* in businesses.[11] In particular, investors may depend on distributed dividends for their return on investment, while managers who set the dividend may be compensated for performance on a different basis. This can lead to a difference in incentives.[12]

Other authors describe models that fit within the income approach and are more complex than the dividend discount model. We discuss a few more variations in Chapter 14, "Practical Applications of the Income Method."

Situations Where Income Methods Commonly Fail

In some situations, traditional income methods, in which the base data are centered on historical performance of the firm and the relevant industry, commonly fail to produce good valuation estimates. These include the following:

- New businesses
- Distressed businesses
- Businesses with substantial real options
- Businesses dependent on intellectual property, innovation, or brand identification
- Businesses that have incurred major changes in policy or key personnel
- Businesses that have endured changes in the industrial or regulatory regime or in the prevalent technology

The difficulties in using the income method in these cases start with the fundamental task of forecasting income. Extrapolating past experience is always risky in business valuation, and naively doing so is one of the most common errors in the field. In any of the preceding situations where conditions have changed, the folly of assuming that past performance will continue unabated is obvious.

The income method may also fail when applied to businesses with restrictive equity structures, including some closely held companies, partnerships, and LLCs, as well as start-up companies with strong financing covenants. The issues raised in the earlier discussion of the dividend discount model are often acute for investors in these firms.

Applications of the Income Method

In Chapter 14, "Practical Application of the Income Method," we present income-approach valuation estimates of the subject firms and further develop this topic.

14 PRACTICAL APPLICATION OF THE INCOME METHOD

An Introduction

In this chapter, we focus on the workhorse income approach to valuation and discuss the following essential steps:

1. The forecasting of future business revenue
2. The identification of income arising from that revenue
3. The discounting of that future income for time and risk

Each of these tasks is important. We argue that the first—forecasting business revenue—is often the most important.

We also discuss the following:

- Information necessary to value a firm
- Common errors in using the income approach
- Rules of thumb

Finally, we include valuations using the income approach of the three sample firms used as subjects throughout the book. These analyses, which were done by different analysts and only lightly edited, illustrate the data used as the basis for the calculations and the many professional judgments and subjective adjustments necessary to complete the valuation exercise.

INFORMATION NECESSARY FOR A VALUATION ESTIMATE

Organizing Information

The information useful to a person attempting to estimate the value of a firm could include the following:

1. The accounting statements for the firm.

2. The business plan for the firm, and description of its management structure, key personnel, major customers and suppliers.

3. The list of prototype state variables in Chapter 16, "The Value Functional: Applications," under the section titled "State and Control Variables in the Value Function Approach"

4. Information pertaining to the market(s) in which the firm operates (such as geographic, demographic information or workforce characteristics)

Broad Categories of Information

At the least, valuation professionals should consider the following categories of information:

1. Information on the economy and industry
   - Characteristics of the industry
   - Current and expected relevant economic conditions
   - The technology for producing and distributing products in the industry

2. Information on the firm
   - Accounting information, including historic income statements and balance sheets
   - Important performance and financial metrics
   - Description of the management team, workforce, suppliers, and customers

3. Information on products, prices, and competitors
   - Key competitors
   - Key products or services sold
   - Prices in the markets for these products and services
   - Important licenses, franchises, brands, trademarks, or patents

4. Information on the market
   - Characteristics of the local market(s)
   - Ability to enter other markets and remain in existing markets

REALISTIC ASSUMPTIONS ABOUT THE MARKET FOR PRIVATE FIRMS

Realistic Assumptions About the Firm

Throughout this chapter, we make realistic assumptions about private firms and the markets in which they operate. In particular, we make the following assumptions:

1. The business being valued is a *bona fide* firm.

2. The firm generates revenue primarily from operations.

3. The firm has a record of legal operation, a management structure, and financial records that allow for an analyst to evaluate its finances and operations.

This rules out a subset of businesses and business assets, including bankrupt firms, traded commodities, passive investments, nonoperating companies, initial start-ups, and entities that fit the legal or accounting definition of a firm, but not the economic definition. However, it encompasses most of the private and public firms in the United States and many other nations.

Realistic Assumptions About Investors

We also make realistic assumptions about investors in these firms. In particular, we assume the following:

1. Investors are also consumers and have the normal preferences of consumers, including an aversion to risk. Consumers choose to invest in order to secure future consumption for themselves and others.
2. Investors often have labor income as well as investment income.
3. Investors display *bounded rationality*, meaning that they expend limited time and effort attempting to improve their financial position and consider the costs of information as well as its value.

It is important to note that we do *not* make a number of the assumptions often made in mathematical finance, such as the following:

- A strictly defined utility function
- A restriction to the mean and variance as the relevant indicators of risk or return
- Similar preferences among investors, or the existence of one representative investor
- Zero transaction costs

Realistic Assumptions About Markets

Furthermore, we do *not* enforce assumptions that are commonly asserted in the field of economics and finance, such as complete markets or no arbitrage. Similarly, we do not assume the firm is publicly traded. Holding such assumptions effectively rules out most firms operating in the United States and most other countries.

PRACTICAL TASK 1: FORECASTING REVENUE

Revenue and the Value of the Firm

Without revenue, a firm cannot have value. Even start-up firms require the *prospect* of revenue; what investor, lender, or employee would join a business that did not at least plan to earn revenue in the near future?

Because of this primacy, we argue that forecasting revenue is the most important of the three essential tasks in the practical application of the income method. It is often, sadly, the most neglected in practice. The other two tasks often involve existing historical data, an extensive academic and professional literature, and steps that are simplified by the existence of spreadsheet and other models. Forecasting revenue, however, requires hard thinking about the economy, the industry, the firm's management and business plans, the firm's competitors, and the firm's products. As we demonstrate shortly, no easy formula or spreadsheet model will do this.

Key Factors Underlying Revenue Growth

We present the factors that underlie business revenue growth, which can be categorized into *economic, accounting,* and *management* factors, in Exhibit 14.1. These factors all affect the future growth of the firm's revenue, and all should be considered when estimating the value of a firm. Note that each factor directly affects the future path of revenue and therefore must be considered if the income approach is used.

Of course, some factors are more important than others in distinguishing a particular firm from the rest of the industry and the rest of the private economy. Identifying the most important factors is an essential part of the valuation analyst's job. Failure to identify these—as discussed next—is a frequent error.

EXHIBIT 14.1
Key Factors for Estimating Revenue Growth

1. Economic assumptions
   - General economic conditions, including trend output growth, interest rates, inflation, and employment
   - Economic conditions in the industry, including costs, regulations, and technology important in the industry
   - Economic conditions in the geographic trade area
   - Economic value of franchises, licenses, and intangible assets
   - Competitors

2. Accounting information
   - Historical revenue by product line
   - Historic cost of goods sold and operating costs
   - Capital structure and costs of financing, including sources of debt and equity
   - Dividends paid on stock, interest rate paid on debt, and any other key financing sources

3. Management policies
   - Management structure and senior management individuals
   - Important management policies
   - Business plans, including any plan for expansion or contraction

Source: Adapted from Anderson (2004a, chap. 10).

Historical Growth; The Error of Extrapolation

It is unfortunately common to see valuation analyses that are done almost entirely on the basis of assuming that historical growth rates will continue. However, simply using the past—extrapolating rather than analyzing the causes and predicting—can cause serious errors, because it implicitly assumes that the future will be exactly the same as the past. Invariably, it is not. Furthermore, potential buyers do not assume the future will simply be a glide path from the past, so the market for the business interests does not follow a simple extrapolation.

Furthermore, at least as far back as 1959, the IRS has insisted that causal economic factors be considered when estimating the value of the firm, including the economics of the industry.[1] These same factors are now included in other standards as well. The naive use of extrapolated revenue is listed as a common error in valuation in both Anderson (2005b) and Pratt (2008, chap. 9).

Frequent Error: Cut-and-Paste Analysis

Another frequent error seen by the author in professional valuation work is the use of what might be called *cut-and-paste analysis*. Such "analysis" of the economy or industry is essentially a reprinting (sometimes without attribution) of another person's report on the general economic or industry outlook. Whether such a report bears any relation to the subject company is often not addressed.

Growing Error: Computer-Generated "Analysis"

One emerging source of error is the misuse of computer software to generate detailed valuation "analyses." These can include impressive-looking schedules and objective-sounding narrative. As with the error of cut-and-paste analysis, this raises serious ethical and professional concerns.

Notes on the Literature: Factors to Consider

Nearly all the valuation texts oriented toward professional audiences describe the process of forecasting income. However, this is one area where the background of the authors frequently becomes apparent. One of the weaknesses in the most prominent professional texts oriented to accountants is that they offer little insight about predicting the future revenue growth rate.

Hitchner (2003) mentions using GDP growth, industry growth, and expected inflation. Damadoran (2002) considers historic growth, firm-specific information that has become public, macroeconomic information, information from competitors, and other information about the firm. Pratt and Niculita (2007) even provide a sample report in which an economic discussion is presented. None of these provide much guidance beyond these very limited suggestions.

Economics-oriented texts, such as Gaughan (2003) and Anderson (2004b), are much more specific on this matter, as might be expected from the authors' backgrounds. Both give methods for incorporating economic and industry data into revenue forecasts for specific firms.

PRACTICAL TASK 2: IDENTIFYING "INCOME"

What Is "Earnings" to an Owner?

The accounting income statement is designed to supply detailed information on the operation of the firm, the financing of the firm, and the disposition of the revenue gained from its operations. Therefore, it contains many elements of cost and a number of potential measures of profit or earnings. Thus, one practical task is identifying the proper measure of earnings for valuation purposes.

In general, the relevant measure is the earnings that are available to the owner. Note that the classic dividend discount model and the modern value functional approach both focus on the specific reward to the shareholder.

One can argue (as did Modigliani and Miller) that the dividend policy is "irrelevant" because stockholders can synthesize earnings from other portfolio changes.[2] However, in this chapter we primarily discuss privately held firms, to which the M-M propositions clearly do not apply.[3]

Form of Ownership and Estimating Earnings

Much has been written in the professional valuation literature about the differences between the value of traditional corporations (C corps) and *pass-through* entities such as S corps, most LLCs, and most partnerships. These sources correctly note that C corps pay taxes, as do investors receiving dividends, leading to a double taxation burden that does not exist for pass-through entities. Unfortunately, much of that literature ignores the practical reality of a pass-through entity, in which the owner is required to pay taxes on the imputed earnings *whether the income was distributed or not*.

Thus, the dividend policy decision directly affects the shareholder's earnings (or losses) after taxes. This undercuts the broad claims of an *S corp premium*.

The value functional approach in Chapter 15, "The Value Functional: Theory," is especially useful in dealing with this issue, as it makes explicit the kind of control aspects that often become important in smaller and pass-through entities. The dividend discount model, although often eschewed by modern valuator practitioners in favor of more completed DCF models, is at least specific about what income stream brings value to an investor.

Apportioning Expenses

Historical income statements are an excellent starting point for apportioning income when they are available from operating companies. However, they are just a guide, as the relevant question is how the company will incur expenses *in the future*.

PRACTICAL TASK 3: SELECTING A DISCOUNT RATE

Introduction: The Devolution of Debate on Discount Rates

Probably no topic in economics and finance devolves so quickly into a morass of opinions, argument, and abdication than discount rates. The individual's time preference is an essential part of the neoclassical model, so there is no lack of a theoretical basis. We also have voluminous empirical data on actual interest rates on loans, bank deposits, and bonds, plus volumes of data on rates of return on equity investments. Nobel Prizes are issued for theories on the topic.

Yet with all this knowledge, we are confident of very little when it comes to the discount rates actual investors apply to expected earnings from private firms. As a result of this information overload and underwhelming understanding, practitioners are often confronted with one of two situations:

1. *Unresolved conflicting opinions.* Quite often in practical work, different analysts produce widely different discount rates for the same subject company.[4] Such a situation sometimes arises even when both analysts claim to use the same theory *and* empirical data sets!

In other instances, they produce similar estimates from quite divergent viewpoints. For example, one analyst may use a CAPM method to estimate a discount rate for a firm she considers to be in a cyclical industry, while another may use a build-up method for a firm he claims is in a noncyclical industry and arrive at a similar value. Such enormous variation in usage has resulted in entire sections of professional valuation texts being devoted to common errors in the estimation of discount rates.[5]

2. *Abdication on the question.* The converse often occurs in the academic economics and finance literature, where the most common treatment of discount rates is to simply assume that one exists and denote it with a convenient symbol. Classics in the literature follow this approach, including the famous Modigliani-Miller and Black-Scholes articles. Others often focus on rejecting or confirming a *theory*, rather than on identifying the actual discount rates used by investors. Numerous tests of CAPM and the efficient markets hypothesis are examples of this.

Practical Information on Rates of Return

Practitioners often turn to one of a handful of excellent sources on historical rates of return on publicly traded securities in the U.S. markets, and similar sources where available in other countries. These sources include the following:

1. The data compiled by Ibbotson Associates on stock market returns, compiled in the *Stocks, Bonds, Bills, and Inflation* volumes published annually.

2. The data maintained by the University of Chicago Center for Research in Security Prices (CRSP).

3. The Federal Reserve Board and member banks in the United States, and similar authorities in other countries. The Federal Reserve Bank of St. Louis has a

particularly noteworthy history of providing economic and monetary data on the US economy.

4. Stock exchanges in the United States and other countries.[6]

5. Numerous vendors of financial market data, including Bloomberg, Global Financial Data, Standard & Poor's, and Yahoo! In recent years, the profusion of consumer-based investing and Internet use has driven the expansion of these services to consumers and small investors.

6. A small number of historical sources, such as Cowles (1939) and Shiller (1989).[7]

These sources vary in their coverage and focus. Most contemporary records rely on one of a small number of historical sources, often the early work of Alfred Cowles.[8]

Remark: Problems with Historical Data

There are serious questions of selection and survivor bias in these historical compilations. These biases arise from the preferences of researchers for available data series and those with a long tenure. To some degree, such biases are unavoidable. However, such questions are quite important when considering the application of these data to estimating discount rates for investments in small, start-up, distressed, or private firms.

Iterative Cost-of-Capital Estimates for the Firm

We can identify two variations of the practical income method of estimating the value of income-producing firms:

1. Discounted earnings *to the firm*

2. Discounted earnings *to equity*, including the classic dividend discount model

Both require forecasting a stream of earnings and discounting that stream using an appropriate discount rate.

Problem: Incorrect Weights for the WACC

In the case of earnings to the firm, the appropriate discount rate reflects the entire financing side of the balance sheet, including all debt and equity financing. The most common technique to estimate this discount rate is to calculate a weighted average cost of capital (WACC) based on the relative weights of debt and equity and the discount rates for each component.

A straightforward and common manner of doing this is to use the accounting balance sheet to generate the weights. Unfortunately, it is wrong. The error arises from using the book value of debt and equity, rather than the *market value* of debt and equity. For most operating firms, the market value of equity is typically higher than the book value, meaning that equity constitutes a larger share of the total capitalization than the accounting balance sheet implies.

In many cases involving profitable, operating firms, using the balance sheet to generate weights results in a *substantial overestimate* of the market value of a firm. This overestimate arises from the fact that, in most cases, the cost of equity is much higher than the cost of debt, and the actual (market value) of equity is much higher than the book value. Assigning an incorrectly low weight to the high cost of equity leads directly to an incorrectly high net present value of future earnings.

One Possible Solution: Iterative Methods

One alternative to using book value weights is an iterative method, such as the following:

1. Use book value to prepare a first guess of weights to use in estimating the weighted average cost of capital.

2. Use this initial estimate of WACC to, in turn, prepare a second guess of market value of the firm as a whole.

3. Use the second guess of market value to prepare the second guess of WACC.

4. Continue until the resulting market value estimates are close enough to each other to warrant no further iterations. In practice, this often occurs within twenty iterations.

These iterations are not difficult to perform manually on a standard spreadsheet, and Abrams (2001, chap. 6) describes such a method. The entire process can be programmed into a mathematical model, described by Anderson (2004a, chap. 10). Pratt (2002, chap. 7) also describes the iterative method and highlights how failure to properly weight the capital structure can produce serious errors in value estimates.

SHORTHAND INCOME VALUATION METHODS

Shorthand

This section discusses the theoretical and practical bases of a handful of commonly used valuation methods, which we will term *shorthand* because they do not have a fundamental economic basis. That is not to say they are not useful—the prevalence of their use disproves that notion. It is important for valuation practitioners and those interested in understanding how investors actually behave to understand these methods, their motivation, and their limitations.

Earnings Multiples

The *multiple* is a common shorthand for rule-of-thumb valuations in which the current (or expected) market value is expressed as a multiple of some measure of earnings. The precise definition of *earnings* and the scope of the value estimate often vary by industry.

The P/E Ratio

Sometimes the multiple in use is the well-known price/earnings (P/E) ratio, which is one of the ratios used in the methods discussed in Chapter 13, "Traditional Valuation Methods," under the section titled "The Market Approach: Theory." As the P/E ratio is the price of the traded equity divided by its earnings, when the earnings are those of the past year, it is more accurately known as a *backward-looking* P/E ratio. A *forward-looking* P/E ratio has an analyst's forecast as the denominator of the ratio.

The P/E ratio also has a heuristic value (a practical learning benefit). The reciprocal of this ratio is an implied discount-net-of-growth rate on equity investments in the firm.

Limitations

A heuristic is not a definition or a method by itself. One obvious problem with a P/E ratio is that the implied discount rate cannot be decomposed from the earnings estimate for the future. Another is the implied assumption that future growth and discount rates will be constant, or at least vary together in a constant manner. These are in addition to the inherent limitations of any discounted cash flow methodology, particularly those involving fixed costs, real options, and asymmetrical risks.

In addition, using a forward-looking P/E ratio as an indicator of value is a tautology— the multiple in such an *ersatz* calculation is a forecast itself, and the known price is the actual value.

As long as the analyst is aware of both the shortcomings and the usefulness of such a multiple, an earnings multiple is a handy heuristic.

Value Driver Models

Some valuation models within the income approach rely on decompositions of certain accounting ratios for an operating firm and assessments of how these ratios are likely to change over time. These are often called *DuPont models* after a method pioneered by the E. I. du Pont de Nemours corporation in the early part of the twentieth century. They involve breaking down a profitability ratio (typically return on equity [ROE] or return on investment [ROI]) into parts, and then evaluating each component. For example, ROE (net income/assets) can also be expressed as the product of profitability (net income/assets) and financial leverage (assets/stockholder equity). Subjective judgments or other forecasts about the future can then be made about each of these component parts, and the resulting forecasts can be combined to form a value estimate.

I call these *value driver models* because the analyst's opinion about what drives value is expressed in one or more of the components and then forecasted into the future. Value driver methods have the obvious benefits of any shorthand method, as well as the obvious drawbacks. In particular, they rely on the presumption that the value drivers and the other forecasted indicators are the only factors changing. This typically leaves out market, institutional, accounting, macroeconomic, technological, and managerial factors that do change over time. However, for a class of large companies in stable industries where the analyst has strong evidence of specific trends, value drivers models can be a handy shorthand.

Technical Indicators

Another class of indicators arises from what is commonly called *technical analysis*. Technical analysis is distinguished from *fundamental analysis* in that it focuses on the *movements* of price, often displayed on charts, rather than the *causes* of those price moves. The following is an indicative definition of technical analysis by a practitioner of that approach:

> The technical approach to investment is essentially a reflection of the idea that prices move in trends that are determined by the changing attitudes of investors toward a variety of economic, monetary, political, and psychological forces. The art of technical analysis, for it is an art, is to identify a trend reversal at a relatively early stage and ride on that trend until the weight of the evidence shows or proves that the trend has reversed.[9]

This approach is often criticized as having no theoretical basis, and indeed it is not based on a theory of fundamental causes leading directly to investor decisions. It is difficult, and to some extent impossible, to empirically test some technical trading strategies, because they depend on what a technical analyst sees when he or she looks at a chart.[10]

Instead, it is based on the notion that whatever causes investment behavior, those causes are largely captured in past price trends. Following this logic, technical analysts (some say *technicians*) use the trends to forecast future behavior. There are dozens of technical indicators, such as various calculations of *momentum, lines of support,* and *breakout points.*

The origin of technical analysis is often credited to the writings of Charles H. Dow (1851–1902), one of the founders of the modern company Dow Jones, which publishes (among many other things) stock market indicators. The famous Dow Jones Industrial Average (DJIA) is probably the best-known indicator of the U.S. stock markets.[11]

The *Dow theory* was never outlined by Charles Dow himself but instead is a synthesis assembled by others that largely follow the teachings of Charles Dow. The theory is sometimes summarized as a series of observations about bull and bear markets, phases of a market, and trends that are shared across stock markets.[12]

Although this book, by its very title, focuses on the actual economics of value—meaning the underlying causes of people's investment behavior—we do not dismiss technical analysis completely. Indeed, every time you hand-draw a trend line to simplify a chart of historical prices, you are engaging in a primitive form of technical analysis.

Industry Rules of Thumb

Individuals knowledgeable in specific industries commonly use algorithms that rely on specific industry metrics and historical patterns of purchase prices related to those metrics. These are often called *rules of thumb* because they encapsulate a number of factors into a relatively easy-to-use indicator of value.

For example, wholesalers of products often discuss the market value of the business as a multiple of the product's sales over the past twelve months. However, the market value may be for the essential operating assets (such as some facilities), or just the rights to distribute the products, or for the entire company. Similarly, the sales over the last year may be confined to the main categories of products and are often adjusted to net out any returns of products and other factors.

Looking deeper into the category of retail franchisees illustrates this. An automobile dealership may have its value estimated with a rule of thumb based on the product of the number of cars sold the previous year and a dollar amount per car. These rules of thumb have variations based on the brand or type of product sold, and within those brands considerable variations occur over the business cycle. A Cadillac dealer may be worth more per car than a Chevrolet dealer because the per-vehicle profit on a high-priced car is usually more than on a low-priced car; on the other hand, a Honda dealer may be worth more per car than a dealer selling brands that cost more, but where the viability of that brand is in question.

The author has seen similar rules of thumb for beer distributors (dollars per case sold), rental car agencies (dollars per car on the lot), high-tech start-ups (dollars per employee), repair shops (dollars per repair person or per repair bay) and for other industries.

Economic Rationale for Rules of Thumb

It is easy to dismiss rules of thumb as unscientific or simplistic. However, remember that a rule of thumb in common use will wither away if it has no informational value. Therefore, a commonly used rule of thumb must be given some credibility, if only because potential buyers and sellers consider it when they make their decisions. Understanding the basis for the rule of thumb allows a careful analyst to use it properly.

Limitations on the Use of Earnings Multiples; Failures or Abuses

Earnings multiples tend to be descriptive and useful *when used properly within the proper industry*. Alas, improper use of earnings multiples is common in practical valuation work. This author has seen credentialed valuation experts make serious mistakes of this type, and do so multiple times. For example, some experts have valued firms as a multiple of past sales (or even potential sales) as if the firm were a top performer in the industry, when in fact the firm had ceased operations, was near bankruptcy, lacked financial statements, or was selling a product with little or no track record. In such cases, the professional failure to understand the industry (or the ethical failure to tell the truth) swamped all other factors.

On the other hand, the author has also seen noncredentialed but industry-knowledgeable people estimate with great accuracy the value of firms, franchises, and investment opportunities within their area of expertise. Indeed, a knowledgeable industry person *often* beats a general valuation expert in such matters.

Compilations of Rules of Thumb

Rules of thumb are sometimes assembled into references. One excellent reference for businesses in the United States is the annual *Business Reference Guide*, published by Business Brokerage Press.[13] This contains rules of thumb for numerous industries, assembled from economists, accountants, business owners, brokers, and others that are knowledgeable about the industries. The same publication also gives a partial list of experts that the publisher believes are knowledgeable in certain industries.[14]

The information in this and similar publications is subject to the same cautions and limitations as any rule of thumb. It is also interesting to note that, on occasion, different experts recommend contradictory rules of thumb.

The Sanity Test

A good use for the rule of thumb method is to establish a "sanity test" (or, reasonableness test) for a value estimate done by other means. If, for example, a common industry rule of thumb is $1,000 per unit sold the previous year, and you estimate the value of a business in that industry at $2,000 per unit sold the previous year, you should consider whether any unusual factor for the subject business explains the discrepancy. If not, you should consider whether the market conditions that gave rise to the rule of thumb had changed, or your estimate itself is unreasonable.

Accurate rules of thumb must change when relevant market conditions change. Rules of thumb are just that—rules of thumb. They offer a quick reference. They are not value; they are not even a reliable *estimator* of value. However, they are a useful heuristic and a good basis for a sanity check.

VALUATION APPLICATIONS: INCOME METHOD

We present next sample valuation estimates, using an income method, for each of the sample firms described in Appendix C, "Description of Subject Companies." As in the examples in the previous chapter, these highlight the methodology and the use of subjective adjustments by the valuation analysts (whose work is only lightly edited by the author here).

S. H. Importers

This analysis was prepared by a practitioner guided by professional business valuation standards published by one of the credentialing organizations within this field, the National Association of Certified Valuators and Analysts. The analyst has also been S. H. Importers' accountant since its first years in business and thus had access to additional financial information.

The analyst believed that the best traditional valuation method for a smaller company such as S. H. Importers would be to discount the company's future expected income. Like most small closely held firms, however, S. H. Importers does not generate reliable projections of its operations or income. Therefore, historical earnings were used in lieu of projected earnings. These earnings were then divided by a capitalization rate to compute the company's estimated fair market value.

Income Stream to Be Capitalized

The analyst noted that the proper measure of income to be valued is one that best measures the financial return to an investor in the stock of the company. The analyst deemed that to be net cash flow available to stockholders, as it best approximates the amount of earnings that could be paid out to stockholders, while still leaving enough cash in the company to finance continued operations, replace capital assets, and maintain an adequate level of working capital. Net cash flow to stockholders (sometimes called *net cash flow to equity*) is defined as net income after taxes and debt payments, plus depreciation, minus cash required for the replacement of capital assets and changes in working capital (Table 14.1).

TABLE 14.1
S. H. Importers: Net cash flow to shareholders

Net income after tax[a]	$131,340
+ Depreciation	0
− Replacement of capital assets	0
− Change in working capital	0
Net cash flow available to stockholders	$131,340

[a] Net income after taxes and debt payments, adjusted average for 2002–2006.

The analyst used the following data and adjustments to estimate the trend in cash flow available to shareholders:

- Average net income for the eight years 2002 through 2009 was $83,130, whereas for the five-year prerecession period of 2002 through 2006, average net income was $131,340. The analyst believed that S. H. Importers was well positioned to recover from the recent recession, and the company's prerecession earnings history was a more reasonable estimate of future long-term earnings prospects than the most recent actual earnings.

- Management estimated that historical depreciation expense is a good indication of future capital expenditures, which the analyst found reasonable.

- Working capital (current assets less current liabilities) is the amount of money a firm must keep on hand to carry on its day-to-day operations. Historically the company has had excess working capital available. The analyst accepted the management's forecast that they would not require any immediate additional working capital to fund the operation.

Discount Rate; Use of the Build-Up Method

The cost of capital varies from business to business based on such factors as industry and company size as well as from period to period. To determine the discount rate for S. H. Importers, their accountant used the build-up method, defined as follows (Ibbotson Associates, 2006):

> an additive model in which the return on an asset is estimated as the sum of a risk-free rate and one or more risk premia. Each premium represents the reward an investor receives for taking on a specific risk. The building blocks are summed arithmetically to form an estimate of the cost of capital. (Ibbotson Associates, 2006, p. 37)

The analyst's estimate of the discount rate, using the build-up method, is shown in Table 14.2. (The analyst's notes for each of these, including the data on industry premiums and other indicators, are reprinted in the *Solutions Manual* described in Appendix B, "Description of Subject Companies.") For the company-specific risk, the analyst's reasoning is presented in Table 14.2.

Company-Specific Risk

The analyst used an adjusting premium based on a comparison of the risk level of the company with the risk of the industry as a whole. The analyst felt that the other build-up

TABLE 14.2
S. H. Importers: Discount rate

Risk-free rate	*3.7%*
Equity risk premium	7.1%
Firm size premium	6.4%
Industry premium	−0.4%
Company-specific risk	1.5%
Discount rate for equity investors in the firm	18.3%

NOTE: Estimated using method described in text.

components were based on objective empirical data, while this company-specific risk premium was based on the valuator's professional judgment. The analyst identified the following key factors underlying the company-specific risk premium for S. H. Importers:

• Market presence: *Low risk.* S. H. Importers has been operating in the same area in Southern California for more than twenty-five years, and while sales have fallen sharply during the current recession, several area competitors have closed. The company continues to provide its full complement of services and is well positioned to participate in any economic and industry recovery.

• Financial strength: *Less risk than what is typical for the industry.* S. H. Importers is well capitalized and has little or no debt, and any debt or rent payments are due to the company's principal.

• Supplier base: *No additional risk.* S. H. Importers is not dependent on only one or a few suppliers. Inventory is sourced both locally and overseas from numerous independent vendors, wholesalers, and auction houses. The firm has been increasingly sourcing inventory from consignment sales from individuals and other dealers.

• Management: *Modest increase in risk.* The management team has been in place for the last ten years with no immediate plans to retire. The founder's son is in his late thirties and has been groomed as a successor for years. Nonetheless, the founder continues to be closely involved in day-to-day management, especially in purchasing and merchandising. The founder's sudden departure for any reason would have a significant detrimental impact on sourcing saleable quality inventory. However, the founder believes the firm could continue to run in her absence.

The analyst noted that there is no objective mechanism for assigning numerical values to the risks associated with the preceding factors. The company appears to be superior to the industry financially, and about average for the industry as far as market share, supplier base, and management, but there does appear to be some additional investment risk because of a possible senior management succession problem. Based on these factors, the analyst assigned a company-specific risk premium of 1.5 percent.

Conclusion: Discount Rate

Based on the considerations just discussed, the valuation analyst concluded that an equity investor in S. H. Importers would require a discount rate (rate of return on their investment) of 18.28 percent.

Long-Term Sustainable Growth Rate

The analyst forecasted a long-term sustainable growth rate, composed of "real" growth (determined by professional judgment) plus inflation. Over the previous twelve years (1997–2009), S. H. Importers had an average annual sales growth rate of 4.07 percent. Looking only at the nine prerecession years of 1997 through 2006, the average annual growth rate was 11.98 percent. Recent forecasts for furniture store sales varied from 4 percent to 9 percent, depending on assumptions made about the speed of recovery from the current recession. Taking an average of these two forecasts gives 6.5 percent; in light of the prerecession actual annual growth of 11.98 percent, the analyst forecasted a long-term sustainable growth rate of 7.0 percent.

Capitalization of Income

The forecasted annual income stream to shareholders, divided by the capitalization rate (the discount rate less the growth rate), indicates the present value of that stream. The capitalization of income method within the income approach relies on the assumption that this present value is the estimate of the value of the equity in the company. Using this method, S. H. Importers' equity is estimated to be worth $1,246,000. See Table 14.3.

A & A Consulting

To estimate the value of A & A Consulting, the valuator used fair market value as the standard of value and included all necessary tangible and intangible assets, excluding working capital in excess of that required for operations. The analyst used the close of business for the year, January 1, 2010, as the valuation date.

The analyst carefully looked over the firm's historic income statements and normalized them to adjust for unusual conditions. Using those normalized statements, a discounted cash flow schedule was created for the years 2010 through 2017. The DCF analysis is shown as two schedules, with different growth rates and other adjustments noted at the bottom. See Tables 14.4 and 14.5.

The analyst forecasted faster revenue growth rate and higher total expenses for the immediate four years (15 percent and 89.5 percent) than for the later years (10 percent and 85 percent). The analyst's discount rate of 18.5 percent reflected an assumption of higher risk than many large publicly traded firms, but less risk than a thinly capitalized firm or one in an unstable position.

Using this method, the practitioner concluded that the fair market value of A & A Consulting was $1.94 million.

TABLE 14.3
S. H. Importers: Capitalization of earnings

Annual income stream		$131,340
Capitalization rate (discount rate less growth rate)	18.3% − 7.0%	11.3%
Valuation estimate		$1.26 million

TABLE 14.4
A & A Consulting: DCF valuation, 2010–2013

	Growth rates	2010	2011	2012	2013
Revenue	15%[a]	$1,921,329	$2,209,528	$2,540,958	$2,922,101
Total expenses	89.5%[b]	1,719,582	1,977,519	2,274,147	2,615,269
Operating profit		$ 201,747	$ 232,009	$ 266,811	$ 306,832
Allowance: Federal and state taxes	35.0%[c]	(70,612)	(81,203)	(93,384)	(107,391)
Net after-tax cash flow		$ 131,135	$ 150,806	$ 173,427	$ 199,441
Present value at equity cost	18.5%				
	Period	1	2	3	4
Present value rate		84.4%	71.2%	60.1%	50.7%
Present value		$ 110,663	$ 107,395	$ 104,223	$ 101,144

[a] Includes inflation and business expansion, assuming 15% annual growth between 2010 and 2013.
[b] Total expenses includes interest, depreciation, and amortization. 89.5% is the average of 2006, 2007, 2008, and 2009 (see historical income statements).
[c] Current federal corporate tax rate with state income tax rate adjustment. A & A is an S corp; allowance reflects planned distribution to members for imputed taxes.

TABLE 14.5
A & A Consulting: DCF valuation, 2014–2017

	Growth rates	2014	2015	2016	2017	
Revenue	10%[a]	$3,214,311	$3,535,742	$3,889,317	$ 4,278,248	
Total expenses	85.0%[b]	2,732,165	3,005,381	3,305,919	3,636,511	
Operating profit		$ 482,146	$ 530,361	$ 583,398	$ 641,737	
Allowance: Federal and state taxes	35.0%[c]	(168,626)	(185,626)	(204,189)	(224,608)	
Net after-tax cash flow		$ 313,395	$ 344,735	$ 379,209	$ 417,129	$4,019,609[d]
Present value at equity cost	18.5%	5	6	7	8	
Present value rate		42.8%	36.1%	30.5%	25.7%	25.7%
Present value		$ 134,122	$ 124,502	$ 115,571	$ 107,281	$ 1,003,801
DCF value estimate[e]		**$ 1,938,702**				

[a] Includes inflation and business expansion, assuming 10% annual growth after 2013.
[b] Total expenses includes interest, depreciation, and amortization. Assumes 15% operating profit margin after 2013.
[c] Current federal corporate tax rate with state income tax rate adjustment. A & A is an S corp; allowance reflects planned distribution to members for imputed taxes.
[d] Final PV calculation: (2017 Net After-Tax Cash Flow) * $(1 + g)/(r - g)$. Assumed 7.5% annual growth for the terminal value calculation, with a capitalization rate of 11% (18.5% − 7.5%).
[e] Value is the sum of the terminal and preceding eight periods of present value.

ExxonMobil

Exxon's huge scale and market capitalization mean that numerous financial analysts produce assessments of the company's likely earnings and estimated intrinsic value. There are also many competitive firms for which ratios and similar profitability information are available. Thus, the traditional income method is likely to work relatively well.

The difficulty arises in attempting to estimate the value of the company's real options. Traditional methods have no tools for this, other than educated guesses, comparisons with firms with similar options, or misuse of financial options formulas. Furthermore,

ExxonMobil faces substantial currency risks, political risks, and technology risks. Traditional income methods, and indeed any backward-looking method, will fail to properly consider these.

The analyst concluded that the market method, given the wide availability of recent transactions, was the preferable method, and did not attempt to duplicate the many other income-based analyses available for the company.

15 THE VALUE FUNCTIONAL: THEORY

- Human transversality conditions that we assert apply to nearly all bona fide firms.

- Two important propositions: a unique solution to business value functional equations exists; and it can be found.

THE FIRM, CONTROL, AND MAXIMIZATION OF VALUE

Three Criteria for a Firm

Recall the three-criteria definition of the firm we introduced in Chapter 4, "The Nature of the Firm"—an organization with the following characteristics:

- a separate legal identity
- a motivation to earn profits for its owners
- a set of replicable business processes

A separation between the firm and its owners is established by the first criterion. That implies a separate objective for the firm. In neoclassical economics and modern finance, that objective is assumed to be profit maximization. However, unlike in the neoclassical model of the firm, this new definition requires the following:

1. A set of replicable business processes
2. A motivation to *earn* profits for the investors

This insight allows for a novel application of what is known as *control theory* to the firm. In particular, we can capture much more of the complex motivations and actions of the entrepreneur and business manager than is possible with a model of the firm that is inhibited to focus on profit maximization.

CONTROL THEORY

Control Theory and the Firm

Control theory focuses on the ability to control a *dynamical system*, or a system that changes according to some laws of motion. Such a system can be represented by a set of equations that include both *state variables* (representing the current situation) and *control variables* (representing possible actions). These equations, in mathematical terms, often are *differential equations*, meaning that the *rate of change* of one variable is related to the magnitude of another.

When a firm (as properly defined) exists, the basic elements of a dynamical system are all present:

- state variables (describing the current situation for the business)
- control variables (reflecting management decisions)
- laws of motion, or transition rules, that govern how the firm's activities today result in changes in its situation at a later time

In the case of the firm within a market economy, the laws of motion are largely established by the accounting conventions and budget constraints of the firm, the physical limitations of production and other technologies, and other institutional and resource factors. The state and control variables are also established by these laws of motion, as well as the particular industry, technology, and form of the enterprise.

The firm then becomes, in the parlance of control theory, a dynamical system. The controller of this system is the entrepreneur or business manager. The manner in which the entrepreneur or business manager can control the firm is dependent on these laws of motion, state variables, and the replicable business practices of the firm.

Control Theory: A Whirlwind History

Some control theory enthusiasts, with an uncharacteristic immoderation, date its beginning to the writings of Aristotle.[1] However fanciful that claim, Roman engineers clearly used certain control elements in the design of waterworks such as baths and aqueducts. It was the industrial revolution, however, that brought forth engineering applications of control theory. Dutch mathematician Christiaan Huygens designed clocks that controlled the speed of a pendulum in the seventeenth century; his contributions (along with those of Robert Hooke) were used by windmills. The development of steam engines by James Watt in the eighteenth century increased the need for mechanical control mechanisms, as humankind had now developed powerful machines that would, and did, simply explode if not properly managed. Watt and others developed governors that kept the engine going at the right speed, slowing it down or speeding it up as necessary.

The mathematical basis for control theory was demonstrated in an 1867 exposition by the Scottish physicist James C. Maxwell (whose equations Einstein used as a basis for his relativity theories) on steam-engine governors.[2] Modern control theory (sometimes also called *mathematical* or *engineering* control theory) developed at the interchange of engineering and mathematics in the latter half of the twentieth century and has also been applied in physics, electronics, biology, sociology, and economics. Many of the tools that allowed for its application in social sciences were not developed until the 1950s or later, including the dynamic programming algorithm of the American mathematician Richard Bellman, the filtering mechanism of the Hungarian-American engineer Rudolf Kalman, and the theory of the maximum by the Russian mathematician L. S. Pontryagin. Our use of control theory depends heavily on these later contributions, which bridged control theory and mathematical economics and finance. We discuss these next.

Modern Use in Mathematical Economics and Finance

Of these three pioneers, Bellman had the insight to describe possible applications in the social sciences. (Kalman's work led directly to improvements in aerospace engineering. He was later awarded the 2008 National Medal of Sciences for, among other things, helping to establish the intellectual basis for the guidance system that allowed the Apollo spacecraft to reach the moon.) Bellman (1957) described a particular method of *dynamic programming*, and a core functional equation used in dynamic programming and related methods is often called a *Bellman equation* today. Although early texts on the subject (including Bellman [1957] and Dreyfus [1965]) described thought experiments involving costs and revenues for theoretical firms, the first notable use in economics arose in Robert C. Merton's seminal 1973 article on the intertemporal capital asset pricing model. In that model, theoretical investors choose between income today and future income.[3] The 1989 publication of the Nancy Stokey and Robert Lucas book *Recursive Methods in Economic Dynamics* led to the introduction of control theory into higher-level economics curriculum. (Because solving control theory problems often involves a recursive set of calculations, the approach has sometimes been called a *recursive method.*) Stokey and Lucas proved a set of theorems that established the existence of solutions to functional equations under certain assumptions.

Uses in theoretical models of finance, and the theoretical superiority of dynamic programming over discounted cash flow analysis when options are present, were proposed by Avanish Dixit and Robert Pindyck (1994). The use of recursive techniques in macroeconomics was further developed by Lars Ljungqvist and Thomas J. Sargent (2000, 2004), who describe its growing use in economics as an example of intellectual "imperialism."[4] Applications outlined by Ljungqvist and Sargent include the search for employment, pricing among monopolists, savings and investment in model economies with different features, monetary regimes, and other topics. Significant progress on the computational difficulties was demonstrated in the last decade, including numeric computational methods and a host of examples described by Miranda and Fackler (2002). Alexander Vollert (2003) proposed the use of such techniques for valuing real options available to businesses.

The use of dynamic programming for the valuation of private businesses as a whole, including the idea of the firm as a controlled entity, was introduced by Patrick L. Anderson (2004a). Brief discussions of the use of the technique also appear in Anderson (2005b, 2005c, 2009) including a simplified example of an actual business valuation, the use of the technique in calculating damages, and an intuitive argument applied to the gross value of private businesses in the United States.

THE IDEA OF A FUNCTIONAL EQUATION

Importance of the Concept

Understanding the notion of a functional is essential to understanding the value functional method. To ensure that we properly cover this idea, we introduce it three ways: an informal definition, a slightly formal definition, and finally an illustration. More rigorous treatments are provided in the cited references.

The Idea of a Function

A real-valued *function* is a correspondence (or rule, or map) that relates one set of numbers to a specific real number. (Finite real numbers do not include concepts such as infinity or imaginary numbers such as the square root of negative one.) The set of numbers that serve as inputs to the function are commonly known as the *arguments*. The function itself could involve simple arithmetic or complicated algorithms of algebra, trigonometry, statistics, calculus, and other branches of mathematics.

For example, the function max(*a*, *b*, *c*) selects the single largest number among the set {*a*, *b*, *c*}. The function *net present value* relates a set of numbers (a discount rate, a set of future cash flows, and the time indexes of those cash flows) to a single real number.

The Idea of a Functional

The Functional: An Informal Definition

A *functional* can be considered an extension of the familiar mathematical concept of a function. A rule relating a set of numbers to a single number is a function. A rule that relates a *set of functions* to a single number is a functional. It is a "function of functions."

A simple metaphor illustrates this difference. The dynamic programming pioneer Stuart Dreyfus (1965) described a functional as a rule relating *curves* to a single real number.[5] If one considers a curve to be an illustration of a function, the intuition behind this description should be clear. Dreyfus's explanation from nearly a half century ago inspired the graphical illustrations presented in Figure 15.1 and Figure 15.2.

A Slightly Formal Description of Functional and Vector Space

More formally, a functional is a real-valued function on a *vector space.*

A *vector* is an ordered group of numbers that can represent multidimensional quantities such as magnitude and direction, or income and net worth, or sales of several products this month for each of several divisions of a company. Each column in the quarterly income statement of an operating business is a good example of a vector, although it is rarely described as such. A row of quantitative data in a spreadsheet (which might be the same line in an income statement over several time periods) is also a vector.

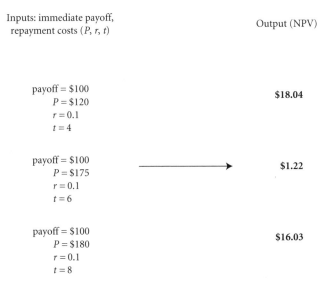

Inputs: immediate payoff, repayment costs (P, r, t)	Output (NPV)
payoff = $100 P = $120 r = 0.1 t = 4	**$18.04**
payoff = $100 P = $175 r = 0.1 t = 6	**$1.22**
payoff = $100 P = $180 r = 0.1 t = 8	**$16.03**

Figure 15.1   Illustration of a function: NPV of an investment

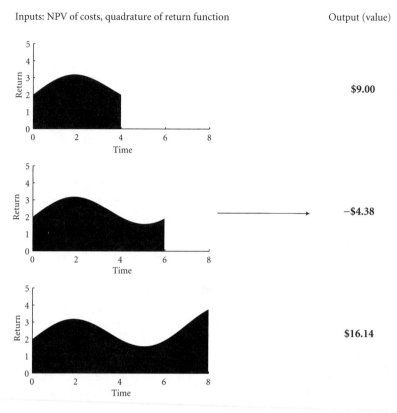

Figure 15.2   Illustration of a functional: Value of an investment

Vectors that consist of numbers alone are frequently shown as surrounded by brackets, such as [1, 2, 3]; these may be displayed as rows or columns. Two- and three-dimensional vectors are also commonly visualized as a line in space (such as an arrow drawn on graph paper). This visualization technique fails when the number of elements is larger than three, as we lack an effective way to show all the information on a standard graph. However, vectors can contain any number of elements. By convention, a single-element vector is called a *scalar*.

Though vectors are often ordered groups of numbers, a vector space is a broader concept. A vector space could include sets of numbers, sets of vectors, sets of sequences of numbers, or sets of functions. To be a true vector space, operations such as addition, subtraction, and multiplication have to be well defined and *closed*, meaning that the result of one of these operations on elements of the vector space must be part of the vector space. Functionals are real-valued functions that operate on this space, meaning they can take as inputs vectors, sets of numbers, and functions.

Differential Calculus; Calculus of Variations

The standard calculus taught in many colleges deals with functions. A common use of this calculus is to find the maximum or minimum point of a function. To do so often requires differentiation or integration of a function. These types of problems are the province of what is commonly called differential calculus.

The *calculus of variations* is a 300-year-old related branch of mathematics that examines questions such as how to minimize the area under a curve generated by a function, or how to find the shortest line between two points.[6] These kinds of questions require a vector space that is the space of functions, hence the use of the term *functional* to describe a function of functions. We use other concepts that originated in the calculus of variations in Chapter 16, "The Value Functional: Applications."[7]

Function Versus Functional: A Valuation Example

The following example illustrates the difference between a function and a functional in valuing an investment opportunity.

Three Example Investment Opportunities; Two Investors

Consider three different business opportunities available to two investors. Each opportunity involves receiving an immediate payment (such as the proceeds from a loan) and the obligation to make repayments over time of different amounts. Both investors have a known discount rate of 10 percent. There is uncertainty about the timing and amounts of repayments, as they depend on the performance of the company and other economic variables. There are empirical bases for making projections about these future conditions, but complete markets do not exist, so the investor will bear some risk that cannot be insured in the marketplace.

Two Approaches

The two investors have the same information and are knowledgeable enough about financial calculations. However, they take different approaches to evaluating the three opportunities.

1. *Net present value function.* The first investor knows the repayments are uncertain but makes an educated guess of the time and amounts that would be required. For the first example, he expects to repay $120 in four years; for the second, $175 in six years; for the third, $180 in eight years. Using the net present value function, he calculates the present value of those future expenditures and subtracts it from the immediate payment.[8]

This set of calculations maps individual real numbers to a single real number; in other words, it is a function. This is illustrated in Figure 15.1, where on the "input" side we see the numbers that go into the net present value calculation, and on the "output" side we see that all three of the investment opportunities produce positive expected net present values for the investor.

2. *Value functional equation.* The second investor also recognizes the uncertainty about the future but considers the likely repayment schedule to be a function of the changing economic conditions. She expects that these conditions will fluctuate around a positive growth trend. Rather than modeling this as a lump-sum repayment at a particular time, the investor models it as a fixed payment plus a variable payment that depends on the economic

conditions. The latter portion she models as a linear function of the path of an index of the relevant business conditions, where the area under the curve represents the effect of those conditions on the company's profitability.

This set of calculations maps functions (the curve representing economic conditions, the quadrature of the area under the curve, and the linear combination of these) to a single real number. It is a functional. This is illustrated in Figure 15.2, where on the "input" side there are a series of curves showing the expected path over time of the economic conditions index. (Not shown are the other inputs.)[9] On the "output" side, we see the solution to the value functional equation. Note that two of the three opportunities appear to be worth pursuing.

Additional Comments

This example reveals two additional insights worth mentioning:

1. The use of a functional allowed for the inputs to the investor's calculations to be functions themselves, and those functions could take into account much broader information about market conditions.

2. The use of a value functional rather than a net present value function causes the investment advice to switch from positive to negative for one of the examples. This suggests that the additional information used in that method was helpful to the investor.

WHY A VALUE FUNCTIONAL FOR BUSINESSES?

Is a Functional Equation Necessary?

One may ask if the use of such a novel mathematical concept is really necessary, when the standard finance curriculum has featured discounted cash flow models for approximately fifty years. The answer is yes, if we are to use the following innovations:

- The notion of a business as a controlled entity (or dynamical system). This is consistent with the definition of a firm in this book, but quite different from the concept of stable earnings from established assets that is the assumption underlying the Modigliani-Miller propositions.

- The recognition of a transition function for state variables. This is superior to a simple projection that underlies most discounted cash flow analyses.

- The use of a reward function, rather than a specific cash-flow calculation, to express current benefits to the owner.

The transition and reward functions are described further below.

Management of Curves—Not Numbers

Recall Dreyfus's description of a functional as a function whose arguments are curves. This leads to an important observation about management. When using the value functional method, we are assuming that the manager of the firm attempts to maximize its value, with the maximization occurring over *functions* of variables as well as variables themselves.

Think of the first of these—the reward function—as a set of curves drawn in the space created by mapping a single state variable to a single reward variable. Assume the state variable is the firm's revenue, the reward variable is the firm's distributed profits, and the control variable is the share of the resulting profits reinvested by the firm. We may expect that distributed profits will go up as revenue increases, but go down as the share of profits is reinvested.

If we hold the share of profits distributed constant, we could illustrate the reward function by a curve. Changing the share of profits distributed would create another curve.

An entrepreneur could—and almost certainly would—consider those curves when managing the firm. Thus, an input to the entrepreneur's informal valuation logic would be the curves that were drawn by the function of two variables just described. The entrepreneur would undoubtedly also have other such curves in mind while managing the firm.

Thus, part of his or her management calculus would be a function of functions, or a functional. It would not be management by the numbers, but management by the curves.

INTRODUCTION TO DYNAMIC PROGRAMMING

Introduction: The Multiperiod Maximization Problem

In this section we introduce a method of modeling the decisions of people who consider their welfare over multiple time periods, where that welfare can be formed into a value functional equation. We use the term *dynamic programming* for this technique for historical reasons.

Dynamic programming is based on the insight of the American mathematician Richard Bellman in his brilliant original work on multiperiod optimization problems.[10] Bellman considered the task of an individual who seeks to maximize the benefits from some activity over time, when the choices made during one period affect the ability to enjoy benefits in the future. This situation occurs every single day in the life of an entrepreneur, investor, or manager, and anyone that manages a household budget.

Optimizing Consumption: The Cake-Eating Problem

The classic economic illustration of this technique is known as the *cake-eating problem.*[11] In this problem, a person is given a cake and must decide how much of the cake to eat each day. To make the problem straightforward, we assume that the person has quite normal views about eating cake: he or she knows that each bite today reduces the size of the cake for tomorrow, considers the enjoyment of eating the third piece of cake in any given day to be smaller than that of eating the first, and also considers enjoyment of eating one piece of cake today to be larger than the enjoyment of eating one tomorrow.[12]

We now ask the following two questions:

1. What is the value of the cake to a cake eater?
2. How much cake should be eaten today?

This is a multiperiod optimization problem in which the eater tries to maximize the gratification of eating the cake over multiple days. We use it to evaluate the traditional net present value approach to value and an alternate dynamic programming approach.

Variables for the Cake-Eating Problem

To use this new approach, we identify the amount of cake left as the *state variable*; all that you need to know about the state of the world (at least for this problem) at any one time is captured in the size of the cake. The amount of cake eaten during each time period is the *control variable*; it is the factor under direct control of the cake eater. How the state evolves is described by a *transition equation*. Given our simplifying assumptions of no spoilage or refrigeration costs, the transition equation simply reduces the size of the cake (the state variable) by the amount eaten each day.

We also add the following:

- a boundary condition that ensures that at the end of the time period, all the cake and no more has been eaten
- a (fixed) discount factor that is nonnegative and less than one
- a finite time limit for the cake to be eaten

These are listed in Equation 15.1.

Equation 15.1 Variables in the Cake-Eating Problem

C_t = amount of cake remaining at time t (state variable)

c_t = amount of cake eaten at time t (policy variable)

$C_t = C_{t-1} - c_t = C_0 - \sum_{t=0}^{t} c_t$ (transition equation)

$C_T = 0$ (boundary condition)

$0 \leq \beta < 1$ (discount factor)

$t = 0, ..., T$ (time index)

We now need to define two additional variables: the value of the cake given the state, and the enjoyment of eating a piece of cake (Equation 15.2).

Equation 15.2 Value and Enjoyment of Cake

$V(C_t)$ = value of cake at time t

$f(c_t)$ = enjoyment of eating cake at time t

Using these variables and equations, we can try the classic NPV valuation method and an alternative.

Cake Eating: An NPV Approach

We may attempt to answer the two questions (value of the cake and how much to eat) with a classic net present value equation (Equation 15.3).

Equation 15.3 Value as NPV of Cake

$$V(C_{t=0}) = E_{t=0}\left[\sum_{t=0}^{T}\beta^t f(c_t)\right], \text{random } \{c_t\}$$

$$V(C_{t=0}) = \left[\sum_{t=0}^{T}\beta^t f(c_t)\right], \text{known } \{c_t\}$$

This equation sets the value of the cake as the expected sum of the discounted stream of gratification from eating the cake. All the pieces of the cake add up to exactly one cake, and we add up the enjoyment (discounted for time) of eating each piece. We drop the expectation operator and simplify the equation because the amount of the cake eaten is not a random variable; it is directly controlled by the cake eater.

If we add the additional assumption that the gratification function is linear (meaning two pieces of cake always taste twice as good as one), the formula is a direct analogy to the $E(NPV)$ approach to valuation, with the net present value of cash flows replaced by the net present value of cake crumbs.

Although this equation works as a value estimate—we have indeed added up all the benefits and taken a net present value of them—it is actually quite useless for the cake-eating problem. It is useless because it tells us either to eat the entire cake immediately (when the discount rate is more than zero), or that it does not matter when you eat the cake (when the discount rate is zero). If we were to adopt the "magic refrigerator" version of the problem, where the cake grows overnight by a constant fraction, then we could again have the cake eater completely indifferent as to when to eat the cake even with a positive discount rate.[13]

Cake Eating: A Value Functional Approach

Now consider the same equation with two vital innovations:

1. Seek the solution of the problem in terms of a *policy* (decision rule) about how much to eat given the size of the cake.
2. Make the problem tractable by considering only how much to eat in the *current period*, and then revisit the same question in the next period.

With these innovations, we can produce the core functional equation or Bellman equation that describes the value of the cake (Equation 15.4).

Equation 15.4 Bellman Equation for the Cake Eater

$$V(C_t) = \max_c\{f(c_t) + \beta E[V(C_{t+1})]\}$$

Here we have a tractable problem: we maximize the gratification from eating the cake over the range of policy actions available to us, which in each period consists of a choice to eat none, some, or all of the remaining cake. Eating is the control, and the remaining cake is the state variable.

Now we can ask mathematically what we ask in practice: how much cake do I eat today? This Bellman equation equates the *value* of having the cake to the optimization, over the policy choices available to the cake eater, of the sum of cake-eating enjoyment today and the expected discounted cake-eating enjoyment in the future.

If you like cake but your gratification from eating it becomes smaller after each piece, this approach gives you a usable solution: eat the cake over a small set of days.

THE VALUE FUNCTIONAL MODEL OF THE FIRM

Illustrating Recursive Decisions: An Entrepreneur's Problem

We can use the same recursive structure of the cake-eating problem to model an entrepreneur's problem.

This time, assume that the "cake" is the capital of a fledgling business, and "eating the cake" is taking money from the company (or taking leisure time rather than working). This being a company rather than a cake, the entrepreneur can also add to the capital in the firm—but such additions are costly. Given this backdrop, every day the entrepreneur decides how much to work and how much to take in the form of salary, benefits, or distributions.

Furthermore, a host of management decisions must be made. Most of these decisions will not produce immediate earnings, and some immediately cost the company money. Obvious examples are expenditures for training, advertising, and capital investments, all of which cost the company far more in the early time periods than they produce in revenue.

Finally, the entrepreneur observes a state of affairs, much of which appears to be the outcome of random events, and other parts which seem to be the direct consequence of her actions. Other parts of the state of affairs she ignores because it is too costly (in terms of time and the costs of information) to evaluate them. However, decisions must be made.

After one round of decisions, the state of the world changes. She again looks at the factors she thinks are important, and makes similar decisions with more information. In particular, she considers the state of the business, and her own desire to take a salary. Regardless of the decisions made last period, she evaluates the current state of affairs and makes new decisions.

This is the cake eating of entrepreneurial life. Add a substantial dose of risk, liquidity constraints, demands for time, and excitement, and you have a good model of the entrepreneurial challenge. In particular, you have incorporated the essential tension between the need to reinvest in the firm and the need to distribute money to the entrepreneur. This tension is omnipresent in start-up firms, a large fraction of which do not survive their first several years.

Elements of the Value Functional Model of the Firm

We now formalize the value functional model, which contains the following elements:

1. *A definition of the firm.* We defined the firm as an organization with three characteristics: separate identity from its workers or owners; profit motivation for the owners; and a set of replicable business practices. This definition is essential to the value functional

method. If the firm is not separate from its owners, does not have a profit motive, or does not have replicable business practices, the model may either be indeterminate or have a trivial answer.

2. *Identification of state variables.* The state variables include the relevant factors that establish the environment for the company's operation. For many operating firms, the revenue of the company, economic conditions in the industry, and the existence of stable and experienced management are natural state variables.

Note that the absence of state variables would mean that the firm is like an airplane flying on autopilot. One of the most common mistakes in business valuation (and many other fields) is assuming that past trends continue forever. The value functional method requires that key state variables be made explicit.

3. *Identification of control variables.* The control variables are the elements that are under the control of the firm's managers or owners and affect the current reward given to them. The amount of money reinvested in the firm is a natural control variable, as are investment decisions (including decisions to undertake research and development [R&D], improve training, advertise, and postpone making expenditures as well as make them). The same observation about state variables made previously applies also to control variables; ignoring them is tantamount to assuming that the company runs on autopilot forever.

4. *A transition equation for the state variables.* The world changes over time; a proper model of business valuation explicitly takes this into account. The transition equation relates the current state and control variables (and any random elements) to the state variables in the next period.

Making the transition function explicit highlights the ability of the firm's management to adapt to changing circumstances. Note that the combination of control and state variables, and a transition equation, makes the model recursive.

5. *A reward function.* This function expresses the earnings or other benefits received by the firm's owners.

6. *A value functional equation for the entrepreneur.* This functional equation relates the value of the firm at a certain time, given a certain state of affairs, to functions of state and control variables, and possibly random processes.

This functional equation also incorporates the entrepreneur's objectives in a recursive manner that matches the actual decision making of the entrepreneur. In particular, it recognizes when information arrives to the entrepreneur, how the entrepreneur can act on that information, and how such actions affect the present and the future.

The Bellman Equation for a Private Firm

The functional equation (or Bellman equation) shown in Equation 15.5 establishes the value of a firm to an entrepreneur, given the state of affairs at a certain time.

Equation 15.5 Bellman Equation for a Private Firm

$$V(s, t) = \max_{x}\left\{ f(s_t, x_t) + \beta E\left[V(s_{t+1}, t_{t+1}) \right] \right\}$$

where:

$V(s, t)$ = value at time t given state s

$f(s_t, x_t)$ = a reward function given state and action

t = 0, ..., T is a time index

s_t = s_0, ..., s_T are state variables

x_t = x_0, ..., x_T are control variables

$0 < \beta < 1$ is a discount factor

In this equation, the reward function $f(s, x)$ relates the amount of benefit provided to the entrepreneur at any one time to the control choices made at that time and the state of affairs at that time. An example of this is the combination of the profit function of a firm and its dividend policy, given the state of the industry and the management decisions of the firm. The one-period gross discount that investors apply to future earnings appears as the parameter β. The expected future value of the firm is shown as $E[V(s_{t+1})]$.

Note the maximization operator applies to the *sum* of current rewards and expected discounted value. Note also that the maximization of the control variable is over feasible possible values.

The Transition Equation

Along with this functional equation, we also need a *transition equation* to describe how the state evolves over time (Equation 15.6). The transition equation expresses the effect of the actions that are taken on the future value of the state variables.

Equation 15.6 Transition Equation for a Private Firm

$s_{t+1} = g(s_t, x_t)$

where:

$g(s_t, x_t)$ is a Markov process

$x \in X$, the finite action space

$s \in S$, the finite state space

The transition equation has the Markov property, which intuitively means that all the information useful to predict the next time period is contained in the information available in the current time period.

Recursive Decisions

Observe the recursive nature of the decisions involved using this model: the investor-manager decides how to run the firm in the initial period, including how much in salary to pay and how much earnings to distribute to shareholders. Those decisions affect the value of the firm at the beginning of the next period. When that point in time is reached, the investor-manager again examines the state of the world, makes a new set of decisions, and

TABLE 15.1
Expanding a firm: Possibilities of action

Possible action	Likely long-term result	Likely immediate effect
Shrink operations	Reduces state value	Reward increases
Maintain operations	State remains the same	Reward remains the same
Expand operations	Increases state value	Reward reduces

goes forward earning a reward and considering the greater (or lesser) value of the firm at the end of that time period.

Note that this approach does not require the counterintuitive notion of time-separable utility. Instead, it assumes only recursive utility.[14]

An Example of States and Control; "Euler Tension"

A strength of the value functional model is that it can include multiple states and actions. For the purposes of this text, we have limited the number of states and actions to a handful. However, even a small number of states and actions often allow a powerful analysis of an important business decision. Table 15.1 describes a common dilemma facing many businesses: when is a good time to expand? The table gives three policy possibilities (actions) and their likely result and effect on the firm's immediate reward.

Note that the effect of a particular action is considered in two ways: its immediate effect and its long-term consequences. Often, people are faced with choices that increase short-term rewards but result in lower long-term benefits. The recursive nature of the value functional approach matches this real-world dynamic.

In a quantitative model of business value, these choices create what I call *Euler tension*, after the Euler equation that can be derived from some functional equation problems. A hallmark of the value functional approach is making this tension—between benefits today and expected benefits tomorrow—explicit.

DIFFERENCES BETWEEN RECURSIVE AND DISCOUNTED CASH FLOW METHODS

Key Differences: The Equation

It is useful to pause and ask an obvious question. Stripped of the recursive formulation, the use of control variables and an explicit transition function, isn't a Bellman equation really a fancy discounted cash flow schedule?

To examine this question, consider Equation 15.7, in which the discounted cash flow analysis for a firm is summarized in a parsimonious fashion, using the same variables and format as for the functional equation shown in Equation 15.5.

Equation 15.7 DCF Valuation as a Parsimonious Equation

$$V_{\text{DCF}} = E_{t=0}\left[\sum_{t=0}^{\infty} \beta^t \pi(s_t)\right] \text{ (infinite horizon) or}$$

$$V_{\mathrm{DCF}} = E_{t=0}\left[\sum_{t=0}^{T}\beta^{t}\pi(s_{t}) + \beta^{T}R_{T}\right] \text{ (discrete period)}$$

where:

t $= 0, ..., T, ..., \infty$ is a time index

$E_{t}[\,\bullet\,] =$ expectation given information at time t

V_{DCF} $=$ DCF method value estimate at time t given state s

$\pi(s_{t}) =$ the profit function given state s at time t

s_{t+1} $= g(s_{t})$ is the transition function

R_{T} $=$ the scrap or terminal value at time T

s_{t} $= s_{0}, ..., s_{T}$ are state variables

Even if we assume the profit function and state variable are identical for both methods, significant differences in their equations remain:

- The DCF equation contains an expectation taken at time $t = 0$ because the sum of expected future discounted cash flows is calculated at that time.

- In contrast, the value functional equation implies a recursive set of decisions and a persistent next-period expected-value variable. This is a set of expectations taken at successively later periods. At each period, the manager can decide to scrap, expand, buy, or sell.

- The discounting occurs on the *value* in the next period for the value functional approach, rather than on an entire stream of expected cash flows as in the DCF approach.

Key Differences: The Firm

We also consider how the concept of the firm is different between the two models.

1. *The firm is a human organization, not a portfolio of assets.* The firm must be separated from a portfolio or other set of assets that can be traded. Firms are not simply an aggregation of workers; neither are they simply financial assets.

2. *Management, and policy, are integral to the value of a firm.* One key advantage of the value functional method is its assertion of the importance of management policy. Traditional valuation methods often assume a passive role for managers. This passive assumption matches the implicit assumptions in the standard neoclassical economics and the neoclassical finance models.

In contrast, the value functional method puts management policy front and center. The manager is assumed to *optimize* the sum of current earnings and discounted future value. This may, or may not, be the "profit maximizing" decision. The mathematics of solving such models, while arcane and difficult, at least have the cardinal virtue of mimicking the actual incentives of business owners.

3. *The small firm is different from a scaled-down large firm.* This definition of the firm used in this approach recognizes that most firms—closely held small companies in which the manager is also a major equity owner—operate within an envelope that cannot be defined by stock market returns and risks. Furthermore, most such firms do not have access to the type of borrowings, or broad class of equity holders, that are typically assumed to exist in modern portfolio theory and neoclassical finance. The value functional method can describe the decision found by the entrepreneur as well as the publicly traded corporation.

4. *Euler tension affects most critical decisions.* A fundamental feature of the consumer's savings problem is the tension between consuming now and saving so that greater consumption can occur later.

A similar essential tension exists in business. The entrepreneur's policy decisions, at each recursion, are his or her resolution of that tension. The need to resolve it is explicit in the maximization of value over a feasible set of actions. Such a tension is commonly either ignored entirely or subsumed in a trend analysis in the standard discounted cash flow model.

Key Differences: The Entrepreneur and the Investor

5. *Human capital and entrepreneurial spirits are part of the value functional model.* Firms are started, grow, struggle, and sometimes survive. Joseph Schumpeter called this *creative destruction.* Two key elements in this creative destruction are the human capital of the entrepreneur and the entrepreneurs' "animal spirits" in John Maynard Keynes's colorful turn of phrase. Such spirits are missing in complete-market models (there being no security labeled *animal spirits*). They are also missing in the Modigliani-Miller model that underlies much of corporate finance (which is limited to just assets and risk classes).

The value functional equation recognizes both animal spirits and the human capital of the entrepreneur in a manner that matches our observations about actual behavior. In particular, the entrepreneur can rationally choose to reinvest in human capital in a manner that would appear irrational in a profit-maximizing, net-present-value world. Furthermore, the entrepreneur can decide to forgo income in order to persevere even when the odds against a firm's success appear low to the rational observer.

6. *Investors are released from rigidly specified utility functions.* The value functional approach does not restrict the considerations of the investor to quadratic preferences, von Neumann–Morgenstern utility, a certain "risk class," or the mean-variance framework. Similarly, the risks of default, bankruptcy, loss of key employees, departure of investors, and other major events are not subsumed into an assumption of a large number of independent, small risk factors.[15]

Neither the risks entrepreneurs face nor their apparent willingness to face them fits neatly into the traditional models. The value functional model, on the other hand, accepts them readily.

7. *The method allows a reasonable time frame for investors.* Both the neoclassical and the modern portfolio theory models are essentially one-period models. The complete-market model requires the existence of securities that, in practical terms, could rarely be more than

a few periods away from maturity. The traditional income approach assumes that the net present value of future earnings—regardless of when they actually arrive—is what really matters.

On the other hand, in the real world, finite multiyear time horizons are the rule. Most firms are privately held, and investors in such firms usually cannot quickly enter and exit. Furthermore, no securities exist that allow them to rebalance their portfolios or hedge private-firm risks in the same manner as an investor with a large stock portfolio often can. Thus, their time horizon is normally beyond one or two years.

For struggling entrepreneurial firms, using a ten-year time horizon for financing and operating the firm can be a struggle. *Most* start-up firms do not survive for five years, as evidenced by data from multiple countries summarized in Chapter 5, "The Organization and Scale of Private Business." Indeed, an investor-manager of such a firm could lose money for several years, in the hopes that the fledgling business (for which no lenders or other equity investors have appeared) will eventually succeed. "Eventually" for many of these entrepreneurs appears to be something shorter than ten years.

Key Differences: Real Options

8. *Recursive decision making natively incorporates real options.* The net present value rule routinely fails to provide proper guidance when a firm faces financial or real options. In particular, the NPV rule (and the related notion that the value of the firm is the expected net present value of the earnings on its assets) often suggests value-reducing investment decisions when a firm has options to learn, to wait, or to abandon. To adjust for this deficiency, various forms of expanded and adjusted net present value rules have been proposed.

Recursive decision making allows for real options to be considered naively. In particular, the option to wait is a natural consideration in a recursive model and does not exist in a net present value model. Thus, recursive models can often take advantage of existing options without the need to expand or adjust the results of another calculation.

Key Differences: The Market

9. *Private firms are within the proper market for the value functional approach.* The Roll critique of CAPM and factor models has been around for decades, establishing the fact that these models consider only a fraction of the investment portfolio available in the world. However, it is quite common to see CAPM and factor models used uncritically to value private firms.

There are difficulties with the notion of discount rates in any model. However, the value functional model does not repeat the error of assuming that stock market data on publicly traded companies establish the discount rates for investors in private firms, or that liquid stock market investments are similar to interests in closely held firms.

10. *The value functional approach does not rely on untenable market assumptions.* Such untenable assumptions include complete markets, low transaction costs and bid-ask spreads, and unlimited ability to borrow and short-sell stock.

EXISTENCE OF SOLUTIONS TO VALUE FUNCTIONAL EQUATIONS

A Technique That Does Not Solve All Problems

The technique known as dynamic programming can theoretically solve value functional problems that are well defined and fall within certain limitations. These qualifications—which fall easily off the tongue when reading so many mathematical texts—must be taken seriously. Indeed, we should be clear: for some value functional problems, there are *no well-defined solutions*. For others, solutions probably exist, but they have not been found within a practical limit of time and effort. We consider a few examples next.

Examples: Problems Without Solutions

The observation that some problems do not have solutions is not unique to this method. A rigorous examination of other methods reveals that in some cases, solutions do not exist, or they imply implausible results.

Here are three examples:

1. Consider a business valuation problem with the discounted cash flow form shown in Equation 15.7. Assume that there is a known, finite current-period profit that must be either distributed to shareholders (a reward this period) or reinvested in the firm (and become part of the next period's value). Assume further the counterintuitive notion of perpetual, known rates of return and discount rates. If the gross discount rate was smaller than the inverse of the gross rate of return, then it appears to make sense to perpetually postpone any reward and hence never produce any return for the shareholders.

2. Using the same model, consider the same firm with the converse problem: a high current-period reward and a discount rate that is close to one. In such cases, it may make (mathematical) sense to choose a high reward right now and then close down the company.

3. Again using the same model, consider a firm with a reward or transition function with a kink or hole in it (meaning that it has no defined value for some plausible state and action pair). For such firms, it may be impossible to calculate any result.

4. Now consider the traditional income valuation approach. Within that approach, the commonly used perpetual-capitalization formula known as the *Gordon growth formula* $[\pi(1 + g)/(d - g)]$ provides a notorious platform for producing implausible results. Since the denominator in the ratio is the difference between trend growth in profit and the discount rate, setting the growth rate equal to the discount rate produces an undefined result (because it would require division by zero). Assuming that a recent period of fast growth will be continued into the future may make $(d - g)$ very small, and therefore the calculated value very large. Yet it is quite possible that the discount rate for some firms is approximately equal to the firm's likely growth rate, at least for some time periods.

5. The complete-market approach to pricing assets (from the neoclassical finance school) relies on the existence of a replicating portfolio of assets. Assembling such a replicating portfolio means that under the no-arbitrage assumption, the only price allowed in the market for an asset is the one equivalent to the replicating portfolio. However, in *incomplete* markets, there is no replicating portfolio. Hence, there are many possible prices for such assets.

Existence of a Solution to a Value Functional

The question of when solutions exist to the functional equation problem defined previously has been theoretically addressed only recently. Richard Bellman's 1957 treatise introducing the dynamic programming method was careful to describe certain conditions for a solution and was sober in its assessment of practical problems such as the *curse of dimensionality*. It fell to others to show how, and under what conditions, a unique solution could be found.

Blackwell's Theorem on Contraction Mapping

The great African-American mathematician David Blackwell provided the seminal breakthrough in 1965. He proposed that two conditions established the existence of a *contraction mapping* in a functional equation problem: *discounting*, and *monotonicity*.[16] Blackwell's *sufficiency theorem* and its components are important enough to present, at least in conceptual terms, to anyone interested in the value functional method:

- Discounting causes the implied value of a quantity to be received in the future to be smaller than the same quantity received today. A common example of this is the use of a discount factor between zero and one to adjust for the net present value of a future expected payment to an investor. Note that discounting does not require time-separable utility, constant discount rates, or any specific assumption about risk aversion.

- Monotonicity is a property of a function in which a larger input consistently produces a larger output. This is a common but not universal condition of many economic activities; for example, having more people buy a product tends to produce higher sales revenue.

  Note that this assumption does not mean constant returns to scale, and that diminishing (but still positive) marginal returns are common in economic applications. Furthermore, the monotonicity assumption (for the purpose of establishing a contraction) applies to the functional equation as an operator, and not necessarily to the reward and transition functions.

- A *contraction* is a device that makes things smaller. A *mapping* is a correspondence between one set of concepts (in this case, functions) and another. Thus, a *contraction mapping* is a correspondence between one set of functions and another set, where the distance between the two gets progressively smaller each time an operation occurs.

- An *operator* is the device that performs the mapping or correspondence. A functional equation of the type in Equation 15.5 is one type of operator.

Blackwell proved that if a functional equation or any other operator met the discounting and monotonicity conditions, it was a contraction mapping. This has an important consequence: repeatedly using an operator that produces a contraction mapping eventually forces a convergence toward a specific result. That result can be made arbitrarily close to the theoretical exact solution.

This, along with some other assumptions described before and after this discussion, allows us to assert the existence of solutions to many business value functional equations. It also motivates the discussion of what we call human *transversality conditions* shortly.

Development for Use in Economics and Finance

It took approximately two and a half decades for value functional equations to become introduced to a broad audience in economics.

One difficulty was the abstract conditions under which the functional equations were defined and the tenuous connection to real-world problems. This was finally addressed through a rigorous effort involving measure theory, real analysis, and more familiar mathematical economics by Nancy Stokey and Robert Lucas in their 1989 book *Recursive Methods in Economic Dynamics*. We rely heavily on Blackwell's theory of sufficient conditions for a contraction mapping, and on the Stokey and Lucas theory of existence of a solution to functional equations in economic settings, in the following section.

Human Transversality Conditions and Functional Equations for a Business

We are focused on a specific class of functional equations: those that describe a *firm*, as we have defined it.

Returning to that definition, we note that it involves a separate human organization with a separate legal identity, a profit motive for the investors, and a set of replicable business practices. We also asserted a set of institutional requirements for the operation of firms, such as property rights and enforcement of contracts. Given these observations about human organizations and human-created institutions, we propose a set of transversality conditions. These are contained in Exhibit 15.1.

Transversality in Mathematical Economics

Transversality conditions have a particular rationale in mathematical economics; they are used to ensure that dynamic optimization problems have solutions. One purpose is to prevent a model from "blowing up" by, for example, trying to add to infinity, divide by zero, or continue in an endless loop. Another is to tie down the optimization region to one that is known, at least at the outer reaches. An example of this purpose is to limit the amount of capital purchases a firm could plausibly make to what its budget and liquidity constraints could possibly allow.

These human transversality conditions reflect commonsense observations about business and economic history. Nothing in these is based solely on mathematics, or on technology, or on the physical world. They are all based on human nature.

EXHIBIT 15.1
Human Transversality Conditions

For any firm and all investors in firms, we assume the following:

- *Finite, nonnegative time period:* The operating time periods for all persons are limited in duration: *Time is indexed by $t = 0, \ldots, T$. T is a finite, nonnegative real number.*

- *Discounting:* Investors consider future net benefits to be worth less than current net benefits: $0 < \beta < 1$.

- *Expectations conditioned on available information:* For any investor and firm, expectations about future conditions are conditioned on information on the economy, the firm, the industry, and the institutions available at or before the time the expectation is formed: $E(X) = E(X \mid \Omega_t) = E_t(X)$, *where X is any variable, $t = $ a specific time period, and Ω_t is the information available at time t.*

- *Costly information and transactions:* For any firm and all potential investors, acquiring information relevant to management and investment decisions imposes a positive cost. For any investment in a firm, a positive transaction cost is borne by the firm or the investor:

- *Available information always incomplete:* The information set available to any investor and all firms is a subset of the information that could assist in the prediction of future events that affect the relevant state variables: For all expectations of state variables $E_t(X) = E(X \mid \Omega_t)$, Ω_t is a subset of the complete information set.

- *Bounded, finite earnings:* The reward that can be distributed to owners of a firm is always a finite number under an upper bound. $f(s, x) < U$ *for some upper bound U.*

- *Bounded, finite state variables:* The underlying state variable for any transition function is always a finite real number within upper and lower bounds: $\{s_t, s_{t+1} = g(s, x)\} << U$ *for some upper bound U and $\{s_t, s_{t+1}\} >> L$ for some lower bound L, period $[t, t + 1]$.*

- *Long-run growth is less than long-run discounting:* For any firm and investor, the expected long-run growth rate of distributable earnings for the firm is less than the corresponding long-run discount rate of the investors. *Either $(d - g) > 0$ or $\lim_{t \to \infty} (d - g) > 0$, where $\{d, g\}$ are either constants or geometric averages of varying discount and growth rates.*

- *Existence of limited liability and counterparty risk:* For any firm and group of investors, there are limits to the liability of the investors for the actions of the firm. For all contracts between the firm and other persons (including other firms and governments), there are nonzero risks that affect the earnings and performance from those contracts: $f(s, x) > L$ *for some lower bound L.*

- *Incomplete markets:* For at least one relevant state variable, the market is incomplete.

Consequences of Ignoring Human Transversality

I know of no similar existence propositions (or related human transversality conditions) in the seminal works of the professional valuation literature or modern portfolio theory.[17] To be sure, each has its peculiar institutional assumptions (such as the existence of the wealth portfolio for the CAPM, the full-rank tableau of securities in neoclassical finance, and the availability of perpetual growth and discount rates in the traditional income method). However, the question of the existence of solutions often is assumed to be obvious, appears as an afterthought or technical question, or is left to a critique.[18]

The consequences of these omissions can be observed by the frequency with which the embedded assumptions are violated in traditional valuation models. Additional examples can be seen in the examples listed earlier, the quandaries posed at the beginning of this book, and in the discussion of behavioral finance.[19]

Conditions for the Existence of a Solution to a Business Value Functional

We briefly discussed earlier the general requirements for a solution to functional equation problems. We then introduced transversality conditions that placed restrictions on such concepts as the maximum earnings a company could distribute to its shareholders and the plausible range of values for a discount rate, as well as establishing the existence of both counterparty risk and limited liability for shareholders. These conditions were tied directly to the definition of the firm introduced in this book.

Given these, we can now identify *specific* conditions for the existence of a solution to a class of value functional equations: those that estimate the value of a business. These are contained in Exhibit 15.2.

We can immediately observe that most of the requirements for existence of a solution are fulfilled by the statements in Exhibit 15.1. However, in order for there to be a value functional

---

EXHIBIT 15.2

Proposition I: Existence of a Solution to Functional Equation

Consider a firm and its investors that fulfill the human transversality conditions in Exhibit 15.1, and a set of functional and transition equations and related parameters of the form in Equations 15.5 through 15.6.

If the following conditions are also true within a plausible range of values for $\{s, x\}$:

a. Positive and increasing returns: $f(s, x) > 0$ and $f'(s) > 0$ for some plausible $\{s, x\}$.

b. Well-defined, approximately continuous and differentiable, real-valued f and g.

then the functional equation has a solution, which includes a real-valued value function $V(s)$ and an implicitly defined policy function $x = h(s)$.

problem of any interest, we also have to establish that there is something of value to an investor. Furthermore, to use the method requires that there be a value functional equation with some content. Hence, the conditions require that there be a state transition equation and a reward equation, and that the value of the enterprise be partially determined by the state of affairs.

It is important to note that these conditions *do not* exclude the following:

- Start-up companies
- Companies with substantial real options
- Companies that are currently bankrupt
- Companies that are privately held
- Companies without good accounting records
- Companies in new industries or using untested technologies

Such companies are often difficult to value using traditional methods. Furthermore, these conditions do not preclude typical investors or impose upon them restrictive assumptions about their risk aversion or utility function.

VALUE FUNCTIONAL PROBLEMS: FINDING A SOLUTION

Bases for Concluding the Existence of a Solution

Let us assume that a value functional problem is well defined and fulfills the conditions that are necessary for there to be a solution. What methods are available to actually *find* that solution? Can the solution be found?

Fortunately, the general theoretical results mentioned earlier and the specific conditions in Exhibit 15.2 provide the basis for concluding that a solution can be found, at least given sufficient time and effort. Furthermore, we can identify at least three methods for finding it. This assertion is discussed next.

Proposition II: Ability to Find Solution to Functional Equation

Consider a firm and its investors that fulfill the human transversality conditions in Exhibit 15.1, and a set of functional and transition equations that meet the conditions stated in Exhibit 15.2. Given sufficient time and effort, a solution can be found to a value functional equation for the firm through the use of one or more of the following methods:

- Value function iteration
- Policy improvement
- Backward recursion

Two Cheers for Eventually Finding a Solution

Proposition II tells us that, at least for problems that meet the conditions stated earlier, there are at least three possible ways to find a solution. It also asserts that if we expend enough time and effort, we will eventually find that solution.

This may be underwhelming to those used to calculating results immediately. Most readers of this book have watched calculators or spreadsheet programs calculate a net present value of a whole row of numbers in the blink of an eye. Publicly available web sites calculate the Black-Scholes option formula nearly immediately. Handheld devices perform thousands of calculations each second in order to produce the impressive graphics featured in any number of games.

Unfortunately, we do not have the ability—at least today—to match that speed of calculation, even for nicely organized sample value functional problems.

Remember, the net present value algorithm was invented approximately five hundred years ago. Dynamic programming was invented about fifty years ago. Business value functional equations were invented about five years ago. It may take some time to make them work quickly!

PROBLEMS AND LIMITATIONS OF THE VALUE FUNCTIONAL MODEL

Limitations of New Theories

This chapter presented the theory of the value functional method. The next chapter presents a series of applications of the method. It is worth pausing now to recognize some limitations and weaknesses of the method.

All theories have inherent limitations and weaknesses. Also, any novel theory suffers from the fact that it has not had years of development to fill in gaps and address practical difficulties. We therefore roughly split the problems and limitations into two categories: those that are inherent in the method, at least for now; and those exist today but are likely to be addressed with more development over time.

Inherent Weaknesses of the Value Functional Method

1. *The value functional equation may not have a solution.* Depending on the specification of the value functional equation (including the transition equation, the discount rate, and any random elements), there may or may not be a solution.

We addressed earlier the theoretical conditions under which a solution is known to exist and outlined certain conditions that ensure that a solution exists for valuation functionals applied to privately held firms.

2. *The discount rate is determined outside the model and is difficult to estimate.* This weakness is inherent in nearly every valuation model.[20] For example, a common implementation of the income method is to create a discounted cash flow schedule and use the CAPM (and data on publicly traded firms) to estimate a discount rate—even if the CAPM and stock market data are inappropriate for the company being valued.

3. *It will be difficult to calculate the expected value of future relevant events.* This limitation applies equivalently to every method that requires estimating future economic conditions. In other words, it applies to any method where the price is not immediately apparent in the market.

The value functional method has two advantages: First, it requires only a one-period-ahead expectation. That is much less complicated than the idea of expecting future events over a multiyear period, which is common in standard DCF models. Second, it does not restrict the analyst to only nice, symmetric distributions of random events.

4. *The value functional model requires that a small number of relevant factors be explicitly identified as control and state variables.* This, like the lack of a known discount rate and impossibility of knowing future events, is an inherent problem with nearly every valuation method. There are always variables that are more important than others. Distilling the relevant factors down to one or two is always difficult in real-world situations.

However, explicit identification of control and state variables is usually a more difficult task than creating a projected discounted cash flow schedule from past accounting income statements.

Practical Problems with the Value Functional Method

5. *The curse of dimensionality is a constant issue.* The major computational issue in dynamic programming arises from the *curse of dimensionality,* which is the potentially vast number of possible actions and variable changes that must be considered before an optimal decision can be made. As Richard Bellman noted in his original presentation of dynamic programming, the size of the problem grows exponentially with the number of state and control variables.

Even with extremely fast computers, this curse remains with us, albeit in a more manageable form than twenty years ago. Its existence is one of the reasons why we present multiple algorithms for solving value functional problems.

6. *Few algorithms are available for solving value functional problems.* The NPV algorithm can be implemented on many handheld calculators if the number of cash flows is small, and on nearly any personal computer or similar device equipped with rudimentary financial software. Some people (I'm privileged to work with a few) can actually do the calculations in their head!

On the other hand, there are only a handful of known algorithms for calculating the solution of a value functional problem, even if the problem is known in advance to have a solution.

7. *No off-the-shelf software or calculation tools currently exist for the method.* As of this writing, none of the known algorithms for solving a value functional equation have been compiled into an off-the-shelf software application. Of course, if the method proves useful, demand for its use should provide an incentive for one or more companies to create one. I therefore expect this practical difficulty to be overcome.

8. *There is little experience with the method, no common rules of thumb, and few practical examples.* This is the most obvious difficulty, and one that afflicts every novel method, in every discipline. This book is intended to fill some of this gap.

VI APPLICATIONS

16 THE VALUE FUNCTIONAL: APPLICATIONS

Purpose and Requirements

The purpose of this chapter is to introduce and demonstrate practical methods of using the value functional approach to estimate the value of an operating business.

The previous chapter introduced the idea of a functional equation and the theory of the value functional method of business valuation. It also described state and control variables, and stated propositions for the existence of a solution to a functional equation for the value of a business. Familiarity with those concepts is necessary to understand the content in this chapter.

Elements of This Chapter

This chapter includes the following:

- A discussion of state and control variables for representative operating businesses.
- A presentation of four different ways to formulate and solve a value functional problem:
  a. The dynamic programming (also called *stochastic control*) method for continuous-valued state and control variables.
  b. The Markov decision problem (MDP) method for discrete-valued state and control variables.
  c. The Hamilton-Jacobi-Bellman (H-J-B) method, for certain cases in which differential changes in value from specific causes can be identified and estimated separately.
  d. "By hand."
- Computational designs for the dynamic programming solution algorithms, along with observations on the practical difficulties of using them.

- Example valuations using these approaches.

- A discussion of the differences between the value functional and standard discounted cash flow methods of estimating the value of a company.

Some of these techniques were only recently developed, and much of the material in this chapter appears here in published form for the first time.

STATE AND CONTROL VARIABLES IN THE VALUE FUNCTION APPROACH

Key Variables for Reward and Control of a Business

The general value functional model does not specify the state and control variables or the reward function. For a general business valuation problem, it seems obvious that earnings available to shareholders (including any capital gains or requirement for additional capital) are a reward, and likely that reinvestment in the company is a control variable.

This formulation is a direct analogy to the cake-eating problem for the consumer: distributing earnings ("eating the cake") is one policy option, while reinvesting in the firm (which could be seen as buying another cake) is another. Trading off benefits from the current period to the next requires only the modest assumption of recursive utility.[1]

In many situations, a limited set of control and reward variables works quite well. The selection of these variables is the topic of the rest of this section.

State and Control Variables Derived from the Firm

The value functional approach relies on a definition of the firm as a controlled entity, with certain attributes and one specific motivation. It is worth reviewing the following elements of the definition of a firm used in this book:[2]

- *Organization* and *separate legal person* imply a distinct management structure and an entity that captures its own revenue and absorbs its own costs.

- *Motivation to earn profit for investors* implies a reward function and a method for distributing the reward to the owners of the firm.

- *Replicable business processes* implies a business structure and production function. This is the basis for assuming that a reward can be generated and some type of transition function defined. *Replicable business processes* also implies the existence of state variables, and (along with the institutional factors) further implies that certain economic conditions, management policies, and business structures are stable or evolve slowly from one period to the next.

Parsimonious List of State and Control Variables

Given the preceding discussion, we identify a parsimonious list of state and control variables relevant to most operating companies in Equation 16.1. These factors cover the key economic and market conditions, business assets, technology and management considerations, and available management and investor actions for most operating firms. For any specific company, a handful of these will be much more important than the others.

Equation 16.1 State and Control Variables in the Entrepreneur's Value Function

$$
\text{state} = s = \begin{bmatrix}
h_1 \text{ (human capital committed by owner)} \\
y_1 \text{ (general economic conditions)} \\
y_2 \text{ (industry or local market conditions)} \\
c_1 \text{ (competitive conditions)} \\
k_1 \text{ (cash or current assets)} \\
k_2 \text{ (net worth)} \\
k_3 \text{ (investments in plant and equipment)} \\
l_1 \text{ (current liabilities)} \\
n_1 \text{ (employees)} \\
t_1 \text{ (technology, patents, intellectual property)}
\end{bmatrix}
$$

$$
\text{action} = x = \begin{bmatrix}
x_h \text{ (commit owner's time)} \\
x_l \text{ (borrow or repurchase debt)} \\
x_a \text{ (advertise)} \\
x_p \text{ (change pricing)} \\
x_k \text{ (invest or expend on R\&D)} \\
x_n \text{ (hire employees)} \\
x_t \text{ (acquire technology or intellectual property)}
\end{bmatrix}
$$

Discussion: Information in the State Variables

If we have accurately identified the important control and state variables for a firm, then we should expect that the firm's managers and investors will want to receive information on these variables on a regular basis. Thus, a first test of the prototype list of state and control variables (and an implicit test of the value functional methodology) is whether firms (or their investors, lenders, or customers) actually use these data.

A quick scan of the elements of the prototype state vector produces the following observations:

1. The first element in the prototype state variable vector is the human capital of the entrepreneur. This is a critical variable and frequently watched by other employees, customers, investors, and (of course) the entrepreneur herself.

2. The second set of elements includes general economic conditions and the competitive conditions in the relevant marketplace.

3. The third set contains balance sheet information, including some measure of liquidity, debt, net worth, and invested capital. Such information is a subset of that reported in periodic accounting statements and is clearly on the minds of managers, investors, and lenders.

4. The fourth set includes employees and technology or other intellectual property.

Of course, specific companies have specific state and control variables that reflect their management structure, industry, market, and production technology. However, at a broad level of generality, the prototype state vector passes the information test.

Discussion: Relevance of Control Variables

A related test can be conducted on the vector of control (or *action*) variables. These variables reflect the exercise of management powers that affect the operation of the firm and ultimately the reward that passes to the investors. (We do not, at this point, state exactly *how* each variable affects the reward given to investors.)

It is interesting to note that some elements of the state vector do not have corresponding elements in the control vector. These are, of course, elements that are important to the business, but outside the control of the company. General economic conditions, market condition in the local area, and other such factors are generally uncontrollable and therefore are absent from the control vectors of almost all firms.

Discussion: Measuring State and Action Variables

At this point, we have not detailed how any of these variables could be constructed from available information. This is not a trivial matter—either in this valuation methodology or in the others that have been discussed.[3] All models involve simplifications, and the most useful models achieve simplification while maintaining power.

For some of these variables, a simple number (such as *net borrowing* or *total advertising expenditures*) may suffice. For others (such as *general economic conditions*) any number of qualitative or quantitative indicators could be used. Certain action variables may be stated as binary variables, particularly those that involve a onetime action such as selling a stake in a firm, exercising an option, or irrevocably investing or scrapping an investment.

SOLUTION METHODS FOR VALUE FUNCTIONAL EQUATIONS

Different Analytical Methods for the Value Functional Approach

In the following sections of this chapter, we present analytical tools that are useful or necessary for solving value functional equations, including the following:

1. *Dynamic programming (DP) or stochastic control (SC) algorithms.* The continuous-state dynamic programming problem has attracted much mathematical attention over the

past few decades, mostly in fields other than economics. As a result, a number of specific algorithms can be used, albeit with difficulties that were often foreseen by the pioneers of the technique a half century ago.

We discuss these algorithms further in Chapter 15, "The Value Functional: Theory," under the section titled "Existence of Solutions to Value Functional Equations." An example of one of the solution algorithms is also presented later in this chapter.

2. *The Markov decision problem (MDP) formulation.* Some value functional programs can be cast as decision problems with a limited number of discrete states and actions, and where the transition equation has the Markov property. In such cases, we can use some of the dynamic programming algorithms to solve for the optimal policy.

One could classify this as a special case of dynamic programming, but I classify it separately because it places significant demands on the structure of the problem that do not exist for general dynamic programming problems.

We use this technique later in this chapter, under the section titled "An Example Using a Markov Decision Problem (MDP) Method."

3. *The Hamilton-Jacobi-Bellman (H-J-B) equation.* In many situations, though not all, a business or investment can be modeled as a return-generating function of a state variable that follows a stochastic process known as a *diffusion*. In such cases, it may be possible to adapt a technique from physics and stochastic calculus to focus on separable concepts of return and risk that sum to an instantaneous total return for the firm.

We discuss this later in this chapter, under the section titled "An Example Using the Hamilton-Jacobi-Bellman Equation."

4. *Closed-form solutions for certain value functional problems.* For some problems with well-defined (and convenient) assumptions, closed-form solutions may be available. Not coincidentally, these are often found in academic treatises on dynamic programming or in theoretical problems in economics.

5. *Solutions drawn "by hand."* Because of the difficulty in quantitatively modeling the various components of a dynamic programming problem in practical situations, in some cases it is best to set up the problem "by hand," meaning identifying a relatively few choices available to the manager and estimating directly the value or returns available for certain states or time periods.

SOLUTION METHODS: DYNAMIC PROGRAMMING

Possible Algorithms for Solving Dynamic Programming Problems

A number of methods can be used to solve dynamic programming problems of the type described in Chapter 15, "The Value Functional: Theory," under the section titled "Existence of Solutions to Value Functional Equations." These algorithms include the following:

1. *Backward recursion.* If the problem is simple enough, it may be possible to recursively solve the problem backward from a known terminal value. This is known as *backward recursion.*

2. *Policy iteration (PI).* Iterating on the values created at each step with variations in the *policy* created by the application of the control variables is known as *policy iteration* or *Howard's policy improvement algorithm.*

3. *Value function iteration (VFI).* Specifying an initial set of values for all variables, calculating the value function at these points, and then iteratively searching for higher values until such searches yield no further improvement is known as *value function iteration.*

We summarize these algorithms in Exhibit 16.1. We present the underlying functional and transition equation, along with the key iterative calculations of these methods, in Equation 16.2.

EXHIBIT 16.1

Selected Algorithms for Solving Dynamic Programming Problems

Backward Recursion

a. Start with known best terminal-period result (value and reward).

b. Choose optimal decision at time $T-1$ given known optimal result at time T.

c. Repeat for periods $T-2$ to 1, until solved completely.

Policy Iteration

a. Make initial guess of best feasible policy function $x = h(s)$ (action, given state) at time $t = 0$.

b. Compute the tentative value of operating forever using that policy. The resulting $j = 0$ iteration of this calculation is V_0.

c. Try a large number of alternate policies, intended to represent all alternative policies available, and generate a new policy that solves the two-period problem. Designate the new policy h_{j+1} and the new estimate of value V_{j+1}.

d. Repeat (iterating on j) until convergence.

Value Function Iteration

a. Make initial guess of value at $t = 0$; call it V_0.

b. Choose the best feasible action in each state, and tentatively calculate the sum of current reward and discounted next-period value, with the next-period value being the last iteration of V. Designate the tentative value at each iteration V_j.

c. Repeat (iterating on j) until convergence.

Equation 16.2 Policy Iteration and Value Function Iterations

Functional and Transition Equations

$$V(s) = \max_{x \in \Gamma}\{f(s,\, x) + \beta V(s_{+1})\}$$

$s_{+1} \quad = g(s,\, x) \; (s = \text{state},\, x = \text{action})$

$\beta \quad\ \ = \text{discount factor}; \eta = \text{convergence tolerance}$

Policy Iteration Algorithm

$x \qquad = h_0(s)$

$$V_j \quad\ = \sum_{t=0}^{T} \beta^t f[s_t,\, h_j(s)]$$

For $j = 0$ to N,

$\quad s_{j+1} = g[s,\, h_j(s)]$

$\quad V_{j+1} = \max_{x \in \Gamma}\{f(s,\, x) + \beta V_j(s_{+1})\}$

$\quad x \quad = h_{j+1}(s)$ where $x \leftarrow \text{argmax } V_{j+1}$

End when $\left\| V_{j+1},\, V_j \right\| < \eta.$

Value Function Iteration Algorithm

$V_0 \qquad = 0$

For $j = 0$ to N,

$\quad V_{j+1} = \max_{x \in \Gamma}\{f(s,\, x) + \beta V_j(s_{+1})\}$

$\quad s_{+1} \quad = g(s,\, x)$

End when $\left\| V_{j+1},\, V_j \right\| < \eta.$

Notes on Solution Algorithms

The algorithms listed in Exhibit 16.2 should be understood with the following in mind:

1. Each of these algorithms is *iterative*, meaning a tentative result is calculated and compared with the previous result, and then a new result is calculated, multiple times. Practical considerations (including the availability of computing resources and the precision of the algorithms) place a limit on the number of these iterations.

2. In general, for continuous-valued state vectors and value functions, it is not practical to physically calculate the solution at every point, even with modern computing technology. Hence, methods of *discretizing the state space* have been developed that allow for an approximate solution to be calculated in many cases. The references listed shortly discuss this important step.

3. To evaluate each tentative solution requires the calculation of the *distance* between two functions. (Recall that this is a functional equation, not a function.) To calculate

this distance requires a *norm*; here we use the *supremum norm*, which is defined more clearly in Appendix A, "Key Formula and Notation Summary." In the equations, the norm (measurement of distance between two vectors) is shown as a pair of double vertical brackets.

4. Each of these algorithms has been adapted for computer programs in various ways. The boundaries between the mathematical algorithms and the computer programs implementing the algorithm are sometimes blurry. See the references listed in the following section and in the *Solutions Manual* described in Appendix B, "Guide to the Solutions Manual," for more information.

References on Dynamic Programming Techniques

The underlying mathematics of these algorithms and numerical approaches to implementing them are discussed in a handful of references. Stokey and Lucas (1989) outline the theoretical basis for concluding that a solution exists to certain value functional problems. Numerical techniques to solve them are described in Judd (1998, chap. 12), Miranda and Fackler (2002), and Ljungqvist and Sargent (2004, chap. 3). The application to business valuation was introduced by Anderson (2004a, chap. 10). Additional resources are discussed in the *Solutions Manual* described in Appendix B, "Guide to the Solutions Manual."

AN EXAMPLE USING A MARKOV DECISION PROBLEM (MDP) METHOD

Introduction: Profitable Retail Business

In this section, we use the value functional approach to assist S. H. Importers in making an investment decision. S. H. Importers is an actual company, described further in Appendix C, "Description of Subject Companies." We are basing our analysis on a business-cycle-adjusted income statement. This allows us to use this methodology with a company with growth options (and shrinkage options).

Here, we assume the following:

1. Profits in the closely held retail firm, which has been in existence for more than twenty-five years in the same area of California, have been consistent the past few years.

2. The company's founder is contemplating investing additional funds to expand its business. In particular, the firm could lease additional space for retail sales and hire additional workers to sell at those locations. This would leverage the firm's creative talent and supply base, although it would possibly strain its management, logistics, and finances.

3. Alternatively, the company could remain at its current scale or decide to allow its business revenue to decline while enjoying higher profits.

This is a classic small and medium-sized business problem. Many successful firms face this type of challenge repeatedly.

MDP Method: Event Tree and Action Space

Within the value functional approach, we selected a Markov decision problem method. The MDP method of implementing the value functional distills the random events, policy choices, and all other institutional, economic, and industry considerations into a small set of states and actions. Thus, one must identify a set of discrete states of nature that could occur because of both random events and policy choices. In addition, one must select a discrete set of actions that the firm could take.

In this case, we structured the problem as follows:

- There are three possible actions for the firm: shrink, maintain, or expand operations. Each has a related immediate cost.
- There are four possible states of nature in which the firm could operate, numbered 1 through 4, with the current (baseline) state being number 2. For both descriptive and analytical purposes, each of the states is labeled with the scale of operation and revenue that would be associated with it. For example, state 3 has expanded revenue from the same operation.

To illustrate the potential movements among states, we use the event tree shown in Figure 16.1. Note that the company is currently in state 2, with the potential to move up to a more desirable state, regress to a less desirable state, or remain the same. Note also that the event tree does not allow the company to move more than one state up or down per time period, as discussed further shortly.

Reward and Costs for Each State-Action Pair

In the value functional approach, the state of nature and the firm's immediate rewards are determined by both random factors and the firm's own policy choices, in a recursive

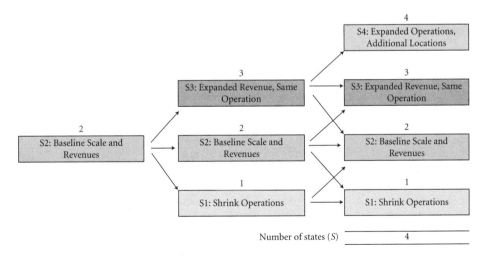

Figure 16.1   S. H. Importers' four states of nature

fashion. Each state-action pair could produce different immediate rewards and likelihoods of moving to a different states.

Euler Tension in the Management Decision

In this case, the policy choice is expressed as an investment expenditure, which obviously affects the amount of profits that can be distributed to shareholders. If the company does not invest, its shareholders reap immediate higher rewards. Thus, we have the essential Euler tension of a value functional problem: choosing higher rewards today reduces the expected value tomorrow, and vice versa.

Method of Estimating Rewards: Income Statements for Each State-Action Pair

A value functional requires a reward function; for the MDP method this is formulated as a reward matrix. The elements of this are the reward for each policy choice in each state of nature. In this three-action, four-state MDP, that means calculating twelve different elements of a reward matrix.

Because we are solving this value functional problem for an actual company, we must calculate these potential rewards using information available to the management of the company. The method we developed for this purpose included the following steps:

1. We created an income statement for each state, reflecting the scale of operations and revenue in that state. We estimated these using the firm's historical information, as well as projections for the future. States 3 and 4 were based on results from previous years with high revenue (occurring before the Great Recession); state 2 was based on a recent, sluggish-economy-year's income statement.

For firms without comparable historical information for all states, one may be able to estimate the income statement for certain states using operating or financial ratios, plus management advice; using professional judgment to adjust from the current state; using comparable data on other firms; or using other methods.

2. In addition to the relevant lines from the income statement, the most important financial and operational variables were similarly projected to ensure that the calculated rewards are reasonable given the assumed state and action.

3. Within the income statement for each state, we model the policy choice (in this case, discretionary investments) as it affects income and expenditures.

4. The benefits that accrue to the firm's shareholders are typically the net proceeds to those persons; these are the elements of the reward matrix. In the case of a business valuation problem, care must be taken to ensure that these are rewards only for ownership of the firm. Any implicit wage earnings or special owner benefits must be taken into account separately.

We show the income statements for state 2, with a column for each action, in Table 16.1. Note that the operating and financial ratios differ, even in the same state, depending on the action. In particular, we expect higher operating expenses as a share of revenue for action A (shrinking operations). This is consistent with both business intuition and from historical evidence for the firm.

TABLE 16.1
S. H. Importers income statement: State 2

Income statements for state	S2: BASELINE SCALE AND REVENUES		
	Action A: Shrink operations	Action B: Maintain operations	Action C: Expand operations
Revenue	$ 1,992,239	$ 1,992,239	$ 1,992,239
Cost of goods sold	570,786	570,786	570,786
Subtotal: Gross margin	$ 1,421,453	$ 1,421,453	$ 1,421,453
Operating expenses[a]	876,585	844,368	844,368
Net capital expenditures and other expenses	52,829	52,829	52,829
Pretax profit	$ 492,039	$ 524,256	$ 524,256
Taxes	147,612	147,612	147,612
Net profit	**$ 344,427**	**$ 376,644**	**$ 376,644**
Additional policy income (expenditure), after-tax effects	10,000	—	(20,000)
Distributed profits	**$ 354,427**	**$ 376,644**	**$ 356,644**
Ratios			
Pretax/revenue	31%	26%	23%
Distributed profits/revenue	23%	19%	16%
Operating expense/revenue	44%	42%	42%

[a] Although action A is a choice to shrink operations, operating expenses are slightly higher due to a lessening of economies of scale.

TABLE 16.2
S. H. Importers immediate rewards given each action possibility

Current states	STATE × ACTION		
	Action A: Shrink operations	Action B: Maintain operations	Action C: Expand operations
S1: Shrink operations	$256,517	$261,517	$251,517
S2: Baseline scale and revenues	354,427	376,644	356,644
S3: Expanded revenue, same operations	402,604	372,604	322,604
S4: Expanded operations, additional locations	682,640	652,640	602,640

Reward Matrix

The resulting elements (one for each state-action pair) are assembled into the reward matrix shown in Table 16.2. Observe that the rewards shown for state 2 in the matrix are the results of the income statement calculations for that state shown in Table 16.1.

Transition Function

Thus far, we have identified specific states of the world, specific actions that could be taken in each, and the resulting rewards in each state-action pair. Now, we must model how the combination of policy decisions, current state conditions, and random events cause the subject company to move from one state to another over time. The transition function maps the current state and current actions to a future state, and may do so using random events as well.

TABLE 16.3
S. H. Importers transition matrices

	NEXT-PERIOD STATES			
Current states	*S1: Shrink operations*	*S2: Baseline scale and revenues*	*S3: Expanded revenue*	*S4: Additional locations*
ACTION A: SHRINK OPERATIONS				
S1: Shrink operations	1			
S2: Baseline scale and revenues	0.8	0.2		
S3: Expanded revenue, same operation	0.25	0.5	0.25	
S4: Expanded operations, additional locations		0.25	0.5	0.25
ACTION B: MAINTAIN OPERATIONS				
S1: Shrink operations	0.8	0.2		
S2: Baseline scale and revenues	0.1	0.8	0.1	
S3: Expanded revenue, same operation		0.15	0.7	0.15
S4: Expanded operations, additional locations			0.25	0.75
ACTION C: EXPAND OPERATIONS				
S1: Shrink operations		0.8	0.2	
S2: Baseline scale and revenues		0.1	0.8	0.1
S3: Expanded revenue, same operation			0.25	0.75
S4: Expanded operations, additional locations				1

This requires a careful look at the firm's specific situation and the circumstances of the market, as well as an assessment of what uncontrollable events can be modeled as random occurrences.

For an MDP, we formulate the transition function as a *transition matrix*, which captures the probability of moving from one state to another, given an action. There is a transition matrix for each action; it shows the likelihood of each possible next-period state given that action. Because the elements of a transition matrix are probabilities, they must sum to one for every current state. Following our convention of each current state being displayed in a row, this means each row of the transition matrix sums to one. We show the transition matrix for this example valuation in Table 16.3.

Discipline and Judgment in the Transition Matrix

Much of the power of the value functional approach is in the proper structure of the states and the transition function (or transition probability matrix). Here we can incorporate knowledge of the business, economy, competitors, management, and so on by isolating how specific actions in specific situations affect the subject company.[4]

In this particular case:

- We estimated the transition probabilities for *each* state and action pair. We believed this firm could usually move up or down by only one state per period; in other cases a larger potential movement would be plausible.

- We recognized that the firm could not expand operations without investing. This is shown among the transition probabilities as zero entries, which encapsulates the statement "The probability of expanding operations when you are trying to shrink them is zero."
- Conversely, the probabilities of increasing the scale of the operation are much higher when the action is "expand," which is shown in the lower pane of the table.
- One way to quickly read these transition matrices is to observe how the probabilities tend to "lean" to one side (from the diagonal), depending on the action.

Structure of MDP Value Functional; Existence of Solution

Recall the general structure of a value functional equation for a business:

1. The manager must decide how to run the firm in the initial period, including how much salary to pay herself and other managers, and how much earnings to distribute to shareholders or reinvest back into the company.

2. Those decisions (plus any random events) affect the reward given to the investors and the value of the firm at the beginning of the next period.

3. When the next period is reached, the investor-manager examines the state of the world again and makes a new set of decisions based on the information available at that time.

4. We expect the investor-manager to choose a policy that maximizes the sum of the current reward and the expected discounted value of the firm the next period. The premise of the value functional approach is that such an optimization provides the investor-manager with the value of the business to that particular investor in that particular state.

In the case of the MDP method within the value functional approach, we have distilled down the number of states and actions and explicitly identified a transition matrix that establishes the probabilities (given each current state and action) of moving to each state in the next time period. We now need to ensure, if possible, that the problem is formulated in a way that guarantees the existence of a solution. Fortunately, the problem as outlined meets the conditions identified in Chapter 15, "The Value Functional: Theory," under the section titled "Existence of Solutions to Value Functional Equations," such as those in Exhibit 15.12 and Exhibit 15.13. In particular, note that we assume a positive discount rate; that the state variables and rewards are bounded; and that Euler tension exists between the current reward and the value in the expected next-period state.

Next we present the solution of this MDP.

Results Using the Markov Decision Process Method

Solution Algorithms

We asserted in Chapter 15, "The Value Functional: Theory," under the section titled "Existence of Solutions to Value Functional Equations," that given enough time and effort,

TABLE 16.4

Results for S. H. Importers investment opportunity

	Algorithm 1 (VFI)	Best policy	Algorithm 2 (PI)	Best policy
State 1	$ 3,829,808	C (expand)	$ 3,829,808	C (expand)
State 2	$ 4,078,189	C	$ 4,078,189	C
State 3	$ 4,262,417	C	$ 4,262,417	C
State 4	$ 4,620,241	C	$ 4,620,241	C

a solution could be found to a value functional problem that met the nontrivial conditions referenced earlier, and listed three possible algorithms.

For this problem, we used two of these algorithms: value function iteration and policy improvement. The structures of these algorithms were presented earlier in this chapter, under the section titled "Solution Methods." To implement them, the author created a set of custom routines for use within a vector-processing mathematical software environment.[5] This causes both a value function iteration and policy improvement solution to be calculated for each initial state. Finding these solutions took over 150 iterations for the VFI algorithm and less than 5 for the PI algorithm. Theoretically, in cases where a unique solution exists and enough time is spent searching for a solution, these two solutions should be approximately equal.[6]

Solution Using These Algorithms

We display the results for S. H. Importers' investment opportunity in Table 16.4. The table shows, for each state, the value of the firm in that state, and the optimal policy.

We can immediately observe the following:

- As theoretically anticipated, the solutions under each algorithm are the same, at least rounded off to the nearest integer.

- As expected by the structure of the model, the estimated value of the firm is highest when the state is higher, meaning when revenues and operations are expanded.

- In each state, the recommended policy is to expand, and this policy produces the largest value. However, the policy producing the highest value is different from the policy that maximizes current-period profits. (See Tables 16.1 and 16.2.)

Comparison with Naive Income Methods

Although not illustrated here, we also calculated for benchmark purposes a value estimate using a naive income method. In particular, we calculated the value of a perpetuity of the immediate reward amount, using the assumed discount and growth rate. This is the equivalent of using the common Gordon growth formula, or of simply extrapolating the results from the most recent period.

One can verify by hand calculation that, assuming a $376,000 profit in the current year, a discount rate of 16 percent, and a growth rate of 3 percent, the perpetual capitalization amount is approximately $3 million. The naive income method does not take into account any growth (or shrinking) options, any aspect of management flexibility, or random events beyond that incorporated in the trend growth and discount rate.

Explicit Estimation of Growth Options; Comparison with DCF

In this case, the MDP method, which explicitly identified growth options and incorporated an optimal policy of exercising them, produces a value estimate of approximately $4 million, which is $1 million higher than the naive DCF estimate. The starting assumptions (including the financial information for the firm, current status of the industry, current management policies, and trend discount and growth rates) are the same for both methods. The key difference is that the value functional method recognizes the value of the growth option, and the DCF method ignores it.

A practitioner using the traditional income method who wishes to recognize the value of the growth option would face a dilemma: either ignore the growth option, or adjust the schedule to force the value estimate produced by the DCF model to meet his or her actual beliefs regarding the market value. The latter is a common practice, as identified in Chapter 3, "The Failure of the Neoclassical Investment Rule." It may also be an honest choice, if the practitioner clearly states the rationale and existence of the adjustments. However, where possible, I recommend choosing a model that explicitly recognizes an important real option, rather than adjusting a model that does not.

Note on Including Only Plausible Actions

It is important to note that the value functional method recognizes management flexibility and estimates the value of the firm *assuming that the firm's manager is willing to take the best action.* Thus, one should not include within the action set an action that the manager or owners are unwilling to take, is prevented by financial or other constraints, or is otherwise implausible. Similarly, one should not ignore any implicit penalties involved in taking such actions.

The same guidance, of course, should also be followed when using traditional income methods. However, the traditional income method typically contemplates only one course of action.

The Autopilot Calibration Test

A practical test of the value functional method is sometimes available for profitable, operating firms with reasonable stability; I call it the *autopilot test.* It jointly tests whether the discount and growth rate assumptions are approximately correct, and that other aspects of the problem are not grossly incorrect. The test is a comparison, without any subjective adjustments, of two results:

- A constrained value functional estimate, using the baseline policy and current state (the autopilot value)
- A capitalization of current earnings that reflect the baseline policy and current state where the capitalization is done using the same discount factor and growth assumptions as with the constrained value functional estimate (the naive DCF value)

In the limited cases where this test is available, a result that is similar for the two methods indicates that the discount and growth rates are roughly calibrated to model and to each other.

Note that using the value functional approach while ignoring management flexibility makes no sense except as a calibration exercise or error check.

Calibration Test Results for This Example

Performing this test on this example company suggests that the MDP model is approximately calibrated correctly.

THE DISCOUNT RATE IN A VALUE FUNCTIONAL PROBLEM

The Discount Rate

The value functional method requires a discount rate that distinguishes the value of the next-period value from the current-period benefits, which is incorporated in the Bellman equation. Note that the use of a discount rate does not imply the use of time-separable utility, nor that the method is the same as a traditional DCF analysis.

In value functional equations, the time preference normally enters through a gross discount rate, in the form of $\beta = 1/(1 + d)$ where d is the net discount rate, such as 15 percent.

In the case of an MDP where the reward matrix is assumed to be stationary over time in either a real or nominal sense, we can use a discount rate that incorporates the nominal discount rate, the nominal growth rate of the economy and industry, and the expected rate of price inflation. In this case, we set $d = 16$ percent and $g = 3$ percent and used $\beta = 1/(1 + [d - g])$. This implies a Euler tension between \$1 in reward today and \$0.885 in value the next period.

Difference from Discount Rates Commonly Used in DCF

The use of variables for trend growth and the nominal discount factor in the value functional approach is not the same as the common use (and abuse) of perpetual capitalization formulas such as the Gordon growth formula in standard DCF analysis. The Gordon growth formula implies a *perpetual* single-state, single-action scenario. It also implies that institutional factors (including relevant tax rates and other government burdens) remain the same.

In the value functional approach (including the MDP method), we explicitly contemplate that the state *will change* over time, and that managers *will* react accordingly. Furthermore, a well-designed value functional contemplates the possibility of unusually bad outcomes, including in some cases bankruptcy. Perpetual-capitalization formulas usually ignore these risks.

Compounding; Discrete Versus Continuous Discounting

The standard convention for income methods applied to business valuation, at least in the United States, is to use full-year income statements and full-year discount and growth rates as the basis for forecasting future earnings. One often sees DCF schedules with annual periods and the *midyear convention* applied to approximate discounting throughout the year. Standard accounting and finance texts illustrate the differences that apparently minor changes in discounting conventions can have on such DCF calculations. Most economics references largely ignore this topic and often assume continuous discounting.

In the case of value functionals, it is important to match the timing of the management control points with the recursion schedule. For example, if the firm regularly reevaluates its investment policies every quarter, and opportunities change significantly within that time frame, a quarterly recursion can be established (with appropriate quarterly discount and trend growth rates). If conditions change, and management responds, on an annual basis, an annual recursion is a reasonable periodicity for the model.

With some exceptions, the author's experience suggests that practical business valuations can often be performed with annual recursions. (One alternative, which uses continuous discounting, is the method described later in this chapter, under the section titled "An Example Using the Hamilton-Jacobi-Bellman Equation.")

No Convention Yet; Future Development

Because the use of the value functional approach to business valuation is so new, there is no convention yet on the use of discount rates or the best method of incorporating price inflation and real growth in a discrete-state setting such as an MDP. This is clearly an area where future development has the potential to improve the technique.

Criticisms of Discount Rates in Dynamic Programming

Dynamic programming in general has been criticized for the fact that a discount rate must be supplied exogenously.[7] This criticism is valid, in the sense that the value functional approach involves a gross discount rate that is not determined by the model itself. Thus, as with almost every other practical valuation method, the value functional analyst must provide a discount rate.[8] It is usually not clear exactly what discount rate to use, and the selection of one often requires much thought and some risk of error.

To put this criticism in perspective, one should also observe the unfortunate prevalence of naive and incorrect use of discount rates with other methods, such as the common abuse of CAPM and build-up models to estimate discount rates for private companies. (See Chapter 3, "The Failure of the Neoclassical Investment Rule," under the section titled "Six Failings of the NPV Rule" and the Roll critique discussed in Chapter 11, "Portfolio Pricing Methods," under the section titled "Limitations of CAPM and Factor Models.")

A Proper Discount Rate Involves Idiosyncratic Preferences

Because the value functional method involves an optimization for a particular person or set of persons, the proper discount rate can be determined by both idiosyncratic preferences and market conditions. This, in my opinion, is a strength of the method rather than a weakness. For example, two prospective owners of equity in a closely held but profitable, firm are likely to have different subjective beliefs on time preference and need for liquidity. It makes less sense to assume that they both operate like representative stock market investors than to be informed by their actual behavior, stated desires, and observed risk tolerances and financial resources.

AN EXAMPLE USING THE HAMILTON-JACOBI-BELLMAN EQUATION

Continuous-Time Functional Equation Dynamics

The Bellman equation presented in this chapter is normally expressed as a discrete-time equation, with the units of time conveniently expressed as annual (or perhaps quarterly) periods. However, there is a continuous-time analogue to the discrete Bellman equation, which can provide a useful alternative technique in certain situations.

We also compare this technique to the perpetual-capitalization formulas that are commonly used in practical valuation work, such as the Gordon growth formula.

Discrete-Time Perpetual Capitalized Earnings

It is common in applied work to see the Gordon growth formula used as a shortcut income approach valuation method, as a calculation for terminal values in a DCF schedule, and even sometimes as the primary valuation method. Of course, this formula relies on the assumption that profits will grow *in perpetuity* with constant discount and growth rates, thus implicitly assuming no uncertainty. This is, almost everywhere, an incorrect assumption when applied to an actual business.

See Equation 16.3, where we define the value of perpetuity of profits *Vgg* as the net present value of that stream of income. We include the state variable as an argument to the profit function, to emphasize the embedded assumptions that the state changes over time at a constant rate and that the profit function exhibits constant returns to scale.

Equation 16.3 Value of Perpetuity; Decomposition

Value of Perpetuity:

$$V = \sum_{0}^{\infty} \frac{\pi(x_t)}{(1+d)^t}$$

$$Vgg \equiv \frac{\pi(x_0) \cdot (1+g)}{d-g}$$

where:

$\pi(x_t)$ = profit at time t, given state variable x_t

$\quad = \pi(x_0)(1+g)^t$

$g \quad$ = constant growth trend in $\pi(x_t)$

$d \quad$ = constant discount rate; $0 < g < d < 1$

Decomposition:

$(d-g)Vgg = \pi(x_0) \cdot (1+g)$

$d \cdot Vgg \quad = [\pi(x_0) \cdot (1+g)] + [g \cdot Vgg]$

However, the *Vgg* formula can be decomposed in a manner that illustrates the portions of total return under these ideal conditions. As shown in the bottom part of the equation, the total return is the product of the discount rate and the current value and equals the sum of two concepts: the current *flow return* of profits and an implicit capital gain on the increasing value of the asset. Because there is no uncertainty, there are no other components of total return.

The Total Return When the State Is a Diffusion

Now consider the value of a perpetual stream of income, again in a theoretically near-perfect world (with no transaction costs and complete markets), where the income is also derived from a profit function of a state variable. The state variable itself $X(t, \omega)$ is a diffusion with parameters μ and σ, and the inclusion of two arguments reminds us that its path is determined by both a random and deterministic components. It may be a geometric Brownian motion of the type anticipated in the Black-Scholes-Merton model and other models of mathematical finance. We model this in continuous time, with the value of this perpetual stream defined as the expected discounted future sum of the future profits, as shown in Equation 16.4.

Equation 16.4 Value of a Perpetual Stream of Income from a Diffusion

$$v(x_0) \equiv E\left[\int_0^\infty e^{-\rho t}\pi(x_t)dt\right]$$

where:

$\rho > 0$ is a discount rate

$\pi(x_t)$ is a continuous, bounded profit function of the state variable x_t

$x_t = X(t, \omega)$ is a diffusion with parameters $\mu(x)$ and $\sigma(x)$

ω is a stochastic process

$t = 0, 1, \ldots \infty$ is a time index

At this point, we have not introduced any management decisions or other human elements into the mythical income-producing asset, so this equation is not equivalent to the value functional equation for a firm. It is, however, conceptually equivalent to the perpetuity equation for a hypothetical asset we presented earlier, with the critical distinctions of being in continuous time and having a state variable that is a diffusion.

The H-J-B Equation

Using results from stochastic calculus, we can derive from Equation 16.4 and its assumptions the following stochastic differential equation, known as the *Hamilton-Jacobi-Bellman equation*, which I abbreviate as H-J-B.

The derivation is essentially a Taylor expansion of the value function in Equation 16.4 around the point x_t, and makes use of the celebrated Itô-Döblin formula.[9] Because time does not enter directly into that function, we dropped the time subscripts in Equation 16.5.

Equation 16.5 Hamilton-Jacobi-Bellman Equation

$$\rho v(x) = \pi(x) + \mu(x)\, v'(x) + \frac{1}{2}\sigma^2(x)v''(x)$$

where:

ρ > 0 is a discount rate and $\pi(x)$ a continuous bounded profit function

x_t = $X(t,\,\omega)$ is a diffusion with parameters $\mu(x)$ and $\sigma(x)$

$$v'(x) = \frac{dv}{dx}$$

Decomposing the H-J-B Equation for Total Return

The H-J-B equation provides a basis for decomposing the total return to a valuable asset, when the total return is produced from the returns generated from a state variable that is the stochastic process. In particular:

- $\pi(x)$ is the current profit (flow return) from current operations.
- $\mu(x)v'(x)$ is the trend change in the state variable, multiplied by the derivative of value with respect to the state variable. There is an intuition for this: the marginal change to the value of the firm just because of a change in the state. This is equivalent to the implied capital gain in the decomposition of total return in the discrete time, no uncertainty setting.
- The third term, $\frac{1}{2}\sigma^2(x)v''(x)$, recognizes the burden of volatility. The second derivative of the value function $v''(x)$, if the returns exhibited the normal condition of decreasing returns to scale, would probably be negative in at least some range of the state space. This implies that this factor is often negative in practical cases where some volatility exists. If we assume a mythical company where no uncertainty exists about the state variable's path, $\sigma = 0$ and this term drops out of the equation.
- Although not shown in this equation (because the value function includes only the state variable, not time), the H-J-B equation includes an additional term when time is a direct argument of the value function. This term is the first partial derivative of the value function with regard to time. The inclusion of this term is intuitively obvious in cases where a business opportunity, revenue inflow, or cost is triggered solely by the movement of time. We consider a case involving an expiring real option that illustrates this.

Thus, the H-J-B is a direct analogy to the decomposition of the total return from a perpetuity expressed in discrete time, but it has additional terms reflecting any volatility burden and time-sensitive real options.

H-J-B Method: First Example Valuation Application

The H-J-B equation has not been used in practical business valuation work before, probably because there was no matching theory of a firm or of a value functional approach to the value of a firm. However, it has been used in the theoretical development of pricing formulas for some return-producing assets and for financial options.

We present the following example of its use to solve a value functional problem for a simplified example of an operating firm.

Assumptions: A Firm with a Linear Profit Function and Some Uncertainty

For illustrative purposes, consider a firm with a profit function that is a simple linear function of the state variable. A firm that earned a consistent net profit margin on its sales and could scale up or down fairly quickly would be an example of a firm that operates like this.

Assign the firm and the market the following assumptions, which differ slightly whether we are using discrete time or continuous time:[10]

- discount rates: $d = 0.15, \rho = 0.14$
- growth trends: $g = 0.05, \mu = 0.0488$
- a state variable at the initial time period of $x_0 = 1.5$ million
- a profit function of $\alpha_1 * x$, where $\alpha_1 = 0.20$ in U.S. dollars per unit of the state variable
- a volatility factor of $\sigma^2 = 0.10$

Using this information, we can calculate the total return using the decomposition of the Gordon growth discrete-time formula, and the H-J-B formula in continuous time:

- The values Vgg and $VcapC$ were calculated at $3.14 million and $3.29 million, respectively. Note that differences between discrete and continuous compounding are responsible for some of this small discrepancy.

- The total returns estimated using the discrete perpetuity formula and the H-J-B method (with two variations) were $returnGG = \$470,000$; $returnHJB^A = \$453,000$; $returnHJB^B = \$460,000$.

- Recall that we assumed the value function was linear in the state variable $[v''(x) = 0]$, meaning that the volatility burden did not enter into the equation. Similarly, we assumed trend growth without a termination date, so no time-dependent real option existed. In other cases, these assumptions would not be tenable.

An illustration of this result is shown in Figure 16.2.

H-J-B: Second Example Valuation

Next we demonstrate a second application of the value functional approach, this time using a much more complicated subject: an actual firm, in an actual industry, operating under actual conditions of uncertainty and the presence of real options. We also examine in this example how the value functional approach allows for an implicit evaluation of certain competing management policies, if these policies are explicitly modeled in the value functional equation.

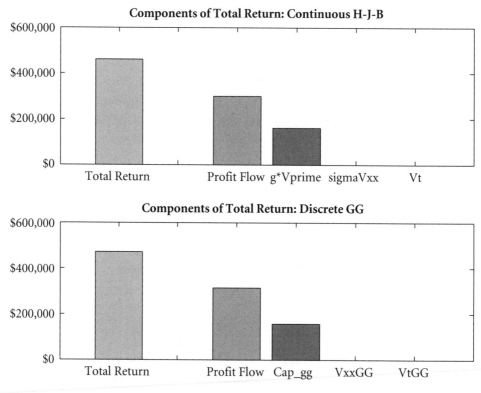

Figure 16.2   Illustration of H-J-B and Gordon growth methods

Value Functional Approach: A & A Consulting

As described in Appendix C, "Description of Subject Companies," A & A Consulting is a professional services firm with annual revenue of approximately $2.0 million that has been operating for more than a decade and has two offices. Like most firms of this type, it has a certain "key man" risk related to the reputation of its founder, although this risk has diminished over time as the firm acquired a stronger group of managers and consultants. The firm has operated in a manner that recognizes this risk, investing heavily in developing management and training consultants. However, such a policy is expensive in terms of reducing current earnings.

Assumptions

The key assumptions used in the analysis are shown in the top panel of Table 16.5. Here the state variable is identified as trend demand, stated in terms of nominal gross revenue. By *trend demand*, we mean the revenue that the company expects it would earn if the effects of temporary factors (including the business cycle) were averaged across multiple periods.

In the case of A & A Consulting, the trend demand was set at a lower level than the actual revenue for the previous year, because the firm's management believed that it had received a larger share of onetime business than was typical during that period.

TABLE 16.5

Value functional approach: Key assumptions using the H-J-B method
for A & A Consulting

Concept	Symbol	Value
Time increment [periodicity]	Δt	1 year
Net discount rate/period [ρ]	ρ	0.15
Gross discount rate [$\beta = 1/1 + \rho$]	β	0.87
State variable (trend demand revenue)	s	$2,000,000
Trend growth rate in s/period	g'	0.06
Flow profit at typical control policy (pre-discretionary expenditures x)	$\pi(s, x)$	$ 325,000
Action variable (discretionary expenditure to secure management in future)	x	$ (75,000)
Volatility in state	$\sigma^2(s)$	0.2
State-change effect on value	$V'(s)$	1.0
Volatility burden effect on value	$V''(s)$	0.1
Time-dependent option values		
Time-dependent option 1, value at expiry ("key man" eventual retirement)	V_{t1}	$ (250,000)
Time to expiry	T_1	10
Time-dependent option 2, value at expiry (management investment)	V_{t2}	$ 200,000
Time to expiry	T_2	5

VALUE FUNCTIONAL AND TRANSITION EQUATIONS

$V(s, x) = \max\{\pi(s, x) + \beta \cdot E[V(s_1, x_1)]\}$
    maximization is over feasible set for x; $s_1 = g(s_0, x_0)$

H-J-B DECOMPOSITION

$\rho \cdot V = \pi(s, x) + g'(s, x) \cdot V'(s) + 1/2\sigma^2(s) \cdot Vss + Vt$

The action variable is identified as discretionary investments, meaning expenditures that are not necessary to maintain capital stock or current policies regarding compensation, marketing, and other operating expenses. In this case, discretionary investments are focused on increasing management depth. Note that two time-dependent real options are explicitly modeled: the eventual retirement of a "key man" and the management investment necessary to increase the revenue of the firm without the "key man." These are shown as nominal amounts to be received (or paid) at different future dates. We model these as *real options*, although, as in the case of the eventual retirement of any human, many events are inevitable.

Calculations

The value functional equation and its H-J-B decomposition are shown conceptually in the top panel of the table. In Table 16.6, we present the primary valuation and an alternative, using that decomposition with estimated values for the actual subject company.

1. The primary valuation assumes that the company continues to follow the current management policy of making discretionary investments. The flow profits are only $250,000, which is less than the available profits of $325,000. The state-change gain is another $120,000. If we had stopped at this point (which would be the case if we assumed no uncertainty, no

TABLE 16.6

Value functional approach: H-J-B calculations for A & A Consulting

VALUE FUNCTIONAL APPROACH: H-J-B DECOMPOSITION, STANDARD POLICIES

Total return $(\rho \cdot V)$	Flow profits $\pi(s, x)$	State-change gain $g'(s, x)V'$	Volatility burden $1/2\sigma^2 \cdot Vss$	Time-dependent options
	Income before discretionary x $\$ 325,000$	$g'(s, x) = g \cdot s$ 0.06	$1/2 \cdot \sigma^2(s)$ 0.2 0.5	
		$\$ 2,000,000$	0.1	V_{t1}: E(NPV) $\$ (55,783)$
	Discretionary control expenditures $\$-75,000$	$\$ 120,000$	$Vss = 0.1 \cdot s$	
			0.1	V_{t2}: E(NPV)
		$V' = 1$	2,000,000	
		1	$\$ 200,000$	$\$ 94,473$
$\$ 428,691$	$\$ 250,000$	$\$ 120,000$	$\$ 20,000$	$\$ 38,691$

Implied value: $ 2,857,938

VALUE FUNCTIONAL APPROACH: ASSUMING DIFFERENT MANAGEMENT POLICIES

Management policy assumption:
Accept loss of V_{t2}; save 1/2 of discretionary spending

Total return	Flow profits	State-change gain	Volatility burden	Time-dependent options
	$\$ 325,000$ $\$ (37,500)$			$\$ (55,783)$
$\$ 371,717$	$\$ 287,500$	$\$ 120,000$	$\$ 20,000$	$\$ (55,783)$

Implied value: $ 2,478,116

real options, and perpetual growth), we would have the equivalent of a traditional income method using a decomposition of the Gordon growth equation.

However, in this case we incorporate a volatility burden (which is positive, reflecting the fact that the company expects that it would earn higher marginal profits on incremental revenue), and the net result of two time-dependent options. Note that the options mature at different times and that the net amount is slightly positive. The amounts considered at the future time are the (continuously) discounted present values, assuming exercise of the option on a consistent basis. As a whole, this method produces a total return figure of nearly $429,000, implying a market valuation of $2.8 million under this management policy.

2. The second valuation is identical except for the treatment of the real options and the management policy that treatment represents. If the firm chooses not to make the discretionary investments, its flow profits are higher. However, its total return is lower because the eventual retirement of the "key man" reduces the value of the company faster than the additional profits. Thus, the total return and the resulting valuation are both smaller by a factor of about 15 percent.

The valuations here, done without any subjective adjustments, show how an actual company can be analyzed effectively with the value functional approach. They also illustrate a powerful advantage of this approach: the ability to reveal the effects of management policies on the value of the firm.

Observations on the Value Functional Approach and the H-J-B Method

The value functional approach is novel, and the H-J-B method is both novel and difficult to implement. The biggest difficulty is defining the profit and value functions, which must be identified in enough detail that their first and second differentials can be estimated. The second difficulty is expressing these in terms of increments of the state variable. The third difficulty is in converting from discrete to continuous time, or at least short-increment time. However, as the previous two examples demonstrate, the method does work. In particular:

- Given the same information about a (mythical) company with perpetually growing profits, it produced the same approximate answer as the traditional income approach.

- Given the same information about an actual operating company, with real options, uncertainty, and pending management decisions, it produced a *better* answer than a traditional income method.

- Of course, a skilled practitioner could make subjective adjustments (to the discount rate, future expected revenues, expenses, and earnings, and to add various discounts and premiums) to the estimate from a naive traditional income model, to account for various issues. However, the value functional approach makes many of these issues *explicit parts of the model* and therefore is both more powerful and more transparent.

This example demonstrates that valuation problems involving companies with complicated situations (such as real options dependent on time, differing volatility burdens, and different forms of implicit production functions) can also be attacked with this technique.

EXAMPLE USING DYNAMIC PROGRAMMING

Introduction: A Firm with Eroding Market Position and Real Option to Scrap

In this example, we estimate the value of a firm with the following characteristics:

- It is steadily profitable at its current scale of operations.
- It operates in an industry with relatively stable conditions.
- The underlying conditions supporting its business are steadily eroding, at least in real terms.

This erosion could be due to any number of factors, such as the following:

- The impending or eventual retirement of a "key man" in the organization, such as a founder, rainmaker, or other individual for whom no close replacement can be found
- The expiration of a patent, license, or franchise or the loss of important access rights or intellectual property
- A technological change already on the horizon

- A change in laws or regulation
- The growth of a powerful competitor, or a competing technology

While this erosion is occurring, the company remains in business and—at the current time—profitable. It can choose to exit the business and gain a payoff that may be termed a *salvage value*, or remain in business. The company could make a certain number of management or production changes that would adjust their costs somewhat. However, no plausible technological, scale, or other management change would dramatically change their business prospects.

Purposes of the Exercise

The following example illustrates these facets of valuation:

- The existence and use of a real option
- The existence of limits to current business operations
- The use of value functional methods that incorporate recursive decision making by a firm's manager
- The difference between a naive valuation (including standard DCF and income-multiple methods) and one done recognizing managerial flexibility
- The additional information that a value functional method can provide the management of the firm and potential investors

Assumptions for the Real Options Problem

Quantitative Assumptions

- We discussed earlier the assumption that the firm is now profitable under steady management, has good accounting records, and operates in an industry with fairly stable technology.
- The most important aspect of the company's business can be captured in a variable that captures the state of the underlying security, revenue stream, asset, or other basis for the real options discussed previously. For example, if the real option involves the selling of a mine, the state variable could be the amount of proven natural resource reserves remaining.
- An examination of the company's operating and financial records indicates the following values: the state variable $s = 250$; distributable profits $\pi = 316$. The profit measure considered here is the profit distributed to investors, after the company makes required debt and tax payments and reinvests enough in the business to retain the planned working capital levels and maintain the physical capital of the company. (Although we do not show the derivation from the income statement here, this concept is equivalent to net cash flow to equity in the professional valuation literature.)

- In the past, the firm's revenue was growing at a steady rate over many years. However, management recognizes that the state variable is now trending downward at a slow but steady rate. It can be modeled fairly accurately as an arithmetic Brownian motion process, with $\mu = -2$ per period. On a year-to-year basis that trend is largely obscured by other random factors affecting all businesses in the industry. Given that $s = 250$, this process suggests that the underlying state will erode at slightly less than 1 percent per year for the next couple of decades.

- Management judgment and recent historical data indicate that there are positive returns to scale within the plausible range of production quantities, with reducing marginal returns at some point above the current production rate, and a lower-production point at which fixed costs overwhelm profits. This pattern is consistent with the information available for most midsized and larger companies in most industries.

- Within a narrow production range, the net profit margin of the firm is stable given the current operating structure. The management believes it can increase its profits by another 2 percent if it were to implement cost-savings efforts that would take approximately a year.

- The firm is largely equity financed and held by a relatively small group of investors. Their agreed-upon discount rate for equity investments in the firm is $d = 15$ percent, although the steady management, strong capitalization, and tenure of the firm suggest that the actual discount rate should be a bit lower. Although we do not investigate this assumption further here, we note that it is close to the standard rule of thumb for equity investments in the U.S. stock market for the past few decades.

- The growth rate of revenue in the industry is about 3 percent per year, reflecting the fact that demand grows similarly to the real economy and that any inflationary price changes are approximately offset by slow efficiency and technology improvements on both the production and consumption side.

- The operation (plant, mine, extraction field, or other set of facilities), if shut down on an orderly fashion, has a net salvage value of $S = 1900$. This is expected to remain constant in nominal terms over time, implying a slow decline in real terms given the inflation assumption.

The expected state path, returns, and discounted returns over time are shown in Figure 16.3.

Questions to Be Answered

The valuation and management questions we examine in this example are the following:

1. How much is the firm worth today?

2. How long does the firm have to operate, if it wishes to remain in business, before the business conditions deteriorate to the point that it should shut down?

3. What are the indicators that it is optimal to sell the business and take the salvage value?

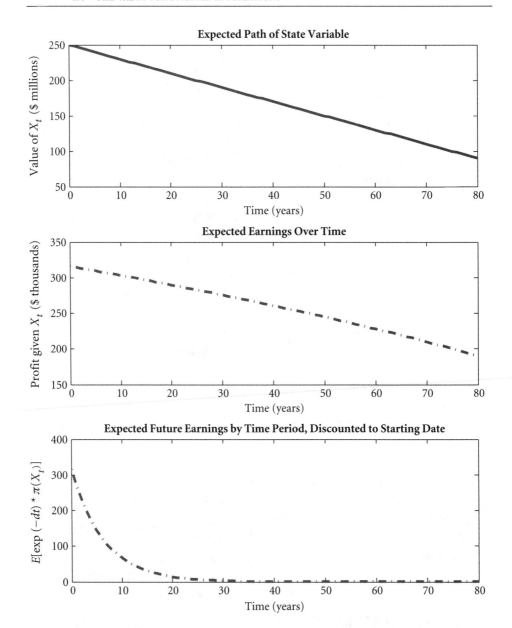

Figure 16.3   Expected state path and return, real options example

Value Estimates: Naive Methods

The standard methods, which I classify as naive to emphasize that they ignore valuable information, can be used readily with the preceding information. Direct calculations using these methods and the preceding assumptions provide the following set of value estimates:

• A starting point is the salvage value of $S = 1900$. Traditional valuation theories provide no insight about when to take the salvage value, other than the neoclassical microeconomics notion of shutting down when the operation can no longer cover its variable costs.

• A simple perpetual-capitalization (Gordon growth) formula, assuming growth trend $g = 0$ and discount rate $d = 15$ percent, produces a value estimate of $Vgg = 2107$. An analyst providing this estimate could assert that it is very conservative because it assumes no change in the revenue in the future, even as the economy grows and inflation occurs. The same analyst could demonstrate that a weighted average of growth rates during a selected set of recent years was near zero.

• An alternative set of assumptions is that profits will grow at a trend of 3 percent per year and that the discount rate is actually a lower figure of 14 percent. An analyst making such a projection could note that inflation had historically been 2 percent and that nominal GDP growth had been about 6 percent, so that a 3 percent revenue trend assumption was still conservative. The perpetual-capitalization formula using these optimistic assumptions is $Vgg\text{-}o = 2959$.

• A spreadsheet model, with more detailed expense breakdowns and proposed cost-savings measures (increasing profits by 2 percent) implemented in the second year produces a slightly higher value estimate. These assumptions increase the value estimate to $Vss = 2938$.

• A review of publicly traded companies in the industry suggests that large operating companies have stock market capitalizations that are about 15 times their current earnings. That implies a value estimate of $Vmult = 4740$. A rule of thumb in the industry is that operating companies that are interested in expanding typically pay between 2 and 2½ times the salvage value; this implies that $Vmult\text{-}s$ is within the range $3800 - 4750$.

Thus, a group of skilled analysts using traditional methods and very good information could produce value ranging from 2107 to 4750 — a potential variance of more than 100 percent.

Value Estimates: Value Functional Method

The value functional method requires explicitly stating the state, control, and reward functions. Using the same quantitative and qualitative assumptions stated earlier, we can implement this method as follows:

• Model the production function of the firm as a quadratic function of the state variable. This has a shape consistent with the management observation and recent historical data.

• Model its distributable profits as the same share of revenue as in the standard DCF model, although only when in the same production range.

• Use an arithmetic Brownian motion assumption for the state variable, with no uncertainty. This is a relatively modest adjustment given the fact that the uncertainty about the state variable is small and that it appears to provoke small changes in profits that are of similar magnitude of a large number of random events that affect all businesses in the industry.

• Use an implementation of a recursive solution calculation structured as described in Exhibit 16.2 to solve for the time at which to exercise the real option, or alternatively, the state value at which to exercise the option.

• The critical decision factor is a form of Euler tension: the company should not continue to operate when the profits for current operations are less than the discounted salvage value

$(d * S)$. Note that this encapsulates the logic that the forgone earnings from postponing the exercise of the option to scrap is the interest rate times the salvage value. Hence, once the firm's current earnings fall below this, the investors should exercise the option. The analytical structure of this problem was outlined by Stokey (2009, sec. 6.1).

The results from using this method, as well as the key assumption and the results from using traditional methods, are shown in Table 16.7, "Results of Real Option Valuation Example."

• The assumptions listed here, and in the computational routine of the type described in Exhibit 16.2, demonstrate that the calculation of the estimate using the value functional method is $vf_{xd} = 2052$, which can be decomposed into a continuation value of 1996 and an option premium of 56.

These calculations can be confirmed by an *ad hoc* quadrature of the earnings over the time period up to the calculated stopping time plus the discounted salvage. This alternate calculation produces an estimate of $QdiscT = 2010$.

TABLE 16.7
Results of real option valuation example

Estimation method	Value (at time t = 0)	Note
NAIVE METHODS		
Perpetual capitalization		"Gordon Growth" formulas; standard and
Vgg	2,107	optimistic assumptions
Vgg-o	2,959	
Spreadsheet DCF with cost adjustments		Assumes cost savings appear in second year; then evaluated using perpetual-capitalization formulas
Vss	2,938	
Earnings multiple		Multiple derived from publicly traded firm
$Vmult$	4,740	data
Multiple of salvage value		Professional judgment of brokers
$Vmult$-s	3,800–4,750	
Time to shutdown	No information or ignore completely	Perpetual-capitalization formulas implicitly assume no shutdown; standard microeconomics indicates shutdown when revenue cannot cover variable costs
Time to sell (exercise real option)	No information or ignore completely	
VALUE FUNCTIONAL METHOD		
Value functional with real option to abandon, no uncertainty	2,052 v-continue: 1,996 v-option: 56	Value functional formulas can decompose the value into the continuation and option-related parts
Time to sell (exercise real option) Tb	23	
GENERAL ASSUMPTIONS		
Initial state and growth trend	250	Modeled as arithmetic Brownian motion with little uncertainty
S_0		
μ	–2/year	
Company: Fiscal period	Year	
π_0	316	
d	15%; 14% (optimistic)	These values are typical of private firms; the range between "optimistic" and regular assumptions is not very large
g	0%; 3% (optimistic)	
S	1,900	Salvage value is received after shutdown and is net of costs
Production and profit function	Power function with scale and exponent parameters $A = 20$; alpha $\cdot$ eta $= .5$	Exhibits positive but declining returns to scale in relevant range of state variables

EXHIBIT 16.2

Computational Design: Value Functional Method; Operating Company with Real Options

Auxiliary Routines

- Return function (of state variable, with firm- and industry-specific parameters)
- Transition function (with parameters for drift and possibly diffusion)
- Perpetual-capitalization formula

Main Routine

A. INITIALIZE

- Establish plausible range for state and action variables.
- Establish assumptions regarding discount rates, and maximum number of time periods.

B. PRELIMINARY CALCULATIONS

- Calculate return at current state.
- Compare with returns calculated at lower and upper bounds of state variable.

C. ESTABLISH DECISION RULE

- Operate while: $\pi(s) >$ discounted salvage.
- Stop when: $\pi(s) = \pi(b^*) =$ discounted salvage

  where: $Tb =$ stopping time

  $\qquad b^* =$ stopping state value.
- Calculate discounted salvage (or discounted real option exercise value).
- Check to see that calculated return is:

  Consistent with actual income statement at current or recent state value.

  Above lower and beneath upper thresholds for immediate exercise of real options.

D. CALCULATE STOPPING TIME

- Solve for stopping time as (inverse) function of return function, expected trend of state variable, and recursive decision threshold rule. Solve for stopping value of state.

E. ESTIMATE VALUE

- Project optimal policy for manager, given expected path of state.
- Project returns along expected state path, if following optimal policy.
- Using Tb, b^*, S, d, and expected path of state variable, returns, and salvage value, calculate discounted rewards over optimal path calculated earlier. Set to estimated value.

The estimated time to exercise (stopping time) is $Tb = 23$ years, at which time the state value would have dropped to $bstar = 203$.

Results; Observations

From these results, one can observe the following:

1. Using traditional methods produces a large range of possible values; in this case two different traditional method estimates were double or more the estimate of the value functional method.

2. If one ignores the slow declining trend (perhaps from optimism, random deviation, or unrealistic expectation that traditional capitalized income methods are accurate), one can produce a greatly exaggerated value estimate. This can be seen from the *Vgg-optimistic* estimate of nearly 50 percent higher than the value functional estimate.

3. Of course, it is possible, using traditional methods *and the correct subjective adjustments*, to come up with an estimate of value similar to the value functional estimate. Presumably, it would also be possible to produce an even more misleading estimate using traditional methods and incorrect subjective adjustments.

4. The benefits to the firm's management from using the more powerful value functional method are not limited to receiving an accurate value estimate; they also benefit from an estimate of the amount of time until the company should exercise the salvage option.

5. The observation of Dixit and Pindyck in 1994 is demonstrated again: ignoring real options in valuation can produce an answer that is not only wrong, it is *very* wrong.

17 APPLICATIONS: FINANCE AND VALUATION

OUTLINE OF THIS CHAPTER

In this and the following chapter, we frequently refer to techniques and theories presented in the earlier parts of the book. Careful readers will ensure that they have reviewed those chapters before plunging into the valuation of, say, their local professional sports team.

Start-Ups and Bankrupt Firms as the Typical Case

Remember that small firms, start-ups, and distressed firms are the *rule*, not the exception! Thus, one can view a discussion of these firms as a discussion of the typical firm. In this chapter, we do the following:

- Pose the question of whether start-up firms have value.
- Discuss the applicability of traditional valuation methods to start-up firms.
- Discuss valuation methods applicable to firms in and near bankruptcy.

Franchises and Sports Teams

We also discuss application of valuation techniques to an interesting subset of companies: franchises (including franchisees and franchisors) and sports teams. In particular, we discuss the following:

- The definition of a franchise, a franchisor, and a franchisee.
- The key drivers of value for franchises.
- How different valuation methods can be used to estimate the value of franchised companies.
- Major league sports franchises and their market values.

START-UP FIRMS

Do Start-Up Firms Have Value?

We reviewed in Chapter 5, "The Organization and Scale of Private Business," the empirical evidence on business creation and destruction. We found that half or more of new firms in the United States go out of business within the first five years of their existence, and most new firms in European countries (where data are available) seem to disappear within about five years as well. We also noted strong evidence that most recently started firms lose money, and that entrepreneurs often work for reduced pay—and dip into their family savings—to keep operating.

Despite these apparently grim statistics, entrepreneurs continue to start firms and work long hours to keep them going. Furthermore, "being your own boss" remains part of the American dream, as well as the dream of many people the world over. Clearly, entrepreneurs throughout the world strongly believe that the fledgling firms they start have value.

Valuing Start-Up Firms: Comparison of Methods

How can entrepreneurs believe that start-up firms have value, when empirical evidence suggests that *most* of these businesses will lose money and go out of business? This question is an important test of valuation methods.

In Table 17.1, we consider how each of four different methods would estimate the value of a newly formed business with the common attributes of a start-up firm, including no profits, only one or two employees, and significant start-up expenses. The table summarizes

TABLE 17.1

Comparison: Valuation of start-up firms using different methods

Type of firm	Asset	Market	Income	Value functional
New inventor firm (no saleable intellectual property yet, but promising technology under development; no sales revenue or royalty income yet)	Zero or small value Value would become positive only after a contract or revenue was produced	Zero or small value Intellectual property may have small market value independent of inventor	Zero or small value, unless heroic forecast made With a contract, could forecast income that establishes basis for positive value	Small positive value in the market; significant positive value to inventor given faith in abilities and desire to work in this manner
New consulting firm (firm with two experienced employees, a handful of contracts, but not yet profitable when salaries are accrued)	Positive, though small Owners could manipulate estimate by adjusting salaries	Close to zero, unless owners are valuable as employees of another firm, or if firm acquires valuable market position	Positive, though small Proper application of method requires adjustment for salaries	Positive value that probably exceeds that estimated under either the market or income approach Value functional recognizes growth potential and benefits of "being own boss"

Assumptions: Naive application of each method to classic example of first-year firm of each type.

the likely conclusion of a straightforward application of the traditional asset, market, and income approaches, along with the value functional approach, all done without subjective adjustments.

Observations on Methods: Theoretical and Practical

Table 17.1 also illustrates how the traditional methods are aligned with the dire side of the aggregate statistics about business survival: they consistently show little or no market value for a typical start-up firm. The value functional methodology, however, is aligned with the optimistic side of those same statistics: it consistently shows some value for such firms. This matches the opinion and decision of actual entrepreneurs.

As these entrepreneurs are actually financing and starting firms, and a share of these are also receiving financing from others, a superior method would recognize the value that the market itself has confirmed. At least theoretically, the value functional method is superior to the traditional methods in this respect.

In practical cases, the facts often dictate that one valuation method is better than others, especially given data limitations and the knowledge of the person doing the value estimation. Based on both theoretical and practical consideration, I offer the following advice on valuing start-up firms:

- An income approach may be useful if the new business has sound projections of business income and evidence supports the projections. Of course, the mere existence of a business plan or cash flow projection can be meaningless if the plan or projection is divorced from the facts.

- Accounting records rarely establish future earnings potential, but they can establish convincingly the amount of effort and investment put into the new business by the entrepreneur and other investors. They also can show the strength of the business management (or reveal its inadequacies).

- Market methods are unlikely to produce a sound estimate of the value of a new business, except in the unusual case where actual market transactions for comparable firms (or offers for the subject business) are available. However, a market method may provide an upper bound or other indication of the plausible range.

- Since the success of most new businesses is based heavily on their ability to exercise real options, real options methods should be considered. However, guard against double-counting the value arising from real options and that arising from natural growth.

- The value functional method is the closest match to the actual tension of an entrepreneurial firm. Furthermore, it correctly recognizes the importance of management control. Hence, if the information necessary is available and the expert is capable of using the method, it should be considered.

- The skill and knowledge of the person estimating the firm's value will probably be critical. His or her professional judgment may, in the case of relatively few hard facts, be the most important factor in the valuation.

- The plausible range of potential market values is likely to be relatively large compared to the range for established firms.

- Management always matters in a business valuation. When management decisions can result in the life or death of the enterprise, management means even more. A large firm can often survive an incompetent CEO for a few years. A small firm usually cannot.

DISTRESSED AND BANKRUPT FIRMS

What Is Bankruptcy?

It is important to define *bankruptcy* in order to properly understand the value of firms that may be in, or near, bankruptcy. We define, in general terms, bankruptcy for a firm as follows:[1]

A firm is bankrupt when:

a. It is an operating firm.

b. Its financial obligations exceed its ability to satisfy them under its existing business and operational structure.

c. It declares bankruptcy under the applicable laws of the state in which it operates.

d. That state has adopted a bankruptcy code.

This definition incorporates the institutional factors of limited liability for stockholders,[2] a bankruptcy code,[3] and the economic definition of the firm. These are all important topics themselves.

Going Concern Principle

An important accounting convention has largely been adopted, in practical terms, by the economics, finance, and professional valuation communities: the *going concern principle*. This is a presumption that the company can function without fear of liquidation for the foreseeable future, which is often interpreted to mean at least one year. Such a premise is implicitly incorporated in nearly all analytical models in economics and finance. Without this premise, it would be difficult for other parties to contract with the firm, and for lenders and investors to finance the firm.

The going concern presumption allows the firm's financial affairs to be presented using normal accounting rules, including the rules for accruing income and expenses. These normal accounting rules also allow for the calculation of *book value* or accounting net worth of the firm, which is the excess of assets over liabilities. Such a calculation does not predict the market value of the firm, but it does provide investors with a useful indication of the firm's solvency under the relevant accounting rules.

Value of a Distressed Firm

A distressed firm may no longer fulfill the premise of a going concern, although the issue is often a matter of some ambiguity. However, we focus on the value question: does a formerly profitable firm that has become distressed still have value?

The answer for most such firms, at least conceptually, is clearly yes. In general, distressed firms have valuable assets, they have the potential to become profitable again, and they may be attractive acquisition candidates for investors or competitors. Valuation methods used for distressed firms should recognize these facts.

Value of a Bankrupt Firm

Now consider a bankrupt firm, where the ongoing concern premise is not fulfilled and where the company has filed a bankruptcy petition indicating that it is insolvent and can no longer operate in a normal fashion. Could such a firm have any value?

From an accounting basis, the firm has negative net worth. However, such a bankrupt firm could have *business value*, because such a firm (or a successor firm that acquires its key assets, employees, or technology) could earn profits in the future from replicable business processes it possesses.

Situations in Which Bankrupt Firms Often Have Business Value

There is an identifiable set of business situations in which bankrupt or distressed firms often have significant business value. These include the following:

1. *Failed expansion; successful core.* Consider a firm that operates profitably for many years. It has an opportunity to dramatically expand and believes that such an expansion is likely to result in higher future profits. The expansion carries risk; the management of the firm weighs the risks and proceeds ahead. Unfortunately, the expansion effort encounters large unexpected costs, and the firm becomes unprofitable. It cannot sustain the expanded operations but could sustain the core operations that preceded the expansion. It files a bankruptcy petition and seeks to reorganize, shedding the expanded operations.

2. *Successful expansion; failed core.* The converse example also occurs with some frequency. Consider a firm that extends its operations into new markets. The new markets develop nicely, with the support of the core operations. Eventually, the core operations fail and push the firm into bankruptcy. The firm tries to radically change its core operations and retain its new-market operations. If that fails, it may shut down its core operations entirely, and reorganize to focus on its new-market operations.

3. *Catastrophic business events.* A firm may operate profitably for many years and then suffer a catastrophic event that causes losses beyond its capacity to absorb. In such cases, the firm may have some value once the source of the disaster is removed from the corpus of the firm.

4. *Strong brand, bad business.* A firm that created a strong brand, but whose business practices and costs had failed to allow it to operate profitably, may have some value even in bankruptcy. Such firms may have a customer base that, even though diminished by bad business practices, still is connected to the brand.

Bankruptcies Without Good Prospects of Emergence

There are also examples of businesses that fail without a clear basis for ongoing business value. Such firms may fail, not because of any extraordinary event, but because of a funda-

TABLE 17.2
Advice on methods for valuing distressed firms

Method	Advice
Traditional asset	May be useful if assets are separable and all have identifiable value
Traditional income	Rarely usable unless dramatic adjustments are made
Market	Rarely useful for specific assets; can be useful in plotting exit from bankruptcy
Value functional	Usable, though difficult, if reliant on information from other methods

mental imbalance between costs and the market price, the inability of the firm to achieve the necessary scale, the inability to attract investors and lenders, the failure of a promising invention or idea to prove viable, or the loss of key employees. They may also fail because of a fundamental change in the market or economy that causes a large number of previously valuable firms to simply disappear.[4]

In such situations, there is often little prospect that the firm can emerge from bankruptcy as an operating company.

Advice on Valuing Distressed and Bankrupt Firms

In Table 17.2, we provide advice on methods that can be used to value distressed and bankrupt firms. Note that institutional factors—including the bankruptcy code and the particular agreements between key employees and the firm, the firm and its lenders, and the firm and its customers and suppliers—are always critical features of a proper valuation of a distressed or bankrupt firm.

FRANCHISES AND SPORTS TEAMS

What Is a Franchise?

An Introduction

A franchise is a business model in which specific branded products or services, and a specific mode of operation, are replicated among many businesses. These businesses contract with each other through a set of franchise agreements.[5]

Franchises dominates certain sectors of the U.S. economy, such as automobile and truck retailing, fast-food restaurants, hotels, alcoholic beverage distribution, automobile rental, and copy centers. In a franchise, one business (known as a *franchisor*) creates a brand identity for a product or service, outlines a method for providing the service, and appoints separate companies (known as *franchisees*) to provide the goods and services. In exchange for these services, the franchisor receives some type of fee, royalty, or license payment from the franchisees.

The underlying economics of the franchise is critical to the value of franchisees and franchisors. The study of franchises also highlights particular aspects of the value of all businesses and helps isolate value components in nonfranchise businesses.

Essential Elements of a Franchise

The three essential characteristics of a franchise system are as follows:

1. *Trademark.* The franchisor creates a brand identity for a product or service. This brand identity normally includes trademarked symbols or names.

2. *Significant control.* The franchisor exercises significant control over the franchisees' operations. This typically includes following certain standards for service, product delivery, and overall representation of the brand.

3. *Required payment.* In return for the use of the trademarked product or service and other benefits of being part of the franchise system, the franchisee pays a royalty, license payment, or other fee to the franchisor.

Other Typical Characteristics of Franchises

In addition to the three essential elements, many franchises share the following characteristics:

4. A written agreement between the franchisor and franchisee that outlines the obligations of the franchisee and franchisor. This may be called the *distribution agreement, sales and service agreement,* or *franchise agreement.*

While this may seem a commonsense requirement, our experience indicates that many business arrangements that are clearly franchises operate without a comprehensive written franchise agreement.[6]

5. The franchisee is normally granted the primary or exclusive right to represent the brand within a certain area, subject to performance and market standards. This territorial grant is an important aspect of traditional franchises.

However, the degree to which the franchisee truly has *exclusive* rights to represent the brand varies considerably. In practice, customers are almost always free to purchase a product or service from a franchisee of their choice, regardless of whether they are located in its designated market area.

Statutory Requirements for Franchises

Franchise as an Economic, Not Legal Concept

The franchise business model is fundamentally an economic model, not a legal fiction. Governments often impose specific requirements on businesses that meet their definition of a franchise. In the United States one of the most important is the FTC Franchise Rule. This rule uses the three-element test described earlier to define traditional franchises, and subjects them to disclosure requirements.

Valuation Factors for Franchises

At the top level of analysis, a franchisee business is no different from any other. It purchases products and resells them, hopefully at a profit. In franchisee businesses, however, there are certain specific factors that must be considered, and an additional set of risks.

TABLE 17.3
Key franchise elements in valuation

Element	Franchisor valuation	Franchisee valuation	Notes
ESSENTIAL FRANCHISE ELEMENTS			
Trademark or "brand"	Very important	Very important	Both parties share in the cultivation of the brand. Valuation should consider the durability and risk associated with the brand itself, which may not be the same as the business risk of either party.
Quality control	Important	Important	Quality control is important for both parties; however, franchisees are vulnerable to abuse through "control" requirements.
Fee	Very important	Important	Fee revenue is the dominant source of earnings for the franchisor, and a smaller part of the franchisees' expenditures. Structure of fee is often as important as amount.
OTHER ELEMENTS			
Number of locations (for sales, service, or distribution)	Very important	Important	Size of franchise system is important to both parties, as strength of brand is critical to both parties.
Advertising and other brand support by franchisor	Low to high importance, depending on product or service	Low to moderate importance	Varies significantly by product category.
Product development by franchisor	Low to high importance, depending on product or service	Low to moderate importance	Varies significantly by product category. Very important for new products; less important for well-established products.
Competing franchises	Important	Very important	For traditional retailers of developed products, local competition with competing franchisees may be a dominant factor in their market. New franchisors may find it difficult to compete against established sales and service networks of existing franchisors.
Ability to designate new locations or control franchise in that area	Important	Very important	This "growth option" can be valuable for a franchisee; franchisors typically rely on motivated franchisees to grow and hence are reluctant to cede control in this area.

The key factors that should be considered in franchised businesses include the following:

- Control, or lack of control, over product pricing
- Quality control of the product across the entire franchisee network
- Extent of the network and strength of marketing efforts
- Benefits of the brand or brands associated with the franchise, and landscape of competing brands

- Any growth option in the brand or variants of the brand
- Any growth option for new franchisees, such as rights to emerging markets
- Risk that the brand itself may decline or the franchisor may cease doing business

The relative importance of these elements is discussed in Table 17.3.

SPORTS FRANCHISES

Private Businesses and Civic Institutions

Most sports franchises are private businesses. However, many occupy a place in American society quite close to civic institutions. This status has given major league sports franchises access to direct and indirect taxpayer subsidies, and even a *de facto* exemption from the major antitrust laws.

Major revenue sources of a sports franchise are ticket and luxury suite sales; advertisement and sponsorship income; media rights; sales of licensed products such as jerseys, hats, and T-shirts; and other royalty income. Major expense items of a sports franchise are salaries of players, stadium and other facility costs, nonplayer employee salaries, advertising, and meal and travel expenses.

Some authors assert that the value of sports franchises is not determined in the same manner as that of other businesses. For example, Soonhwan Lee and Hyosung Chun presented this argument in a 2002 article in *Sport Journal*:

> Unlike industrial or financial business, which is generally valued on cash flow and assets, sport franchises are valued on their revenues. There are two reasons for this. First, in the long term, the operating expenses within each league are about the same for every team. Second, revenues most closely measure the quality of a team's venue and track athletic performance, ultimately the two most critical elements in team evaluation (Ozanian, 1994). Professional sport team values have risen over the past decade and are expected to rise to unpredictable levels for the next few years. The reasons for this rise are the revenues from the leagues, including gate receipts, broadcasting right fees, luxury boxes, club seats, concessions, advertising and membership fees. (Lee and Chun, 2002)

Other economists reject that argument, at least implicitly. For example, Phillip Miller (2006) makes a conventional claim that the value of a sports franchise is simply the discounted expected future stream of profits.

> Suppose the owner and prospective buyer are negotiating over the sale price of a team. Both seek maximum profits and both have perfect foresight. The owner would not rationally accept less than the present value of the team's future profit stream and the prospective buyer would not rationally pay more than the present value of the team's profit stream. If the owner and prospective buyer discount future returns at the same rate and the revenues and costs are the same under either ownership group, the sale price of the franchise equals the present value of its profit stream. Under the assumptions, the team's franchise value measures the present value of its profit stream.[7]

There are, however, substantial vagaries in these declarative statements, including whether the value in question is merely a rule of thumb for discussion purposes or an actual market value.[8] To some extent, the looseness of the term *value* when applied to sports franchises is simply an extension to the general vagueness of the term we lamented in Chapter 1, "Modern Value Quandaries."

Estimates: *Forbes* Values

Two well-known publications have published estimates of sports franchise values on a regular basis in the United States: *Financial World* magazine and *Forbes* magazine. It appears that both relied heavily on the work of one researcher, Michael Ozanian, to develop their estimates. The published *Forbes* estimates have been accompanied by considerable data, including indicators of revenue from various business enterprises associated with a sports team, information on television and royalty revenue, and player salaries. Furthermore, they have been published on an annual basis for a number of years, during which some market transactions also occurred. Although no specific methodology has been claimed for these various estimates, it appears that professional judgment is the dominant factor.

The *Forbes* estimates have become public benchmarks of value, even though they are not market values and in some cases are hotly disputed by both the owners of the specific teams and the leagues. In the case of Major League Baseball, the league has a track record of "lambasting" the estimates.[9] Certainly, the release of bits and pieces of information on privately held firms can misportray the actual finances of a club.[10] The same, of course, is true of selective reading of similar data by others involved in the sports industry, including players' unions, local sports committees, municipalities, and stadium authorities. The tension in the industry between these parties, especially at times when contracts or stadium leases are being negotiated, colors many of the public statements on team finances.

Evidence from Actual Transactions

U.S. Sports Teams

A handful of recorded transactions involving U.S. teams provide a basis from which to compare estimates with actual market values and to consider whether a naive income method works well for such firms. The sale of the Boston Red Sox in 2002 was one example. In this case, a naive income method would have implied little worth in the apparently money-losing club, while the professional judgment method used by *Forbes* correctly implied a value in the hundreds of millions.[11]

Geckil and Anderson (2007) compiled data on a set of U.S. major league franchises for which published value estimates and transaction prices were available and adjusted several of the reported transaction prices to make them comparable with the estimates. Their data support the notion that a naive income method fails to predict actual transaction values and instead suggest that other factors (including those identified by the *Forbes* researchers) were in play. However, for most of the transactions, the previously published estimate differed from the transaction price by a significant margin. They conclude that at least three factors account for this degree of variation:

1. There is a powerful "ego factor" at work in these transactions, implying that team owners are paying for more than future earnings.[12]

2. The *Forbes* estimates appeared to take into account winning percentage. However, Anderson and Geckil propose an explicit "contender factor," which is discussed further below.[13]

3. Sports team finances are clouded by arrangements for stadium leasing, parking and other concessions, league revenue sharing, and other factors, thus making the transaction prices less than completely observable.

These issues are in addition to the normal difficulties in estimating the value of private firms.

European Sports Franchises

Unlike U.S. major league sports franchises, many European franchises are publicly traded. This provides a transparent data source on franchise values. Anderson and Geckil (2007) used data on market capitalization of these organizations to test a hypothesis that "sportive performance" as well as current earnings affects the value of a sports franchise.[14] They conclude that there is a strong relationship between a team's performance in recent seasons and the current value of the sports team. They identify a "contender factor" separate from average winning percentage, and assert that investors appear more interested in a franchise that consistently has a chance to win a league or conference championship than one with a similar average winning percentage.

Case Study: The Chicago Cubs

The same researchers, along with a Chicago-area collaborator, undertook a similar study of the Chicago Cubs baseball team in 2007. At that time, the team invested significantly in new playing talent and upgrades to the venerable Wrigley Field ballpark.[15] They predicted that the club, strengthened enough to be a contender for the league pennant, would be worth $600 million—a significant increment over the previously available estimate from *Forbes*.

The same report also listed potential buyers, one of which later purchased the Tribune Company, owner of the Cubs franchise in Chicago, for $8.3 billion.[16] The sale price included many more assets than the Cubs sports teams, including the stadium and media interests. By January 2009, the Cubs baseball team along with related assets, including Wrigley Field, was sold for $900 million. If one deducts about $250 million from this sales price for Wrigley Field as a separate entity, the implied 2009 sale price of $650 million closely corroborates the 2007 value estimate for the team alone.

18 APPLICATIONS: LAW AND ECONOMICS

In this chapter, we consider the effect of government policy on business decisions, and the use of valuation techniques to estimate damages incurred due to breaches of contracts and violations of laws governing commerce and property rights. In contemporary terms, this chapter deals with the field of law and economics. In classical terms, it would be within the field of political economy.

Policy Evaluation: Government Policies and Business Hiring Decisions

The first application is to examine the effect of government policies on business decisions. In particular, we examine whether government policies that may increase labor costs in the future discourage employers from hiring workers. We use both the traditional neoclassical economics model and the value functional model, and discover that they suggest quite different responses by private employers.

Economic Damages

The second application is the estimation of economic damages, which is a topic at the intersection of business, valuation, and the law. In this chapter, we do the following:

- Briefly survey many centuries of laws on economic damages.
- Review the modern doctrine of economic damages arising from breaches of contract and other causes. Such losses when incurred by businesses are commonly called *commercial damages*.
- Suggest valuation methods for estimating different categories of commercial damages.

Intellectual Property

The third application is the extraction of the value of *intellectual property* (IP), which has become increasingly important in the modern economy. In this chapter, we do the following:

- Outline categories of intellectual property by the legal mechanisms that can secure rights to the property, including patents, trademarks and copyrights.

- Discuss briefly the importance of intellectual property in valuing a firm.

- Provide advice on methods of estimating commercial damages due to the infringement of intellectual property.

GOVERNMENT POLICY AND HIRING DECISIONS

An Admonition; An Opportunity

Economic models are effective tools for policy evaluation only when they reflect the actual incentives of the people who are affected by the policy. Too often, economic models (as well as those originating in other social sciences) miss the actual incentives of the relevant people and instead focus on aggregate responses of the broader economy and the effect on large government institutions.[1] Policy evaluation should be approached with this admonition in mind: whenever you use an economic model to evaluate a government policy, be sure you have captured the incentives of those affected by the policy.

The development of the value functional model presents an opportunity to evaluate policies in a manner that preserves a much richer mix of incentives, fixed costs, information asymmetries, and other factors than allowed by traditional models. Much of this benefit stems from the recursive nature of the underlying behavior, which matches the manner in which human beings make decisions. More of the benefit comes from the greater amount of information processed in the model, again compared with a standard model. In this chapter, we demonstrate the use of the value functional model of the firm to analyze questions of public policy.[2]

The Problem of Persistent Unemployment

The causes of persistent unemployment are a matter of longstanding debate in the economics profession. For more than two centuries, classical, neoclassical, Keynesian, monetarist, and real business cycle theorists have introduced competing theories on the topic.[3]

The Great Recession of the late 2000s challenged economic orthodoxy once again. In the United States, it triggered dramatic federal intervention in the economy. However, such intervention failed to arrest persistent high unemployment in the first years of the recovery, even as inflation and interest rates remained historically low, government expenditures surged, and neither commodity prices nor trade and tax policies changed dramatically. This led to a wide-ranging political and economic debate over the causes of persistent unemployment and the best policies to combat it. We consider one hypothesis for a cause, from both neoclassical and value functional approaches.

The policy uncertainty hypothesis asserts that government policies that threaten to impose substantial cost burdens on employers discourage private-sector employers from hiring workers because of uncertainty about future cost burdens. Unfortunately, the standard neoclassical model of firm behavior fails to adequately capture how policy uncertainty affects business decisions. (We describe this model in some detail in Chapter 8, "Value in

Neoclassical Economics.") In particular, the neoclassical model assumes that managers solve one-period optimization problems in complete markets. Such models do not incorporate uncertainties that are not spanned or priced in the real or financial markets, but that nonetheless affect management decisions. Clearly, current costs affect the profit-maximizing decision of business managers in a neoclassical world. However, the neoclassical model fails to contemplate incentives for firms to expand or delay expansion of their operations because of uncertainty about *future* costs of employing workers, when such costs are not reflected in current market prices.

Testing the Hypothesis with a Value Functional Model

Theoretically, the value functional model of the firm captures a broader array of the actual risks faced by the business manager, and includes a mechanism for a rational response to those risks. In the value functional model, a manager observes important events (such as changes in political trends and likely future economic policies) and reacts to them in a rational manner. Those reactions are intended to maximize the value of the firm, even if they are contrary to the profit-maximizing principle of the neoclassical model, or are based on risks that cannot be handled by the complete-market model.

We outline next a methodology to test the policy uncertainty hypothesis, using a value functional model of the firm. This methodology also indirectly tests whether a value functional model can capture incentives faced by business managers that are not reflected in market prices, and hence would be missed by neoclassical and complete-market models.

Specifying the Model
The essence of the model is the specification of multiple states reflecting different government policies and scales of operation, with the latter reflecting past hiring decisions by the firm and the former outside the control of the manager. We then consider two different policy regimes represented by two different sets of transition probabilities. These reflect a baseline uncertainty regarding government policy, and an alternative uncertainty incorporating a higher chance of government-imposed costs remaining in place in the future.

These are shown in the following exhibit and tables:

1. The model of a representative firm is described in Exhibit 18.1.

2. The likelihood of the next state, given the current state and the action of the firm, is summarized in a transition probability matrix for two different policy regimes: a baseline case and an alternative persistent-cost case. These are presented in Table 18.1 later in this chapter.

3. The income that the firm could expect to earn in each state of affairs, for each possible action by the firm in that state, is contained in a reward matrix presented in Table 18.2 later in this chapter.

Running the Model

First, we attempt to find a solution to the question of the value-maximizing actions for the representative firm, in each possible state, using the baseline transition probability

EXHIBIT 18.1
Value Functional Model: Unemployment and Uncertainty

1. *State vector s.* The state consists of current economic conditions (including the economic burden of current government policies) and the current employment level for the firm.

   In this model, we use four-element state vectors to capture all combinations of high and low policy costs, as well as big and small scale.

2. *Action vector x.* The subject company has three elements within its action set: hiring workers, keeping the same number of workers, and laying workers off. These directly affect the scale of the firm. We also assume that the firm cannot control government policy.

3. *Reward matrix R.* The reward matrix represents the reward of distributed profits and capital gains to the shareholders of the firm while operating in each possible combination of state and action. As the state vector is size $S = 4$, and the action vector is size $A = 3$, the reward matrix must be size $S \times A = 4 \times 3$.

4. *Transition probability matrix P.* The transition function controls how the state changes over time, including the effect of decisions (actions) taken by the firm's manager and random elements. In this case, the firm's action to hire, or not hire, directly affects the scale of the firm's operations, which is part of the state vector. We assume a random distribution of policies, which in the baseline is centered on the current policy.

5. *Discount factor β.* We use a discount rate that is consistent with equity returns from publicly traded firms, the likely form of ownership for small and medium-sized firms, and a trend growth rate in the economy. We assume $0 < \beta < 1$.

6. *Optimization problem.* The firm optimizes the following value functional equation, which is a two-period Bellman equation:

$$V(s) = \max_{x \in \Gamma} \left\{ R(s,\ x) + \beta \left[V(E(S_{t+1})) \right] \right\}$$

$$E(S_{t+1}) = E[P(s_{t+1} \mid s_t,\ x_t)]]$$

The rational manager observes the states s_t and chooses an action x_t to maximize the sum of this period's reward $R(s_t, x_t)$ and the next period's expected, discounted value. The rational manager knows that the next period's state (and hence the next period's value) depends on the actions taken this period and random events. These transition probabilities are summarized in the P matrix. Note that restricting the maximization of x to feasible values ($x \in \Gamma$) rules out extreme and implausible choices, such as selling all the assets on the last day of the year.

matrix, which affects the baseline policy regime. Although not shown here, the plausible assumptions incorporated in the representative firm's income statement and discount rates ensure the existence of this solution.

We then run the analysis a second time with the transition matrix that reflects the persistent-cost policy regime and compare the results as follows:

1. First, examine the value of the firm in each state across the two regimes. Recall that we do not change the reward matrix or the discount factor, so the profits of the firm in each state-action pair are exactly the same. Therefore, the profit-maximizing policies in each state are also the same. This is the result implied by the standard neoclassical model. Furthermore, the capitalized future profits of the firm, assuming a continuation of the current state and action pair, also remain the same.

This is an indirect test of the value functional method. If, as would be implied by the neoclassical investment rule, there is no difference between the values of the firm under the two (transition probability) regimes, then the value functional method has no power to improve on the neoclassical model.

2. Second, examine the optimum policy in each state and compare them across the two regimes. This is a similar indirect test of the value functional method.

3. Directly test the policy uncertainty hypothesis. If the optimum policy in low-cost states remains the same under both regimes (as would be the case in a neoclassical, profit-maximizing model), then the results do not support the hypothesis. If it changes from *hire* to *maintain* or *lay off*, then it supports the hypothesis.

Transition Probabilities

The transition function accepts as arguments the current state, current action, and any random elements; it produces the next period's state. In Exhibit 18.1, the transition function was implicitly shown as part of the expectation of the manager for the next period's value.

As we have specified the state and action spaces in discrete terms, the transition function in this case is a transition matrix. Here, we need a probability of reaching each state from the current state, for each possible action. That implies a transition matrix of size $S \times S \times A$, which in this case is $3 \times 3 \times 4$.[4] As these are probabilities, the sum of each row (which indicates the probability of moving to other states from one current state, given one current action) must equal 1, and no element can be negative. The transition matrix for the baseline policy regime is shown in Table 18.1.

For example, if the action is to maintain (Frame 2) and the current state is high cost/small scale (second row), the probability of remaining in that state is 80 percent (second column). However, if the action is to hire (Frame 3), the second row indicates an 80 percent chance of moving to high cost/big scale and a 20 percent chance of moving to low cost/big scale.

For the persistent-cost policy regime, a similar transition matrix (with probabilities weighted toward high-cost states persisting over time) was used. In that matrix, the probability of high-cost states persisting was 95 percent rather than 80 percent.

TABLE 18.1
Baseline policy regime transition matrix

	HB	HS	LB	LS
FRAME 1: LAY OFF				
HB	0	0.8	0	0.2
HS	0	0.8	0	0.2
LB	0	0.2	0	0.8
LS	0	0.2	0	0.8
FRAME 2: MAINTAIN				
HB	0.8	0	0.2	0
HS	0	0.8	0	0.2
LB	0.2	0	0.8	0
LS	0	0.2	0	0.8
FRAME 3: HIRE				
HB	0.8	0	0.2	0
HS	0.8	0	0.2	0
LB	0.2	0	0.8	0
LS	0.2	0	0.8	0

NOTE: Each row is a current state, each column is a next-period state, and each frame represents the result of one action.

Policy Intuition

The policy intuition behind this model is based on the experience of business managers with government-imposed cost burdens. In the United States and many other democratic countries, business managers are familiar with a cycle of events that result in government policies that fluctuate over time. In this case, we focus on the United States after 2008, when a serious recession coincided with the election of a new president and supportive congressional majority, who enacted laws that created a national health care system and expanded state unemployment insurance benefits. However, income tax rates—a standard indicator of policy direction and a direct cost burden for employees and employers—did not change dramatically. Furthermore, the costs of the national health care policy and expanded unemployment insurance benefits were not immediately imposed on employers and were subject to considerable uncertainty.[5]

We distilled these observations into two policy regimes:

1. A baseline regime, reflecting a view that government-imposed cost burdens would fluctuate over time. Such a view is roughly consistent, for example, with the fluctuations in federal income tax rates in the United States between 1950 and 2010.

2. A persistent-cost regime, reflecting a view that once government programs imposing payroll burdens on employers are created, the likelihood that the costs would be eliminated in the future is very small. Such a view is roughly consistent with the gradual expansion of Social Security, Medicare, and unemployment insurance programs in the United States during the same time period mentioned earlier. It is also consistent with the structure of the national health insurance program enacted in the United States in 2010.[6] Thus, at least some employers presumably adjusted their

view of the policy regime from the baseline (fluctuating-cost) view to the persistent-cost view, around the year 2010.

Note that both policy regimes were modeled as probabilistic statements about future cost burdens, and not as different cost burdens. Thus, the profit-maximizing decision of an employer in any one time period would be the same under both regimes. The value-maximizing decision, and the value of the business, however, could be different.

Reward Matrix

The reward matrix incorporates the distributable profits of the firm for each combination of state and action. This means the R matrix is size $S \times A = 4 \times 3$. We used the following method to generate the R matrix:

1. For the baseline we selected the *maintain current employment* action in the *low policy cost* states. Here we used the profit of a representative profitable medium-sized firm in the United States, which could choose to hire more workers and operate at a larger scale. Assuming continued low policy costs, the representative firm would expect to earn larger profits after absorbing some costs of expansion.

2. For *high policy cost* states, we adjusted for higher costs of employing workers, again for the *maintain* action.

3. From these entries (which formed the center column of the R matrix) we created the *hire* and *lay off* action columns, with the adjustments reflecting the costs or savings from doing these actions, and the costs being higher under the *high policy cost* states.

The reward matrix is shown in Table 18.2. Here the matrix size is $S \times A$ and each row is a current state, each column a current action. For example, if the current state is *low cost/small scale* (fourth row) and the action is *maintain* (second column), the reward is 65.

Results

The results of the analysis are summarized in Table 18.3. We used both a value function iteration and a policy iteration algorithm to solve for the value function of the firm in each possible state. The same solution provided an optimum policy for the firm's manager in

TABLE 18.2
Reward matrix

	Lay off	Maintain	Hire
HB	$47	$50	$45
HS	$47	$50	$45
LB	$65	$75	$65
LS	$55	$65	$60

NOTE: State space is $s = \{HB, HS, LB, LS\}$ where H and L mean high and low costs, and B and S mean big and small scale.

TABLE 18.3
Results

State	V_{vfi}	V_{pi}	p_{vfi}	p_{pi}
TRANSITION MATRIX: BASELINE FLUCTUATING COST				
HB (high cost, big scale)	$516.6	$516.6	2	2
HS (high cost, small scale)	$511.6	$511.6	3	3
LB (low cost, big scale)	$569.9	$569.9	2	2
LS (low cost, small scale)	$554.9	$554.9	3	3
TRANSITION MATRIX: PERSISTENT COST				
HB (high cost, big scale)	$463.2	$463.2	2	2
HS (high cost, small scale)[a]	$459.0	$459.0	2	2
LB (low cost, big scale)	$537.5	$537.6	2	2
LS (low cost, small scale)	$522.5	$522.6	3	3

NOTES: $g = 0.03$; $d = 0.16$; rho $= 0.13$; beta $= 0.88496$.
[a] Indicates a switch in optimum action between two policy regimes.
vfi = value function iteration; pi = policy iteration; p = policy; V = value
Policy 2 is "maintain employment"; policy 3 is "hire workers."

each state. We completed this analysis for the baseline and persistent-cost regimes. These results proved robust to minor changes in the discount rate and implicit transaction costs in the reward matrix.[7]

These results confirm the intuition that the value of profitable firms is not destroyed by policy fluctuations that affect the profitability of the firm, but not the foundations of its operations. This can be seen by the fact that the firm has value in every state and both policy regimes, given that the reward matrix shows positive profits in every state-action pair.

However, the value of the firm is clearly lower in the persistent-cost regime than in the baseline regime. This decline in value—which would typically not be revealed in any one period's income statement—is a real loss in wealth for the business owner. Furthermore, the loss in value could affect the owner's ability to finance current operations, and almost certainly reduces the ability to finance future expansions. This is one avenue through which policy uncertainty negatively affects hiring.

The results for optimum policy are also consistent with economic intuition. In the baseline case when costs are low, we expect the firm to hire workers, seeking to grow the scale of the firm. When costs are high, managers should maintain their workforce. The calculated optimum decisions reflect this value-maximizing objective. However, as can be observed from Table 18.2, the value-maximizing decision to hire is not the profit-maximizing decision.

In the alternative policy regime, in which managers expect that government-imposed costs are more likely to persist over time, the optimal policies are sometimes different. In particular, the optimal policy for a manager with a small scale and high costs is not to hire workers but instead to maintain the workforce as it is. (This is indicated in the table by a switch from optimum *action* = 3 to *action* = 2 under the two regimes.) This directly supports the policy uncertainty hypothesis: some firms will refuse to hire workers because of the risk of higher government-imposed costs in the future, even if such costs are not currently imposed on them.

It is interesting to observe that of the four possible states, the optimum policy switches for only one. This suggests that some firms are much more affected by policy uncertainty than others. Intuition suggests that the smaller firms, for whom the transition and compliance costs are more severe, would be more affected. If this is correct, it reinforces the severity of the policy-uncertainty problem, because these smaller firms are likely the ones that have the inclination to hire additional workers.

Note on Limitations

The focus in this chapter is on methodology, rather than results, so we have not fully discussed limitations, data sources, sensitivity tests, other potential causal factors, and alternative hypotheses. Two specific qualifications bear noting: First, the results support the existence and the direction of the policy uncertainty effect but do not indicate its magnitude or its duration. Second, we did not explore the degree to which business managers ascribe benefits to potential government-imposed policies that exceed their costs.

COMMERCIAL DAMAGES

Introduction

Ancient Commercial Damages Doctrines

The concept of damages paid to resolve disputes is at least as old as the Code of Hammurabi, which promised "an eye for an eye, a tooth for a tooth."[8] Although sometimes seen today as a code of revenge, in fact the Code of Hammurabi was a relatively civilized notion, in which damages were allowed only in compensatory magnitude.[9] This contrasted with the cycle of revenge and blood feuds that had allowed—and tragically still does allow—an escalation of violence that claims more and more innocents.

Hammurabi's Code also dealt with what we might call commercial damages. Sections 53 through 59 of the Code, translated into English, state the following:

> 53. If any one be too lazy to keep his dam in proper condition, and does not so keep it; if then the dam break and all the fields be flooded, then shall he in whose dam the break occurred be sold for money, and the money shall replace the [grain] which he has caused to be ruined.

> 54. If he be not able to replace the [grain], then he and his possessions shall be divided among the farmers whose corn he has flooded.

> 55. If any one open his ditches to water his crop, but is careless, and the water flood the field of his neighbor, then he shall pay his neighbor corn for his loss.

> 56. If a man let in the water, and the water overflow the plantation of his neighbor, he shall pay ten *gur* of corn for every ten *gan* of land.

> 57. If a shepherd, without the permission of the owner of the field, and without the knowledge of the owner of the sheep, lets the sheep into a field to graze, then the owner of the field shall harvest his crop, and the shepherd, who had pastured his flock there without permission of the owner of the field, shall pay to the owner twenty *gur* of corn for every ten *gan* [of land].

58. If after the flocks have left the pasture and been shut up in the common fold at the city gate, any shepherd let them into a field and they graze there, this shepherd shall take possession of the field which he has allowed to be grazed on, and at the harvest he must pay sixty *gur* of corn for every ten *gan*.

59. If any man, without the knowledge of the owner of a garden, fell a tree in a garden he shall pay half a *mina* in money.[10]

Other ancient moral codes, such as the biblical book of Exodus, also contain statements requiring compensatory payments by those that immorally caused damages to another's property or body.[11]

Commercial Damages: Current Era

In the current era, the classical period of Roman law (from AD 1 to AD 250) led to the famous *Corpus Juris Civilis* ("Body of Civil Law") of the Byzantine emperor Justinian I, proclaimed from 529 to 534.[12] Among many other facets of the Justinian Code were limits on the recovery for debt and provisions for the enforcement of contracts, including monetary and in-kind damages.[13]

Early codes outside Europe include the *Arthashastra* by the Indian sage Kautilya, which was written about AD 150. Kautilya outlines a law of contracts, limitations on pledges and mortgages, a system of accounts for a government, and the importance of strong administration and tax collection to the health of society and the preservation of the state. Kautilya, like Hammurabi and Justinian, did not envision a utopia; his rules of statecraft recognized human weaknesses. As in the Code of Hammurabi, the punishments were balanced with the severity of the crime, given the sentiments of the age. Kautilya also knew well the weaknesses of government officials; his work includes a schedule of "twenty-eight of the forty ways of stealing" in an extensive discourse on "Financial Misbehavior of Government Servants."[14]

Modern Commercial Damages Doctrines

The critical doctrine of compensation for lost property and loss of the ability to enjoy the property was illustrated in the founding documents of the United States. England's lack of compensation for quartering soldiers on the property of colonial citizens was a grievance stated in the Declaration of Independence of 1776.[15] In 1789, compensation for property confiscated by the government was fixed into the U.S. Constitution.[16]

Compensation for damages suffered—even when the perpetrator is a sovereign government—was a revolutionary concept in the eighteenth century. It still generates resistance today.

"Making Whole" and Compensatory Damages

English Common Law Tradition

In the previous section, we discussed the long history of economic damages in the human experience. Almost all of the early history took place in parts of the world we now consider to be in the East or in the Middle East. In this section, we consider economic damages from the perspective of the English legal tradition.[17]

The Principle of Making Whole

The fundamental principle of commercial damages is *making whole* the wronged party. If one person was wrongly deprived of the benefits of their work or their possessions, what would compensate them sufficiently to make their situation equivalent to what it would have been without the wrongful action?

Compensatory and Exemplary Damages

Making whole means compensating for the loss but not punishing the wrongdoer. This is known as *compensatory* damages, in contrast to *punitive, vindictive,* or *exemplary* damages. This distinction is longstanding. For example, the 1856 *Law Dictionary*, sixth edition, by John Bouvier states:

> Damages for torts are either compensatory or vindictive. By compensatory damages is meant such as are given morely to recompense a party who has sustained a loss in consequence of the acts of the defendant, and where there are no circumstances to aggravate the act, for the purpose of compensating the plaintiff for his loss.[18]

Throughout this chapter, we consider compensatory damages, unless directly addressing the issue of deterrence arising from exemplary damages.[19]

LEGAL BASIS FOR CLAIMING ECONOMIC DAMAGES

We briefly discuss in this section important principles in U.S. common law for economic damages. Of course, this is primarily an economic treatise on value, and therefore the discussion of legal principles will be limited to what is necessary to establish a logical foundation.

Three Key Legal Criteria for Economic Damages

In order to claim economic damages because of a specific event under contemporary U.S. legal doctrine, the claim must generally satisfy three criteria:

1. The proximate cause of the damages must be the specific event.[20]
2. The parties must be able to foresee that the event would have caused damages.
3. The fact of damages must be proved with reasonable certainty.[21]

Thus, the modern doctrine—proximate cause, foreseeability, and establishment with reasonable certainty—refines the question that Bouvier in 1856 stated must be handled on a "case ruled by its own circumstances" basis. In particular, damages that may have been peripheral consequences, but were not proximately caused by the specific event in question or that could not have been foreseen by the parties, are often considered by courts to be too remote to justify damages.

In the discussions of methods that follow, we assume that the event, breach of contract, or other action by a person fulfills the operative legal requirement for causing economic damages.

Commercial Damages Methods: Operational Losses

Breaches of contract, or events such as floods, fires, power outages, strikes, and shutdowns, may damage a firm that was planning to operate but was prevented from doing so because of the specific cause of damages. We classify these damages as operational losses.

Concept of Losses: Lost Profits or Diminished Value?

The damages suffered by an operating firm can often be measured as lost profits or as diminished value. In certain simple cases, these are identical. However, it would be a mistake to conclude that lost profits is always the same as diminished value for a firm that suffers damages; this is a complement to the failure of the neoclassical investment rule. One easy example of this is the losses suffered by a firm that is prevented from operating at all; one may claim that the firm never had profits and therefore could not "lose" any of them. However, it is abundantly clear that preventing a company from beginning operations deprives it of much of the value of the firm.

It is worth considering this question carefully when approaching a commercial damages issue.

Concept of Damages: Mitigation

An important (and sometimes overlooked) principle of commercial damages is the doctrine of mitigation. This doctrine requires the injured party to take reasonable steps to limit the damages incurred due to the specific cause. For example, a company that was prevented from operating because of a fire would be expected to take immediate steps to prevent additional damage and to begin restoring operations. If the injured party fails to mitigate its damages, the court may limit the amount of compensation.

COMMERCIAL DAMAGES: LOSS OF INTELLECTUAL PROPERTY

Firms and Intellectual Property

When you define a firm in the strict manner of this book, the intellectual property of the firm is at least partially integrated into the value of the firm.[22] First, the separate legal identity and profit motive for investors implies that the business has some sort of brand or image that the company managers attempt to promote and maintain. Second, the replicable business practices often are unique (or at least individualized) to the firm, and usually one basis for the firm's attempts to earn a competitive advantage over other providers in the same industry. These processes are often intellectual property, even if they are not patentable or trademarked.

Using this concept of the firm, many kinds of practices and intangible assets could be considered important in a business, and the property of a business. Thus, important intellectual property (or "IP") should be considered part of the state space for many firms, and investing in research and development part of their action spaces.

Constitutional Basis for Intellectual Property Rights

The importance of preserving the rights of "Authors and Inventors" to "their respective Writings and Discoveries" was recognized in the U.S. Constitution of 1789, in Article I, Section 8. This constitutional provision is the foundation of legal protections for intellectual property in the United States.

Securing these property rights should be considered part of the institutional factors essential to the operation of a firm, which we discussed in Chapter 4, "The Nature of the Firm." The continuing effort by the United States and European Community nations to enforce IP rights in countries around the world is evidence of the continuing importance of such institutional factors.

Patents

Patents convey a legal monopoly to the owner, giving him or her the exclusive right to market and sell his or her specific invention over a period of years in the country granting the patent.[23] The U.S. Patent Office defines a patent as follows:

What Is a Patent?

A patent for an invention is the grant of a property right to the inventor, issued by the Patent and Trademark Office. The term of a new patent is 20 years from the date on which the application for the patent was filed in the United States or, in special cases, from the date an earlier related application was filed, subject to the payment of maintenance fees. US patent grants are effective only within the US, US territories, and US possessions.

The right conferred by the patent grant is, in the language of the statute and of the grant itself, "the right to exclude others from making, using, offering for sale, or selling" the invention in the United States or "importing" the invention into the United States. What is granted is not the right to make, use, offer for sale, sell or import, but the right to exclude others from making, using, offering for sale, selling or importing the invention. (U.S. Patent Office, *General Information Concerning Patents*, January 2005)

In the United States, *utility patents*—which include most common inventions of machines and manufacturing devices or processes—generally offer protection for twenty years. Through the Patent Cooperation Treaty, U.S. utility patents may be protected in many other countries that are parties to the Treaty. Patents are available only to original inventions. These inventions must be "novel," "unobvious," and "useful."[24]

Before granting a patent, the U.S. Patent Office performs research to determine whether there is *prior art*, or evidence that a similar device or invention has already been in use. However, patent searches do not always discover all prior art, and the determination whether a product infringes on a patent may be made by a court.

Damages in Patent Cases

There are two common measures of damages in cases where a patent has been infringed. They are explicitly contemplated in the U.S. statute governing patent damages:

Upon finding for the claimant the court shall award the claimant damages adequate to compensate for the infringement but in no event less than a reasonable royalty for the use made of the invention by the infringer, together with interest and costs as fixed by the court. (35 U.S.C. § 284)

The determination of an appropriate "reasonable royalty" is generally left to the trial court, and expert testimony is often necessary to establish a reasonable royalty. If an injured party meets certain additional tests—particularly those requiring it to be able to manufacture and sell its product—it may be entitled to lost profits. In general, lost profits *for an operating, profitable firm* are higher than a reasonable royalty on the product the firm is manufacturing and selling. However, this may not be the case when demand for the product is not established, or where the firm is not operating in a stable industry or under regular conditions.

In the United States, two seminal cases are often cited as providing guidance on estimating damages for loss of intellectual property. The first is the 1971 *Georgia-Pacific Corp. v. United States Plywood Corp.* decision, which listed eighteen factors experts should consider when estimating a reasonable royalty.[25] The second is the 1978 *Panduit v. Stahlin Bros.* decision, in which damages of lost profits were allowed under somewhat restrictive conditions.[26] However, neither case provides a road map to the proper estimation of commercial damages in every circumstance, and the mere recitation of these factors by an expert does not make a damages estimate reasonable.

Brands, Trademarks, Trade Secrets, and Other Intellectual Property

Patents are one instrument for securing intellectual property rights. However, other categories of intellectual property bear noting. These include brands, trademarks, and trade secrets. The value of such items often depends heavily on their use in business and the uniqueness and degree of advantage that the particular intellectual property brings the owner. For some such property, there is a particular statute that sets forth the requirements for establishing ownership and a remedy for breaching intellectual property rights of the owner. The U.S. Lanham Act is one such statute for trademarks.[27] Copyrights are also separately protected under specific laws.[28]

For other forms of intellectual property, such as brands that are not adequately protected solely by trademark rights, a more general examination of the industry, laws, and contracts may be required to identify the important intellectual property assets and the potential ways to secure their protection.

METHODS OF ESTIMATING COMMERCIAL DAMAGES

Valuation Methods in General

In general, the methods that can be used to estimate the *loss of value* to a firm are the same as those that can estimate the value of a firm. When the measure of damages is diminished value, this is conceptually straightforward: the difference in the value immediately before the breach of contract (or other cause) and after the breach is the amount that would make the business owner whole.

Therefore, all of the valuation methods described in this book are also potential methods of estimating commercial damages. Of course, each of these has advantages and disadvantages in general and may or may not fit the facts and circumstances of a particular case.

Summary of Advice: Useful Commercial Damages Methods

Table 18.4 summarizes advice on useful damages methods for three categories of damages that may be incurred by an operating firm:

1. Those arising from a breach of contract
2. Those arising from a breach of intellectual property rights
3. Those arising from violations of antitrust law

TABLE 18.4

Usefulness of methods for estimating commercial damages incurred by operating firms

	Breach of contract	Intellectual property	Antitrust
Risk-neutral and arbitrage methods	Unlikely to be useful, except for traded commodities and financial instruments	Unlikely to be useful	Unlikely to be useful, except for traded commodities and financial instruments
Traditional income methods, including DCF	Very useful where income and expense apportionment is possible; often relies heavily on professional judgment	Useful for "lost profits" and "reasonable royalty" measures in patent cases; may be used for trade secrets; case law in the United States suggests "factors" to consider in such matters	May be useful in consumer overcharge cases, and to measure of excess profits; note that evidence in such cases is often lacking and estimation is often difficult
Asset methods	Unlikely to be useful except for disposal of assets or commodities	Unlikely to be useful, unless a strong relationship exists between "book" and market values	Unlikely to be useful, except for infractions involving short-turn-around commodities
Market methods	Often most useful method if bona fide comparables are available; usually they are not	Often most useful method if bona fide comparables are available; usually they are not	Often very useful
Financial or real options; decision tree analysis; Monte Carlo	May be the best available method where breaches cause the business to become impaired or where the chain of events cannot be evaluated in another manner	IP is often a "real option"; DTA may encompass operations and real options	Unlikely to be useful, except in cases where business is terminated or severely impaired, or when market entry is prevented
Value functional	Useful where income and potential actions can be identified; can usually incorporate mitigation directly	Useful where the IP is integral to the operations of the business, or where sustained R&D investment is important	May be useful, but is often more difficult than other useful methods when market price data are available

NOTE: See caution in text regarding specific cases.

Of course, the best methodology for an expert to use in any particular case will depend on the facts of the case, the relevant legal doctrines, and the available data. The table focuses on methods that are commonly useful, and those that are not, for these three categories of damages.

Note on Causality, Historical, and Accounting Records

Recall that the existence of commercial damages depends on proving causality. Therefore, accounting records and other historical records alone rarely establish the amount of damages. However, an expert typically must review some accounting records to establish a baseline of operating performance for the subject firm, along with other sources of information necessary for a valuation of the subject company. (See Chapter 14, "Practical Application of the Income Method," on this topic.) The need to identify causality often dictates a focused examination of one category of information, which may or may not be part of a typical information set for a firm of that type.

Commercial Damages: Lost Opportunities to Begin Operations

The Traditional and Modern New Business Rule

One of the most difficult tasks for an expert in commercial damages is to estimate the value of a business that is just starting operations. For many decades in the United States, the traditional *new business rule* prevented the award of damages on the basis of future lost profits for such firms, on the basis that any forecast of future profits for an unestablished business was speculative. This was an obvious logical error; *every* successful business was a new business at one point. Fortunately, U.S. courts have moved sharply away from the traditional rule on this topic. What might be called the modern new business rule now allows for the recovery of damages in cases where a fledgling business is interrupted or otherwise damaged because of a breach of contract or other cause.[29] In general, the modern new business rule focuses on evidentiary sufficiency, rather than on history, to prove damages.

Potential Methods

In the context of this modern rule, we suggest in Chapter 17, "Applications: Finance and Valuation," under the section titled "Start-Up Firms," certain methods that are likely to be useful in the valuation of newly established firms.

Authorities on Commercial Damages

The measurement and estimation of commercial damages is a specialized topic that requires knowledge of both the economics of business and the law of commercial damages.

A handful of authorities cover these topics directly. These include Gaughan (2004, 2009) and Anderson (2004a). Other references on valuation that contain sections that deal with commercial damages include Hitchner (2003) and S. Pratt (2008, chap. 41). Anderson (2005b) covers new developments in the field. In the United States, the *Journal of Forensic Economics* discusses methodological issues in both commercial and personal damages. Dunn (2005) is a comprehensive summary of case law.

VII   APPENDICES

INTRODUCTION

Purpose

This appendix compiles the symbols, operators, and other notational conventions used throughout the book. It also serves as a handy reference for key formulas used throughout the book. This appendix is not intended as a reference guide. Substantial additional information is available to purchasers of this book in the *Solutions Manual and Reference for Economics of Business Valuation*. The contents of that volume, and instructions on acquiring it, are summarized in Appendix B, "Guide to the Solutions Manual."

Specific Notes on Ambiguous Concepts

This book draws from different literatures, each of which tends to use its own set of nomenclature and symbols. The author attempted to select only one meaning for each term and symbol, but for some concepts a complete avoidance of ambiguity was not possible. We address these shortly.

• *Symbol β and the term* beta. The Greek letter β is nearly universally used for a specific purpose in corporate finance, another purpose in mathematical finance, and yet another in control theory literature. In general, the symbol β implies a gross discount rate, and the term *beta* when describing a portfolio model has a specific meaning in that setting. See Equations A.8 and A.12.

• *Discount rate conventions.* Many variations of discount and interest rate symbols are in use in finance, accounting, and economics. To complicate matters, economists tend to use a symbol for gross return (and gross rate of discount) that is almost absent from the business management literature. We attempted to enforce a consistency on discounting and return symbols throughout the book. See Equation A.8 and Equation A.9.

• *Definition of* profit. Economists frequently use a single variable to describe the profit of a business. At the same time, the accounting and finance literature (and many professional valuation texts) contain a near-riot of acronyms for various measures of income and cash flow. These include such terms as net income, pretax income, NOPLAT, NCF, FCFF, and FCFE, not to mention at least three decompositions of EBITDA. (Some of these are described later in this appendix, under the section titled "Common Accounting and Finance Acronyms.")

Because this book focuses on value, we generally use the term *profit* to refer to the earnings of a firm that are available for distribution to the owners of the firm.

OPERATORS AND SYMBOLS

Equation A.1 Operators and Symbols

$\equiv$ is defined as

$=$ equals (as in an equation)

$\approx$ is approximately equal to

$\gg$ vector inequality; all elements are equal or greater, and at least one element is greater

$\cdot$ scalar multiplication, or vector dot product

$\sum\limits_{i=1}^{n} X_i$ sum of X_i from $i=1$ to $i=n$

$\int\limits_{a}^{b} f(x)\,dx$ Riemann integral of $f(x)$ from $x=a$ to $x=b$

$\int\limits_{\Omega} x\,dp$ Lebesgue integral of X over space Ω using measure P

$\forall$ for any; for all

$\exists$ there exists

$\in$ is a member of the set

$\varnothing$ empty set

$\dfrac{dy}{dx}$ derivative of y with respect to x

$\dfrac{\Delta y}{\Delta x}$ ratio of small change in y to small change in x

MICROECONOMICS; UTILITY

Equation A.2 Preferences

$A \succ B$ A is preferred to B

Preferences are the basis for utility theory. The following characteristics of utility functions implied by typical consumer and investor behavior are useful in the context of valuation theory. Further information on preferences and utility theory is available in the *Solutions Manual.*

Equation A.3 Useful Characteristics of Utility Functions

$u(c)$ utility of consumption c

$u'(c) > 0$ more consumption is desirable

$u'(0) = \infty$ consumers strenuously avoid starvation

$u''(c) < 0$ additional consumption provides diminishing marginal benefit

Note that we sometimes distinguish between "time-separable" utility (which implies that [properly discounted] income received in different periods is equally desirable) and "recursive" utility. (See Chapter 8, "Value in Neoclassical Economics," under the section titled "Time-Separable and Recursive Utility.")

Equation A.4 Euler Equation

$$u'(c_t)R^{-1} = E_t \beta u'(c_{t+1})$$

where:

$u'(c_t) \equiv$ marginal benefit from additional consumption at time t

$R^{-1} = \dfrac{1}{1+r}$ gross rate of return from net interest rate r

$\beta = \dfrac{1}{1+d}$ gross discount factor using net discount rate d

$E_t \equiv$ expectation given information at time t

The Euler equation summarizes the tension between receiving benefits in the current period and forgoing those benefits in anticipation of greater benefits received in the subsequent period. We sometimes describe this in conceptual terms as *Euler tension.*

REVENUE, COSTS & PROFIT

Equation A.5 Profits, Revenue, Costs

$R(a) \equiv$ revenue as a function of action a

$C(a) \equiv$ cost as a function of action a

$\pi = R(a) - C(a)$ profits equal revenue less costs

Note that the Greek symbol π is also used for probabilities in some settings. Note also the ambiguous usage of terms such as *earnings* and *profit* in various literatures, as discussed earlier.

Equation A.6 Marginal Revenue and Costs

$R'(a) - C'(a) \equiv$ marginal revenue minus marginal cost

$\quad \dfrac{d\pi}{da} \equiv$ marginal effect on profit of action a

The term *marginal cost* usually refers to marginal cost *per unit of volume*, although the term *marginal* means the first derivative with respect to any action.

CONSUMER BUDGET VARIABLES: PAYOFFS, RETURNS, AND DISCOUNTING

Equation A.7 Consumer Budget Variables

L_t gross payout on bonds at time t

$L_t > 0 \Rightarrow$ *borrowing*; $L_t < 0 \Rightarrow$ *lending*

N_t net equity shares purchased at time t

p_t price of each equity share at time t

A_t asset value at time t

B_t price of pure discount bond at time t

Equation A.8 Payoffs, Returns, Discounting

$\beta \; = \dfrac{1}{1+d}$ discount factor using net discount rate d

$R \; = \dfrac{x_{t+1}}{p_t}$ gross return on asset

$R^{-1} = \dfrac{1}{1+r}$ gross discount factor using net interest rate r

where:

$x_{t+1} \equiv$ payoff at time $t+1$

$x_{t+1} = p_{t+1} + y_{t+1}$

$p_{t+1} \equiv$ price of asset at time $t+1$

$y_{t+1} \equiv$ income on asset (e.g., dividend) at time $t+1$

Note: *Payoff* here is the total amount paid at a specific time by any security.

CASH FLOWS; SECURITIES AND PORTFOLIOS

Equation A.9 Bonds and Risk-Free Interest Rates

$B_t \equiv$ bond payoff at time t

$R^f = (1 + r^f)$ gross risk-free interest rate

$r^f \equiv$ net risk-free interest rate

This presumes the existence of a risk-free security with zero transaction costs, which can be bought and sold. This assumption may or may not be approximately true in various markets and time periods.

Equation A.10 Cash Flows, Net Present Value

$\{C\} = [C_1, ..., C_T]$ cash flows over time index $t = 1, ..., T$

$NPV(C) =$ net present value of cash flows $\{C\}$

$E[NPV(C)] =$ expected net present value of cash flows $\{C\}$

Equation A.11 Portfolios; Arrow-Pratt Tableau

$\eta = [\eta_1, ..., \eta_n]$ portfolios

$\eta_i =$ weight of security i in portfolio

$G = [g_{ij}] =$ payoff of security i, in state j (θ_j)

$$G = \begin{pmatrix} g_{11} & \cdots & g_{1n} \\ \vdots & \ddots & \vdots \\ g_{m1} & \cdots & g_{mn} \end{pmatrix} = \text{Arrow-Pratt Tableau}$$

PORTFOLIO MODELS

Equation A.12 Portfolio Model Variables and Parameters

R^W = gross return on total wealth portfolio

$R^W_{t+1} = \sum_{i=1}^{N} w_i R^i_{t+1}$; $w_i =$ portfolio weight for security i

W_t = wealth at time t

W^* = subjectively determined level of wealth

$\underline{W}$ = a minimum level of wealth

f_{t+1} = (undefined) factors that predict investment returns

a, b, γ, λ = parameters for portfolio models

β_i = regression coefficients on predictive factors

The use of the Greek letter β here conforms with the common practice in finance of using this as a regression coefficient, and as the shorthand symbol for the portfolio covariance coefficient in the CAPM and other factor models. However, the same letter is commonly used as a gross discount factor in economics, and is also used that way in this book. The italic letter f also appears in two fashions here: first as the symbol for a function, and second (again conforming to finance practice) for linear factors.

STOCHASTIC DISCOUNT FACTOR; BASIC PRICING EQUATION; STATE PRICES; RISK-NEUTRAL PROBABILITY

Equation A.13 Stochastic Discount Factor (SDF) or Pricing Kernel

$$m_{t+1} \equiv \beta \, \frac{u'(c_{t+1})}{u'(c_t)} \text{ stochastic discount factor or pricing kernel}$$

The variables on the right hand side of this equation are described earlier in this appendix, under the sections titled "Microeconomics; Utility" and "Consumer Budget Variables; Payoffs, Returns, and Discounting."

Equation A.14 Payoff Space, State Prices, Set of Real Numbers

$\mathbb{R}^s$ set of possible payoffs in all states

p_s state prices for state s

$\underline{X}$ payoff space

x_i payoff of individual security

Equation A.15 State Density, Risk-Neutral Probabilities

$z \quad = (z_1, \, ..., \, z_m)$ payoff vector for asset in m states

$V(z) = qz$ value of payoff z

$q_i \quad =$ element in pricing vector q

$\pi_i \quad =$ probability

$\tilde{\pi}_i \quad = \dfrac{q_i}{\sum_i q_i}$ risk neutral probability for security i

$\phi_i \quad = \dfrac{q_i}{\pi_i}$ state price density (pricing kernel) for security i

Equation A.16 Correspondence: Fundamental Theorem and Basic Pricing Equation (BPE)

Fundamental Theorem of Finance

$$V(z) = qz$$

where:

$V(z) =$ value (price) of asset with payoff z

$z \quad = (z_1, \dots , z_m)$ payoff vector

$q \quad =$ positive linear pricing vector

$\phi_i \quad = \dfrac{q_i}{\pi_i}$ positive state price density (pricing kernel)

Basic Pricing Equation (BPE)

$$p_t = E(m_{t+1} x_{t+1})$$

where:

$p_t \quad =$ price of asset with payoff x_{t+1}

$m \quad \equiv \beta \dfrac{u'(c_{t+1})}{u'(c_t)}$ stochastic discount factor (pricing kernel)

$x_{t+1} \equiv$ payoff at time $t+1$

Different notation is sometimes used for derivations of asset prices from the fundamental theorem in complete markets and from basic consumer behavior in all markets. The correspondence between the pricing equations from each approach is shown in Equation A.16.

Note that the BPE involves an expectation of a product, while the positive pricing vector is multiplied directly by payoffs across states.

STOCHASTIC PROCESSES; EXPECTATIONS; MEASURE

The use of *random variables* (the result of one or more stochastic processes) presupposes the existence of a probability measure, a norm for measuring, and other concepts that are part of *measure theory*. In this book, we presume the existence of a measure space, norm, and probability measure. This is sometimes summarized as the existence of the triple of a *probability space* of (ω, F, P) where ω is a finite state space of events, F is a *tribe* of these events (including the empty space), and P is a probability measure that applies to the events in the state space.

Equation A.17 State Space, Events

Ω state space of events

ω_i events within space

$\Omega = \left\{ \omega_1, \; \omega_2, \; \omega_3 \right\}$

When stochastic processes exist within the probability space, they produce a *filtration* over time. This use of a time index implies that information known at one time period is contained in the information set at a later time.

Equation A.18 Stochastic Processes

$\{x\} = \{x_0, \; ..., \; x_{t-1}, \; x_t, \; x_{t+1}, \; ...\}$ stochastic process

$P = \left[P_{ij} \right]$ transition matrix for (stationary) Markov process

$i, j \in S$ elements i, j are members of a finite state space S

A *Markov process* is a stochastic process in which the useful information about the probability distribution of the next period's outcome is entirely captured in the last period's value. A *martingale* is a stochastic process in which the expected value of the next period's observation is equal to the current-time observation. Some Markov processes can be described partially by a transition probability matrix.

Equation A.19 Expectations

$E_t(Y)$ $\equiv$ expectation of random variable Y at time t

$E(Y \mid F(t)) \equiv$ expectation conditional on filtration F at time t

$E(X \mid Y)$ $\equiv$ expectation of random variable X given Y

Expectations of random variables presume the existence of a probability measure. The ability to change the measure in many cases is asserted by the Radon-Nikodym theory. This result is necessary for the concept of risk-neutral measure and a risk-neutral discount factor.

Equation A.20 Expectation Under Probability Measure

$E^Q \equiv$ expectation under measure Q

$Z = \dfrac{dQ}{dP}$ = Radon-Nikodym derivative for measures Q and P

STOCHASTIC DIFFERENTIAL EQUATIONS; ITÔ AND WEINER PROCESSES

A stochastic differential equation (SDE) is a common model of asset prices in mathematical finance. These are sometimes informally called *diffusions*; two key parameters for SDEs are often called *drift* and *diffusion*. SDEs typically involve a stochastic process known formally as a *Weiner process* and informally as *Brownian motion*. A general and important category of SDEs are known as *Itô processes*; a common Itô process used in modeling stock prices is known as *geometric Brownian motion*.

Equation A.21 Itô Processes; Geometric Brownian Motion

$$S_T = S_0 + \int_0^T \mu(t)dt + \int_0^T \sigma(t)dz \quad \text{Itô process}$$

$$S_T = S_0 + \int_0^T \mu S_t dt + \int_0^T \sigma S_t dz \quad \text{geometric Brownian motion}$$

$$\frac{dS}{S} = \mu dt + \sigma dz \quad \text{geometric Brownian motion (informal notation)}$$

$$dS = \mu S dt + \sigma S dz \quad \text{geometric Brownian motion (informal notation)}$$

where:

dz = increment of standard Brownian motion process $z(t)$

S_t = value of variable S at time $t = 1, ..., T$

ΔS = change in variable S during short time period

Note that the notation here for Itô processes uses common mathematical shorthand. Abuses of notation are common in the presentation of SDEs in mathematical finance. Consult a technical reference such as Shreve (2004) or Duffie (2001) for a rigorous definition of the elements and properties of SDEs and a discussion of Itô's lemma.

FUNCTIONAL EQUATIONS; NORMS

Equation A.22 Functional Equation Variables

$V(s, t)$ = value at time t given state s

$f(s, x)$ ≡ reward function given state and action

$g(s, x)$ ≡ transition function

t = 0, ..., T time index

s_t = $s_0, ..., s_T$ state variables

x_i = $x_0, ..., x_M$ action or control variables

β = discount factor

ε = random error term

Note: Some sources use square brackets for the arguments of functionals, such as $V[s]$, to distinguish them from the arguments of a function such as $f(x)$. Note that functional equations may or may not have solutions.

A functional is sometimes called a *function of functions*. Comparing two functions is intuitively like examining the distance between two curves. A specific manner of summarizing the distance between two curves, or the length of a vector or size of a matrix, is known as a *norm*. The *supremum norm* is one useful norm.

Equation A.23 Norms, Distance Metric, Supremum Norm

L^{∞} norm for vector $x = [x_i]$

$$\|x\|_{\infty} \equiv \max_i |x_i|$$

A *norm* is an indication of the size, length, or extent of an object. A *distance metric* or vector norm measures the distance or difference between two vectors. The *supremum norm* or L^{∞} *norm* can be used to measure the distance between two curves or vectors.

COMMON ACCOUNTING AND FINANCE ACRONYMS

The following is a glossary of some of the many accounting and finance acronyms commonly used in valuation. This is intended as a quick reference and is subject to two important qualifications: first, the intended subject for most of these metrics is C corporations that are publicly traded and subject to a corporate income tax; and second, actual usage varies to a surprising degree for many acronyms. Good sources, which sometimes differ on the precise definitions and usage of these concepts, include Damadoran (2002), Abrams (2000), Gallagher and Andrew (2007), and Gropelli and Nikbakht (2006). Many other references cover the same topics.

cash flow (CF)
A measure of a company's cash earnings and liquidity, it generally consists of net income plus noncash expenditures and other adjustments, which vary depending on the convention employed. Standard accounting statements include a cash flow schedule that reconciles earnings to cash flow. In general, it is not equivalent to FCFE or CFO.

cash flow from operations (CFO)
A cash flow measure confined to a firm's operations, rather than its operating and financing activities. It can be used to determine the extent to which cash flows differ from operating or net income.

earnings before interest and taxes (EBIT, also called *operating income*)
An indicator of a company's profitability calculated as revenue minus expenses, excluding income taxes and interest paid by the company.

earnings before interest, taxes, depreciation, and amortization (EBITDA)
A widely used, very broad measure of operating cash flow calculated just as the acronym suggests.

economic profit (EP)
The amount by which earnings on operations exceed the cost of capital. This is conceptually equivalent to economic value added. Typically, the "cost of capital" is the expected rate of return for investing in other securities of similar risk.

economic value added (EVA)
The amount of profit remaining after accounting for the return expected by a firm's investors. It is sometimes considered an estimate of true economic profit. (The term *EVA* is a trademark of Stern Stewart & Co.)

free cash flow (FCF, also called *net cash flow* or *NCF*)
The profits from operations that are available ("free") to be distributed to suppliers of the firm's capital, such as company debt holders and preferred and common stockholders. The net cash flow is the amount remaining after cash expenditures, income and other taxes, cash capital expenditures, and new additions to working capital are subtracted from cash revenues.

free cash flow to equity (FCFE, also called *net cash flow to equity* or *NCFE*)
The free cash flow available to stockholders; it differs from FCFF by the amount due to lenders.

free cash flow to the firm (FCFF, also called *net cash flow to the firm* or *NCFF*)
The free cash flow available to bondholders (lenders) and stockholders.

funds from operations (FFO)
A measure of cash flow often used by REITs and other investment trusts. Defines cash flow from operations as net earnings (before any capital gains or losses) plus depreciation and amortization (which are noncash expenses).

generally accepted accounting principles (GAAP)
Accounting standards used by almost all U.S. publicly traded corporations.

net operating profit less adjusted taxes (NOPLAT)
A measure of operating earnings that allows for comparisons of firms as if they were not leveraged (financed without debt).

$$\text{NOPLAT} = \text{operating income } (1 - \text{income tax rate})$$

return on equity (ROE)
Net income as a percentage of shareholder equity

return on invested capital (ROIC)
A measure of the efficiency of using capital to generate earnings. Although usage differs, it is a ratio of operating earnings divided by invested capital. Dividends (and the tax shield effect of borrowing) are sometimes deducted from net income in the numerator. The denominator can be book value of invested capital, total capital, or an adjusted measure of capital.

terminal value (TV)
Expected value of an investment at the end of a time period, taking into account the expected conditions (including trend growth and discount rates) at that time. A terminal value is often used in discounted cash flow schedules (as well as DTA and VF analyses) to represent either the expected proceeds of a future sale or a salvage value.

working capital (WC)
Working capital has a strict accounting definition and a much looser usage in practice.

WC = current assets − current liabilities

AVAILABILITY OF *SOLUTIONS MANUAL*

I have edited and partially written a companion volume to this book, *Solutions Manual and Reference for Economics of Business Valuation*. It includes extensive material to support scholars, readers, and practitioners who have purchased this book. The main topics covered in this companion volume are described in the following sections.

Purchasers of the book may obtain an electronic copy of the *Solutions Manual* by visiting http://www.andersoneconomicgroup.com/books and clicking the link for *The Economics of Business Valuation: Towards a Value Functional Approach.*

EXTENDED CHAPTER MATERIAL

The *Solutions Manual* includes extended discussion of a number of topics that are covered in summary form in this book, including antecedents of the NPV rule; principal-agent and moral hazard problems; other forms of organization for private businesses; history of option contracts; and additional value quandaries such as the existence of the "winner's curse."

PROBLEMS FOR EACH CHAPTER; HINTS TO PROBLEMS

For each chapter, I have prepared a set of questions and problems that develop the material further. These are included in the *Solutions Manual*, along with hints and entire solutions to a number of the problems.

MATHEMATICS OF VALUE

The *Solutions Manual* includes a guide to the mathematics of value covering each of the following topics:

- Important algorithms
- Random variables, stochastic processes, Brownian motion, Itô processes, and Markov processes

- Expectations and measure theory
- Annuities, perpetuities, and cash-flow formulas
- Continuous and discrete-time compounding and discounting
- Preferences and utility functions
- Optimization using differential calculus
- Neoclassical finance and alternate derivations of complete markets pricing formulas

Note that Appendix A in this book, "Key Formula and Notation Summary," contains a summary of notation and a small number of important formulas.

ADDITIONAL BUSINESS DATA

The *Solutions Manual* contains additional data on business forms and business activity in the United States and in other countries, including data on the following topics:

- Statistics on businesses in the United States, included updated information on data used in this book
- Indicators of the value of privately held firms
- Additional information on businesses in other countries

VALUATION STANDARDS

The *Solutions Manual* reprints a set of standards of value and guidance statements that describe the proper methodology. These authorities include the following:

- The *Fair Market Value* (FMV) definition in the U.S. Code of Federal Regulations
- The U.S. Internal Revenue Service Revenue Ruling 59-60 (RR 59-60), which is incorporated in many other authorities
- Professional Appraisal Practice Standards for Federal Agencies (USPAP) for appraisals of an equity interest in a business enterprise
- Financial Accounting Standards Board statement of financial accounting concepts No. 1 (FASB 1)

VALUATION SUBJECT COMPANIES

The *Solutions Manual* includes an extended description of the valuation subject companies, including their histories, competitors, reputations, market position, and management.

INTERMEDIATE RESULTS FOR EXAMPLES

For a number of the examples shown in the text, I include intermediate results in the *Solutions Manual* that allow the reader to follow more calculation steps and inspect additional data.

SOFTWARE FOR BUSINESS VALUATION

Categories of Software

In the *Solutions Manual*, I attempt to list some applications available at the time of writing that could be useful to a scholar, student, or practitioner interested in business and business valuation. The categories discussed in the *Solutions Manual* include the following:

- Vector-processing mathematical software, including the Matlab software that was used in the preparation of many of the examples in this book.[1]
- Simulation software
- Statistics and econometrics software
- Spreadsheet software
- Decision tree and Monte Carlo software, including those marketed as "real options" software
- Software that solves value functional, dynamic programming, or Markov decision process problems (see the note that follows)
- Business valuation software

Of course, all the information on software is provided subject to the limitations caused by changing technology and myriad forms of operating systems and hardware, and the admonition that no software is a substitute for critical thinking.

Specialized Value Functional Software

The examples presented in this book were developed using both standard tools and novel applications. The value functional problems were solved using specialized software tools, which in some cases were developed by the author initially to solve the problems illustrated here. At this writing, these are not commercially available in a form that can be readily used. However, the *Solutions Manual* describes a set of these tools and provides updated information on any available versions.

ERRATA AND ADDITIONAL REFERENCES

Should any errors in the published version be identified, I will note them and provide a correction in the *Solutions Manual*. In addition, any clarifications, additions, or corrections to the references will be included in the *Solutions Manual*.

If you believe you have found an error or a missing citation in the text, please alert us via email at the address listed at http://www.andersoneconomicgroup.com/books. (Click the link for *The Economics of Business Valuation: Towards a Value Functional Approach*.)

SECTION C.1. DESCRIPTIONS OF THREE ACTUAL FIRMS

In this appendix, we describe the three actual firms we use in the valuation examples throughout the book. We wanted to use actual firms, rather than fictitious entities with conveniently assembled accounting statements, as the test subjects. We have been given consent for this purpose by the management of the two privately held firms. The names we assign to those firms are pseudonyms, and certain other identifying information has been obscured.

This sample is roughly representative of firms in the United States and Europe in the sense that a majority of them (two of the three) are privately held, small firms, while one is very large and publicly traded.

We include below a brief description of each firm, as well as their income statements and balance sheets. These descriptions and the notes on the use of traditional valuation methods were compiled by individuals who have received training by valuation-credentialing organizations in the United States, and reflect subjective judgments as well as recitation of facts. They have been only lightly edited by the author of this book. Additional information on these firms is available in the *Solutions Manual* described in Appendix B, "Guide to the Solutions Manual."

SECTION C.2. S. H. IMPORTERS

a. History of Enterprise, Industry, and Management

In 1981, the founder began a sole proprietorship in Southern California, naming it S. H. Importers. The firm retails imported and reproduced antique furniture and furnishings primarily in Southern California. S. H. Importers sells primarily to interior designers (60 to 70 percent). The company also rents furniture and furnishings to the film and television industries and provides customized wood finishing and cabinetry to meet customer specifications.

The company has assembled a wide network of local and international suppliers over the years, which allows it to respond quickly to requests for specific pieces. The company has approximately a half dozen employees, although the number varies with demand, which is common in this industry. A number of the employees are part time. There are two full-time employees, the founder and her son. The business has been managed and operated primarily by the founder for much of its existence. However, over the past decade the founder's son has been trained as a manager and groomed as a successor owner. The son is now skilled at all aspects of the business and deals directly with customers and vendors. The company is, however, very dependent on the founder for purchasing and merchandising. All of the sales staff admit that the company owes a great deal of its success to the fact that customers are "buying the taste" of the founder.

b. Ownership and Financial Performance

The founder of the company still owns 510 shares, representing a 51 percent ownership interest. Her son owns the remaining 490 shares, representing a 49 percent interest. The company was very profitable in 2006 but did not earn sizable profits over the succeeding three years, which included a severe recession. Historical income statements are shown in Table C.1.

TABLE C.1
S. H. Importers income statement, 2006–June 2010

	2005	2006	2007	2008	2009	June 2010
INCOME						
Gross sales	$2,246,392	$2,508,998	$2,169,100	$1,396,017	$1,272,769	$536,448
Discounts	(508,891)	(435,478)	(436,847)	(277,937)	(234,381)	(104,425)
Net sales	1,737,501	2,073,520	1,732,253	1,118,080	1,038,388	432,023
COGS	655,409	789,639	652,947	415,680	396,809	158,314
Gross profit	1,082,093	1,283,880	1,079,307	702,399	641,579	273,709
Movie rental	19,391	38,173	50,714	16,690	11,450	12,748
Custom carpentry	29,371	25,309	30,156	13,820	34,940	12,135
Other income	3,096	5,266	5,569	2,924	2,512	5,365
Total income	**1,133,951**	**1,352,628**	**1,165,745**	**735,834**	**690,481**	**303,957**
EXPENSE						
Depreciation	8,790	5,867	16,329	4,193	4,000	—
Rent	144,765	187,673	192,000	192,000	96,000	72,182
Property taxes	12,510	12,712	12,964	13,206	13,672	6,858
Salaries and commissions						
Officers	44,400	49,042	45,500	50,500	34,250	9,000
Other	326,135	401,400	374,140	296,278	265,471	108,353
Total	370,535	450,442	419,640	346,778	299,721	117,353
SG&A	301,809	284,843	292,118	230,770	193,971	132,071
Total expenses	**838,409**	**941,536**	**933,051**	**786,948**	**607,363**	**328,464**
EBIT	295,542	411,092	232,694	(51,113)	83,118	(24,507)
Interest						
Shareholder	69,805	55,839	45,557	72,054	74,086	37,043
Other	2,228	1,776	1,303	808	285	—
Total interest	72,032	57,615	46,861	72,862	74,370	37,043
Income taxes	3,242	5,192	2,699	800	800	189
Net income	**220,268**	**348,284**	**183,135**	**(124,775)**	**7,947**	**(61,739)**

TABLE C.2
S. H. Importers balance sheet, 2006–June 2010

	2005	2006	2007	2008	2009	June 2010
ASSETS						
Cash	$ 259,071	$ 8,420	$ 76,052	$ 14,851	$ 138,540	$ 49,142
Accounts receivable	165,696	242,862	153,365	18,003	43,077	44,109
Inventory	1,217,227	1,433,384	1,461,791	1,457,878	1,341,793	1,377,166
Other current assets	—	—	2,501	2,920	2,970	1,720
Total current assets	1,641,994	1,684,666	1,693,709	1,493,652	1,526,380	1,472,137
Fixed assets	224,511	224,511	236,261	236,261	236,261	239,584
Accumulated depreciation	(132,145)	(138,012)	(154,341)	(158,534)	(162,534)	(162,534)
Net fixed assets	92,366	86,499	81,920	77,727	73,727	77,050
Total assets	**1,734,360**	**1,771,165**	**1,775,630**	**1,571,379**	**1,600,108**	**1,549,187**
LIABILITIES AND EQUITY						
Current liabilities	68,358	88,938	64,167	56,379	22,650	95,368
Long-term debt						
Due to principals	599,660	398,006	740,857	680,387	746,518	692,234
Other LTD	43,926	33,676	22,953	11,735	115	—
Total LTD	643,586	431,682	763,810	692,122	746,633	692,234
Total liabilities	**711,945**	**520,620**	**827,977**	**748,502**	**769,283**	**787,602**
Shareholders' equity	**1,022,416**	**1,250,545**	**947,653**	**822,878**	**830,825**	**761,585**
Total liabilities and equity	**1,734,360**	**1,771,165**	**1,775,630**	**1,571,379**	**1,600,108**	**1,549,187**

The company's principals own the showroom and workshop facility, so the company has no debt to speak of except for due-to-principals, as shown in Table C.2. This was especially beneficial during the recent economic recession; several competitors had to cease operations when unable to make rent payments or repay debt.

c. Note on Adjusted Income Statement

For the purpose of comparing valuation methods, we use a normalized (for business cycle) income statement in one example valuation. This is based on the 2006 and 2007 actual income statements, with adjustments for distributed profits based on the assumption that professional managers could be substituted for the family members in the business, at a lower cost.

d. Market Transactions

There have some intrafamily transactions involving equity shares for this firm over the past several years. The company does not have access to market data on any truly comparable firms. However, it does have some information on transactions involving publicly traded furniture stores or furniture assembly companies.

SECTION C.3. A & A CONSULTING

a. History of Enterprise, Industry, and Management

A & A Consulting offers business and public policy consulting services, as well as expert testimony. The company was founded in 1996, and after more than fifteen years of opera-

TABLE C.3
A & A Consulting income statement, 2006–2010

	2006	2007	2008	2009	2010
INCOME					
Revenue					
Professional billings	$2,050,152	$2,067,618	$1,935,639	$1,964,809	$3,156,481
Reimbursed expenses	82,868	58,408	41,463	55,247	103,180
Total revenue	2,133,020	2,126,026	1,977,102	2,020,056	3,259,661
Discounts and write-offs	(254,960)	(402,343)	(363,181)	(349,336)	(588,435)
Total revenues after discounts	**1,878,060**	**1,723,483**	**1,613,921**	**1,670,720**	**2,671,226**
EXPENSE					
Payroll and benefit expenses	1,097,770	1,231,934	1,071,051	1,097,063	1,490,229
Insurance, licenses, legal, accounting	2,857	15,297	8,398	11,393	18,053
Office and equipment expense	55,106	59,589	50,826	55,815	74,399
Computer software and data	43,402	40,563	38,996	34,555	47,897
Travel, advertising, and marketing	118,282	191,355	150,633	197,556	143,564
Occupancy expense	67,073	106,211	119,434	133,266	141,563
Total operating expenses	**1,384,490**	**1,644,949**	**1,439,338**	**1,529,648**	**1,915,705**
Operating income	493,570	78,534	174,583	141,072	755,521
Interest, amortization, depreciation, and other	(25,459)	(31,052)	(38,075)	(33,528)	(124,650)
Taxes					
Personal property	2,749	3,271	3,321	3,724	2,113
State business tax	12,177	9,322	15,014	8,314	32,517
Net income	**453,185**	**34,889**	**118,173**	**95,506**	**596,241**

tion it has grown to between a dozen and twenty full-time employees plus a number of part-time employees and contractors.

The company has a diverse list of clients including governments, corporations, nonprofits, trade associations, and small businesses. While the share of business outside its region has been increasing over time, about half of the company's revenue comes from one state, with considerable variation from year to year. A & A Consulting is one of the few consulting firms of its type in the United States that follows a quality assurance program, and it has built a solid reputation for high-quality work. It tends to charge a somewhat higher price than its competitors in the local market, but a lower price than its competitors in New York, Seattle, and Washington, D.C.

The company's founder is a "key man" and brings in a significant amount of business, although a declining share over time. This dependency poses a risk for the company, although it has a well-developed position in a handful of niche markets, built on its excellent reputation.

b. Ownership and Financial Performance

The primary shareholder in the company has been the founder for much of the past decade. Over the past several years, there have generally been two or three shareholders, with the founder owning about 90 percent of the equity. The company adopted a dividend policy in the mid-2000s that has resulted in regular distributions to members, even in the recent recession. Despite the recession, the company has retained a healthy income statement, as shown in Table C.3.

TABLE C.4
A & A Consulting balance sheet, 2006–2010

	2006	2007	2008	2009	2010
ASSETS					
Total checking/savings	$487,295	$228,322	$277,909	$207,343	$536,284
Accounts receivable	241,507	333,124	244,662	305,645	362,780
Allowance, doubtful accounts	(50,000)	(60,000)	(75,089)	(57,500)	(87,500)
Prepaid state business tax	—	6,498	15,979	17,979	—
Total current assets	678,802	507,944	463,461	473,467	811,564
Fixed assets	155,513	216,108	221,775	205,932	207,430
Accumulated depreciation	(68,738)	(109,717)	(139,450)	(145,516)	(143,062)
Net fixed assets	86,775	106,391	82,325	60,416	64,368
Other assets	22,612	23,008	18,062	17,712	17,712
Accumulated amortization	(5,206)	(5,425)	(5,755)	(6,640)	(7,525)
Total other assets	17,406	17,583	12,307	11,072	10,187
Total assets	**782,983**	**631,918**	**558,093**	**544,955**	**886,119**
LIABILITIES AND EQUITY					
Current liabilities					
Accounts payable	3,005	5,472	—	780	43,316
Accrued payable	35,665	19,585	25,582	63,242	38,130
Customer retainers	230,438	183,722	200,839	177,065	261,054
Business taxes payable	16,120	16,523	12,477	13,966	26,872
Note payable	—	—	—	50,397	50,397
Accrual for share repurchase	—	—	79,788	—	—
Total current liabilities	285,228	225,302	318,686	305,450	419,769
Long-term liabilities, note	—	—	89,640	62,996	12,599
Total liabilities	**285,228**	**225,302**	**408,326**	**368,446**	**432,368**
Equity					
Beginning capital	232,617	500,114	411,037	149,767	176,510
Members distributions	(200,699)	(128,964)	(379,418)	(68,764)	(319,000)
Net income	465,837	35,466	118,148	95,506	596,241
Total equity	**497,755**	**406,616**	**149,767**	**176,509**	**453,751**
Total liabilities and equity	**782,983**	**631,918**	**558,093**	**544,955**	**886,119**

A & A Consulting has not acquired much long-term debt, but its balance sheet in Table C.4 does show a decline in overall assets during the recession year, with a rebound after that.

c. Market Transactions

There have been about a half dozen market transactions involving equity shares for this firm over the past several years. These have implicitly valued the company in the range of $1.6 million to $2.3 million. The company does not have market transaction data for shareholder interests in any truly comparable firms. However, it does observe some transactions involving other professional service firms that involve experts (such as management consulting firms), as well as industry analogues among a handful of publicly traded expert witness firms.

SECTION C.4. EXXONMOBIL

ExxonMobil is significantly different from our other two example firms: it is one of the world's largest publicly traded companies.

TABLE C.5
ExxonMobil income statement, 2006–2010 (USD millions, except per-share amounts)

	2006	2007	2008	2009	2010
INCOME					
Sales and other revenue	$365,467	$390,328	$459,579	$301,500	$370,125
Income from affiliates	6,985	8,901	11,081	7,143	10,677
Other income	5,183	5,323	6,699	1,943	2,419
Total revenue and other income	377,635	404,552	477,359	310,586	383,221
EXPENSE					
Crude oil and product purchases	182,546	199,498	249,454	152,806	197,959
Production and manufacturing	29,528	31,885	37,905	33,027	35,792
Selling, general, and administrative expenses	14,273	14,890	15,873	14,735	14,683
Depreciation and depletion	11,416	12,250	12,379	11,917	14,760
Exploration expenses	1,181	1,469	1,451	2,021	2,144
Interest expense	654	400	673	548	259
Sales-based taxes	30,381	31,728	34,508	25,936	28,547
Other taxes and duties	39,203	40,953	41,719	34,819	36,118
Income applicable to minority interests	1,051	1,005	1,647	—	—
Total expenses	310,233	334,078	395,609	275,809	330,262
EBIT	67,402	70,474	81,750	34,777	52,959
Income taxes	27,902	29,864	36,530	15,119	21,561
Net income	39,500	40,610	45,220	19,658	31,398
Net income per common share	$ 6.68	$ 7.36	$ 8.78	$ 3.99	$ 624.00

a. History of Enterprise, Industry, and Management

ExxonMobil is the world's largest publicly traded international oil and gas company, as well as a direct descendant of John D. Rockefeller's Standard Oil Company. ExxonMobil has continued to develop technology to discover oil fields and better refinery methods, which has made it a leader in the energy and petrochemical industry. ExxonMobil operates facilities or markets products in most countries around the world and explores for natural gas and oil on six continents. By operating as an integrated company, ExxonMobil combines upstream activities (involving exploration and production) with downstream operations (through the point of sale), creating a presence in the two main sectors of the oil and gas industry.

b. Ownership and Financial Performance

ExxonMobil is a publicly traded company with wide stock ownership. We show Exxon-Mobil's income statement in Table C.5. As shown, ExxonMobil rebounded nicely from its 2009 slump.

As a whole, ExxonMobil is an extremely solid investment. It had twenty-eight consecutive years of dividend-per-share increases through 2010. We show the balance sheet in Table C.6.

ExxonMobil describes its management system as incorporating best practices developed all over the world and emphasizing project evaluation and execution. It believes that these practices result in superior investment returns despite business cycles. Exxon also emphasizes its commitment to innovative technology and workforce safety as vital components to compete in the industry, as well as meet the growing demand for energy.

TABLE C.6

ExxonMobil balance sheet (USD millions)

	2006	2007	2008	2009	2010
ASSETS					
Current assets					
Cash and cash equivalent	$ 32,848	$ 33,981	$ 31,437	$ 10,862	$ 8,455
Accounts receivable	28,942	36,969	25,272	27,645	32,284
Inventories					
Crude oil, products	8,979	8,863	9,331	8,718	9,852
Materials and supplies	1,735	2,226	2,315	2,835	3,124
Other current assets	3,273	3,924	3,911	5,175	5,269
Total current assets	75,777	85,963	72,266	55,235	58,984
Investments, long-term receivables	23,237	28,194	28,556	31,665	35,338
Property, plant, equipment at cost, less accumulated depreciation and depletion	113,687	120,869	121,346	139,116	199,548
Other assets, including intangibles, net	6,314	7,056	5,884	7,307	8,640
Total assets	**219,015**	**242,082**	**228,052**	**233,323**	**302,510**
LIABILITIES AND EQUITY					
Current liabilities					
Notes and loans payable	1,702	2,383	2,400	2,476	2,787
Accounts payable and accrued liabilities	39,082	45,275	36,643	41,275	50,034
Income taxes payable	8,033	10,654	10,057	8,310	9,812
Total current liabilities	48,817	58,312	49,100	52,061	62,633
Long-term debt	41,427	43,360	47,480	48,219	66,744
Other long-term obligations	11,123	14,366	13,949	17,651	20,454
Equity of minority interests	3,804	4,282	4,558	—	—
Total liabilities	**105,171**	**120,320**	**115,087**	**117,931**	**149,831**
Shareholders' equity	**113,844**	**121,762**	**112,965**	**115,392**	**152,679**
Total liabilities and equity	**219,015**	**242,082**	**228,052**	**233,323**	**302,510**

Exxon is subject to the inherent risks of the oil business, including political risks (which extend to threats of nationalization, expropriation, and piracy) and technological risks (including efforts by many national governments to reduce reliance on fossil fuels), as well as considerable costs related to environmental concerns in the exploration, refining, and transportation of petroleum and petroleum products. In addition, the huge scale of the business means that potentially catastrophic events cannot be ruled out; the wreck of the tanker *Exxon Valdez* more than a decade ago is one example of a single incident that cost the company billions of dollars and contaminated a sensitive area.

c. Market Transactions

ExxonMobil's enterprise value was $403.7 billion as of June 2011.[1] Its market capitalization at that time was $402.4 billion.[2] ExxonMobil distributed more than $19.7 billion to its shareholders in 2010.

NOTES

CHAPTER 1

1. King Hammurabi (sometimes spelled *Hammurapi*) was the ruler of ancient Babylonia beginning around 1792 BC. We will note some of these ancient contributions in Chapter 18, under the section titled "Commercial Damages."

2. Drèze was a lifelong friend of Franco Modigliani and a colleague of Herbert Simon and Merton Miller since the 1950s. His interest in uncertainty generated some of the earliest extensions of microeconomics and finance to this important concept. A fascinating tour through both personal and intellectual history is contained in Dehez and Licando (1996).

3. The conjunction of these statements was identified by Gonçalo Fonseca in "Production: The Cowles [Commission] Contributions," in *History of Economic Thought*, ed. Gonçalo L. Fonseca, available at http://homepage.newschool.edu/~het/essays/get /production.htm.

4. We describe this more fully in Chapter 8, "Value in Neoclassical Economics."

5. We will review the available statistics in Chapter 5, "The Organization and Scale of Private Business," under the section titled "Value of Private Firms in the United States."

6. Recent objects of scorn in the United States, in no apparent order and without commenting on the validity of the criticism, include the oil, pharmaceuticals, automotive, insurance, and telecommunications industries. On top of this, one cannot avoid the metaphor of "Wall Street," which may mean all big businesses, all financial businesses, or some other convenient category.

7. Three points apply here: first, the sheer size of advertising revenue and its importance to several sectors of the economy; second, the importance of marketing by firms that such expenditures reveals; and third, the apparent uncertainty about future demand for firms' products.

8. The numerous examples include Andrew Carnegie, Alfred Nobel, and Henry Ford, and the modern-day Bill Gates and Warren Buffett.

9. This would include income taxes levied on firms, value-added taxes, excise taxes and sales taxes collected by firms on their sales, tariffs on trade, regulatory exactions, real

property tax, and personal property tax. Income and payroll taxes collected from firms, but based on employee earnings, is another category.

Of course, because firms are owned by people, the entire tax burden ultimately falls on people.

10. Gilder's *Spirit of Enterprise* (1984, 1992) even criticizes Adam Smith's "invisible hand" argument for capitalism (which he compares to "trad[ing] greed for wealth") as "hogwash." Instead, he argues that entrepreneurs give to society far more than they take. "Greed," he continues, "leads, as if by an invisible hand, toward ever more government action" (*Recapturing the Spirit of Enterprise*, 1992, chap. 1).

Gilder's biography for the Discovery Institute describes him as "President Reagan's most frequently quoted living author" and notes that "in 1986, President Reagan gave George Gilder the White House Award for Entrepreneurial Excellence" ("George Gilder, Senior Fellow—Discovery Institute," n.d., available at http://www.discovery.org/p/10).

11. George Gilder concluded his 2004 address to the Philadelphia Society on this point:

> It's not greed or self-interest but the service of others that propels the advances of capitalism. Equilibrium economics is an economics of death. Disequilibrium, entrepreneurial economics, the economics of surprise and creativity is the economics of life. The key message of ordered liberty is "choose life." (Discovery Institute, 2004, available at http://www.discovery.org/a/2061)

12. Cantillon (1755, chap. 13); see also the essay by F. A. Hayek (1931) on Cantillon, which notes that he is one of the few authors Adam Smith quotes in *Wealth of Nations*.

13. A footnote that has been omitted from the quotation describes the "revolutions" as "not strictly incessant."

14. George Gilder, in his 2004 address to the Philadelphia Society, made the following connection between information and equilibrium:

> So, information is disequilibrium not equilibrium. This is one of the problems of much economics because economists always tend to favor equilibrium. They seem to believe that somehow the correct system is always in balance. But, I believe that science tells you that economies should have balanced law, families—all these—property rights and stable money. But the basic forces of growth are disequilibrium. The effort to reduce economics to equilibria is deadly and destructive. (Discovery Institute, 2004, available at http://www.discovery.org/a/2061)

15. The critique of Mark Casson (2002) is very clear on this point:

> In their mathematical models of economic activity and behavior, economists began to use the simplifying assumption that all people in an economy have perfect information. That leaves no role for the entrepreneur. Although different economists have emphasized different facets of entrepreneurship, all economists who have written about it agree that at its core entrepreneurship involves judgment. But if people have perfect information, there is no need for judgment.

16. The career path for a university professor requires extended work in academic and research settings. In contrast, multiple-year stints at risky, often low-paid jobs are stand-

ard gateways to entrepreneurial success. Such devotion to "building a business" would almost certainly preclude one from pursuing a teaching position at a university.

Furthermore, nearly all U.S. colleges and universities and a large share of their students depend on government or quasi-government institutions for stipends, loans, or operating revenue. Few entrepreneurial firms do this. Furthermore, bankruptcy is rarely a threat at public colleges and universities, whereas it is a serious risk for start-up firms.

The recent growth of start-up firms near some university clusters in the United States (and the prestige this brings the institutions) may be changing this cultural bias, albeit slowly.

17. See the preceding discussion under the section titled "The Fulsome Importance of the Firm in the Real Economy," as well as Chapter 5, "The Organization and Scale of Private Business."

18. One of the more vivid examples is the fictional Gordon Gekko in the movie *Wall Street*, who encourages investors to make money even at the expense of destroying a company with the statement "Greed is good."

19. We review this school of thought, which ushered into social science "marginalist" analysis and the ubiquitous supply-demand charts, in Chapter 8, "Value in Neoclassical Economics."

20. See Chapter 3, "The Failure of the Neoclassical Investment Rule," under the section titled "Outline of This Chapter."

21. If you can easily obtain information that would improve your decision, it is rational to do so. If, on the other hand, it is very costly to obtain information that would only slightly improve the outcome of a decision, it may be "rationally ignorant" to ignore it.

22. Brealey and Myers (1983, 2006). The sixth edition (2006) includes a section titled "Foundations of the Net Present Value Rule."

Careful readers will note that Stuart Myers also appears as the progenitor of at least two important concepts that are bases for the synthesis I propose here. Those concepts are the "growth options" we discuss in Chapter 12, "Real Options and Expanded Net Present Value," and the use of an adjusted NPV as the basis for a practical investment decision rule.

23. Brealey and Myers (1981, 1985). Repeated in Myers (2001), where Myers argues that there is a "gap" between strategic planning and finance theory and that "we on the financial side need to . . . apply existing theory correctly [and] . . . extend the theory." I will return to Myers's prescient statement in Chapter 3, "The Future of the Neoclassical Investment Rule."

24. In preparing to write this book, I reviewed at least a hundred texts describing, in some technical sense, the "value" of a business asset. I was surprised to find so many different underlying principles used as the basis for value and the apparent obliviousness of many authors to valuation principles used outside their own profession.

I would tentatively date the split in the literature to some time after the early 1960s, after M-M and CAPM were established as frameworks for valuation in the economics and finance fields and Revenue Ruling 59-60 was promulgated by the IRS and began the codification of professional valuation practice. Certainly, the split grew after the 1970s, when mathematical finance pioneers brought forth option valuation and no-arbitrage pricing models.

25. Examples here include the widely used book by Pratt, Reilly, and Schweihs (2000); Koller, Goedhart, and Wessels (2007); and Hitchner (2003). The first two of these have appeared in multiple editions. They are chock-full of cash flow schedules of various types, along with careful derivations of numerous accounting concepts.

26. I include these portfolio theories on the accounting-finance hand, not the economics-finance hand. One could easily switch hands here. However, the main point is the same: a true valuation theory lies outside both hands.

27. A handful of indicative examples that address asset pricing in general include S. Ross (2005), Duffie (2001), and Cochrane (2003). There are also numerous examples that focus on specific mathematical foundations or relatively narrow categories of assets, such as Hull (2008) and Shreve (2004). These excellent references, which I cite numerous times, are almost entirely lacking in accounting statements.

This pattern extends back at least another decade; the one-volume *Finance* edition of the 1989 *New Palgrave: A Dictionary of Economics* contains thirty articles (many by luminaries of the field), but not a single income statement.

28. For example, the valuation of S corps versus C corps, and the degree to which minority interests in a firm should be discounted for marketability, are hotly debated in the professional valuation literature. They are almost completely ignored in the mathematical finance literature. (For example, the Winter 2007 edition of *Business Valuation Review* includes no fewer than three articles debating S corp valuation, whereas none of the mathematical finance texts listed in the note above mention "S corp" in the index or deal directly with the topic [Cochrane 2003; Dullie 2001; Ross 2005].)

Conversely, the contemporary debates among economists over behavioral finance or the equity premium puzzle are like trees falling in an empty forest when viewed from the perspective of the professional valuation literature. One could read dozens of such texts and see only a few mentions of these topics.

29. Two book-length valuation texts from the (small) forensic economics literature are Gaughan (2009) and Anderson (2004a). Other references are listed in Chapter 17, "Applications: Finance and Valuation." Aside from the forensic economics literature, other exceptions include Long and Bryant (2008) and Sharpe (2007).

30. For example, these theories do not suffice to explain holdings in private firms (a large part of the actual wealth of many investors and a very large part of the wealth of entrepreneurs); their implicit or explicit view of investors' attitudes toward risk are, at best, a gross simplification; and they largely ignore the intertemporal adjustments that are primary concerns of actual investors.

We will further explore the usefulness, and the weaknesses, of the CAPM and related techniques in Chapter 11, "Portfolio Pricing Methods."

31. Sharpe continues:

There are strong arguments for viewing mean/variance analysis as a special case of a more general asset pricing theory (albeit a special case with many practical advantages). (Sharpe 2007, p. 4)

32. Consider this statement from their first paper:

We have been the first to stress that our paper was intended to be no more than the beginning of the attack on the cost of capital and related problems; and we have indicated areas both fundamental and applied in which the implications of our model remain to be totally or partially explored. (Modigliani and Miller, 1959, p. 668; see also p. 633)

Modigliani and Miller's modesty here, with fifty years of retrospect, is noteworthy. We discuss the M-M propositions further in Chapter 3, "The Failure of the Neoclassical Investment Rule."

33. Complete-market asset pricing models are described in Chapter 10, "Arbitage-Fuel Pricing in Complete Markets," and the use of the no-arbitrage assumption in the Modigliani-Miller propositions is discussed in Chapter 3, "The Failure of the Neoclassical Investment Rule," under the section titled "Outline of this Chapter."

34. In particular, see Chapter 4, "The Nature of the Firm"; Chapter 5, "The Organization and Scale of Private Business"; Chapter 10, "Arbitrage-Free Pricing in Complete Markets"; and Chapter 12, "Real Options and Expanded Net Present Value."

CHAPTER 2

1. The following definitions are representative examples: *economic value* is "the amount (of money or goods or services) that is considered to be a fair equivalent for something else"; *value, in economics* is the "worth of a commodity in terms of other commodities, or in terms of money" (*Free Dictionary*, 2011).

2. See Chapter 8, "Value in Neoclassical Economics."

3. See Chapter 6, "Accounting for the Firm."

4. See the authorities listed in Appendix B, "Guide to the Solutions Manual."

5. The *intrinsic* value of an asset is its inherent or underlying worth. This may be quite different from the *market* value, which is set by competing buyers and sellers.

6. We will introduce the formal notion of *preferences* and *utility* in Chapter 8. Note that we did not say that people assign value by responding to survey questions or by simply declaring that they like or want something. Actual "willingness to pay" has been demonstrated to be a much firmer basis for value than declaration of preferences or desires.

7. One of the fundamentals of statistics and finance is *measure theory*, which rigorously defines metric spaces, measure norms, and other concepts. See Appendix A under the section titled "Stochastic Processes; Expectations; Measure."

8. A *convenience yield* is an implicit or explicit benefit of having a commodity close at hand, even if it is not used. A *cost of carry* is the cost of keeping a commodity.

9. *Sufficient information* implies adequate information, though not *perfect* information. For example, "sales" of the Brooklyn Bridge would not demonstrate its market value if all the sales were to gullible "buyers" of a worthless piece of paper.

It is worth retelling some of the colorful history of this metaphor. References to selling the Brooklyn Bridge have appeared in American literature for more than a century. Some authors attribute the story to the exploits of William McCloudy and George C. Parker around 1900. They were said to have sold the bridge to recent immigrants, giving the buyer a bill of sale saying "one bridge in good condition." A skeptical but entertaining review of these stories was penned by novelist Gabriel Cohen (2005); less skeptical accounts are from the language scholar Barry Popik (2004) and the Straight Dope (2007), a web site that investigates urban myths.

10. The seminal reference for this definition is the IRS Revenue Ruling 59-60 (1959). These and other standards are described in Appendix B, "Guide to the Solutions Manual."

CHAPTER 3

1. Rubinstein's study of the question motivated this subsection. Note that some translations use the term *Hindu* rather than *Indian*; the area we call India now was commonly called *Hindustan* and its occupants *Hindus* for some time, regardless of their actual religion.

2. Italian-born American economist Franco Modigliani (1918–2003) was awarded the 1985 Nobel Prize in Economics, and American economist Merton Miller (1923–2000) shared the 1990 prize, both for their contributions to financial economics. The original papers were Modigliani and Miller (1959) and Miller and Modigliani (1964), as well as Miller and Modigliani (1961).

3. For example, James Brickley and John McConnell (1991) summarize the intellectual history before and after the publication of the 1961 Modigliani-Miller article. They conclude:

> After a brief flurry of debate, the Modigliani-Miller irrelevance proposition was essentially universally accepted as correct under their set of assumptions.

Brickley and McConnell then discuss various analyses involving the relaxation of the key M-M assumptions. In these, the "value of the firm" is consistently assumed to be equal to the net present value of its earnings. Another excellent survey of the debate and acceptance of these propositions, from a perspective nearly two decades later, is Villamil (2008). Villamil notes many subsequent works that focus on transaction costs, taxes, and bankruptcy.

4. This is especially the case for investments in what are now called options; see Chapter 12 under the section titled "Brief History of Option Contracts." On the "surprisingly short history" of finance as a separate discipline, see the entertaining essay on finance theory in Fonseca (2005).

5. We note specifically the contribution of Irving Fisher and John Burr Williams in this chapter, and that of Harry Markowitz in Chapter 11, "Portfolio Pricing Methods."

6. Keynes (1936, chap. 12, sec. III–IV) states that financial investors, who increasingly are separated from the management of the firms they own, are involved in "a mixed game of skill and chance." He illustrates this by mentioning a number of card games, including Old Maid. He also proposes the famous "beauty contest" analogy, comparing investors to newspaper readers picking out the face that they think most people will find pretty, rather than the face they think is prettiest.

7. These assumptions appear in the following places in the text of the 1958 article: riskless borrowing and perfect markets (p. 268); division of firms into risk classes (which result in their securities being "homogeneous") (p. 266); no asymmetric information or agency problem between managers and investors (p. 266); expectation of infinite streams of profits (p. 265); and uniform rate of capitalization (within a risk class) (p. 267).

8. Modigliani and Miller (1958, p. 296).

9. Modigliani and Miller (1958, pp. 268–269), "Proposition I."

10. Although the M-M propositions do not assume identical (or constantly growing) returns, there are analogies for the $V = X/\rho$ formula based on such assumptions.

The net present value (at discount rate r) of a perpetuity of the amount A, received at the end of each future year, is $PV = A/r$.

The present value of a constantly growing future stream of returns could also take on the form A/r, where r would account for the growth and discount rates. The well-known "Gordon Growth" formula, $PV = A_0 * (1 + g)/(d - g)$, is an illustration.

11. In addition, it is worth noting that Modigliani and Miller themselves called this a *proposition*, not a theorem; were explicit about the "drastic" simplifications and assumptions underlying it; and felt the need to offer support and (given many assumptions) proofs of it. On top of that, they noted that others had proposed Proposition I through intuitive arguments, but that "Proposition II, however, as far as we have been able to discover is new" (Modigliani and Miller, 1958, p. 271).

12. Both the expected value of the future stream of earnings and the discount rate for that class of investments can only be estimated. If one observes the market value of debt and equity and estimates one quantity on the right side of the equation, then the implied estimated value of the other variable can be calculated. This is not a logical proof.

13. They continue:

> To establish Proposition I we will show that as long as the relations (3) or (4) do not hold between any pair of firms in a class, arbitrage will take place and restore the stated equalities. We use the term arbitrage advisedly. For if Proposition I did not hold, an investor could buy and sell stocks and bonds in such a way as to exchange one income stream for another stream, identical in all relevant respects but selling at a lower price.

Here, "relations (3) and (4)" are Proposition I (shown in Equation 3.2) and a restatement of that equation.

14. For example, Modigliani and Miller (1959) argue against a criticism of Durand (1959) by noting that their use of the term *arbitrage* means "(1) simultaneous purchase and sale of (2) perfect substitutes" and that this does not mean *identical* securities.

15. Modigliani and Miller asserted that Proposition I held "in equilibrium," meaning that they were well aware that some kind of adjustment process would occur. However, by assuming away bankruptcy risk and differential interest rates, they also eliminated at least one of the adjustment mechanisms.

See also the following discussion about infinite and predictable stream of profit.

16. If one firm in a class issues a dividend and the other retains its earnings, the M-M model sees no difference at all in the value of the firm:

> As will become clear later, as long as management is presumed to be acting in the best interests of the stockholders, retained earnings can be regarded as equivalent to a fully subscribed, pre-emptive issue of common stock. Hence, for present purposes, the division of the stream between cash dividends and retained earnings in any period is a mere detail. (Modigliani and Miller, 1958, p. 266)

17. To salvage the equivalence-through-arbitrage result, there would have to be complete markets that include securities that span the risks to the profit stream of the individual firms. (See Chapter 10, "Arbitrage-Free Pricing in Complete Markets.") As long as there are a small number of risk classes, this seems plausible. Once firms are exposed to an array of individual risks, it is clearly implausible.

18. Rubinstein (2005, p. 7) cites Joel Dean's *Capital Budgeting* (1951) as the progenitor for a wave of later corporate finance books that use NPV as a fundamental tool. This is corroborated by Harry Roberts (1957), who wrote that Dean's book "has had great influence on the development of what is now generally called 'capital budgeting.'"

However, Roberts bemoans the "confusion" about the "unfortunate term 'cost of capital.'" He also cites Friedrich and Vera Lutz's *Theory of Investment of the Firm* (1951) as both more clear and more careful about the term than Dean.

19. Fumio Hayashi and other authors cite Jorgenson (1963) and Tobin (1969).

Avanish Dixit and Robert Pindyck (1994, chap. 1) also describe the neoclassical approach, citing these two authors, as "the orthodox theory."

20. Heijdra and van der Ploeg (2002, pp. 41–42, including formula [f]), with the firm subscript i omitted. Here, π is the cash flow of the firm, and T is the terminal time period, which may tend toward infinity.

Note that the formulation here is exactly the same as the DCF formulation used as a comparison against dynamic programming in Chapter 15, under the section titled "Differences Between Dynamic Programming and Discounted Cash Flow Methods."

21. Brealey and Myers (1981, p. 732) extend the NPV rule for project investment to the price investors will pay for shares in a company:

> In well-functioning financial markets, all equivalent risk-bearing assets are priced to offer the same rate of return. By discounting at the opportunity cost of capital, we calculate the price at which investors in the project could expect to earn that rate of return. . . . The NPV rule allows thousands of shareholders, who have vastly different levels of wealth and attitudes toward risk, to participate in the same enterprise and to delegate its operation to a professional financial manager. They give the manager one simple instruction: "Maximize present value."

22. Other editions of the text by Pratt and colleagues include the same statement.

23. It is interesting to note that these authors are actually quoting an earlier edition of Frank Reilly's investment analysis book (quoted earlier), thus confirming the ubiquity of the principle in both finance and accounting.

24. In addition to those cited earlier, see the references cited in the section titled "Failure 4: Decision Makers Fail to Follow the Rule."

25. It is common in finance to assume that the probability distribution of random events can be described by just two measures: the mean (expected value) and the variance. (It is also a convenient assumption for approaches such as the mean-variance framework.) However, this is unusual among statistical distributions. Most useful distributions of natural events have such characteristics as "leaning" to one side (known as *skew*) or a bulge or narrowness of shape (known as *kurtosis*).

Failure to know the key indicators of the distribution (including the mean, variance, and skew, and potentially the kurtosis) of important random events would mean that a manager probably could not actually follow the $E(NPV)$ rule, because he or she wouldn't know what the $E(NPV)$ of earnings would be.

26. Stewart Myers (2001) lists "four chief problems" with DCF, even when applied well: estimating the discount rate, estimating the project's cash flows, estimating the

project's impacts on the firm's *other* assets, and estimating the project's impact on future investment opportunities.

27. In particular, see the Modigliani-Miller assumption of an unstated (but apparently known) discount rate that is the same for both lenders and borrowers; Chapter 9, "Modern Recursive Equilibrium and the Basic Pricing Equation," for a presentation of the stochastic discount factor; Chapter 11, "Portfolio Pricing Methods," for a summary of modern portfolio theory; Chapter 13, under the section titled "The Income Method," for a discussion of the use of cost of capital in traditional income methods; and Chapter 10, "Arbitrage-Free Pricing in Complete Markets," on the risk-neutral rate used in complete-market pricing models.

28. For example, the risk-free rate used in complete-market models assumes the availability of a short-term, widely available, highly liquid bond or bank deposit with no risk of default. U.S. Treasury bills often fit this role nicely, though not exactly, but only for a narrow class of investors. A second example is the theoretical wealth portfolio available to investors in the classic CAPM, which represents the entire universe of investable assets. The market for publicly traded securities does *not* fit this assumption. See the discussion of the Roll critique of the CAPM in Chapter 11, under the section titled "Limitations of CAPM and Factor Models."

29. For examples, think of the efficient frontier in modern portfolio theory, or the normal distribution that underlies financial models that range from Bachelier's random walk to the Black-Scholes model. The assumption of normality is often based on the central limit theorem, which holds that a very large number of independent, random events, when summed together, produces a normal distribution.

On stochastic distributions, see the resources discussed in Appendix B, "Guide to the Solutions Manual."

30. An expected value can be defined for a variable that takes a range of potential values for which a known probability distribution exists. If the relevant variable is *not* randomly distributed (such as a variable controlled by a manager or investor), then there is no probability distribution in the normal sense of the term.

31. The role of strategy in business, and the tools that businesses can use to evaluate strategic options, is the subject of the recent book *Applied Game Theory and Strategic Behavior* (Geckil and Anderson, 2009).

32. This is a version of the first maxim of business economics: "Remember: it's a social science!" See Anderson (2004a).

33. Brealey and Myers (1981, p. 238, 1985). Repeated in Myers (2001, p. 26).

34. Among the evidence: a recent survey of chief financial officers of large American corporations (members of the *Fortune* 1000) by Patricia and Glenn Ryan (2002). Interestingly, they concluded that the survey results showed that contemporary managers are much more aligned with the academic literature than they were in the past. They summarize the academic literature as strongly favoring the use of NPV for capital budgeting, using a discount rate of weighted average cost of capital (WACC). Ryan and Ryan (2002) cite nine past studies, the earliest being Ronald Williams (1970) and the latest being that of Marc Ross (1986). The Ross study is discussed further shortly.

35. This is particularly evident from an interesting study led by an author completely outside the fields of economics and finance: University of Michigan physicist Marc Ross.

The purpose of his survey (Ross, 1986) was "to evaluate tax incentives for industrial energy conservation" and the methodology used relied on extensive interviews (one to three days in length) with actual managers at firms.

Ross concludes that all of the firms evaluated used some form of a DCF analysis of proposed investments with a hurdle rate that was close to a cost of capital for the firm. Perhaps because his background is in another field, and perhaps because of the extensive interviews (and the anonymity granted the subjects and their firms), he does not flinch from concluding that the decisions made at the firms varied considerably from those that the prevailing finance theory would expect.

More extensive reviews were completed by Myers (2001, p. 27) and Trigeorgis and Mason (2001), who report criticisms that extend back to the 1980s. A number of important "real options" articles are collected in Schwartz and Trigeorgis (2001).

36. I include here only adjustments that reflect actual uncertainties about future events and a plausible range of potential outcomes. The temptation to overestimate cash flows in attractive investment opportunities (or add fudge factors to the discount rate to account for subjectively risks) is common enough to merit mention in one of the most common corporate finance textbooks; see Brealey and Myers (1985, pp. 220, 272).

37. The latter two factors probably weigh the heaviest on chief financial officers at large firms, who were the recipients of some of the reported surveys. The regulatory concerns of a CFO at a publicly traded company in the United States (or in other countries with laws requiring disclosure of financial issues) are especially serious; a CFO who reported anything other than a rigorous capital budgeting process would probably lose his or her job.

38. See, for example, Chirinko and Schaller (1995), quoting Tinbergen (1939) and Meyer and Kuh (1957); they also report empirical data on the effect of liquidity constraints drawn from more than two hundred firms.

39. We review the evidence from multiple countries on new business survivorship rates and related concepts in Chapter 5, "The Organization and Scale of Private Business."

40. If we attempted to do this calculation, we would break the new businesses into some kind of risk classes and look at the empirical record of failures at, say, one-, three-, and five-year periods, then add in the other costs and expenses for the appropriate term.

41. Two pioneers in this were Dixit and Pindyck (1994) and Stokey (2009). We discuss this further in Chapter 15, "The Value Functional: Theory."

42. Brealey and Myers (1981, p. 350) note that the M-M propositions had been anticipated by J. Williams (1938) and by Durand (1952). We discussed earlier in the chapter Modigliani and Miller's response to Durand's (1959) criticism of their original article.

Rubinstein (2006) calls Williams's book an "insufficiently appreciated classic" and goes on to note that Markowitz himself cited it as an inspiration for his Nobel Prize–winning work. (See also the interview with Markowitz reported by Wasendorf and Wasendorf [2008].)

43. Fisher (1930, chap. 7, sec. 11). He further describes, in terms that are the basis for most contemporary finance texts, the analysis required:

> In general, the rate of return over cost has to be derived by more complicated methods. As already indicated, the rate of return over cost is always that rate which, employed in computing the present worth of all the costs and the present worth of all the returns, will make these two equal. Or, as a mathematician would prefer to put it, the rate which, employed in computing the present worth of the whole series of differences

between the two income streams (some differences being positive and others negative) will make the total zero.

If the rate, so computed, were taken for every possible pair of income streams compared as to their advantages and disadvantages, it would authentically decide in each case which of the pair is to be preferred. That one which compared with the other shows a rate of return on sacrifice greater than the rate of interest would be preferred and the other rejected. (Fisher, 1930, chap. 7, sec. 9)

44. See Fisher (1930, chap. 9, sec. 2).

45. J. Williams (1938), quoted by Rubinstein (2006).

46. The argument appears in Modigliani and Miller (1958, p. 271, including notes).

47. These authors cite Jack Hirshleifer as the modern reinterpreter of the Fisher theory, in particular his article "On the Theory of Optimal Investment Decision" (1958) and his book *Investment, Interest and Capital* (1970). See also Gonçalo Fonseca's essays "Finance Theory" and "Irving Fisher's Theory of Investment" in *History of Economic Thought* (2005); and LeRoy (1991).

48. See, for example, Fisher's *Theory of Interest* (1930, chap. 9 and 17).

CHAPTER 4

1. Although the book insightfully discusses the difference between a "business" and a "pile of assets."

2. For example, *business* is defined as follows in nontechnical dictionaries:

"any activity or enterprise entered into for profit" (*Free Dictionary*, 2011)

"enterprise," which is further defined as "a unit of economic organization or activity" (*Merriam-Webster Dictionary*, 2011).

"an industrial, commercial, or professional operation" (*Collins English Dictionary*, 2011)

"the purchase and sale of goods in an attempt to make a profit," or "a person, partnership, or corporation engaged in commerce, manufacturing, or a service; profit-seeking enterprise or concern" (*Random House Dictionary*, 2010)

3. Spulber (2009). The new definition proposed later in this chapter was first published in Anderson (2009).

4. See Spulber (2009, chap. 5):

Entrepreneurs are the genesis of firms. Through the actions of entrepreneurs, firms obtain their initial missions, goals, business definitions, employees, financing, technology, and organizational structure. The economic theory of the firm must therefore recognize that entrepreneurial decisions endogenously create firms.

5. In particular, Spulber (2009, p. 5) argues that entrepreneurs create additional firms as long as the gains from intermediation (internalizing the transactions) given the number of consumers exceed the gains from making the same transactions without the intermediation provided by firms.

6. Spulber (2009, chap. 2). An alternative, and more limited, modern neoclassical definition is provided by Sengupta and Sen (2004, chap. 8):

A firm is *an institution that organizes production by internalising the transactions* necessary to produce an output.

This definition captures the intermediation incentive for the organization of firms but ignores the separation criterion and, like other neoclassical definitions, does not include a business practices criterion.

7. In general, business organizations in the United States are organized under state laws, which vary among the states. This variance in laws produces a variance in firm behavior. For example, many larger corporations are incorporated in Delaware, which has a relatively small economy but a tradition of predictable legal decisions on corporate governance matters.

8. Such business "persons" are sometimes distinguished in law from *natural persons*, which are human beings.

9. Defining limited liability for shareholders to be a fundamental characteristic would imply that sole proprietorships and some partnerships were not businesses. We consider these to be valid business forms. A separate legal identity, not limited liability, is a fundamental characteristic of a firm.

10. The bankruptcy laws in the United States, as well as other state and federal laws, govern this. Attaching the assets of an equity owner of a company is sometimes called *piercing the veil* of the company.

In this matter, as in others, sole proprietorships blur the distinction between worker and business. In general, a sole proprietor as an individual is liable for the debts of the sole proprietorship business.

11. Spulber (2009, sec. 2.1.2).

12. Coase (1937, sec. II). On the lack of a definition of the firm in Coase's theory and further insight into the failings of neoclassical theory, see also Demsetz (1997b, essay 1), where he wryly observes that "the existence of the firm seemed not to be recognized as a problem in need of addressing by the literature surrounding the neoclassical theory."

13. George Stigler (1988) recounts the famous Chicago dinner meeting at which Coase convinced Milton Friedman and twenty other economists of the validity of his theorem.

14. The resource-based theory of the firm is attributed to Edith Penrose (1959). A retrospective on the contributions of Penrose was edited by Christos Pitelis (2002). The categorization of assets here follows the outline of Sengupta and Sen (2004, chap. 8).

15. The description of proprietary assets is attributed to Richard Caves (1996, 2007). One could observe some ambiguity in the concepts of "strategic" versus "proprietary" assets, especially with regard to trademarks and patents.

16. Caves (2007, p. 4; citing Nelson and Winter [1982]).

17. Note that replicable processes need not be unique, just replicable. Thus, firms that sell similar products are all still firms.

18. Jensen and Meckling (1976); reprinted in Jensen (2000).

19. The notion of minimum efficient scale may be attributable to Italian economist Piero Sraffa (1898–1983), who clearly delineated the notion of natural monopoly. See, for example, Sraffa (1926).

20. Classic works on military strategy such as Sun Tzu's *Art of War* (c. 600 BC), Musashi's *Book of Five Rings* (c. 1645), and Clausewitz's *On War* (1873) are sometimes recommended for their insight into business competition and strategy.

21. Dozens of business tracts use—or abuse—the metaphor of the company as a sports team, including employees as players, the executive as the coach or manager, the reporting period as the season, and the competition with other businesses as the game.

22. We discuss a few shortly: the incentive to achieve a certain scale (size) of firm. Other reasons include the following: workers need human capital (skills, experience, informal advice) to become highly productive, and groups of people organized as a firm provide this; limits exist on the information available to an individual that is not part of a firm; and individuals desire social interaction in the workplace and accept lower wages if they work in a firm that provides it.

23. Michael E. Porter is often credited with propounding a theory of business success based on strategy (Porter, 1980).

24. John Kay outlined, and supported with empirical examples, a theory of comparative advantage applied to relevant markets (Kay, 1993).

25. John W. Deming brought American-originated concepts to Japan after World War II, and Japanese companies in turn brought those concepts back to the United States later in the century.

26. *In Search of Excellence* by Tom Peters and Robert Waterman (1982) is a classic work on entrepreneurship, culture, and management motivation. As a classic, it also attracted a range of revisionists and critics, including some who noted how many of the original "excellence" companies later failed.

27. Joseph Schumpeter, who identified the "creative destruction" wrought by entrepreneurs, was a lonely midcentury voice in economics who recognized the role of the entrepreneur.

George Gilder is largely responsible for the modern reintroduction of the entrepreneur as a *moral* character in the broader intellectual and political culture of the United States. His 1981 *Wealth and Poverty*, and more specifically the 1984 *Spirit of Enterprise*, are contemporary expositions of the entrepreneur as engine of human progress. Indeed, Gilder's 1984 work quotes Smith's "invisible hand" statement directly on this point.

28. Of the dozens of possibilities, I select several that have passed the test of time and were clearly written by the named authors. First, one of the most influential books written about both American business and society in the twentieth century was Dale Carnegie's *How to Win Friends and Influence People* (1937). Two other examples of management advice from the make-friends-and-build-relationships school are Harvey MacKay's *Swim with the Sharks Without Being Eaten Alive* (1996) and Mark McCormack's *What They Don't Teach You at Harvard Business School* (1986). Decidedly different schools are represented by bare-knuckles guides such as Robert J. Ringer's *Winning Through Intimidation* (1975) and lessons-from-history guides such as Wess Roberts's *Leadership Secrets of Attila the Hun* (1989).

29. There are too many authors in this category to list here. For example, the first selection I identified in quick perusal of the business section of an online bookseller was *The 21 Irrefutable Laws of Leadership*, by John C. Maxwell, with a foreword by Zig Ziglar (Nelson, 1998). Between the two of them, Maxwell and Ziglar—both master storytellers—have written more than a hundred published titles on philosophy, business, faith, leadership, and success.

30. Many Americans underappreciate the debt they owe to the efforts of English patriots to achieve these freedoms. Early Americans, including those who debated and later

adopted the Constitution and Bill of Rights in the eighteenth century, reflected a more appropriate appreciation in many recorded debates, writings, and court decisions. For a thorough study by one of the foremost scholars on property rights in America, see Siegen (2001). An authoritative eighteenth-century description of English common law is William Blackstone's *Commentary on the Laws of England* (1915), which is based on lectures first given at All-Soul's College in 1753. Chapter 1 of this work states a "scheme of Anglo-American law" that includes "private property" as a right of persons, and includes many detailed derivations and examples of the right to private property.

31. Private property includes *intellectual property* such as patents and trademarks. For example, theft of intellectual property is a major problem for U.S. and European companies operating in China and other parts of Asia.

32. Probably the most influential contemporary author on the topic of private property, free enterprise, and liberty was Milton Friedman. His *Capitalism and Freedom* (first published in 1962) is still a seminal work.

33. A thorough survey of the economics of incomplete markets by the European authors Michael Magill and Martine Quinzii (1996, chap. 1, sec. 2) includes an extensive review of the literature on contracts.

Their summary begins by noting the importance of contracts to commerce and highlights Napoleon's Civil Code of 1804 and the Roman emperor Justinian's Code of 533. They call Justinian's Code "one of the really significant contributions of the Roman Empire to modern civilization." Their recent citations include seminal works in the law and economics literature such as Posner (1992) and Cooter and Ulen (1988).

34. Magill and Quinzii (1996, chap. 1, sec. 2) give the following "historical note":

> It should be recognized that the young field of economics only became a subject in its own right when it learned to separate itself from the much older field of law—and this separation lasted for some two hundred years. What is surprising is that it has taken so long for economists to recognize the fundamental importance of law and above all of contracts for the proper understanding of the functioning of an economy.

See also Chapter 10 under the section titled "Incomplete Market."

35. At least as far back as Adam Smith, government commitments to property rights, enforcement of contracts, and trade policy were known to affect the motivation of investors. Tax, fiscal, and monetary policies also affect investor motivation and have figured in national political debates in Western countries for at least the past century. (The contributions of economists such as Keynes, Schumpeter, Hayek, and Friedman, all cited elsewhere in this book, greatly informed those debates.)

36. Alfred Marshall, writing in *Principles of Economics* (1890), presaged his profession's trend toward undervaluing "customs":

> For the sake of simplicity of argument, Ricardo and his followers often spoke as though they regarded man as a constant quantity, and they never gave themselves enough trouble to study his variations. (appendix B.23)

His criticism is even more severe in later passages:

> They were aware that the inhabitants of other countries had peculiarities of their own that deserved study; but they seemed to regard such differences as superficial and

sure to be removed, as soon as other nations had got to know that better way which Englishmen were ready to teach them. (appendix B.23–24)

37. This is quite clear in macroeconomics, where the dominant models largely ignored individual opinions about institutions, at least until the rational expectations critique (originated by Robert Lucas) and subsequent research into the credibility and reputation of central banks gained acceptance late in the twentieth century.

In microeconomics and finance, only in recent decades have models of specific firms or investors that incorporate institutional factors, except in primitive fashion, become part of the mainstream literature. See, for example, Tirole (2006, sec. 16.3) and Ljungqvist and Sargent (2005). Some part of the behaviorist critique can also be traced to the ignorance of institutions in many standard economic models.

38. A recent survey article is De Haan, Lundström, and Sturm (2006). These authors find that market-oriented institutions and policies are strongly related to economic growth. They focus on studies using the economic freedom indicator of the Fraser Institute, although they recognize shortcomings of empirical studies using this index.

See also the historical note cited earlier in Magill and Quinzii (1996).

39. Gwartney and Lawson (2007).

40. Jensen and Meckling (1976). They cite works by Coase (1937, 1960); Alchian and Kessel (1962); Demsetz (1967); McManus (1975); and others.

41. It does not include criteria of replicable business practices or a separation between the firm and the relevant workers.

CHAPTER 5

1. SBA estimates are based on data from the Census Bureau and other sources. Small Business Administration, "Frequently Asked Questions," http://app1.sba.gov/faqs.

2. SBA, *The Small Business Economy (2006)*, p. 8.

3. SBA, *The Small Business Economy (2006)*, p. 8, citing the SBA Office of Advocacy. The same report states on page 13 that "even obtaining the number of firms can be daunting."

4. According to the methodology description listed by *Fortune*, to be eligible for listing, a firm must have its financial information reported to the U.S. government to be considered for ranking. This implies (and the implication is confirmed by the tagline of "America's largest corporations") that the eligible firms must be publicly traded corporations in the United States.

5. *Fortune* calculates that only about 1,800 companies have been on the list of the top five hundred in the more than fifty-five years that the magazine has published the list. The archives are found online at http://money.cnn.com /magazines /fortune /fortune500 _archive.

6. "Fortune 500: A Changing Landscape," available at http://money.cnn.com /magazines /fortune /fortune500/2010.

7. The 2010 *Forbes* list, filtered to include only U.S. companies, lists many of the same companies as *Fortune* in its top twenty-five list of (American) firms. However, there are differences; for example, Berkshire Hathaway is listed eighth among the top *Forbes* firms, but eleventh among the *Fortune* firms, even though both magazines report the same $112 billion revenue figure. See DeCarlo (2010).

8. The smallest *Forbes* Global 2000 firm on the 2010 list was Vulcan Materials Company, traded on the NYSE under the symbol VMC.

9. Murphy and Ray (2009).

10. The criteria used for the 2009 listing excluded foreign companies, companies that did not pay income tax (such as tribal gaming authorities), mutual companies (such as large mutual insurers), cooperatives, companies with fewer than a hundred employees, and companies that were more than 50 percent owned by another firm. In addition, they excluded auto dealer and real estate investment or management firms.

11. Reifman and Wong (2006). There were 394 private companies with revenues in excess of $1 billion that made the 2006 *Forbes* Largest Private Companies list. *Forbes* estimated that these firms employ 4.4 million people and generate $1.25 trillion in sales annually.

12. The three Michigan firms were Chrysler LLC, GMAC Financial Services, and Meijer. If General Motors had been included in that year (2009), Michigan would have claimed four out of the top twenty-one. Note that we classified GMAC Financial (sold by General Motors in 2006 and renamed Ally Financial in 2010) as a financial firm, not an automotive firm.

13. Among the top twenty U.S. firms in the *Forbes* Global 2000 list for 2010, JP Morgan, General Electric, and Goldman Sachs are in the top ten; IBM, Johnson & Johnson, and Pfizer are in the next ten. Note that we classified these firms by location of the operating headquarters rather than by state of legal domicile.

14. See the discussion on the relationship between total receipts of businesses and the U.S. GDP, in this section of the chapter.

15. U.S. Census Bureau (2010).

16. The likelihood of an overestimate can be seen most easily by the fact that this employment categorization includes more than 1,900 firms, where by definition the "big corporations" list could not exceed one thousand.

17. The gross domestic product (GDP) of a country is the market value of all the goods and services produced from labor and property located in that country. It is the standard measure of the size of a nation's economy.

18. Popkin (2002).

19. Indeed, they are consistent across multi-decade periods. For example, for 1990–1991, the SBA reports 541,141 births and 546,518 deaths, matching the 1:1 ratio reported for the years in the decade beginning in 2000.

20. Although we did not investigate this further, some portion of firms declaring bankruptcy eventually reorganize and emerge from bankruptcy.

21. Headd, Nucci, and Boden (2007). Note that these data focus on "establishments" rather than firms, although the ratio of establishments to firms was approximately 1.08 to 1.00.

22. This statement is widely repeated in published research, often without data to support it. For example, the summary in the *OECD Small and Medium Enterprise Outlook, 2002* (p. 8) states that the share of new jobs in the United States attributed to small firms was "up to three-quarters" in the 1990s and that firms with fewer than twenty employees now account for "up to one-half of the net new jobs."

23. Among the memorable examples in ancient and modern literature: in Greek mythology, the craftsman Daedalus and his son Icarus, who fashioned wings to fly off the island of Crete (with Icarus perishing because he flew too close to the sun); the starving playwrights in Puccini's opera *La Bohème*, who burn their manuscripts one night just to keep warm; and the sculptor in the contemporary Dire Straits song "In the Gallery," who dies before his work becomes discovered.

24. Perhaps the strongest comparison is with Canada, whose economy is partially integrated with that of the United States and which shares the North American Industry Classification System (NAICS). The next tier of comparisons is with other OECD countries, which include many developed, relatively open economies with trading relationships with the rest of the world. For some EU countries and Canada, where value-added taxation is common, the data on shares of GDP by size class may be superior to that of the United States, at least for firms that report and pay taxes.

25. Statistics Canada (2008).

26. Morrison (1999).

27. Note that these data compare employment in small, private firms with *all* employment (including government and military employment) and therefore are not directly comparable with the U.S. and Canada ratios listed previously.

28. *OECD Small and Medium Enterprise Outlook, 2002.*

29. European Commission (2009).

30. The OECD researchers noted a strong correlation between exit and entry rates among these countries. See Scarpetta (2003).

31. Morrison (1999).

32. The description below is based on common practice, as well as state laws, national laws, and tax codes in multiple countries. Obviously, such laws change periodically, and this presentation does not cover all circumstances for individual investors or companies.

33. Very large firms such as these often set up subsidiaries and have investments in other firms that have a variety of forms of organization. The assertion in the text refers to the best-known portion of the company. Note that during the time this book was being written, General Motors Corporation declared bankruptcy and became effectively owned by the U.S. government, and then reorganized and emerged from bankruptcy as General Motors Company. It was the world's largest automaker (by sales) in 2011.

34. For example, historically many professional service firms created by doctors, accountants, and lawyers were partnerships.

35. The IRS describes a PTP as follows: "A publicly traded partnership is any partnership an interest in which is regularly traded on an established securities market regardless of the number of its partners. This does not include a publicly traded partnership treated as a corporation under section 7704 of the Internal Revenue Code." See the IRS web site at http://www.irs.gov/businesses/small/international/article/0,,id=105070,00.html. See also the National Association of Publicly Traded Partnerships web site, which lists entities in most states, at http:///www.naptp.org.

36. S corporations are limited to a hundred shareholders, which must be natural persons, estates, certain trusts, and certain exempt organizations. Shareholders must also be citizens or residents of the United States. There may only be one class of stock. This places

both a practical and a legal obstacle to public ownership. See, for example, *2006 CCH U.S. Master Tax Guide*, Section 305.

37. An interesting question is the form of business for an enterprise involving illegal or informal activity. In the example of the individual ticket scalper, the business form is likely a sole proprietorship. However, criminal syndicates may involve more complex ownership and management structures. We will not settle this question here.

38. This often surprises new filers. As of 2007, U.S. Internal Revenue Code section 1401 imposed a self-employment tax of 12.4 percent for OASDI (Social Security) up to an inflation-adjusted cap, and an additional 2.9 percent tax for hospital insurance (Medicare); a partial deduction is allowed for the OASDI portion. This roughly matches the payroll tax burden on employees (including the portion paid by the employer).

On this and related S Corp compensation tax issues, see Koski (2007).

39. Evidence of this scrutiny includes the additional filing requirements (sole proprietorships typically must use Schedule C, which requires much information; wage and salary earners simply attach a W-2) and the existence of targeted audit programs. Even with these additional requirements, the IRS "tax gap" estimates contained in the GAO report of July 2007 attributed $68 billion in annual underpayment of income taxes to sole proprietors. See GAO (2007).

40. See Anderson (2009) for further discussion, including observations about the well-known phenomenon of consumers underestimating their income when responding to surveys. Federal Reserve Board research on the 2009 *Survey of Consumer Finance* (Kennickell 2010) discusses the reasons for nonresponse among some intended survey participants.

CHAPTER 6

1. Luca Pacioli (1447–1517) was a Franciscan monk and a mathematician of renown. His seminal work, *Summa de arithmetica, geometrica, proportioni et proportionalità*, published in 1494, contained a section titled "*Particularis de computis et scripturis*." This can be translated as "Details of Accounting and Recording" or "Details of Calculating and Recording," depending on whether the translator wishes to emphasize Pacioli's mathematical or accounting contributions.

Pacioli's work described a system of recording transactions that was used in Venice. Pacioli did not claim to invent the system, which is known to have been employed as early as 1305 by a merchant firm in Siena, Italy; see Nobes (1982). However, the publication of his work roughly coincided with the enormously important developments of movable type and the European discovery of America by Columbus. Thus, the *Summa* is often regarded as the first modern accounting text of wide distribution, and Pacioli the "father of accounting."

2. On Pacioli, see, for example, Linehan (1911) or Rubinstein (2006); see also Yamey (2004), discussed shortly.

3. Basil Yamey (2004), writing in Spain, adopts a skeptical tone about the use of Pacioli's work as an accounting treatise. However, he confirms that the work had tremendous influence on mathematicians across Europe. He cites Manzoni's *Quaderno doppio* (1540) as a more substantial treatise on the actual accounting entries. He also credits Hugh Oldcastle's *A Profitable Treatyce* (1543) and other works published in England as indica-

tive of the spread of the ideas in the English-speaking world, as well as other evidence of the use of double-entry accounting outside Italy by the sixteenth century.

Yamey also notes that some of the early treatises in English on accounting bear close similarity to Pacioli's and yet do not credit him. Yamey (1979) calls this a four-hundred-year-old plagiarism scandal.

4. Alexander (2007); Alexander attributes this to the late accounting scholar Ananias C. Littleton.

5. Supporting this argument are Mattessich (1998) and Sihag (2004). Most Western scholars, however, date accounting to the Italian Renaissance and cite Pacioli specifically.

6. An interesting notion raised by Mattessich is the alleged resistance by Europeans to the notion of negative numbers—an affliction that he feels the Indians never suffered. Mattessich identifies this as one of the reasons why the ancient Indians could readily accept the concept of debt as a "negative asset" and therefore create a prototype of the modern balance sheet centuries before Pacioli.

7. Kautilya listed numerous ways in which government officials could be corrupt, dishonest, or incompetent, as well as numerous ways to incentivize and punish them.

8. Sihag (2004), although supporting the claim of Kautilya as the true father of accounting, makes this point about Kautilya. Indeed, the scope of topics in the *Arthashastra* is much more like that of *Wealth of Nations* than of any mathematical treatise.

On the other hand, the title of Pacioli's *Summa de arithmetica, geometrica, proportioni et proportionalità* can be loosely translated as "everything about arithmetic, geometry, and proportions." The "father of accounting" claim stems from the chapters about "reckonings and writings."

9. Coffee (2005) examines possible explanations for the observation that more accounting scandals occur in the United States than in Europe, despite the apparently greater degree of standards for U.S. accountants. Tirole (2006, sec. 1.3) describes codes of governance among various countries and describes motivations for financial misrepresentation and other faults.

10. Larson, Miller, and Garrison (1993), p. 23.

11. See, for example, FASB (1980, para. 120), citing Opinion no. 20 of the Accounting Principles Board, a predecessor of the FASB that was established in 1959. FASB was established in 1973. It is interesting to note that VisiCalc, the first commercial spreadsheet software, wasn't introduced until 1979.

12. FASB explicitly contradicts the notion that precision is either possible, or even desirable:

Reliability does not imply certainty or precision. Indeed, any pretension to those qualities if they do not exist is a negation of reliability. (FASB, *Principles of Financial Accounting Concepts No. 2*, 1980, para. 72; see also para. 73–75)

13. The 2006 Basel Framework report (BIS, 2006, p. 1) describes the Committee as follows:

The Basel Committee on Banking Supervision is a committee of banking supervisory authorities that was established by the central bank governors of the Group of Ten countries in 1975. It consists of senior representatives of bank supervisory authorities and central banks from Belgium, Canada, France, Germany, Italy, Japan, Luxembourg, the Netherlands, Spain, Sweden, Switzerland, the United Kingdom, and the United States. It usually meets at the Bank for International Settlements in Basel, where its permanent Secretariat is located.

14. The recently adopted FAS 157 (Financial Accounting Standards Board, *Statement of Financial Accounting Standards 157*, September 2006) requires publicly traded companies and others to mark to market (using "fair value") many financial securities and contracts. FAS 157 has generated controversy, with some critics claiming it will simply make work for accountants. Others claim it is causing artificial losses to appear on company balance sheets and may threaten the solvency of otherwise sound firms. Still others claim it is just bringing more transparency into financial statements.

There were other "mark to market" requirements before FAS 157, including FAS 133 (1998), dealing with derivatives; FAS 133 was amended with FAS 161 (2008).

In addition, FAS 161 notes that the International Accounting Standards Board pronouncement IFRS 7, *Financial Instruments: Disclosures* (2005), also requires specific disclosures of market-based value estimates. The IASB also began requiring certain "mark to market" requirements (such as reporting "fair value through profit or loss") more than a decade ago, including IAS 32 (1995) and IAS 39 (1998).

15. International Accounting Standards Board, IAS 1, *Presentation of Financial Statements* (1997). The IASB describes itself as follows:

The IASB was established in 2001 and is the standard-setting body of the International Accounting Standards Committee (IASC) Foundation, an independent private sector, not-for-profit organization.

CHAPTER 7

1. References are to the edition edited by M. Cannan, first published in London in 1961. Many similar editions exist.

2. See Dobb (1973, chap. 4, sec. 1). In chapter 3 he notes how Ricardo himself subtly revised the wording of the key passages in *Principles* with each edition, moving toward the later neoclassical ideas. Despite criticisms, key Ricardian principles are still apparent two centuries later.

3. Roy Weintraub summarizes this as follows:

By the middle of the nineteenth century, English-speaking economists generally shared a perspective on value theory and distribution theory. The value of a bushel of corn, for example, was thought to depend on the costs involved in producing that bushel. The output or product of an economy was thought to be divided or distributed among the different social groups in accord with the costs borne by those groups in producing the output. This, roughly, was the "Classical Theory" developed by Adam Smith, David Ricardo, Thomas Robert Malthus, John Stuart Mill, and Karl Marx. (Weintraub, 1993)

4. This topic is discussed in some detail in Waldauer, Zahka, and Pal (1996).

5. Kautilya, *Arthashastra* (circa 350 BC), Book II, chapter XXXIII.

6. Karl Marx (1818–1883) devoted his efforts to both political economy and political agitation. Some of the scholarly works attributed to him (such as Volume 3 of *Das Kapital*,

published in 1894, well after Marx was dead) were actually written by Friedrich Engels. See, for example, Prychitko (2004). For a discussion of Marx's life that comments on his talents and political efforts, see Johnson (1989).

7. The revolutionary call exists in many of Marx's works, most memorably in *The Communist Manifesto* (1848), which calls for an end to private property rights for land and for confiscation of property from "rebels" and others, and closes with the famous slogan "Working men of all countries, unite!" Marx's call for revolution follows the famous slogan of the French anarchist Pierre-Joseph Proudhon, "Property is theft." See Proudhon (1840).

8. Dobb (1973, chap. 6, sec. 2) lists the following luminaries in the economics profession that rejected Marx in this manner: Eugen von Böhm-Bawerk, Alfred Marshall, John Keynes, Francis Edgeworth, Paul Samuelson, and ("more categorical than any") Ludwig von Mises. He notes only Joseph Schumpeter as respectful because of "the totality of his vision," which makes him interesting to "friend as well as foe."

It is not clear that Marx considered himself an economist. Prychitko quotes Marx (in Volume 1 of *Das Kapital*) himself in this regard: "Classical political economy *nearly* touches the true relation of things [emphasis added]."

9. The Marxist concept of a centrally planned economy (in which the government controls much of the property used for production of goods and services) has also been largely discredited. On the "information problem," see Hayek (1844, 1988). Empirical evidence of its failure is manifest in the relative poverty of the communist countries of Eastern Europe compared to their Western European counterparts in the decades after World War II.

CHAPTER 8

1. Some authors identify the beginning of neoclassical economics with the publication of William Stanley Jevons's *Theory of Political Economy* (1871), Carl Menger's *Principles of Economics* (1871), and Léon Walras's *Elements of Pure Economics* (1874). See, for example, Campus (1991). See also Dobb (1973, chap. 7), who argues that Jevons "completed the reaction against Ricardo" and cites George Stigler as naming him "the forerunner of neoclassical economics."

2. Alfred Marshall's *Principles of Economics* was first published in England in 1890 and republished in different editions into the 1920s. Among other contributions, Marshall popularized the ubiquitous supply-and-demand charts that occupy so much of economic pedagogy. Almost all contemporary introductory and intermediate economics textbooks continue to follow Marshall's general outline of the neoclassical model, including the introduction of consumer preferences and utility; supply and demand "curves" based on marginal benefits and costs; substitution for less expensive goods by both consumers and businesses; and a theory of industrial organization in which monopoly firms maximize profits.

See the excerpt in the text from the 1890 edition, along with the note on the "Marshallian" supply-demand "scissors."

3. Even in the eighth edition (1920), Marshall devoted the entire Appendix I of *Principles* to this topic, quoting at length from the various authors.

4. See, for example, Weintraub (1993).

5. It is interesting to note that, in a footnote, Marshall attributes the word *marginal* to von Thünen's *Der isolierte Staat* (1826), noting that the term was commonly used by German economists and that he preferred it to the term used by his fellow English economist William Stanley Jevons. Von Thünen is considered the father of spatial economics, and later editions of his landmark work related the marginal productivity of land to the rent for the land.

Although I attribute the format of the ubiquitous supply-demand graphs to Marshall, some scholars [e.g., Humphrey (1992)] claim that Antoine-Augustin Cournot originated the device as far back as 1838.

6. John Hicks, writing in the 1930s, stated that the equilibrium of the firm had already been discussed *ad nauseam*.

7. Readers may also wish to consult contemporary microeconomics texts such as Varian (1992); Mas-Colell, Whinston, and Green (1995), or the seminal treatment of Debreu (1959).

8. This is often attributed to Paul Samuelson (1938), who summarized it as follows: "If an individual selects batch one over batch two, he does not at the same time select two over one." Much more formal mathematical treatments are summarized in Varian (2006).

9. One influential description of this process has been provided in prospect theory, which models expected utility differently. See the discussion in this chapter, under the section titled "The Behaviorist School."

10. For example, in the neoclassical consumer welfare model, consumers choose to purchase goods at a single market-clearing price. A moment's reflection reveals that a single market-clearing price requires information to be distributed nearly instantly and at zero (or uniformly low) cost to market participants.

11. For example, it is impossible to accurately forecast interest rates for next year, yet almost all businesses and households are sensitive to changes in interest rates. (Note that even if you are not borrowing, you are probably "lending" to the bank or other depository institution. Furthermore, most workers and many firms also have pension or other plans that are sensitive to investment earnings.) Similarly, almost all households and businesses are sensitive to the business cycle.

12. We say we *can* incorporate time, even though many microeconomic models essentially ignore time.

13. The equation shown is nearly identical to the one used in Barro and King (1984), although the standard model they discuss also includes a budget constraint (which includes interest paid on savings) and an income process. They note that the findings would have been the same if their infinitely lived households had been subject to a finite time horizon.

14. Barro and King (1984) discuss the prevalence of this assumption and its effects on macroeconomic models, including the permanent-income model of Milton Friedman (1957). In particular, they note that this assumption minimizes the effect of information about future government policies or economic conditions on current decisions.

15. See Chapter 9, "Modern Recursive Equilibrium and the Basic Pricing Equation," under the section titled "Recursive Decision Making: Consumer Savings."

16. See, for example, the survey article by Backus, Routledge, and Zin (2008); the more formal treatment by Skiadas (1998); or the extended discussion by Kreps (1988), which includes many examples of violations of the "expected utility" model.

17. Note that we are not considering here compulsive gambling or other compulsive or addictive behavior that truly endangers the health and well-being of the individual or his or her family.

18. The cited passage is from Marshall (1920, p. 347). See also Vickers (1994, chap. 6). Vickers also quotes Walras acknowledging that "production . . . requires a certain lapse of time." As we noted earlier, Walras was completely honest when he stated that he simply ignored this dimension in the neoclassical model. Vickers's analysis of Joan Robinson's work including her later clarifications—is similarly revealing.

19. In real markets information is revealed over time, and decisions must be taken on the basis of partial information *at the time*. Thus, assuming multiple-period models, but not considering how people could be affected by uncertainty about the prices in the next period, means that the model ignores uncertainty.

20. This was pointed out by Simon (1964, p. 4). See the discussion that follows.

21. Simon (1964). Later works by Simon, including Simon (1982) and the collected works in Simon (1997), develop this theme further.

22. The following excerpt from Demsetz (1997) provides a beautiful synopsis:

> If contemporary theorizing about firms shares the weakness of Coase's views on the existence and importance of firms, it has nonetheless improved knowledge of institutional arrangements in other respects. This it has done by rejecting the assumptions used by neoclassical theory in its core model of the competitive firm: (i) markets function freely, (ii) prices and technology are known by all interested parties, and (iii) owners are effective in controlling the use of their assets. In their place, contemporary theory substitutes positive information cost. This creates a productive role for management where none exists in neoclassical theory.

23. Lucas (2003, p. 201). Lucas associates the neoclassical (marginalist) theory of pricing with economists, and the "full cost" (accounting system cost information plus a manager-determined markup) approach to accountants. He notes the widespread acceptance of a "reality gap" between the marginal cost–related pricing advocated by both managerial accounting authorities and economists and the actual behavior of firms.

24. The seminal criticism emerged from a survey of businesses reported in Hall and Hitch (1939), which described a process of price-setting in firms dubbed "full cost pricing." To address this criticism, Milton Friedman (1953) offered the "instrumentalist" argument that firms acted as if they were neoclassical profit-maximizers, even if there was no empirical evidence that they compared marginal costs to marginal revenue. Edwards (1952) argued that there were numerous "informal and unrecorded stages in the price fixing process" in which marginal cost and marginal revenue information were introduced in an effort to reach the neoclassical profit maximization goal. On this, see, for example, Mongin (1997).

25. Some sources report that the largest ship ever built, the *Jahre Viking* (also known as the "seawise giant"), had a capacity of 550,000 long tonnes of deadweight. Illustrating the risks of this industry, the ship was attacked during the Iran-Iraq war in 1988 and heavily damaged. Reconstruction took almost three years and sixty million dollars. (It was then renamed the *Happy Giant*.) See, for example, Visser (2011).

26. These have all happened in this industry. For example, more than one oil-producing nation effectively confiscated ("nationalized" is one explanation) the assets of a foreign oil company; the 1989 *Exxon Valdez* crash was both an environmental and financial disaster for Exxon; occasional "windfall" taxes and other exactions are levied on oil producers; and John D. Rockefeller's Standard Oil was the subject of antitrust prosecution resulting in a government-ordered breakup early in the twentieth century.

27. The original proposition is attributable to John Muth (1961). It was developed extensively by Robert Lucas, Thomas Sargent, and others. See, for example, Ljungqvist and Sargent (2004).

28. The concept is often attributed to the American social scientist Herbert Simon (1916–2001), whose thoughts were so wide-ranging that it would be unfair to characterize him solely as an economist, political scientist, or sociologist. He was awarded the Nobel Prize in Economics in 1978 "for his pioneering research into the decision-making process within economic organizations."

It is interesting to note that Herbert Simon and John Muth were colleagues at Carnegie Mellon University in the late 1950s and early 1960s and collaborated on research. In retrospect, both Simon's bounded rationality and Muth's rational expectations triggered changes in thought much later in economics. Simon and Robert Lucas (who originated the rational expectations critique of Keynesian economics, and who regularly cited Muth) won well-deserved Nobel prizes. Muth did not. Lucas later observed (in Klamer [1984]), "It must be quite an experience to write papers that radical and have people just pat you on the back and say 'that's interesting' and nothing happens."

29. We do not need to describe precisely how bounded is the rationality of investors or managers, nor the specific manner in which taxpayers view government policies or acquire information about them.

30. For example, another list of principles (assembled by Dawnay and Shah, 2005) is the following:

1. Other people's behavior matters.
2. Habits are important.
3. People are motivated to "do the right thing."
4. Self-expectations influence behavior.
5. People are loss averse.
6. People have poor skills at computation.
7. People "need to feel involved and effective to make change."

31. See Chapter 9, "Modern Recursive Equilibrium and the Basic Pricing Equation," under the section titled "Bubbles, Puzzles, and Troubles."

32. Kahneman and Tversky (1979) and Tversky and Kahneman (1992) outline this theory.

33. See Frydman and Goldberg (2007, sec. 9.1), citing Tversky and Kahneman (1991).

CHAPTER 9

1. The recursive model is described at length in Ljungqvist and Sargent (2000, 2004) and summarized in the survey article by Mehra (2006, 2008). Stokey and Lucas (1989)

provide the mathematical bases for optimization in a recursive setting, including the dynamic programming algorithm introduced in Chapter 15, "The Value Functional: Theory," under the section titled "Introduction to Dynamic Programming."

Numerous applications of recursive methods in economics are presented in Miranda and Fackler (2002). Their use in finance and investment was pioneered by Dixit and Pindyck (1994), and their use in business valuation by Anderson (2004a). Bellman (1957) outlined the recursive decision-making process in broad mathematical terms.

2. The presentation of these results is modeled after Ljungqvist and Sargent (2004, chap. 13).

3. Mehra's (2006, 2008) survey article shows, using a recursive model that is somewhat more detailed than the one presented here, that the decision rule in a recursive growth model ("of course, simply maximize . . . period profits") is the same as the neoclassical model, if one assumes that all markets are perfectly competitive.

4. This is also called the *Euler-Lagrange differential equation*, which is a fundamental equation of the calculus of variations. See Appendix A, "Key Formula and Notation Summary," under the section titled "Stochastic Discount Factor; Basic Pricing Equation; State Prices; Risk-Neutral Probability." See also the related information in Appendix B, "Guide to the Solutions Manual," under the section titled "Mathematics."

Applications of Euler equations in finance are described in Ljungqvist and Sargent (2004, sec. 13.3) and Stokey and Lucas (1989, sec. 4.5).

5. Cochrane (2001) provides an excellent and accessible presentation of the stochastic discount factor approach to asset pricing, and we adopted the payoff notation and some observations about the usefulness of the SDF pricing equation from this text. The survey of research on the equity premium puzzle by Mehra and Prescott (2003, p. 902) also follows this derivation, noting that it has been used in seminal papers dating from the late 1970s, as well as advanced textbooks in the 2000s.

6. The term *basic pricing equation* is from Cochrane (2001), whose emphasis on the generality of the result is adopted here. Ljungqvist and Sargent (2000, 2004, sec. 1.3.9) develop the same result and use it to introduce recursive applications in both macroeconomics and finance.

However, versions of this equation (sometimes called *fundamental equations*) were derived under different and more restrictive conditions by Rubinstein (1976), R. Lucas (1978), Breeden and Litzenberger (1978), and others decades ago; see, for example, Constantinides (1989) for a survey.

7. This is the intuition behind the mathematical assumption that $\lim_{c \to 0} u'(c) =$ infinity.

8. Broadening this observation to real consumers requires broadening the definition of *savings* as well as *eating*. Actual consumers, at least in the United States, have access to a variety of savings and investments (including their home equity, as well as investments in private businesses); access to borrowing (including credit card and other short-term, unsecured debt); and a government and private safety net. Thus, the observed savings rate calculated using the U.S. national income and product accounts may move close to zero for certain time periods.

9. The original statement is from Milton Friedman (1957). Meghir (2004), in a retrospective on the theory, notes that it was originally described in Friedman and Kuznets

(1954) and concludes that the idea was simple and powerful and had stood the test of time.

The permanent income theory is often combined with a related concept, the life cycle theory of income, for which Ando and Modigliani (1963) and Hall (1978) are the seminal references. Both theories explain how consumers smooth their consumption patterns, compared to more variable income patterns. Many macroeconomics texts discuss these theories; see, for example, Ljungqvist and Sargent (2004, sec. 1.3.1).

10. Robert Lucas (1978, p. 1432) states that this concept of equilibrium is exactly the same as the "standard, Arrow-Debreu equilibrium" in which the commodity space is all possible realizations of the future income stream.

11. This is a form of an Euler equation, in which the marginal rate of temporal substitution (the *discount rate* on consumption) equals the marginal rate of transformation (investment returns). Euler equations are discussed above and in Appendix A, "Key Formula and Notation Summary," under the section titled "Stochastic Discount Factor; Basic Pricing Equation; State Prices; Risk-Neutral Probability."

In this particular model, this is a *stochastic Euler equation*; see Lucas (1978, p. 1434). As stochastic difference equations were unknown to Euler, this is not precisely the same as the Euler equation of the calculus of variations.

12. Indeed, Robert Lucas derives a variation of the "efficient market" theory in his model and derives a returns formulation of the asset price equilibrium. See Lucas (1978, p. 1443). Ljungqvist and Sargent (2004, sec. 1.3.8) compare the use of the Euler equation logic in the Lucas model with those of other recursive models.

13. See the summary of research in Cochrane (2001, chap. 21). This view contrasts sharply with that of Ross (2005), who wonders what the fuss is about. A retrospective of Mehra and Prescott (2003) contains an excellent summary of the various explanations, from the perspective of the authors who originally decided there was a "puzzle."

14. That does not mean *rational* in the inhumanly narrow way in which it is sometimes used in social science, where human beings are placed into a humorless straitjacket of profit maximization and portfolio optimization. Rational human beings give money to charity, throw away their mail unread, gamble in casinos, do risky things they enjoy, pay for status and pay to avoid hassles, and do all the other things that entertain, annoy, frustrate, and thrill each other.

15. The circumstances are important here; the "motivated and prepared" speculator in the example would have the capital and expertise to engage in this kind of speculation, and the discipline to do so within limits. Even then, the speculator would lose on many trades and, in some circumstances, lose a lot.

This illustrates the difference between the mathematical condition of "no arbitrage" and the practical description of the circumstance in which speculators "should" purchase a security. Very low risk is *not* the same as zero risk, and so these trades are not true arbitrages.

16. Such an analysis explains a good part of the late-1990s tech bubble, as shown by Pastor and Veronesi (2004). See the note on different meanings of the word *bubble* that follows.

17. Note Cochrane's (2001, sec. 20.1) admonition that the word *bubble* can mean at least two different things: any large movement in prices, and any large movement not corresponding to a present-value model with constant expected returns. Perhaps anticipating

a reexamination of even the Dutch tulip mania, he cites Garber (2000) as questioning whether even that episode is a true bubble.

CHAPTER 10

1. This chapter deals with the direct application of the no-arbitrage principle in traded (often assumed to be complete) markets. One of the common abstractions used in economics is that of assuming that all assets can be bought and sold in a market filled with many buyers and sellers, without impediment or large transaction prices. This is clearly not true for most assets, as we discuss below in this chapter.

2. Ingersoll (1989) refines the claim by saying that Ross was the "first to prove the equivalence of the absence of arbitrage and the existence of a linear pricing rule." However, the historical record is not completely clear on this point. Differing accounts are offered by Duffie (2001, chap. 1); S. Ross (2005, p. 1), who dates the "discovery of risk neutral pricing" to Ross (1973); and Rubinstein (2006, pp. 116, 277), who emphasizes the underappreciated contribution of Drèze (1971). Other scholars point to Harrison and Kreps (1979), Harrison and Pliska (1981), and Dybvig and Ross (1987). More obscure references include Fischer (1972) and Beja (1971), who was cited at least as early as Rubinstein (1976).

3. The key mathematical innovations included an application of the Reisz representation theorem from functional analysis, which tied together the NA assumption with the existence of a positive linear pricing operator (Ross, 1973), and its later development by Harrison and Kreps (1979). Dybvig and Ross (1987) are responsible for much of the nomenclature, including the "fundamental theorem of finance." The seminal paper on option pricing, which relies on the no-arbitrage assumption as well as other strong assumptions, was Black and Scholes (1973).

4. Rubinstein (2006) says that Arrow's 1953 paper, written in French, "may be the most important paper ever written for financial economics." He also notes that many of the practical difficulties in applying the complete-market assumption were anticipated by Arrow very early. Arrow won the 1972 Nobel Prize in Economics for these and other contributions.

5. Recall the neoclassical model synthesized by Debreu and others, in which demand arises from consumer preferences—not no-arbitrage conditions.

6. Similar definitions occur in numerous texts. However, Arrow (1953) is probably the basis for the definition. A more rigorous definition that incorporates the matrix of payoffs is provided by Magill and Quinzii (1998, sec. 9, definition 22.1).

7. In such models, short-selling is also implied, including "naked" short-selling. Very few brokerage firms would allow regular investors to short securities without limitation.

8. The rank of a matrix of size (m, n) can be no larger than $\min(m, n)$. A square matrix is *invertible* only if the matrix is of full rank. A more technical definition of rank is based on the *dimension* of a vector space. See, for example, Weisstein (2011).

9. Probabilities of events occurring, based on the past record of such occurrences, are sometimes called *frequentist* because they are based on the relative frequency of an outcome, such as the fraction of times that a tossed coin lands heads or tails. There are also other sources of probabilities, such as subjective beliefs.

10. These fulfill the requirements of a probability measure, including having nonnegative values and summing to one. See Appendix A, "Key Formula and Notation Summary," under the section titled "Stochastic Processes; Expectations; Measure."

11. Alternatively, one may also include either the prices or the risk-neutral measure (implied by the prices) as arguments to this operator. Information on alternate derivations of these formulas is discussed in Appendix B, "Guide to the Solutions Manual," under the section titled "Mathematics."

12. Dybvig and Ross (1987) are responsible for much of the nomenclature of this school, including the term *fundamental theorem of finance*. The same theory is sometimes described as *asset pricing* or *arbitrage-free pricing*. See the preceding discussion of the origin of the approach.

13. Two possible ambiguities are (1) the *all assets* phrase (which implies either a universal application in which the no-arbitrage condition applies or a narrow application in which at least one investor has a finite optimal demand) and (2) the existence of a positive linear pricing rule (which may mean a rule that *uniquely* prices all assets). A third ambiguity is the meaning of *optimal demand*; clearly, the existence of one buyer who is satisfied with his or her purchases does not create a market with no arbitrage.

14. This formulation is from Sharpe (2006, p. 84). A shorter—and somewhat ambiguous—formulation of this appears in S. Ross (2005, p. 2):

> The law of one price (LOP) is the most important of the special cases of NA. . . . The LOP holds that two assets with identical payoffs must sell for the same price.

The "law" dates from the early years of development of the complete-market approach. For example, Rubinstein (1976) states that the "single-price law of markets" requires that securities "that yield the same dividends in every future state" must have the same current price. Rubinstein also notes that the existence of transaction costs undermines the "law."

15. This presentation is based on Cochrane (2001, sec. 4.1). The key result is derived with more rigor in Magill and Quinzii (1998, sec. 9).

16. See the section in this chapter titled "Mathematics of Complete Markets."

17. The Green Bay Packers football club is unique in many ways; one is that the club is a publicly owned company with unusual limitations on the shareholders and the firm. This is a good illustration of the contingencies that cannot be insured in incomplete markets. It would be nearly impossible to purchase enough stock to control the Packers board or, say, try to move it out of Wisconsin to a larger media market.

It would also be difficult to purchase a half-share of Microsoft. Thus, to actually fulfill the portfolio formation assumption used here, we would have to choose different quantities, different securities, or both.

18. The Riesz theorem is discussed in Ljungqvist and Sargent (2000, chap. 10), and Stokey and Lucas (1989). The theorem (actually one of a set of theorems named for the late Hungarian mathematician Frigyes Riesz) holds that a bounded linear functional can be represented as the inner product of a random payoff with some scalar random variable. The use of the term *functional* is introduced in Chapter 15, "The Value Functional: Theory," under the section titled "The Idea of a Functional Equation."

19. An excellent summary of efforts to extend this idea is Ingersoll (1989); Cochran (2001) and other cited references also cover the topic well.

20. See, for example, Lengwiler (2004, sec. 6.2.1). The original sources are Kreps (1982) and Guesnerie and Jaffray (1974). See also Ingersoll (1989).

21. See Lengwiler (2004, sec. 5.3.7) for an extended discussion and welfare implications.

22. The seminal essay is Shiller (1994). Shiller and Athanasoulis (2000) provide some analytics on what securities would provide the most social benefit. Lengwiler (2004, sec. 5.3.7) discusses this briefly along with "quasi-complete" markets.

23. As of 2008, at least one company (MacroMarkets LLC) had begun offering such securities, Robert Shiller is one of its founders

24. Monday, October 19, 1987, is known as Black Monday for the enormous crash in stock markets in many Western and Asian countries, including Hong Kong, Spain, the United Kingdom, and the United States. By some measures, Black Monday's decline was the largest one-day drop in stock market values in U.S. history. The many—and still disputed—possible causes for the crash include a proposal from the congressional Ways and Means Committee to increase taxes on certain investment activities, excessive speculation, program trading in the United States, confluence of option expiration dates, unanticipated connections among markets around the world, and market psychology. See, for example, Carlson (2007) and Presidential Task Force on Market Mechanisms (1988, the "Brady Report").

25. Long Term Capital Management (LTCM) was a large and highly leveraged hedge fund that engaged in technical trading strategies, in which the firm attempted to exploit near-arbitrage opportunities. The firm lost more than 90 percent of its capital in 1998 and nearly collapsed because of rapid changes in the interest rate spreads that LTCM attempted to exploit. A consortium that was encouraged by the Federal Reserve Bank of New York took over the fund in the fall of 1998.

Among the reports on the spectacular collapse of LTCM are two prepared by the U.S. Government Accounting Office, GAO (1999) and GAO (2000). They detail, among other failures, how the participation of two Nobel laureates and a former Fed vice chairman in LTCM created a "halo effect" that, along with early successes of the fund, encouraged lenders and counterparties to relax their diligence.

26. Fannie Mae and Freddie Mac were placed under a U.S. government conservatorship in September 2008. The distinction between these government-sponsored entities and actual firms was discussed in Chapter 5, "The Organization and Scale of Private Business," under the section titled "Types of Businesses: Publicly Traded Corporations."

27. See S. Ross (2005, p. 3, footnote).

28. For example, consider a real estate speculator. She may purchase real estate from a seller in distress if she perceives the risk of holding it until she can find a buyer to be small given the difference between the quick-sale price and the (anticipated future) market price. If she is consistently correct, she earns a healthy profit even after the significant transaction costs. However, it is not a risk-free profit. This is practical arbitrage combined with savvy marketing, not mathematical arbitrage.

29. The *central limit theorem* in statistics is a powerful tool in such instances, although it is often used conveniently when the assumptions are not completely fulfilled.

30. On the exclusion of privately held firms from the wealth portfolio in the common treatment of MPT, see Chapter 11, "Portfolio Pricing Methods," under the section titled "Limitations of CAPM and Factor Models."

On the practical ignorance of privately held firms, see the financial pages of almost any major newspaper as of the time of this printing, as well as the common online financial web sites. These are devoted almost exclusively to publicly traded securities.

31. It is not uncommon for disability insurance to cover only a small fraction of the annual income of business managers. Insurance contracts that cover entrepreneurial risk, to my knowledge, do not exist.

32. Koopmans is quoted in Ingersoll (1989), which includes other useful notes on the difficulty in achieving complete markets through various technical means. We discussed the latter topic earlier in this chapter, under the section titled "Technical Rehabilitation of Complete Markets."

33. See, for example, Cochrane (2001, sec. 4.2); Cvitanic & Zapatero (2004, sec. 7.6.4); Sharpe (2007, sec. 4.9.2); and Lengwiler (2005, sec. 3.4).

34. This aspect is explained clearly in Lengwiler (2004, sec. 3.4.1).

35. On this, see Lengwiler (2005, section 3.5). The relevant risks that cannot be insured include human capital risks (for managers and employees), search costs for employment, and information costs for shareholders. To illustrate just one conflict, consider the employee who wants higher wages. However, it is costly to search for a new job, and there is no way to hedge the risk of failing to find one. (No "Sally finds a job" security exists.) Thus, she may stay at an underpaying job, or leave it and remained unemployed for a long time. The employer may overpay employees to discourage them from leaving, or underpay and rely on the search costs to keep them there. All these result in firms that do not achieve a maximum profit, as well as workers and investors who are unhappy.

36. Almost all actual markets involve a large group of potential buyers and sellers who are simply "out of the market" at any one time. Remember that the fair *market* value presumes that a market exists and that the participants in the market set the value. Thus, there must be a fairly large number of potential buyers and sellers to warrant an assumption of active bidding and therefore a well-defined "market price."

CHAPTER 11

1. The use of means and variances to analyze risk and return appeared in Markowitz (1952), independently and around the same time as Roy (1952). The use of what is now called mean-variance portfolio analysis was presented in Markowitz (1959). The work of James Tobin was also instrumental in its development, particularly Tobin (1958), in which he introduced borrowing at a risk-free rate into the potential actions of an investor. This results (within the significantly limiting assumptions of the model) in a separation of the portfolios into one of borrowing and one of equity purchases. An excellent intellectual history of the mean-variance framework and the CAPM appears in Rubinstein (2006).

2. The CAPM appeared in various forms in papers by Sharpe (1964), Lintner (1965), and Mossin (1966). Some authors, including Sharpe, include the work of Treynor (reprinted 1999) as an original source. Rubinstein (2006) has an extended discussion of the genesis of the CAPM.

3. Two seminal references are S. Ross (1976) and Merton (1973a); we discuss the intellectual history further in Chapter 10, "Arbitrage-Free Pricing in Complete Markets."

4. Markowitz states this flatly in the introduction to his 1959 monograph: "A second salient feature of security investments is the correlation among security returns." (The

first salient feature was uncertainty.) He continues: "One hundred securities whose returns rise and fall in near unison afford little more protection than the uncertain return of a single security."

A contemporary account, such as Cochrane (2001, sec. 9.3), similarly emphasizes how modern asset pricing theory "starts" with the recognition that investors really care about the returns from their overall portfolio more than those of specific assets.

Stephen Ross (2005, chap. 1) lists specifically the arbitrage pricing theory (APT), the capital asset pricing model (CAPM), and the consumption beta model (CBM) as asset pricing theories that depend on the primacy of the portfolio. Note that prices in this school are often described in terms of risk premium, and risks in terms of volatility and covariance.

5. Markowitz (1959, introduction) states that "two objectives . . . are common for all investors. . . . They want "return" to be high. . . . They want this return to be dependable, stable, not subject to uncertainty." The investors about whom Markowitz is concerned are further defined as "not for such speculators" as those betting on horse races, or otherwise preferring more risk to less. Utility functions are introduced in Chapter 8, "Value in Neoclassical Economics," under the section titled "Consumer Welfare and Preferences."

6. The analogous Euler equation for consumers is presented in Chapter 9, "Modern Recursive Equilibrium and the Basic Pricing Equation," under the section titled "Recursive Decision Making: Consumer Savings." Euler equations in general are described in Appendix A, "Key Formula and Notation Summary," under the section titled "Stochastic Discount Factor; Basic Pricing Equation; State Prices; Risk-Neutral Probability."

7. This particular form of the quadratic value function looks odd because it has a negative sign in front of it. This follows the practice in finance noted by Magill and Quinzii (1998, sec. 17) of allowing utility functions to be defined for positive and negative real numbers, to reflect the disutility of investment losses.

See, for example, Brandimarte (2006, sec. 2.4.1) for a different version of quadratic utility that has a positive quantity added to the (negative) quadratic term. Depending on the scale factor and the size of the variables, the marginal value function of that variant may be close to that of the variant in Equation 11.7. It also looks odd because the bliss level is subtracted; however, squared deviations are exactly the same whether the deviations themselves are negative or positive.

8. The growing deviations from the bliss point in quadratic utility mean that after a certain point, more wealth makes someone unhappy. This is hard to justify. Also, the bliss level of consumption or wealth (the deviations from which form the basis for the utility) must change over time for a consumer, worker, or investor. Third, quadratic utility implies that wealthier people are more risk averse; empirical data strongly support the notion that wealthier people accept more risk in their investments, not less.

9. Alternative derivations are provided in different settings in Lengwiler (2004), Cochrane (2001), Cvitanic and Zapatero (2004), and Duffie (2001).

10. Critiques of the abuse of CAPM appear in, for example, Anderson (2004a, 2005b) and even (delicately) in Sharpe (2007). A handful of the critiques of multifactor models are noted in the survey by Campbell (2000) as well as Cochrane (2001), who warns against using CAPM and related factor models as a "fishing license." Several critiques of the CAPM are also summarized in this chapter.

11. Because stock prices are strongly correlated with each other, the standard CAPM regression equation (with individual stocks on one side and the stock market as a whole on the other) almost always produces an impressively high *R-squared* statistic, which indicates a goodness of fit.

12. Similar summaries of the assumptions used in CAPM derivations include those by Goetzmann (2006, chap. 4); Brigham and Daves (2006); and Elton, Gruber, Brown, and Goetzmann (2006). I interpret the term "security" in this list as including private firm equity, which may not be the case for all authors.

13. Many consumers can borrow small amounts of money at relatively low rates by increasing their mortgages (sometimes through home equity loans) or secured loans such as automobile loans. They can also lend at very low rates through leaving more money in certain checking or savings accounts or money market accounts. If they have enough capital, they can purchase U.S. government Treasury bills, but they cannot issue similar securities.

If we convert the returns on these instruments into prices for (hypothetical) pure-discount bonds, we observe that a significant spread exists. For example, a home equity loan at 6 percent would have a different price than a money market account yielding 1 percent. Consumers who can purchase T-bills can achieve a lending rate very close to the theoretical risk-free rate (the differential being commissions and bid-ask spreads).

14. For examples of this, see, for example, Cochrane (2001, sec. 9.1).

Brennan (1989) gives a summary of empirical and theoretical critiques reported at that time. Many other texts contain summaries of empirical results from the numerous CAPM tests.

15. Roll (1977). Note that there are actually two Roll critiques of the CAPM: the absence of much of the true wealth portfolio and the joint-statistical-test problem. It is interesting to note that most contemporary summaries of the Roll critique include as other assets human capital, real estate, artwork, and commodities—and often neglect to mention private firm equity.

16. For brief discussions of data snooping problems in empirical research about asset returns, see, for example, Cochrane (2001) or Campbell (2000). Contemporary concerns about data snooping frequently arise, alongside debate about the validity of a model *and* the data and methodology used to test it, in empirical work involving the equity premium puzzle.

17. A widely cited estimate of survivor bias was calculated for mutual funds by Elton, Gruber, and Blake (1996). Subsequent research largely confirms its existence but varies in terms of the definitions used and the size of the bias. The Center for Research in Security Prices at the University of Chicago, the source for much of the data used in contemporary stock market research in the United States, now markets a "survivor-bias-free US mutual fund database."

CHAPTER 12

1. Among authorities on this subject, Hull (2002) states flatly that the fact that an option holder has the right to do something but does not exercise it "is what distinguishes

options from forwards and futures, where the holder is obligated to buy or sell the underlying asset." See Hull (2002, sec. 1.5).

2. Evidence of commercial disputes on these matters exists in cuneiform tablets (on display at the British Museum) from circa 1750 BC! See Poitras (2000; 2008).

3. See, for example, Smitka (1998) and Osaka Securities Exchange (2008).

4. The use of financial options in England at least since the 1690s is documented, meaning at least three hundred years of development and use. See, for example, Anne Murphy (2005), McKenzie (2003), and the sources cited later in this chapter.

5. The East India Company had been chartered by Queen Victoria of England in 1600 and given near-monopoly power on trade with the subcontinent. In the early 1700s it was a joint-stock company engaged primarily in commerce; after 1757 it became the de facto colonial administrator of much of India. Poitras (2008) recorded the financial speculation in the company's shares.

The example here is analogous with that of the Mississippi Scheme in the United States, in that the financial speculation occurred primarily in Europe, while the activities of the companies themselves were primarily in British colonies.

6. See, for example, McKenzie (2003, p. 836).

7. See Poitras (2008) on European events.

8. See Poitras (2000; 2008). Many of the ancient and early modern contracts allowed a merchant receiving goods under a forward contract to refuse to accept them if they were not of satisfactory quality and timely delivery. Indeed, the cuneiform tablets mentioned earlier deal with a dispute regarding the acceptance of goods.

9. The Black-Scholes-Merton model is based on Black and Scholes (1973) and Merton (1973b); Merton's collaboration on this work is well known and careful scholars refer to the formula in a manner crediting all three authors; see the following note for historical references.

10. The academic contemporaries of these pioneers were not always well received. Bachelier did not get high marks for his dissertation and labored for years before receiving a relatively modest professorship. Contemporary finance texts often fail to mention Boness or Castelli. Even Black and Scholes's paper was initially rejected by two different journals! Historical notes on option pricing appear in Shreve (2004, vol. 2, sec. 4.9), Rubinstein (2006, p. 235), and McKenzie (2003).

11. A standard reference in the United States is Hull (2002). The notation here is close to that used by Hull. A thorough mathematical treatment oriented toward mathematicians and economists is Shreve (2003).

12. See Hull (2002, sec. 12.8) for this argument and the risk-neutral derivation.

13. See, for example, Hull (2002, sec. 12.11).

14. The mathematical model in this section is based on that of Duffie (2001, chap. 11), although I have extended the description of economic and institutional factors. Note that the assumptions of $A_t > 0$ and the stock is priced as an option imply that the value of debt cannot drop below zero.

15. Geometric Brownian motion is summarized in Appendix A, "Key Formula and Notation Summary," under the section titled "Stochastic Differential Equations; Itô and Wiener Processes."

16. Recall Modigliani and Miller's Proposition I (the value of a firm is the capitalized expected future income on its assets), which was presented in Chapter 3, "The Failure of the Neoclassical Investment Rule," under the section titled "The M-M Propositions."

17. See, for example, Vollert (2003, sec. 2.2).

18. Formally, a lattice is an algebra $\{L, \wedge, \vee\}$ that contains a nonempty set L with binary operations that are named here $\wedge$ and $\vee$. These operations follow certain familiar properties such as transitivity. The operator symbols can be intuitively considered *up* and *down* for the purpose of ordering prices of assets over time. Lattices are a natural way to formalize any ordered set of objects or events in a partially ordered set. They have a particularly useful property of always having a least upper bound (*supremum*) and greatest lower bound (*infimum*). See, for example, Insall and Weisstein (2011).

19. Cochrane and Saá-Reuquejo (2000). The technique is also presented in Cochrane (2005, section 18.2). Related "bounding the pricing kernel" techniques are summarized in S. Ross (2005, chap. 2).

20. The Sharpe ratio is defined as

$$S = \frac{E[R-R_f]}{\sigma} = \frac{E[R-R_f]}{\sqrt{\mathrm{var}[R-R_f]}}$$

although there is some variation in usage regarding the definition and subtraction of the risk-free rate.

21. Ulam's collaborator Nicholas Metropolis coined the term *Monte Carlo* for the paper they co-authored in 1949 (Metropolis and Ulam, 1949). The invention of the technique is described in Eckhardt (1987).

22. See especially Dixit and Pindyck (1994).

23. These include Vollert (2003), who explicitly describes their use for real options, and Miranda and Fackler (2002), who describe applications for both real and financial options. Anderson (2004a) describes this as a method for business valuation.

24. A Markov process can be defined informally as one in which all the useful information that a decision maker could use to forecast the future is incorporated in the last set of observations. See Appendix A, "Key Formula and Notation Summary," under the section titled "Stochastic Processes; Expectations; Measure."

25. The numerical analysis is from Trigeorgis and Mason (1987). That and other related articles are collected in Schwartz and Trigeorgis (2001); one such collected article is the seminal exposition on the value of waiting to invest by McDonald and Siegel (1986).

26. The expected net present value is $100 = [(.5 * 180) + (.5 * 60)]/(1 + .20)$.

27. The loss in the previous example was $100 - \$104 = -\$4$. In this case, the gross return is $[(.5 * 68) + (.5 * 0)]/1.2 = \$28$. The first term in the numerator is the potential gain if the price of the commodity increases, assuming that the price of the plant rose at the inflation rate during the period (from 104 to 112). The second term is the (null) gain, as the cash payment for the construction is not made if the price of the commodity drops. See the following discussion of the difference between the DTA and CCA result for $t = 1$.

28. See Trigeorgis & Mason (1987, collected in Schwartz and Trigeorgis [2001, p. 51]) for the calculations of risk-neutral probabilities.

29. Fisher (1930, chap. 7, sec. 1). Fisher goes on in this chapter to illustrate how investors choose the investment with the "comparative advantage" over the others, in accordance with the principle that "to induce him to make a change, the rate of return over cost must exceed the rate of interest."

CHAPTER 13

1. See Chapter 1, "Modern Value Quandaries," under the section titled "Quandary 7: Distant and Separate Literatures Cover Business Value Theory."

2. See Anderson (2005b), who cites other critiques and different categorization schemes. See also the discussion on the Bellman equation in Chapter 15, "The Value Functional: Theory."

3. As of 2011, the NYSE Amex exchanges had established a multiple-criteria listing standard, which allowed for various domestic and international companies to "list" their shares on the NYSE or Amex exchange. These criteria include distribution and size criteria as well as financial criteria. Generally it is difficult for publicly traded companies to meet the NYSE criteria unless they have more than 1 million shares outstanding and a market capitalization of $100 million. See NYSE Amex (2011).

4. Two examples follow: First, a partner in a professional services firm may need to sell his or her interest in order to retire. Second, a prospective partner may be compelled by the membership agreement to buy an interest. Neither of these parties is completely free from pressure. Of course, nearly all buyers and sellers are subject to some form of pressure.

5. Often, a small number of prospective buyers (often one) are granted the right to perform due diligence once a confidentiality agreement is signed with the seller. Such expense is avoided by potential buyers of publicly traded companies that produce annual reports and file disclosures with the Securities and Exchange Commission.

6. One complication that affects the price is the *control premium* embedded in prices of equity interests large enough to carry management control as well as title to earnings. In addition, large-share transactions often involve other considerations (such as real estate encumbrances, implied pension benefits, implied salaries and benefits, or personal guarantees), thus rendering the actual equity interest price less apparent.

7. LECG is numerically distant from the rest of the companies. It is an outlier in the respect that its earnings per share and EBITDA are negative. Additionally, its previous closing price was well below that of the other three companies—almost 80 percent less than the smallest.

8. See the discussion of the models underlying the Modigliani-Miller propositions in Chapter 3, "Failure of the Neoclassical Investment Rule," and the option model of the firm in Chapter 12, "Real Options and Expanded Net Present Value." In the latter, equity value was modeled as a call option on the firm's assets, where the call option at maturity is worth $\max(0, A - L)$. In the former, the firm's equity value is modeled as the difference between the *market value* of the firm's assets and liabilities.

9. In particular, firms that have a history of paying dividends and then reducing them are often seen as signaling or confirming financial distress or reduced future earnings potential. For this reason, publicly traded firms may feel pressured to maintain a dividend even when earnings dip.

10. See Chapter 15, "The Value Functional: Theory," under the section titled "The Idea of a Functional," for some interesting applications of this observation and to test the notion of "benefits to the investor are the same" in practical terms.

11. Agency theory is presented in Chapter 4, "The Nature of the Firm."

12. Many companies have attempted to align the incentives of their managers with those of their stockholders through compensation agreements that include equity in the firm, options of equity in the firm, or specific performance targets. This does not eliminate the agency problem but can reduce it. Similarly, many C corp boards of directors insist that board members (who represent the interests of shareholders) have substantial equity stakes.

CHAPTER 14

1. The *Solutions Manual* reprints IRS RR 59-60 (1959) and other standards; see also Appendix B, under the section titled "Valuation Standards." The RR 59-60 factors have also been included in other standards such as USPAP.

2. See Chapter 3, "The Failure of the Neoclassical Investment Rule," particularly the discussion of M-M Proposition I and the role of arbitrage titled "Outline of This Chapter."

3. See again Chapter 3, "The Failure of the Neoclassical Investment Rule," noting that investors cannot assemble portfolios of private company stocks and bonds.

4. In making this statement, I draw on many occasions in forensic economics in which experts are retained by opposing sides in a dispute. For example, I have seen multiple cases where credentialed accountants and economists produce discount rate estimates that differ by large margins—even when they both claim to be using some version of a CAPM and the same stock market data, and where both have the same historical data on the company and the industry. (I ignore for this observation instances in which, in my opinion, one of the experts was either incompetent or consumed by bias.) The same is usually not true for other variables—such as expected revenue growth rates—that have similar effects on the ultimate estimated quantity.

5. The listing in Pratt (2008, chap. 9) includes the following common errors: mismatching the discount rate with the economic income measure; projecting growth beyond what the capital base will sustain; projecting an extrapolation of recent results; discounting terminal value for the incorrect number of periods; inconsistent capital structure assumptions; and incorrect premise of value.

6. For example, the Irish Stock Exchange offers information on both bond and equity markets on its web site, at http://www.ise.ie. The Taiwan Stock Exchange offers similar data on its web site, at http://www.tse.com.tw/en.

7. Cowles (1939); cited in Shiller (1989, chap. 26). Shiller also maintains an updated data summary on his web site at Yale University. See also Goetzmann, Ibbotson, and Peng (2000).

8. See Cowles (1939) and Goetzmann, Ibbotson, and Peng (2000).

9. Pring (2002, p. 2), quoted in Park and Irwin (2007). Park and Irwin further state that "technical analysis includes a variety of forecasting techniques such as chart analysis, cycle analysis, and computerized technical trading systems."

10. We note that empirical tests are further complicated by the fact that the technical analyst has access to the same universe of information that the fundamental analysts also have, and at the same time. Even fundamental analysts draw charts and add their own

versions of trend lines to those charts, so investment advice by an analyst that claims to eschew technical analysis is probably based partially on it.

11. The DJIA is *not* a broad indicator of U.S. stocks, and it is an even narrower view of wealth. However, saying "the Dow went up" is a shorthand way to describe U.S. stock market indicators showing rising prices. See Chapter 11, "Portfolio Pricing Methods," under the section titled "Limitations of CAPM and Factor Models."

12. Early followers of Charles Dow who contributed to the development of the Dow Theory include William Hamilton and Robert Rhea; later proponents were E. George Schaefer and Richard Russell. A nice history on the Dow Theory was compiled by investment advisor Henry To (2004).

13. West (2007) is one edition; later editions were published at least through 2012.

14. This author and his colleagues at Anderson Economic Group LLC have contributed information to past editions and have been recognized as industry experts in selected industries. However, the publisher of *Business Reference Guide* is solely responsible for its content and may change it in future editions.

CHAPTER 15

1. In *Politics*, Aristotle (1885) writes about the necessity of managing a household and illustrates it as follows: "if the shuttle weaved and the [pick] touched the lyre without a hand to guide them . . . chief workmen would not need servants, nor masters slaves" (Book I, pt. 4). Bennett (1979) asserts the Aristotelian origin of control theory in Western literature and traces it through statements from later authors such as Machiavelli, Alexander Hamilton, John Maynard Keynes, and David Hume. However, I distinguish control theory as a mathematical or engineering concept from the philosophical discussion of management and politics.

2. Maxwell (1867). Einstein describes Maxwell's field equations with great respect in his original article outlining the general theory of relativity, published in German in 1916.

3. Merton (1973a). One additional notable observation of the potential for the use of dynamic programming was made by Harry Markowitz in his original (and enormously influential) 1959 dissertation on portfolio management.

4. Ljungqvist and Sargent (2000, 2004).

5. Dreyfus and Bellman collaborated in their efforts to introduce the technique of dynamic programming to mathematicians and other social and physical scientists. I found a copy of Dreyfus's 1965 book at a university math library and marveled at how he succeeded in his efforts to describe this and other concepts in simple terms.

6. The calculus was originated by Leibniz and Newton in the late 1600s. The first textbook in the calculus of variations is thought to be the *Method of Finding Curved Lines that Show some Property of Maximum or Minimum*, published in 1744 and written by Leonhard Euler (1707–1783).

7. These include the Euler tension, the Hamilton-Jacobi-Bellman equation, and control theory.

8. We can calculate this as follows, for example 1:

$$\text{payoff} = \$100$$
$$\text{NPVrepayments} = \$120 * [1/(1 + 0.10)]^4$$

payoff – NPVrepayments = NPVinvestment
NPVinvestment = $18.04

9. The calculations to reproduce this example are much more complex than the preceding example, because much more information is included. The curve was generated as a sine wave around a growth trend similar to real GDP growth in the U.S. economy during the past decade; and the quadrature function is described in many advanced mathematical texts. (*Quadrature* is a method of approximating the area under a curve and is often numerically practical even when a purely analytical effort to solve a definite integral fails.)

10. See Bellman (1957) for the original proposal of the method. Dreyfus (1965) was an early and accessible introduction. Stokey and Lucas (1989) is the authoritative modern treatise on the method, although it is technically demanding. Adda and Cooper (2003) describe applications of the dynamic programming method in economics at a decidedly less rigorous level.

11. The contemporary usage of the cake-eating problem was spurred by Stokey and Lucas (1989). However, the term appeared earlier (e.g., Romer [1986]); Koopmans (1973) and others attribute it to Gale (1967), who used it to examine exhaustible natural resources.

12. Economically minded readers will recognize these as classic assumptions of utility theory: a budget constraint, diminishing marginal utility, and a positive subjective discount rate. Note that we could complicate the model by including preferences that vary over time, storage costs, and investment earnings on the uneaten cake (the "magic refrigerator" version). We could also postulate a whole platoon of potential cake eaters and an arbitrage argument about the prices in the half-eaten-cake market. However, such complications induce no additional insight into the main idea of recursive decision making.

13. This would occur if the gross rate of growth R was the inverse of the gross discount rate β.

14. See Chapter 8, "Value in Neoclassical Economics," under the section titled "Time-Separable and Recursive Utility."

15. The mean-variance framework relies, in general, on one or more of these formulations. See Chapter 11, "Portfolio Pricing Methods."

16. Blackwell (1965, Theorem 5). David Blackwell was the first African-American admitted into the National Academy of Sciences in the U.S.

17. On this question, at least, the pioneers of the economics method were much better. The classical and early neoclassical economists were clear about their assumptions about institutions and human motivations. The neoclassicists later distilled these into mathematical statements of preferences, utility functions, risk aversion, and other concepts. Such mathematical statements often diverge from human nature.

18. Two examples are the Roll critique of the CAPM in the corporate finance literature and the allowance that some markets are not complete in the neoclassical finance literature.

19. See the preceding section titled "Examples: Problems Without Solutions." See also the discussions about profit maximization and the ignorance of the entrepreneur, including the notes, in Chapter 1, "Modern Value Quandaries," under the section titled "The Quandaries." See also the discussion of bounded rationality and prospect theory, again

including the notes, in Chapter 8, "Value in Neoclassical Economics," under the section titled "The Behaviorist School."

20. Exceptions include the complete-market, no-arbitrage model, where it really does not matter because the price is set by the replicating portfolio.

CHAPTER 16

1. We introduced the cake-eating problem in Chapter 15, "The Value Functional: Theory," under the section titled "Introduction to Dynamic Programming." Recursive utility was introduced in Chapter 8, "Value in Neoclassical Economics," under the section titled "Time-Separable and Recursive Utility."

2. The definition of a firm is summarized as follows in Chapter 4, "The Nature of the Firm," in Exhibit 4.3:

An organization with:
1. A separate legal identity from its workers, managers, and owners
2. A motivation to earn profit for its investors
3. A set of replicable business processes

3. For example, consider any of a number of models of valuation used in the field of finance, such as "value driver" models or the traditional income approach. Note carefully the variables for income and discount rate. Now, look at a complete set of accounting statements for a firm. Which lines in what accounting statements correspond directly to these two variables in the finance model? Similar questions are addressed in Chapter 14, "Practical Application of the Income Method."

4. Note that standard DCF analysis does not contemplate all these dimensions of analysis, or it relegates them to the professional judgment of the analyst. Furthermore, methods (such as those based on modern portfolio theory) in which the mean and variance are the critical factors and imply no analysis of additional dimensions.

5. At the time of writing, no commercially available software existed to solve these problems. The software environment and related routines used by the author are sketched in Appendix B, "Guide to the Solutions Manual," under the section titled "Software for Business Valuation." Because this area is likely to change rapidly, Appendix B also refers readers to the *Solutions Manual* and a set of web sites where I expect that updated information, including information on future commercially available software, will be posted in the future.

6. Because both (value function iteration and policy improvement) are iterative algorithms, they theoretically produce solutions that are within an arbitrary threshold. In the author's experience, this threshold can usually be set below the measurement precision of the state variables. However, see the following note about convergence and practical difficulties.

7. See, for example, Dixit and Pindyck (1994).

8. It is possible that, using the market or neoclassical finance (complete-market) approaches, existing prices and securities in the market uniquely determine the market value of a business. This would avoid the requirement of supplying a discount rate.

9. This result is derived in a number of texts, including Miranda and Fackler (2002, chap. 10), Stokey (2009, chap. 3), and Dixit and Pindyck (1994, chap. 4). Note that the H-J-B equation, when the value function has time as an argument, has an additional term of dV/dt. On the addition of the name of W. Döblin (a French soldier in World War II whose work was discovered sixty years later) to what has traditionally been called "Itô's Lemma," see Shreve (2004, vol. 11, chap. 4).

10. The lower values for ρ and μ reflect the fact that they are continuously compounded rates, whereas d and g are annually compounded rates.

CHAPTER 17

1. Recall the definition of a firm from Chapter 4, "A New Definition of the Firm." Under our definition, a firm must have a separate legal identity, a motivation to earn profits for investors, and replicable business processes. This rules out a number of firms that may be subject to bankruptcy codes, including individuals (personal bankruptcies), nonprofit firms, governments and many quasi-government organizations, and businesses that do not fulfill our definition of a firm.

2. This assumption would cover most U.S. corporations (including S and C corps), limited liability companies, and some partnerships and similar organizations such as REITs. It would also cover similar forms of organization in other countries.

3. For the purposes of this chapter, we assume that the bankruptcy code governing the firm has the following features: a petition requirement; protection of the assets of the firm from demands by creditors after the filing of the petition; ability to reorganize its operations, including the ability to dissolve existing contracts (*executory contracts* under the U.S. bankruptcy code); the ability to negotiate a plan with existing lenders and other creditors in which individual obligations were reduced or eliminated; supervision by a judge or other official of the process; the ability to reorganize and emerge from bankruptcy; and a process for the orderly liquidation of the existing assets.

The U.S. bankruptcy code (often referred to by two parts of it: Chapter 11 and Chapter 7) contains all these features. Tirole (2006, chap. 1) includes an international comparison of laws protecting investors in bankruptcy situations.

4. Examples include the near-disappearance of buggy-whip and horse-carriage manufacturers once the automobile gained market acceptance in the early twentieth century; mechanical watch manufacturers after quartz watch technology developed in the 1970s; fountain pen manufacturers when ballpoint pens became cheap substitutes; and many men's clothiers when casual business clothing became acceptable in the 1990s.

It is interesting to note that the disappearance of mass producers of these products is often followed, some time later, with the reemergence of boutique manufacturers that cater to collectors and aficionados. Fountain pens and mechanical watches are two recent examples favored by this author, who has somehow avoided the attraction of buggy whips.

5. This section is based on Anderson (2004b); excerpts are used with permission.

6. In the author's experience, this occurs even in industries (such as alcoholic beverage distribution) where state laws typically *require* a written agreement! Despite the legal and business risks involved, many such arrangements have existed over multiple years, proving again that businesses fundamentally operate through people-to-people agreements.

The continued existence of such handshake business arrangements, which may involve millions of dollars of annual sales revenue and a similar scale of investment by both parties, is interesting and, to some degree, comforting.

7. P. Miller (2006). Miller adds an important internal footnote to this selection: "The assumption of perfect foresight is made for simplicity."

8. Lee and Chun use the term *valuing* in a colloquial sense, meaning "estimating the value." Therefore, their statement about sports teams being valued on revenues probably means only that the rules of thumb for estimating those values are based on revenues. Miller's statements about "discount . . . rate," "costs are the same," and "perfect foresight" are enormous qualifications in the practical sense, thus restricting the assertion to an almost purely theoretical argument.

9. See, for example, Colby (2006).

10. As far back as 1998, Ozanian attacked the practice of portraying sports franchise ownership as a barely break-even business:

> A casual reader might think the owners of most sports teams were all headed for Chapter 11. Baseball owners say most of their teams are in the red. By some accounts, as many as 20 hockey teams are losing money.
>
> Even as they pocket an $18 billion TV deal, many football team owners cry poor mouth.

See Ozanian (1998).

11. An excellent example, in which a market transaction proved the value of this general approach, was the sale of the Boston Red Sox in 2002 for approximately $700 million. As pointed out by Ozanian and other journalists at Forbes.com on April 15, 2002, the (estimated) operating loss of $11 million for the Red Sox the previous year was a poor indicator of value. The buyer acquired a team with an intensely loyal fan base and 80 percent interest in the New England Sports Network—which happened to broadcast those same games. See Bandenhausen et al. (2002).

By the fall of 2010, the owners of the Red Sox were in such a strong financial position that their owners, New England Sports Ventures, purchased one of the most famous professional soccer teams in Europe, the Liverpool Football Club. The purchase, at an announced price of $476 million, implied a value that was 40 percent less than the *Forbes* value.

12. The fact that business owners are seeking more than just income is obvious in this market. The same fact in other markets is one of the themes behind the discussion of the true motivation of entrepreneurs, and the failure of the NPV rule, throughout this book.

13. See the following discussion on Geckil and Anderson's review of European sports franchise data.

14. These included Ajax of Holland, Borussia Dortmund of Germany, Fenerbahce of Turkey, Lazio of Italy, and Newcastle United and Manchester United of England.

15. See Geckil, Mahon, and Anderson (2007).

16. Sam Zell, identified as a potential buyer in the report, later purchased the Tribune Company (which included broadcast and media interests as well as the Cubs franchise). Zell soon afterward put the Cubs on the block.

CHAPTER 18

1. Examples of this within macroeconomics are legion. The *rational expectations* critique was one response to the glaring omission within standard Keynesian econometric models of incentives operating on taxpayers. Of course, it is often difficult to model more than one or two incentive effects within a macroeconomic model. However, that does not excuse ignoring them.

2. A small number of works referenced elsewhere in this book also describe the use of recursive techniques to evaluate public policy questions, including Ljungqvist and Sargent (2004), who focus on macroeconomic issues, and Miranda and Fackler (2002), who provide examples in numerous markets and describe both the mathematics of a recursive model and numerical techniques to solve them.

3. This section is based on Anderson (2011).

4. The action space of the matrix is x = {Lay off, Maintain, Hire}. The state space of the matrix is s = {HB, HS, LB, LS}, where H and L mean high and low costs, and B and S mean big and small scale.

5. Health care cost burdens were already difficult to predict for employers; the burdens under the new federal law are complex, subject to varying state implementation by states, and further subject to constitutional challenge. The unemployment insurance burdens, under most state systems, are based on complicated underwriting and solvency formulas that can be varied by both state and federal laws. In general, the cost of expanded benefits paid during a year of high unemployment are defrayed by higher assessments on employers for years into the future.

6. The U.S. Patient Protection and Affordability Care Act, enacted into law in March 2010, imposes fines and taxes and requires employers to provide certain benefits, subject to a schedule that approximately covers the succeeding four years. Perhaps the most expensive portions of the employer mandates are imposed starting in 2014. The law is currently subject to multiple constitutional challenges.

7. Intermediate results are available in the companion *Solutions Manual*; see Appendix B. Although not shown here, a naive net present value method of valuing the firm, when the likelihood of higher costs in the future is properly recognized, also captures some loss in value in a persistent-cost regime.

8. Hammurabi was king of Babylon and wrote his famous laws around 1780 BC. His reign was known as the golden age of Babylonian science, due partially to the stability of his rule.

9. The Code would, of course, fail to fulfill modern standards of justice, as exemplified by the Bill of Rights to the U.S. Constitution. In particular, the social class of the perpetrator and victim were critical to the penalty under the ancient code. For example, the "tooth for a tooth" penalty was only for people of equal social standing.

10. This translation is from Brians et al. (1999). The original translation is by L. W. King (1915). Minor edits have been performed by the author.

11. Chapter 20 of the book of Exodus contains the Decalogue, or Ten Commandments; Chapters 21, 22, and 23 contain laws that establish both punishment and compensation for a large number of offenses, including those involving humans, animals, and

property. The biblical Exodus may have occurred around 1441 BC, or perhaps 1290 BC; some traditions hold that the book of Exodus was written by Moses himself, while other scholars assert that it was written about 500 BC.

12. A German immigrant and former Wyoming Supreme Court justice, Fred Blume, translated the entire Justinian Code into English starting in the 1920s. See Kearly (2007).

13. Blume (1952), pp. 24–26. Blume's manuscript notes that laws passed by both Anastasium and Justinian would not allow the assignee of a debt to collect more than was paid for it and explains that such laws prevented the abuse of weak property owners by powerful dignitaries. Elsewhere (pp. 183–185) he notes the Hellenic and Oriental influence on the Roman law and observes that Roman law changed when the "main capital of the empire" became Constantinople, instead of Rome.

14. Kautilya (c. 150 AD), chap. VI.iii. The title of the discourse may be attributable to the translator, I. L. N. Rangarajan.

15. Among the grievances listed in the declaration were the quartering of soldiers in the homes of citizens and the "[erection of] a multitude of New Offices, and [sending] hither swarms of Officers to harass our people and eat out their substance."

16. I am including the Bill of Rights. Probably the clearest statement of a damages doctrine in the U.S. Constitution is in the Fifth Amendment, which states in part that "no person shall . . . be deprived of life, liberty, or property, without due process of law; nor shall private property be taken for public use, without just compensation."

17. This section is based on Anderson (2005a).

18. Bouvier (1856). A contemporary definition, such as the following from *West's Business Law*, 6th ed. (1996, chap. 19), is quite similar:

Types of Damages
There are basically four broad categories of damages:
1. Compensatory (to cover direct losses and costs).
2. Consequential (to cover indirect and foreseeable losses).
3. Punitive (to punish and deter wrongdoing).
4. Nominal (to recognize wrongdoing when no monetary loss is shown).

19. On the purpose of exemplary damages to deter illegal conduct, see, for example, Anderson (2004a, chap. 11), D. Friedman (2001, p. 211), and Easterbrook and Fischel (1991, chap. 12). Cooter and Ulen (1988, chap. 7) analyze damages for breach of contract.

20. See, for example, Gaughan (2000, chap. 1), citing Dunn (2005) and Cerillo (1991).

21. Note that the *fact* of damages must be proved with reasonable certainty, not the amount. Courts recognize the inherently difficult task of measuring damages, and therefore have a less restrictive doctrine on the estimation of the amount than on the proving of their existence. One U.S. Supreme Court decision from three quarters of a century ago—*Story Parchment Co. v. Paterson Paper Co.*, 282 U.S. 555, 563 (1931)—articulates this clearly, stating that it "would be a perversion of justice to deny any relief to the injured person" if the nature of the tort was "of such a nature as to preclude the ascertainment of the amount of damages with certainty." See, for example, Gaughan (2000, chap. 1), citing Dunn (1997, sec. 1.3).

22. Recall that the three essential elements of a firm are separate legal identity from workers or managers; motivation to earn profit for investors; and replicable business practices. See Chapter 4, "The Nature of the Firm."

23. Congress was given the duty to establish laws "securing for limited times to authors and inventors the exclusive right to their respective writings and discoveries" in the U.S. Constitution, at Article I, Section 8. The first patent act was enacted in 1790.

24. The U.S. Patent Office's *General Information on Patents* pamphlet summarizes the law as follows:

> In order for an invention to be patentable it must be new as defined in the patent law, which provides that an invention cannot be patented if: "(a) the invention was known or used by others in this country, or patented or described in a printed publication in this or a foreign country, before the invention thereof by the applicant for patent," or "(b) the invention was patented or described in a printed publication in this or a foreign country or in public use or on sale in this country more than one year prior to the application for patent in the United States."

This and other requirements for utility patents are often summarized as "novel, useful, and unobvious."

25. *Georgia-Pacific Corp. v. United States Plywood Corp.*, 318 F. Supp. 1116, 1120 (S.D.N.Y. 1970), modified and aff'd, 446 F.2d 295 (2nd Cir. 1971), *cert. denied*, 404 U.S. 870 (1971).

26. *Panduit Corp. v. Stahlin Bros. Fibre Works, Inc.*, 575 F.2d 1152, 1156 (6th Cir.), *cert. denied*, 439 U.S. 856 (1978); *accord, Radio Steel & Mfg. Co. v. MTD Products*, 788 F.2d 1554, 1555, 1556 (Fed. Cir. 1986), *Tate Access Floors, Inc. v. Maxcess Technologies, Inc.*, 222 F.3d 958, 971 (Fed. Cir. 2000).

27. The Lanham Act, enacted in 1946, is codified at Title 15, Chapter 22, of the United States Code (U.S.C. 1051 and following).

28. Among these is the U.S. Copyright Act of 1976, Title 17 of the United States Code. This replaced a number of earlier copyright acts.

29. See Dunn (2005) or Gaughan (2009) for a historical discussion and some recent case law. Note that this area of law is less settled than most others in the commercial damages field.

APPENDIX B

1. Matlab is distributed by The Mathworks (http://www.mathworks.com).

APPENDIX C

1. Enterprise value is often used as an alternative to straightforward market capitalization and is calculated as market cap plus debt, minority interest, and preferred shares, minus total cash and cash equivalents.

2. Market capitalization calculated as the number of common shares multiplied by the current price of those shares.

REFERENCES

SCHOLARLY WORKS

Abrams, Jay B. (2001, 2010). *Quantitative Business Valuation*. McGraw-Hill.

Adda, Jerome, and Russell Cooper (2003). *Dynamic Economics: Quantitative Methods and Applications*. MIT Press.

Alchian, Armen A., and Reuben A. Kessel (1962). "Competition, Monopoly, and the Pursuit of Pecuniary Gain." In *Aspects of Labor Economics*, ed. H. G. Lewis, 777–795. National Bureau of Economic Research.

Alexander, John R. (2007). "Ancient Accounting: Dawn of Man Through Luca Pacioli." Available at http://www.acaus.org/acc_his.html.

Anderson, Patrick L. (2004a). *Business Economics and Finance: Using Matlab, Simulation Models, and GIS*. CRC Press.

——— (2004b). "Valuation and Damages for Franchised Businesses." Anderson Economic Group working paper 2003-12, presented at the Allied Social Science Association conference, San Diego, California, January. Available at http://www.anderson economicgroup.com/Portals/0/upload/Doc488.pdf.

——— (2005a). "Lost Profits, Diminished Value, and Other Measures of Commercial Damages." Anderson Economic Group working paper 2005-11, presented at the Southern Economics Association conference, Washington, DC, November.

——— (2005b). "New Developments in Business Valuation." In *Developments in Litigation Economics* (*Contemporary Studies in Economic and Financial Analysis*, Vol. 87), ed. Patrick A. Gaughan and Robert James Thornton, 267–306. Elsevier.

——— (2005c). "Practical Dynamic Programming for Business and Forensic Economics." Anderson Economic Group working paper 2005-2, presented at the National Association of Forensic Economics International Conference, Dublin, Ireland, May.

——— (2009). "The Value of Private Firms in the United States." *Business Economics* 44: 87–108.

Anderson, Patrick L., and Ilhan K. Geckil (2007). "Sports Franchise Value: The Contender Factor." Anderson Economic Group working paper 2007-1. Anderson Economic Group.

———— (2011). *The Causes of Persistent Unemployment: New Evidence from a New Approach.* Anderson Economic Group working paper 2011-2, July. Anderson Economic Group.

Ando, Albert, and Franco Modigliani (1963). "The 'Life-Cycle' Hypothesis of Saving: Aggregate Implications and Tests." *American Economic Review* 53, no. 1: 55–84.

Aristotle (1885). *Politics*, trans. Benjamin Jowett. Original work c. 350 BC. Reprinted by the MIT Internet Classics Library. Available at http://classics.mit.edu/Aristotle/politics.html.

Arrow, Kenneth (1953). "Le Rôle des valeurs boursières pour la répartition la meilleure des risques." *Économétrie* 11: 41–47. Published in English as Arrow (1964). Also reprinted with new commentary in *Essays in the Theory of Risk Bearing*, 121–133. Markham, 1971.

Bachelier, Louis (1900). "Théorie de la spéculation." *Annales Scientifiques de l'École Normale Supérieure* 3, no. 17: 21–86. Also published in book form as David Gauthier-Villars, *Théorie de la spéculation*, trans. and with commentary by Mark Davis and Alison Etheridge. Princeton University Press, 2006.

Backus, David K., Bryan R. Routledge, and Stanley E. Zin (2005, 2008). "Recursive Preferences." NYU Stern working paper, December 2005. Reprinted in *The New Palgrave Dictionary of Economics*, 2nd ed., ed. Steven N. Durlauf and Lawrence E. Blume. Palgrave Macmillan, 2008.

Bandenhausen, Kurt, Cecily Fluke, Lesley Kump, and Michael K. Ozanian (2002). "Double Play." Forbes.com, April 15. Available at http://www.forbes.com/forbes/2002/0415/092.htm.

Bandenhausen, Kurt, and Michael K. Ozanian (2005). "The Business of Hockey." Forbes.com, November 26. Available at http://www.forbes.com/2005/11/07/ice-hockey-special-report_05nhl_land.html.

Barro, Robert J., and Robert G. King (1984). "Time-Separable Preferences and Intertemporal-Substitution Models of Business Cycles." *Quarterly Journal of Economics* 99, no. 4 (November): 817–839.

Beja, Avraham (1971). "The Structure of the Cost of Capital Under Uncertainty." *Review of Economic Studies* 38, no. 115: 359–368.

Bellman, R. (1957). *Dynamic Programming.* Princeton University Press. Reissued by Dover, 2003.

Bennett, Stuart (1979). *A History of Control Engineering, 1800–1930.* Institute of Electrical Engineers and Peter Peregrinus. Reprinted in 1986.

Black, Fischer, and Myron Scholes (1973). "The Pricing of Options and Corporate Liabilities." *Journal of Political Economy* 81, no. 3: 637–654.

Blackstone, William (1915). *Commentaries on the Laws of England*, ed. William Carey. Bancroft-Whitney. Based on the Hammond edition of 1788.

Blackwell, David (1965). "Discounted Dynamic Programming." *Annals of Mathematical Statistics* 36: 226–234.

Blair, Roger, and Francine Lafontaine (2005). *Economics of Franchising.* Cambridge University Press.

Blume, Frederick H. (1952). *Code of Justinian and Its Value.* Facsimile. University of Wyoming College of Law.

Boness, A. James (1964). "Elements of a Theory of Stock Option Value." *Journal of Political Economy* 81, no. 3: 637–654.

Bowles, Samuel (2006). *Microeconomics: Behavior, Institutions, and Evolution.* Princeton University Press.

Brandimarte, Paolo (2006). *Numerical Methods in Finance and Economics: A MATLAB-Based Introduction,* 2nd ed. Wiley.

Brealey, Richard, and Stewart Myers (2006 [2003] [1996] [1991] [1985] [1983]). *Principles of Corporate Finance.* McGraw-Hill.

Breeden, Douglas T., and Robert H. Litzenberger (1978). "Prices of State-Contingent Claims Implicit in Option Prices." *Journal of Business* 51: 621–651.

Brennan, M. J. (1991). "Capital Asset Pricing Model." In *The New Palgrave Dictionary of Economics,* vol. 1, ed. John Eatwell, Murray Milgate, and Peter Newman, 336–340. Palgrave Macmillan.

Brians, Paul, Mary Gallwey, Douglas Hughes, Azfar Hussain, Richard Law, Michael Myers, Michael Neville, Roger Schlesinger, Alice Spitzer, and Susan Swan, eds. (1999). *Reading About the World,* vol. 1. Harcourt Brace. Excerpts of the writings of Hammurabi are available at http://www.wsu.edu:8080/~wldciv/world_civ_reader/world_civ_reader_1 /hammurabi.html and http://eawc.evansville.edu /anthology/hammurabi.htm.

Brickley, James, and John McConnell (1991). "Dividend Policy." In *The New Palgrave Dictionary of Economics,* vol. 1, ed. John Eatwell, Murray Milgate, and Peter Newman, 896–898. Palgrave Macmillan.

Brigham, Eugene, and Philip Daves (2006). *Intermediate Financial Management,* 9th ed. Southwestern College.

Buffett, Warren E. (1984). "The Superinvestors of Graham-and-Doddsville." In *Hermes,* Columbia University Business School, 4–15.

Butzen, Paul, and Catherine Fuss, eds. (2002). *Firms' Investment and Finance Decisions: Theory and Empirical Methodology.* Elgar.

Campbell, John Y. (2000). "Asset Pricing at the Millennium." National Bureau of Economic Research working paper 7589. Available at http://www.nber.org/papers/w7589.

Campus, Antonietta (1987). "Marginalist Economics." In *The New Palgrave,* ed. John Eatwell, Murray Milgate, and Peter Neuman. Macmillan.

——— (1991). "Book Reviews." *Contributions to Political Economy* 10, no. 1: 88–90.

Cantillon, Richard (1755). *Essai sur la nature du commerce en général.* Thought to have been written in 1730 and originally published in Paris, perhaps by Barrois, although no original editions exist. Later published in English (trans. Henry Higgs) by Macmillan, 1931. Reissued for the Royal Economic Society, 1959. Available at http://www.econlib .org/library/NPDBooks/Cantillon/cntNT.html.

Carlson, Mark (2007). "A Brief History of the 1987 Stock Market Crash with a Discussion of the Federal Reserve Response." Divisions of Research and Statistics and Monetary Affairs Federal Reserve Board, Washington, DC.

Carnegie, Dale (1937). *How to Win Friends and Influence People.* Simon and Schuster. Reprinted in 1981.

Casson, Mark C. (1993). "Entrepreneurship." In *The Concise Encyclopedia of Economics.* Library of Economics and Liberty. Available at http://www.econlib.org/library/Enc1 /Entrepreneurship.html.

Castelli, Charles (1877). *The Theory of Options in Stocks and Shares.* Mathieson.

Caves, Richard E. (1996, 2007). *Multinational Enterprise and Economic Analysis*, 2nd ed. Cambridge University Press.

Cerillo, William A. (1991). *Proving Business Damages.* Wiley Law Publishers.

Chirinko, Robert S., and Huntley Schaller (1995). "Why Does Liquidity Matter in Investment Equations?" *Journal of Money, Credit, and Banking* 27, no. 2 (May): 527–548.

Clausewitz, Carl von (1873). *On War.* Numerous contemporary editions include the English translation by Michael Howard and Peter Paret (Princeton University Press, 1976) and an abridgment by Beatrice Heuser (Oxford University Press, 2008).

Coase, Ronald (1937). "The Nature of the Firm." *Economica* 4, no. 16 (November): 386–405. The essay is now found in different compilations of Coase's work. Available at http://www.cerna.ensmp.fr.

——— (1960). "The Problem of Social Cost." *Journal of Law and Economics* 3 (October): 1–44.

Cochrane, John H. (2001 [2005]). *Asset Pricing.* Princeton University Press.

——— (2008). "A Mean-Variance Benchmark for Intertemporal Portfolio Theory." Working paper, April 6. University of Chicago Graduate School of Business.

Cochrane, John, and Jesús Saá-Reuquejo (2000). "Beyond Arbitrage: Good Deal Asset Price Bounds in Incomplete Markets." *Journal of Political Economy* 108: 79–119.

Coffee, John R., Jr. (2005). "A Theory of Corporate Scandals: Why the U.S. and Europe Differ." Working paper 274, March. Center for Law and Economic Studies.

Cohen, Gabriel (2005). "For You, Half Price." *New York Times*, November 27, CY-4.

Colby, Edward (2006). "Someone Is Lying. Is It *Forbes* or Baseball Owners?" *Columbia Journalism Review* (April 27). Available at http://www.cjrdaily.org/the_audit /someone_is_lying_is_it_forbes.php.

Constantinides, George M. (1989). "Theory of Valuation: Overview and Recent Developments." In *Theory of Valuation*, ed. Sudipto Bhattacharya and George Constantinides, 1–23. Rowman and Littlefield.

Cooter, Robert, and Thomas Ulen (1988). *Law and Economics.* Scott, Foresman.

Cowles, Alfred, III, and Associates (1939). *Common Stock Indexes*, 2nd ed. Principia Press.

Cox, John C., Stephen A. Ross, and Mark Rubinstein (1979). "Option Pricing: A Simplified Approach." *Journal of Financial Economics* 7: 229–263.

Cvitanic, Jaksa, and Fernando Zapatero (2004). *Introduction to the Economics and Mathematics of Financial Markets.* MIT Press.

Damadoran, Aswath (2002). *Investment Valuation*, 2nd ed. Wiley.

Dawnay, Emma, and Hetan Shah (2005). *Behavioral Economics: Seven Principles for Policy-Makers.* New Economics Foundation. Available at http://www.neweconomics.org /publications/behavioural-economics.

Dean, Joel (1951). *Capital Budgeting.* Columbia University Press.

Debreu, Gerard (1959). *The Theory of Value: An Axiomatic Analysis of Economic Equilibrium.* Wiley. Reprinted by Yale University Press, 1971.

DeCarlo, Scott (2010). "The World's Leading Companies." *Forbes*, April 21.

De Haan, Jakob, Susanna Lundström, and Jan-Egbert Sturm (2006). "Market-Oriented Institutions and Policies and Economic Growth: A Critical Survey." *Journal of Economic Surveys* 20, no. 2: 157–191.

Dehez, Pierre, and Omar Licando (1996). "From Uncertainty to Macroeconomics and Back: An Interview with Jacques Dreze." Center for Operations Research and Econometrics, Université Catholique de Louvain. Available at http://www.core.ucl.ac.be/staff/Dreze/InterviewJHD.pdf.

Demsetz, Harold (1967). "Toward a Theory of Property Rights." *American Economic Review* 57 (May): 347–359.

——— (1997a). "The Firm in Economic Theory: A Quiet Revolution." *American Economic Review* 87, no. 2 (May): 426–429.

——— (1997b [1995]). *The Economics of the Business Firm.* Cambridge University Press.

Dixit, Avanish, and Robert S. Pindyck (1994). *Investment Under Uncertainty.* Princeton University Press.

Dobb, Maurice (1973). *Theories of Value and Distribution Since Adam Smith.* Cambridge University Press.

Dreyfus, Stuart E. (1965). *Dynamic Programming and the Calculus of Variations.* Academic Press.

Drèze, Jacques H. (1971). "Market Allocation Under Uncertainty." *European Economic Review* 2, no. 1 (Winter): 133–165.

——— (1985). "Uncertainty and the Firm in General Equilibrium Theory." *Economic Journal* 95, no. 380a (supplement): 1–20.

Duffie, Darrell (2001). *Dynamic Asset Pricing Theory,* 3rd ed. Princeton University Press.

Dunn, Robert L. (2005). *Recovery of Damages for Lost Profits,* 6th ed. Lawpress.

Durand, David (1952). "Costs of Debt and Equity Funds for Business: Trends and Problems of Measurement." In *Conference on Research in Business Finance,* 215–262. National Bureau of Economic Research.

——— (1959). "The Cost of Capital, Corporation Finance and the Theory of Investment: Comment." *American Economic Review* 49, no. 4 (September): 639–655.

Dybvig, Philip H., and Stephen A. Ross (1987). "Arbitrage." In *The New Palgrave Dictionary of Economics,* ed. John Eatwell, Murray Milgate, and Peter Neuman, 100–106. Palgrave Macmillan.

Easterbrook, Frank H., and Daniel Fischel (1991). *The Economic Structure of Corporate Law.* Harvard University Press.

Eatwell, John, Murray Milgate, and Peter Newman, eds. (1987, 1989). *The New Palgrave Dictionary of Economics,* finance ed. Palgrave Macmillan.

Eckhardt, Roger (1987). "Stan Ulam, John Von Neumann, and the Monte Carlo Method." *Los Alamos Science* 15 (special issue): 131–137.

Edwards, R. (1952). "The Pricing of Manufactured Products." *Economica* 19: 298–307.

Einstein, Albert (1916). *Relativity: The Special and General Theory.* Verlag. Translated and reprinted by Methuen, 1954. Reprinted by the Folio Society, 2004. Original articles were published in 1905 and 1916 by *Annalan der Physik* in Germany.

Elton, Edwin J., Martin J. Gruber, and Christopher R. Blake (1996). "Survivorship Bias and Mutual Fund Performance." *Review of Financial Studies* 9, no. 4: 1097–1120.

Elton, Edwin J., Martin J. Gruber, Stephen J. Brown, and William N. Goetzmann (2006). *Modern Portfolio Theory and Investment Analysis,* 7th ed. Wiley.

Fibonacci (Leonardo of Pisa) (1202). *Liber Abaci,* trans. Laurence Sigler. Springer, 2002.

Fischer, Stanley (1972). "Assets, Contingent Commodities and the Slutsky Equation." *Econometrica* 40, no. 2 (March): 371–385.

Fisher, Irving (1930). *Theory of Interest.* Macmillan. Reprinted by the Library of Economics and Liberty. Available at http://www.econlib.org/library/YPDBooks/Fisher/fshToICover.html.

Fonseca, Gonçalo, ed. (2011). History of Economic Thought. Available at http://homepage.newschool.edu/~het/. [Author's note: although Fonseca discourages citation to the text of this web site and warns that it may be revised in the future, I felt the content was influential enough to warrant a general citation.]

Friedman, David D. (2001). *Law's Order: What Economics Has to Do with Law and Why It Matters.* Princeton University Press.

Friedman, Milton (1953). *Essays in Positive Economics.* University of Chicago Press.

——— (1957). *A Theory of the Consumption Function.* Princeton University Press. Also published by the National Bureau of Economic Research.

——— (1962). *Capitalism and Freedom.* University of Chicago Press.

Friedman, Milton, and S. Kuznets (1954). *Incomes from Independent Professional Practice.* National Bureau of Economic Research.

Frydman, Roman, and Michael D. Goldberg (2007). *Imperfect Knowledge Economics: Exchange Rates and Risk.* Princeton University Press.

Gale, D. (1967). "On Optimal Development in a Multi-Sector Economy." *Review of Economic Studies* 34 (January): 1–18.

Gallagher, Timothy J., and Joseph D. Andrew (2007). *Financial Management: Principles and Practice*, 4th ed. Freeload Press.

Garber, Peter M. (2000). *Famous First Bubbles: The Fundamentals of Early Manias.* MIT Press.

Gaughan, Patrick A. (2000). *Measuring Commercial Damages.* Wiley.

——— (2004, 2009). *Measuring Business Interruption Losses and Other Commercial Damages.* Wiley.

Geckil, Ilhan K., and Patrick L. Anderson (2007). "Sports Franchise Valuation: The Contender Factor." Anderson Economic Group working paper 2007-01. Anderson Economic Group.

——— (2010). *Applied Game Theory and Strategic Behavior.* Taylor and Francis.

Geckil, Ilhan, Tim Mahon, and Patrick Anderson (2007). "Sports Franchise Valuation: The Chicago Cubs." Anderson Economic Group working paper 2007-02. Anderson Economic Group.

Gilder, George (1981). *Wealth and Poverty.* Reprinted by ICS Press, 1993.

——— (1984). *Spirit of Enterprise.* St. Vladimir's Seminary Press. Reprinted as *Recapturing the Spirit of Enterprise*, rev. ed. (ICS Press, 1992).

——— (2004). "Market Economics and the Conservative Movement." Speech given to the Philadelphia Society national meeting, Chicago, IL, May 1.

Goetzmann, William N. (2003). "Fibonacci and the Financial Revolution." Yale ICF Working Paper No. 03-28, October 23. Available at http://ssrn.com/abstract=461740.

——— (2006). *An Introduction to Investment Theory.* Available at http://viking.som.yale.edu/will/web_pages/will/finman540/classnotes/notes.html.

Goetzmann, William N., Roger G. Ibbotson, and Liang Peng (2000). "A New Historical Database for the NYSE 1815 to 1925: Performance and Predictability." Yale ICF Working Paper No. 00-13; Yale SOM Working Paper No. ICF-00-13 (July 14). Available at http://ssrn.com/abstract=236982. DOI: 10.2139/ssrn.236982.

Gordon, Myron J. (1962). *The Investment, Financing, and Valuation of the Corporation.* Irwin.

Gropelli, A. A., and Ehsan Nikbakht (2006). *Finance,* 5th ed. Barron's Educational Series.

Guesnerie, R., and J.-Y. Jaffray (1974). "Optimality of Equilibrium of Plans, Prices, and Price Expectations." In *Allocation Under Uncertainty: Equilibrium and Optimality,* ed. J. Drèze, 71–86. Macmillan.

Gwartney, J. D., and Robert Lawson (2007). *Economic Freedom of the World 2007 Annual Report.* Fraser Institute and Economic Freedom Network. Available at http://www.freetheworld.com/2007.

Hall, R. L., and C. J. Hitch (1939). "Price Theory and Business Behaviour." *Oxford Economic Papers* 2: 12–45. Reprinted in *Oxford Studies in the Price Mechanism,* ed. T. Wilson and P. W. S. Andrews (Clarendon, 1951).

Hall, Robert E. (1978). "Stochastic Implications of the Life Cycle–Permanent Income Hypothesis: Theory and Evidence." *Journal of Political Economy* 86, no. 6 (December): 971–987.

Harrison, J. Michael, and David M. Kreps (1979). "Martingales and Arbitrage in Multiperiod Securities Markets." *Journal of Economic Theory* 20: 381–408.

Harrison, J. Michael, and Stanley R. Pliska (1981). "Martingales and Stochastic Integrals in the Theory of Continuous Trading." *Stochastic Processes and Their Applications* 11: 215–260.

Hayashi, Fumio (1982). "Tobin's Marginal q and Average q: A Neoclassical Interpretation." *Econometrica* 50, no. 1 (January): 213–224.

Hayek, Friedrich A. von (1931). "Richard Cantillon." Preface to the 1931 German translation of Richard Cantillon, *Essai sur la nature du commerce en général,* trans. Micheál Ó Súilleabháin. Reprinted in the *Journal of Libertarian Studies* 7, no. 2 (Fall 1985): 217–247. Available at http://www.econlib.org/library/Essays/JLibSt/hykCnt1.html. [Originally written in German in 1931. Introduction and textual comments written for Hella Havek's 1931 German translation of Richard Cantillon's *Essai.*]

——— (1944). *The Road to Serfdom.* University of Chicago Press.

——— (1945). "The Use of Knowledge in Society." *American Economic Review* 35, no. 4 (September): 519–530.

——— (1988). *The Fatal Conceit: The Errors of Socialism.* University of Chicago Press.

Headd, Brian, Alfred Nucci, and Richard Boden (2010). "What Matters More: Business Exit Rates or Business Survival Rates?" *BDS Statistical Brief,* U.S. Census Bureau, May. Available at http://www.census.gov/ces/pdf/BDS_StatBrief4_Exit_Survival.pdf.

Heijdra, Ben, and Frederick van der Ploeg (2002). *Foundations of Modern Macroeconomics.* Oxford University Press.

Hicks, John R. (1939, 2nd ed. 1946). *Value and Capital: An Inquiry into Some Fundamental Principles of Economic Theory.* Clarendon Press.

"High Growth and Failure of Young Firms." (2009). *BDS Statistical Brief,* U.S. Census Bureau (April). Available at http://www.kauffman.org/uploadedFiles/bds_high _growth_and_failure_4-6-09.pdf.

Hirshleifer, J. (1958). "On the Theory of Optimal Investment Decision." *Journal of Political Economy* 66, no. 4: 329–352.

——— (1970). *Investment, Interest and Capital.* Prentice Hall.

Hitchner, James R., ed. (2003). *Financial Valuation: Applications and Models.* Wiley.

Hull, John C. (2000 [2002] 2003 [2008]). *Options, Futures, and Other Derivatives.* Prentice Hall.

Humphrey, T. M. (1992). "Marshallian Cross Diagrams and Their Uses Before Alfred Marshall: The Origins of Supply and Demand Geometry." *Federal Reserve Bank of Richmond Economic Review* 78, no. 2: 3–23. Reprinted in *Alfred Marshall: Critical Assessments,* ed. John Cunningham Wood (Taylor and Francis, 1996).

Ingersoll, Jonathon E. (1989). "Spanning in Financial Markets." In *Theory of Valuation,* ed. Sudipto Bhattacharya and George Constantinides, 117–127. Rowman and Littlefield.

Insall, Matt, and Eric W. Weisstein (2011). "Lattice." Available at http://mathworld.wolf ram.com/Lattice.html.

Jensen, Michael C. (2000). *A Theory of the Firm: Governance, Residual Claims and Organizational Forms.* Harvard University Press. Available at SSRN: http://ssrn.com /abstract=94043 or DOI: 10.2139/ssrn.94043.

Jensen, Michael C., and William H. Meckling (1976). "Theory of the Firm: Managerial Behavior, Agency Costs and Ownership Structure." *Journal of Financial Economics* 3, no. 4: 305–360.

Jentz, Gaylord A., Roger LeRoy Miller, and Frank B. Cross, eds. (1996). *West's Business Law,* 6th ed. (alternate ed.). West.

Jevons, William S. (1871). *The Theory of Political Economy.* Macmillan.

——— (1881). "Richard Cantillon and the Nationality of Political Economy." *Contemporary Review* (January). Reprinted in *Principles of Economics,* by William S. Jevons (London, 1905). Available at http://www.econlib.org/library/NPDBooks/Cantillon /cntNT8.html.

Johnson, Paul (1989). *The Intellectuals.* HarperCollins.

Jorgensen, Dale (1963). "Capital Theory and Economic Behavior." *American Economic Review* 53 (May): 247–259.

Judd, Kenneth L. (1998). *Numerical Methods in Economics.* MIT Press.

Kahneman, Daniel (2002). "Maps of Bounded Rationality." Nobel Prize lecture. Available at http://www.nobelprize.org/nobel_prizes/economics/laureates/2002/kahnemann -lecture.pdf. Similar to "Maps of Bounded Rationality: Psychology for Behavioral Economics," *American Economic Review* 93, no. 5 (December 2003): 1449–1475.

Kahneman, Daniel, and Amos Tversky (1979). "Prospect Theory: an Analysis of Decision Under Risk." *Econometrica* 47, no. 2: 263–291.

Kautilya (c. 350 BC). *The Arthashastra,* trans. I. L. N. Rangarajan. Penguin Books India, 1992.

Kay, John A. (1993). *Foundations of Corporate Success.* Oxford University Press.

Kearly, Timothy (2007). "Justice Fred Blume and the Translation of Justinian's Code." University of Wyoming College of Law. Available at http://uwacabweb.uwyo.edu /blumeandjustinian.

Kennickell, Arthur B. (2010). "Try, Try Again: Response and Nonresponse in the 2009 SCF Panel." Paper prepared for the 2010 Joint Statistical Meetings, Vancouver, Canada, September.

Keynes, John Maynard (1936). *The General Theory of Interest, Employment and Money.* Macmillan.

Klamer, Arjo (1984). *Conversations with Economists.* Rowman and Allanheld.

Koller, Tim, Marc Goedhart, and David Wessels (2007). *Valuation: Measuring and Managing the Value of Companies*, 4th ed. Wiley.

Koopmans, Tjalling C. (1973). "Some Observations on Optimal Economic Growth and Exhaustible Resources." Cowles Foundation Paper 396. Cowles Foundation.

——— (1974). "Is the Theory of Competitive Equilibrium with It?" *American Economic Review* 64, no. 2 (May): 325–329.

Koski, Timothy (2007). "The Application of Employment Taxes to S Corporation Shareholders." *Taxes—The Tax Magazine* (January): 25–31.

Kreps, David M. (1982). "Multiperiod Securities and the Efficient Allocation of Risk: A Comment on the Black-Scholes Option Pricing Model." In *The Economics of Uncertainty and Information*, National Bureau of Economic Research, 203–232. University of Chicago Press.

——— (1988). *Notes on the Theory of Choice.* Westview Press.

Larson, Kermit, Paul B. W. Miller, and Ray H. Garrison (1993). *Fundamental Accounting Principles*, 13th ed. Irwin.

Lee, Soonhwan D. S. M., and Hyosung Chun (2002). "Economic Values of Professional Sport Franchises in the United States." *Sport Journal* 5, no. 3.

Lengwiler, Yvan (2004). *Microfoundations of Financial Economics.* Princeton University Press.

LeRoy, Stephen F. (1991). "Present Value." In *The New Palgrave Dictionary of Economics*, 3rd ed., ed. John Eatwell, Murray Milgate, and Peter Newman, 947–949. Palgrave Macmillan. Stockton. Also in the slimmer volume *The New Palgrave: Finance*. Stockton, 1989.

Linehan, P. (1911). "Lucas Pacioli." In *The Catholic Encyclopedia.* Appleton. Available at http://www.newadvent.org/cathen/11383b.htm.

Lintner, John (1965). "The Valuation of Risky Assets and the Selection of Risky Investment in Stock Portfolios and Capital Budgets." *Review of Economics and Statistics* 47: 13–37.

Ljungqvist, Lars, and Thomas J. Sargent (2000 [2004]). *Recursive Macroeconomic Theory.* MIT Press.

Long, Michael S., and Thomas A. Bryant (2008). *Valuing the Closely Held Firm.* Oxford University Press.

Lucas, Mike R. (2003). "Pricing Decisions and the Neoclassical Theory of the Firm." *Management Accounting Research* 14: 201–217.

Lucas, Robert E., Jr. (1976). "Econometric Policy Evaluation: A Critique." In *The Phillips Curve and Labor Markets*, Carnegie-Rochester Conference Series on Public Policy, vol. 1, ed. Karl Brunner and Allan H. Meltzer, 19–46. American Elsevier.

———— (1978). "Asset Prices in an Exchange Economy." *Econometrica* 46, no. 6 (November): 1429–1445.

Lucas, Robert E., Jr., and Nancy L. Stokey (1989). *Recursive Methods in Economic Dynamics.* Harvard University Press.

Lutz, Friedrich, and Vera Lutz (1951). *Theory of Investment of the Firm.* Princeton University Press.

Mach, Traci L., and John D. Wolken (2006). "Financial Services Used by Small Businesses: Evidence from the 2003 Survey of Small Business Finances." *Federal Reserve Bulletin* (October): A167–A195.

Mackay, Harvey (1996). *Swim with the Sharks Without Being Eaten Alive.* Ballantine.

Magill, Michael J. P., and Martine Quinzii (1998). *Theory of Incomplete Markets*, vol. 1. MIT Press.

Markowitz, Harry (1952). "Portfolio Selection." *Journal of Finance* 7, no. 1: 77–99.

———— (1959). *Portfolio Selection: Efficient Diversification of Investments.* Cowles Foundation Monograph no. 16. Wiley. Reprinted in a second edition with additional comments and bibliography by Blackwell, 1991.

Marshall, Alfred (1890, 1920). *Principles of Economics.* Macmillan. The 8th edition was published in 1920 and reprinted in 1964. Available at http://www.econlib.org/library/Marshall/marP.html.

Marx, Karl (1848). *The Communist Manifesto.*

Mas-Colell, Andreu, Michael D. Whinston, and Jerry R. Green (1995). *Microeconomic Theory.* Oxford University Press.

Mattessich, Richard (1998). "From Accounting to Negative Numbers: A Signal Contribution of Medieval India to Mathematics." *Accounting Historians Journal* 25, no. 2 (December): 129–145.

Maxwell, James C. (1867). "On Governors." *Proceedings of the Royal Society of London* 16: 270–283.

Maxwell, John C. (1998). *The 21 Irrefutable Laws of Leadership.* Thomas Nelson.

McCormack, Mark (1986). *What They Don't Teach You at Harvard Business School: Notes from a Street-Smart Executive.* Bantam.

McDonald, R., and D. Siegel (1986). "The Value of Waiting to Invest." *Quarterly Journal of Economics* (November): 707–727.

McKenzie, Donald C. (2003). "An Equation and Its Worlds: Bricolage, Exemplars, Disunity and Performativity in Financial Economics." *Studies in Social Sciences* 33, no. 6 (December): 831–866.

McManus, J. C. (1975). "The Costs of Alternative Economic Organizations." *Canadian Journal of Economics* 7 (August): 334–350.

Meghir, Costas (2004). "A Retrospective on Friedman's Theory of Permanent Income." *Economic Journal* 114, no. 496 (June): F293–F306.

Mehra, Rajnish (2006). "Recursive Competitive Equilibrium." NBER working paper 12433. National Bureau of Economic Research. Reprinted in *The New Palgrave Dictionary of Economics*, 2nd ed., ed. Steven N. Durlauf and Lawrence E. Blume. Palgrave Macmillan, 2008.

Mehra, Rajnish, and Edward Prescott (1985). "The Equity Premium Puzzle." *Journal of Monetary Economics* 15: 247–257.

————— (2003). "The Equity Premium Puzzle in Retrospect." In *Handbook of the Economics of Finance*, by G. M. Constantinides, M. Harris, and R. Stulz, 889–938. North Holland.

Menger, Carl (1871). *Principles of Economics.* First printing in German, 1871. English version, 2004, published by the Ludwig von Mises Institute. Available at http://mises.org/etexts/menger/principles.asp.

Merton, Robert C. (1973a). "An Intertemporal Capital Asset Pricing Model." *Econometrica* 41, no. 5: 867–887.

————— (1973b). "Theory of Rational Option Pricing." *Bell Journal of Economics and Management Science* 4: 141–183.

Metropolis, Nicholas, and Stanislaw Ulam (1949). "The Monte Carlo Method." *Journal of the American Statistical Association* 44 (247): 335–341.

Meyer, John R., and Edwin Kuh (1957). *The Investment Decision: An Empirical Study.* Harvard University Press.

Miller, Merton, and Franco Modigliani (1961). "Dividend Policy, Growth, and the Valuation of Shares." *Journal of Business* 34 (October): 411–433.

Miller, Phillip (2006). "Private Financing and Sports Franchise Values: The Case of Major League Baseball." Working Paper Series, Paper No. 06-26, International Association of Sports Economists.

Miranda, Mario J., and Paul L. Fackler (2002). *Applied Computational Economics and Finance.* MIT Press.

Modigliani, Franco (1980). *The Collected Papers of Franco Modigliani*, vol. 3, ed. Andrew Abel. MIT Press.

Modigliani, Franco, and Merton Miller (1958). "The Cost of Capital, Corporation Finance and the Theory of Investment." *American Economic Review* 48 (June): 261–297.

————— (1959). "The Cost of Capital, Corporation Finance and the Theory of Investment: A Reply." *American Economic Review* 49, no. 4, 655–669.

Mongin, Phillippe (1997). "The Marginalist Controversy." In *Handbook of Economic Methodology*, ed. John B. Davis, D. Wade Hands, and Utaki Maki, 558–562. Elgar.

Morrison, Andrew (1999). "Small Business in New Zealand." Parliamentary Library Background Paper No. 21, Parliamentary Library of New Zealand (November). Available at http://www.parliament.nz/NR/rdonlyres/6B18101C-61CE-4E86-B97B-707E516BB54D/468/BP21_SmallBusiness3.pdf.

Mossin, Jan (1966). "Equilibrium in a Capital Asset Market." *Econometrica* 34: 768–783.

Murphy, Andrea, and John Ray (2009). "America's Largest Private Companies." *Forbes*, October 28.

Murphy, Anne L. (2005). "Trading Options Before Black-Scholes: A Study of the Market in Late 17th-Century London." Paper presented at the annual conference of the Economic History Society, University of Leicester, April 8. Available at http://www.ehs.org.uk. Published in 2009 in *Economic History Review* 62, no. 1: 8–30.

Musashi, Miyamoto (c. 1644). *A Book of Five Rings* (*Gorin No Sho*). Reprinted, Overlook Press, 2000.

Muth, John F. (1961). "Rational Expectations and the Theory of Price Movements." *Econometrica* 29: 315–335.

Myers, Stewart C. (1977). "Determinants of Corporate Borrowing." *Journal of Financial Economics*, no. 5 (November): 147–175.

———— (2001). "Finance Theory and Financial Strategy." In *Real Options and Investment Under Uncertainty*, ed. Eduardo S. Schwartz and Lenos Trigeorgis, 19–32. MIT Press.

Nelson, Richard, and Sidney Winter (1982). *An Evolutionary Theory of Economic Change*. Belknap Press and Harvard University Press.

Nobes, Christopher W. (1982). "The Gallerani Account Book of 1305–1308." *Accounting Review* 57, no. 2 (April): 303–310.

NYSE Amex (2011). "NYSE Listing Standards." Available at http://www.nyse.com /regulation.

Osaka Securities Exchange (2008). "History [of Osaka Securities Exchange]." Available at http://www.ose.or.jp/e/profile/pr_re.html.

Ozanian, Michael K., and Ronald Fink (1994). "The $11 Billion Pastime: Why Sports Franchise Values Are Soaring Even as Team Profits Fall." *Financial World* 163, no. 10: 50.

———— (1998). "Selective Accounting." *Forbes*, December 14.

Pacioli, Luca (1494). *Summa arithmetica, geometrica, proportioni et proportionalità*. The section on accounting was translated into English by A. von Gebstattel in *Luca Pacioli's Exposition of Double-Entry Accounting: Venice 1494* (Albrizzi Editore, 1994).

Park, Cheol-Ho, and Scott H. Irwin (2007). "What Do We Know About the Profitability of Technical Analysis." *Journal of Economic Surveys* 21, no. 4: 786–826.

Pastor, Lubos, and Pietro Veronesi (2004). "Was There a Nasdaq Bubble in the Late 1990s?" CRSP Working Paper No. 557, December 13. AFA 2005 Philadelphia Meetings Paper. Available at http://ssrn.com /abstract=557061.

Penrose, Edith T. (1959). *The Theory of the Growth of the Firm*. Blackwell. Reprinted by Oxford University Press, 1995.

Peters, Tom, and Robert Waterman (1982). *In Search of Excellence*. HarperCollins.

Pindyck, Robert S. (1991). "Irreversibility, Uncertainty, and Investment." *Journal of Economic Literature* 29, no. 3 (September): 1110–1148. Reprinted in *Real Options and Investment Under Uncertainty: Classical Readings and Recent Contributions*, ed. Eduardo S. Schwartz and Lenos Trigeorgis, 199–250. MIT Press.

Pitelis, Christos (2002). *The Growth of the Firm: The Legacy of Edith Penrose*. Oxford University Press.

Poitras, Geoffrey (2000). *The Early History of Financial Economics, 1478–1776*. Elgar.

———— (2008). "The Early History of Option Contracts." Working paper, Simon Fraser Institute. Available at http://www.sfu.ca/~poitras/heinz_$$.pdf.

Pomykala, Joe (2004). "What Is Behavioral Economics?" Available at http://www.altruists .org/d255.

Popik, Barry (2004). "Buy/Sell the Brooklyn Bridge." Available at http://www.barrypopik .com/index.php/new_york_city/entry/buy_sell_the_brooklyn_bridge/.

Popkin, Joel (2002). "Small Business Share of Economic Growth." *SBA Small Business Research Summary*, no. 2 (January).

Porter, Michael E. (1980). *Competitive Strategy*. Free Press.

Posner, Richard A. (1992). *Economic Analysis of Law*, 4th ed. Little, Brown.

Pratt, Shannon (2001). *Business Valuation Discount and Premiums*. Wiley.

———— (2002). *Cost of Capital Estimation and Applications*, 2nd ed. Wiley.

Pratt, Shannon, with Aline V. Niculita (2008). *Valuing a Business*, 5th ed. McGraw-Hill Professional.

Pratt, Shannon, Robert F. Reilly, and Robert P. Schweihs (2000 [1996] [1989] [1981]). *Valuing a Business: The Analysis and Appraisal of Closely Held Companies.* McGraw-Hill Professional.

Pring, Martin J. (2002). *Technical Analysis Explained.* McGraw-Hill.

Proudhon, Pierre J. (1840). *What Is Property? An Inquiry into the Principle of Right and of Government (Qu'est-ce que la propriété).* Translated from the French by Benjamin R. Tucker (Dover, 1970). English translation originally published by Humboldt, c. 1890. Also available at http://etext.virginia.edu/toc/modeng/public/ProProp.html.

Prychitko, David L. (2004). "The Nature and Significance of Marx's Capital: A Critique of Political Economy." Library of Economics and Liberty, September 6. Available at http://www.econlib.org/library/Columns/y2004/PrychitkoMarx.html.

Reifman, Shlomo, and Samantha Wong (2006). "The Largest Private Companies." *Forbes*, November 9.

Reilly, Frank K. (1994). *Investment Analysis and Portfolio Management*, 4th ed. Dryden Press.

Ricardo, David (1821). *On the Principles of Political Economy and Taxation*, 3rd ed. Murray. First published 1817. Available at http://www.econlib.org/library/Ricardo/ricP.html.

Ringer, Robert J. (1975). *Winning Through Intimidation.* Funk and Wagnalls.

Roberts, Harry V. (1957). "Current Problems in the Economics of Capital Budgeting." *Journal of Business* 30, no. 1 (January): 12–16.

Roberts, Wess (1989). *Leadership Secrets of Attila the Hun.* Grand Central.

Robinson, Joan (1933). *The Economics of Imperfect Competition.* Macmillan. Second edition published by Macmillan, 1969, and collected in *Joan Robinson: Writings on Economics*, vol. 1 (Palgrave Macmillan, 2001).

Roll, Richard (1977). "A Critique of the Asset Pricing Theory's Tests, Part I: On Past and Potential Testability of the Theory." *Journal of Financial Economics* 4, no. 2 (March): 129–176.

Romer, Paul (1986). "Cake Eating, Chattering, and Jumps: Existence Results for Variational Problems." *Econometrica* 54, no. 4 (July): 897–908.

Ross, Marc (1986). "Capital Budgeting Practices of Twelve Large Manufacturers." *Financial Management* 15, no. 4: 15–22.

Ross, Stephen A. (1973). "Return, Risk and Arbitrage." Wharton Discussion Paper. Later edited and published in *Risk and Return in Finance*, ed. I. Friend and J. Bicksler, 189–217. Ballinger, 1976.

——— (1978). "A Simple Approach to the Valuation of Risky Streams." *Journal of Business* 51, no. 3: 453–475.

——— (2005). *Neoclassical Finance.* Princeton University Press.

Roy, Andrew D. (1952). "Safety First and the Holding of Assets." *Econometrica* 20, no. 3 (July): 431–449.

Rubinstein, Mark E. (1976). "The Valuation of Uncertain Income Streams and the Pricing of Options." *Bell Journal of Economics and Management Science* 7, no. 2: 407–425. Collected in *Theory of Valuation*, ed. Sudipto Bhattacharya and George Constantinides, 25–44. Rowman and Littlefield, 1989.

——— (2006). *A History of the Theory of Investments: My Annotated Bibliography.* Wiley Finance.

Ryan, Patricia A., and Glenn P. Ryan (2002). "Capital Budgeting Practices of the Fortune 1000: How Have Things Changed?" *Journal of Business and Management* (Fall): 355–365.

Samuelson, Paul A. (1938). "A Note on the Pure Theory of Consumer's Behavior." *Economica* 5, no. 17: 61–71.

——— (1955). "Brownian Motion in the Stock Market." Unpublished manuscript.

Schumpeter, Joseph (1975). *Capitalism, Socialism and Democracy.* Harper. Originally published in 1942.

Schwartz, Eduardo S., and Lenos Trigeorgis, eds. (2001). *Real Options and Investment Under Uncertainty: Classical Readings and Recent Contributions.* MIT Press.

Sengupta, D. N., and Anindya Sen (2004). *Economics of Business Policy.* Oxford University Press. Reprinted by Oxford India Paperbacks, 2005.

Sharpe, William F. (1964). "Capital Asset Prices: A Theory of Market Equilibrium Under Conditions of Risk." *Journal of Finance* 19: 425–442.

——— (2007). *Investors and Markets.* Princeton University Press.

Shiller, Robert J. (1989). *Market Volatility.* MIT Press.

——— (1994). *Macro Markets: Creating Institutions for Managing Society's Largest Economic Risks.* Oxford University Press.

Shiller, Robert J., and Stefano Athanasoulis (2000). "The Significance of the Market Portfolio." *Review of Financial Studies* 13, no. 2: 301–329. Available at http://ssrn.com/abstract=197650.

Shreve, Steven E. (2004). *Stochastic Calculus for Finance.* 2 vols. Springer Finance.

Siegen, Bernard H (2001). *Property Rights: From Magna Carta to the 14th Amendment.* Transaction.

Sihag, Balbir S. (2004). "Kautilya on the Scope and Methodology of Accounting, Organizational Design and the Role of Ethics in Ancient India." *Accounting Historians Journal* 31, no. 2: 125–148.

Simon, Herbert (1964). "Theories of Bounded Rationality." Complex Information Processing working paper no. 66, March 12. Available at http://www.library.cmu.edu.

——— (1982). *Models of Bounded Rationality,* vols. 1–2. MIT Press.

——— (1984). "On the Behavioral and Rational Foundations of Economic Dynamics." *Journal of Economic Behavior and Organization* 5, no. 1: 35–55.

——— (1997). *Models of Bounded Rationality,* vol. 3. MIT Press.

Skiadas, Costis (1998). "Recursive Utility and Preferences for Information." *Economic Theory* 12: 293–312.

Smith, Adam (1776). *Wealth of Nations.* An edition edited by Edwin Cannan was published in 1907; reissued by the University of Chicago Press, 1976.

Smitka, Michael (1998). *The Japanese Economy in the Tokugawa Era, 1600–1868.* Taylor and Francis.

Spulber, Daniel (2009). *The Theory of the Firm.* Cambridge Univerity Press.

Sraffa, Piero (1926). "The Laws of Returns Under Competitive Conditions." *Economic Journal* 36 (December): 543.

Stigler, George J. (1988). *Memoirs of an Unregulated Economist.* Basic Books.

Stokey, Nancy L. (2009). *The Economics of Inaction: Stochastic Control Models with Fixed Costs.* Princeton University Press.

Stokey, Nancy, and Robert E. Lucas, Jr., with Edward C. Prescott (1989). *Recursive Methods in Economic Dynamics.* Harvard University Press.

Straight Dope (2007). "Has Anybody Really 'Sold' the Brooklyn Bridge?" Staff report, June 14. Available at http://www.straightdope.com/mailbag/mbrooklynbridge .htm.

Sun Tzu (c. 600 BC). *Art of War.* Translated from ancient Mandarin into English in 1910 by Lionel Giles; reprinted in numerous editions in recent years by various publishers, including El Paso Norte Press (2007) and Barnes and Noble Classics (2004). Other translations include one from different sources by J. H. Huang (1993), published by Harper Paperbacks as *Sun-Tzu.*

Thaler, Richard H., ed. (2005). *Advances in Behavioral Finance,* vol. 2. Princeton University Press.

Tinbergen, Jan (1939). "A Method and Its Application to Investment Activity." In *Statistical Testing of Business Cycle Theories,* vol. 1. League of Nations.

Tirole, Jean (2006). *The Theory of Corporate Finance.* Princeton University Press.

To, Henry (2004). "Dow Theory." Available at http://www.marketthoughts.com/dow _theory.html.

Tobin, James (1958). "Liquidity Preference as Behavior Towards Risk." *Review of Economic Studies* 25: 65–85. Circulated in preliminary form as Cowles Foundation Discussion Paper No. 14, July 1956.

——— (1969). "A General Equilibrium Approach to Monetary Theory." *Journal of Money, Credit and Banking* 1 (February): 15–29.

Treynor, J. L. (1999). "Toward a Theory of Market Value of Risky Assets." In *Asset Pricing and Portfolio Performance,* ed. Robert A. Korjczyk, 15–22. Risk Books.

Trigeorgis, Lenos (2003). "Real Options and Investment Under Uncertainty: What Do We Know?" In *Firms' Investment and Finance Decisions: Theory and Empirical Methodology,* ed. Paul Butzen and Catherine Fuss, 153–166. Elgar.

Trigeorgis, Lenos, and Scott P. Mason (1987). "Valuing Managerial Flexibility." *Midland Corporate Financial Journal* 5 (Spring): 14–21. Also collected in *Real Options and Investment Under Uncertainty: Classical Readings and Recent Contributions,* ed. Eduardo S. Schwartz and Lenos Trigeorgis, 47–60. MIT Press, 2001.

Tversky, Amos, and Daniel Kahneman (1991). "Loss Aversion in Riskless Choice: A Reference-Dependent Model." *Journal of Business* 59: 251–278.

——— (1992). "Advances in Prospect Theory: Cumulative Representation of Uncertainty." *Journal of Risk and Uncertainty* 5: 297–323.

Varian, Hal R. (1992 [1978]). *Microeconomic Analysis.* Norton.

——— (2006). "Revealed Preference." In *Samuelsonian Economics and the 21st Century,* ed. Michael Szenberg, Lall Ramrattan, and Aron A. Gottesman, 99–115. Oxford University Press.

Vega, Jose de la (1688). *Confusion de confusiones.* Amsterdam. Reprinted in Spanish by Profit Editorial, 2009; translated into English by Emili Atmetlla (Marketplace Books, 1996).

Vickers, Douglas (1987). *Money Capital in the Theory of the Firm: A Preliminary Analysis.* Cambridge University Press.

——— (1994). *Economics and the Antagonism of Time.* University of Michigan Press.

Villamil, Anne (2008). "The Modigliani-Miller Theorem." In *The New Palgrave Dictionary of Economics*, 2nd ed., ed. Steven N. Durlauf and Lawrence E. Blume. Palgrave Macmillan.

Visser, Auke (2011). *Auke Visser's International Super Tankers*. Available at http://www.aukevisser.nl/supertankers/id133.htm.

Vollert, Alexander (2003). *A Stochastic Control Framework for Real Options in Strategic Valuation*. Birkhauser.

von Neumann, John, and Oskar Morgenstern (1944). *Theory of Games and Economic Behavior*. Princeton University Press.

von Thünen, Johann Heinrich (1826). *Der isolierte Staat* (*The Isolated State*), trans. Carla Wartenberg, ed. Peter Hall. Pergamon Press, 1966.

Waldauer, Charles, William Zahka, and Surendra Pal (1996). "Kautilya's Arthashastra: Neglected Precursor to Classical Economics." *Indian Economic Review* 21, no. 1: 101–108.

Walras, Léon (1874). *Elements of Pure Economics*. Originally published in French as *Éléments d'économie politique pure*. Corbaz and Cie Editeurs.

Wasendorf, Russell R., Sr., and Russell R. Wasendorf, Jr. (2008). "Feature Interview: Harry M. Markowitz, Nobel Laureate." *SFO Magazine*. Available at http://management.ucsd.edu.

Weintraub, E. Roy (1993). "Neoclassical Economics." In *The Concise Encyclopedia of Economics*. Library of Economics and Liberty. Available at http://www.econlib.org/library/Enc1/NeoclassicalEconomics.html.

Weisstein, Eric W. (2011). "Dimension." Available at http://mathworld.wolfram.com/Dimension.html.

West, Tom, ed. (2007). *Business Reference Guide 2007*. Business Brokerage Press.

Williams, John Burr (1938). *The Theory of Investment Value*. Harvard University Press. Reprinted by Fraser, 1997.

Williams, Ronald B., Jr. (1970). "Industry Practice in Allocating Capital Resources." *Managerial Planning* 18, no. 6: 15–22.

Yamey, Basil S. (1979). "Oldcastle, Peele and Mellis: A Case of Plagiarism in the Sixteenth Century." *Accounting and Business Research* 9, no. 35: 209–216. Reprinted in *Further Essays on the History of Accounting* (Garland, 1982).

——— (2004). "Pacioli's *De Scripturis* in the Context of the Spread of Double Entry." *Spanish Journal of Accounting History* (December): 142–154. Also in Spanish as "De Computis," *Revista Española de Historia de la Contabilidad* 1 (December 2004).

STANDARDS, RESTATEMENTS OF LAW, AND REGULATIONS

Appraisal Foundation (2008). *Uniform Standards of Professional Appraisal Practices, 2008–2009 Edition* (USPAP 2008). Available at http://www.appraisers.org/Files/Professional%20Standards/bvstandards.pdf. USPAP 2005 is the preceding edition.

Bank for International Settlements (2006). *International Convergence of Capital Measurement and Capital Standards: A Revised Framework*. Bank for International Settlements, Basel Committee on Banking Supervision.

Financial Accounting Standards Board (1978). *Statement of Financial Accounting Concepts No. 1: Objectives of Financial Reporting by Business Enterprises*.

——— (1980). *Statement of Financial Accounting Concepts No. 2: Qualitative Characteristics of Accounting Information.*

——— (2006). *Statement of Financial Accounting Standards,* including FAS 157.

International Accounting Standards Board, various statements, including IAS 1, IFRS 7.

GOVERNMENT PUBLICATIONS, STATEMENTS, NOTICES, AND BULLETINS

European Commission (2009). *Annual Report on EU Small and Medium-Sized Enterprises.* Available at http://ec.europa.eu/enterprise/policies/sme/files/craft/sme_perf_review/doc_08/spr08_annual_reporten.pdf.

Internal Revenue Service (1959). Revenue Ruling 59-60. 59-1 CB 237.

Presidential Task Force on Market Mechanisms (1988). *Report of the Presidential Task Force on Market Mechanisms.* U.S. Government Printing Office.

Statistics Canada (2008). *Survey of Employment, Payrolls and Hours (SEPH)* (April). Available at http://www.statcan.gc.ca/cgi-bin/imdb/p2SV.pl?Function=getSurvey&SurvId=2612&SurvVer=1&InstaId=13961&InstaVer=92&DispYear=2008&SDDS=2612&lang=en&db=imdb&adm=8&dis=2.

"A Strategy for Reducing the Gap Should Include Options for Addressing Sole Proprietor Noncompliance" (2007). Report to the Committee on Finance, U.S. Senate. GAO-07-1014 (July).

U.S. Census Bureau (2010). "Preliminary Statistics of All U.S. Firms." *2007 Survey of Business Owners* (July). Available at http://www.sba.gov/sites/default/files/files/ovbd_vet_owned_firms.pdf.

U.S. General Accounting Office (1999). "Long-Term Capital Management. Regulators Need to Focus Greater Attention on Systemic Risk." Report to Congressional Requestors, October.

——— (2000). "Responses to Questions Concerning Long-Term Capital Management and Related Events." Report to Congressional Requestors, February.

——— (2007a). "Fiscal Year 2007 Financial Report of the United States Government." Available at http://www.gao.gov/financial/fy2007/07frusg.pdf.

——— (2007b). "Tax Gap: A Strategy for Reducing the Gap Should Include Options for Addressing Sole Proprietor Noncompliance." Report to the U.S. Senate Committee on Finance, July.

U.S. Small Business Administration (2006). *The Small Business Economy: A Report to the President.* U.S. Government Printing Office.

LAWS AND TREATIES

United Kingdom (2006). *Companies Act of 2006.* Available at http://www.legislation.gov.uk/ukpga/2006/46/pdfs/ukpga_20060046_en.pdf.

DICTIONARIES, ENCYCLOPEDIAS, AND DATA COMPILATIONS

AICPA (2007). "International Glossary of Business Valuation Terms." *Statement on Standards for Valuation Services No. 1. Valuation of a Business, Business Ownership Interest, Security, or Intangible Asset.* American Institute of Certified Public Accountants.

Bouvier, John (1856). *Law Dictionary*, 6th ed. Childs and Peterson. Available at http://www.constitution.org/bouv/bouvier_d.htm.

Collins English Dictionary, 10th ed. (2011). HarperCollins.

Discovery Institute. "George Gilder, Senior Fellow—Discovery Institute." Available at http://www.discovery.org/p/10.

Fonseca, Gonçalo L. (2005, 2008). *History of Economic Thought.* New School for Social Research. Available at http://cepa.newschool.edu/het/home.htm.

The Free Dictionary (2011). Available at http://encyclopedia2.thefreedictionary.com.

Ibbotson Associates (2004, 2006, 2010). *Stocks, Bonds, Bills, and Inflation, Valuation Edition.* Ibbotson Associates (published annually). The 2010 edition is titled *Ibbotson SBBI 2010 Classic Yearbook* and is published by Morningstar.

Weisstein, Eric W., ed. (n.d.). *MathWorld.* Online encyclopedia. Available at http://mathworld.wolfram.com.

INDEX

Italic page numbers indicate material in tables or figures.